Here to Stay

Gypsies and Travellers of Britain

Here to Stay

The Gypsies and Travellers of Britain

COLIN CLARK AND
MARGARET GREENFIELDS

University of Hertfordshire Press

First published in Great Britain in 2006 by
University of Hertfordshire Press
Learning and Information Services
University of Hertfordshire
College Lane
Hatfield
Hertfordshire AL10 9AB

British Library Cataloguing in Publication Data
A catalogue record for this book is available from the British Library

ISBN 978-1-902806-33-4

Design by Geoff Green Book Design, CB4 5RA
Cover design by John Robertshaw, AL5 2JB
Printed in Great Britain by CPI Antony Rowe, Chippenham, Wiltshire

For Dr Donald Kenrick

Without the ground-breaking work and activism of Dr Donald Kenrick this book would not have been possible. Donald has been a source of inspiration to both of us and we thank him sincerely for all his hard work, commitment and scholarship over the years. This book is dedicated to him.

Dr Colin Clark and Dr Margaret Greenfields

For my family – both the big people and the little people, especially Rory who wasn't around for the last book. With love. CC.

For my parents: Peter and Barbara Greenfields who taught me to fight for what I believe in and to use my skills to protect those in need; and for Zack, Madeleine and Frank. MG

Contents

List of illustrations

Gypsies & Travellers in their own words is available from Traveller Education Service, West Park Centre, Spen Lane, Leeds LS16 5BE
Tel: 0113 274 8050
Web: www.travellersinleeds.co.uk

Author biographies

Dr Colin Clark currently works as a Senior Lecturer in Sociology in the Department of Geography and Sociology at the University of Strathclyde, Glasgow. Previous to this post he was a Lecturer in Sociology and Social Policy at the University of Newcastle-upon-Tyne. Dr Clark specialises in the sociology of ethnic and racial studies and has published a number of academic journal articles and book chapters within this academic field. He is the co-author with Dr Donald Kenrick of *Moving On: The Gypsies and Travellers of Britain* (University of Hertfordshire Press, 1999).

Dr Margaret Greenfields undertook a first degree in social anthropology and law before qualifying as a lawyer and subsequently transferring into the field of socio-legal policy. Her doctorate focussed on Traveller family issues and engagement with legal processes. She is a Senior Lecturer in Social Policy at Buckingham Chilterns University College where she is involved in a range of research initiatives relating to Gypsies and Travellers and social exclusion, and access to culturally appropriate health and social care for minority ethnic and marginalised communities. She is a module leader for the UK's only M.Sc. course on Gypsy and Traveller Health and with Dr Robert Home (guided by a panel of Gypsy and Traveller activists and elders) devised the 'Cambridge Model' of Gypsy and Traveller Needs Assessment which has been recognised by the ODPM as a model of best practice for assessing need under the Housing Act 2004.

Dr Rachel Morris was an advice worker on the Telephone Legal Advice Service for Travellers (TLAST, 1996-1998), and Co-ordinator of the Traveller Law Research Unit (1998–2002), both based at Cardiff Law School, Cardiff University. She is the author of a number of books and articles on laws and policies relating to Travelling people, and has worked with public and private organisations at all levels from local to international on improving these regulatory frameworks. She is now working in South Korea as a writer, teacher and photographer; examples of her work can be seen at www.mediabistro.com/RachelMorris

Dr Robert Home is a Professor of Land Management in the Law School, Anglia Ruskin University, Chelmsford. A chartered town planner, he has worked and researched for some twenty-five years on the planning aspects of accommodation for Gypsies, and published on the subject in the *Journal of Planning & Environmental Law, Habitat International* and elsewhere. He has also given evidence to government policy reviews of the area, including the 2004 Parliamentary Committee, and undertaken Gypsy accommodation needs assessments for the local authorities of Bedfordshire, Cambridgeshire and Dorset.

Dr Donald Kenrick first came into contact with the Romani language whilst teaching in Bulgaria, eventually completing a Ph.D. on the Drindari dialect. He has made a lasting contribution to Romani history and linguistics and was the first secretary of the WRC Language Commission in 1971.

Acknowledgements

No book of this type could have been written without the help, support and encouragement of numerous individuals. In acknowledging their help we are aware that we may have inadvertently forgotten someone who has provided us with information, emailed a comment, sent us a photograph, told us their story (or that of their family and friends), or kindly passed on data to a third party which has found its way to us in our persistent hunt for up-to-date materials. If you know you are such a person then please forgive us. Any omissions or misinterpretations are solely the fault of the authors. Please feel free to write to us 'care of' our publisher to correct any misapprehensions we have laboured under, or provide us with new information that can be incorporated into any future edition that may appear.

In terms of gathering data and obtaining critical comment from 'people who know' we particularly wish to acknowledge the role of the now sadly defunct 'Traveller-Net', an email list which was for eight years the home of lively exchange, debate and good humour between Gypsies, Travellers, activists, health professionals, lawyers, community and education workers and a range of individuals who were members of, or worked with or on behalf of, different Travelling communities. The debt we owe to members of that list is profound and hard to do justice to.

We also wish to especially thank (in no particular order) the following people who have been overwhelmingly generous with their time, knowledge and assistance, in some cases acting as 'critical readers' of chapters and in others simply being who they are, individuals with a wealth of knowledge and a willingness to share it with the authors and ultimately, the readers of this text: Len Smith, Richard O'Neill, Patrice Van Cleemput, Siobhan Spencer, Thomas Acton, Donald Kenrick, Judith Okely, John Coxhead, Simon Evans,

Bill Forrester, Nicholas Williams, Dominic O'Callaghan, Michelle Lloyd, Andrew Ryder, Emma Nuttall, David Grant, Nettie Edwards, Felicity Greenfields, Ian Taggart, Martin Naughton, Yvonne McNamara, Alan Dearling, Noelette Keane, Robert Home and Rachel Morris.

Photography credits are supplied on relevant pages of this text, but we would like to thank the following people for enabling us to access their photographs, even though in some cases we were unable to make use of their resources: Alan Dearling, Pete Saunders/Leeds TES, Sam Wilson, Friends, Families and Travellers (FFT), Greg Yates and 'the Clearwater Gypsies', Simon Evans, Felicity Greenfields, Tammy Furey, Len Smith, Grant Doe, Frank Blackmore and Richard O'Neill.

We would like to thank our publisher, University of Hertfordshire Press, for having the patience of more than just one saint. In the end this book took far longer to write than we had hoped. Bill Forster fired the starter's pistol a long time ago and we thank him for that, Jane Housham then ran at speed with the baton, especially the last 100 metres, and Kerry Gilliland crossed the finish line with us. All three of them win medals in our book.

Finally, a big thank you to our respective families who have lived with this book for as long as we have (and doubtless know the material as well as ourselves …).

A percentage of the royalties from the sale of this book will be donated to the Travellers Aid Trust.

Foreword

The sedentary community in Britain, as a generalisation, sees Gypsies and Travellers through a plethora of stereotypically tinted spectacles. Romantic, dirty, criminal, musical, illiterate, child-stealing, shiftless, fiddle-footed, tax-avoiding, anti-social – these and many more largely inaccurate concepts of who Gypsies and Travellers are, or how they behave, is what informs the thinking of the average citizen. Rarely are we seen as fellow human beings or deserving of decent and equal treatment under the law, and in fact, to some degree, the law itself throws its weight on the discriminatory side of the scales. This misinformation is reinforced, and sometimes massaged into outright hysteria, by the tabloid press, anxious to pander to particular political leanings or to bolster sales.

This book sets the record straight in a highly detailed and accurate way. By objective scrutiny it debunks the myths and stereotypes and, instead, presents the reality of what it is like to be a Gypsy or Traveller in Britain in the twenty-first century and how history has brought us to this point. It shows Gypsy culture in a real light, with all its positives, and all it has to offer to society as a whole. It shows the recent upsurge in political activity and a new determination to achieve equality and integration, driven, not just by sympathetic non-Gypsies, but by Gypsies themselves, at last beginning to take charge of their own destiny. The creation of the Gypsy and Traveller Law Reform Coalition (G&TLRC), an amalgam of the separate Traveller cultures in Britain, amounts to a 'tectonic shift' in that cause, recognised as such by the winning of the Liberty Human Rights Award in 2004.

Compiled by two of the most respected academics currently in 'the business', this book will inform law-makers; it will inform academics; it will inform activists; and as such will be an important contribution to the understanding of why we should be, and deserve to be, 'here to stay'.

Len Smith
Chair, British Committee on Romani Emancipation
and founder member of the G&TLRC

ODPM new guidance notes

Unfortunately, as any author will tell you, something important always happens just before you are ready to go to print. In our case it wasn't just three metaphorical buses that came along at once, it was four. As a 'last word' in the introduction, it should be noted that at the time of going to press the Office for the Deputy Prime Minister has just published three new guidance notes that cover a range of matters impacting on Gypsies and Travellers as well as a new Circular (01/06) that replaces Circular 01/94.[1] The focus of all four publications is accommodation, planning and enforcement. In part, this rush of ODPM activity has been prompted by the political and media attention which originated in the 2005 General Election and the (on-going) contested issue of retrospective planning permission applications for private Gypsy and Traveller sites. However, we would also (optimistically) argue that the guidance notes and Circular 01/06 represents government acknowledgement of the chaos and misery brought to many Gypsy and Traveller families by the effective criminalisation of nomadism and the removal of the duty on local Authorities to provide sites by the Criminal Justice and Public Order Act of 1994. We would urge all interested parties to read these four documents (which can be downloaded free of charge via the ODPM website) in conjunction with the relevant chapters of this book (for example, chapter 5).

---

1   The three guidance notes – 'Guide to effective use of enforcement powers: part 1, unauthorised encampments', 'Gypsy and Traveller accommodation assessments: draft practice guides' and 'Local Authorities and Gypsies and Travellers: guide to responsibilities and powers' as well as the new planning Circular - 'Circular 01/06: Planning for Gypsy and Traveller Caravan Sites' - can all be accessed via the main ODPM website which is here: < http://www.odpm.gov.uk/index.asp?id=1153486>. They were all published in February 2006.

Introduction
Colin Clark

On 21 March 2005 Michael Howard, then Leader of the opposition Conservative Party, made Gypsies and Travellers front-page news in Britain. This certainly wasn't the first time Gypsies and Travellers had made the headlines and it is unlikely to be the last. However, the vexed issue of retrospective planning applications for Traveller sites in the south of England has been the latest issue to be used by politicians and the media to shine a bright and critical light on the Gypsy and Traveller communities of Britain. The issue of 'illegal' site occupation and retrospective planning applications was used by Howard, in a most simplistic way, to appeal to vague notions of British 'fair play'. In robust exchanges with both Labour and Liberal Parties during an explosive election campaign he suggested that 'special-interest groups', such as Travellers, should not have 'special rights' when it came to sites and accommodation. To this end, he suggested, the Human Rights Act of 1998 would have to be 'reviewed' if the Conservative Party were elected with a view to either 'improving it or scrapping it'. As he said in his speech at the Conservative Campaign Headquarters, 'if you are a Traveller you can use the so-called Human Rights Act to bend planning law – building where you like. That's just not fair. There shouldn't be one rule to [sic] Travellers and another for everyone else.'[1]

Once again during a bitter and ultimately one-sided General Election contest a political football had been found. In 2005 it was not to be asylum and immigration, the NHS, the 'war against drugs' or even inner-city crime that dominated the tabloids for a short while but a collection of relatively small ethnic minority communities collectively known in the tabloids as 'Travellers' that were considered to be 'fair game' for public vilification. In reviewing what occurred during March 2005 it appears to us that a collective assumption was

1

made that attacking Gypsies and Travellers was 'safe ground' and would not be seen as the racism it clearly was. The other assumption that was made, we suggest, is that politicians and tabloid editors thought Gypsies and Travellers wouldn't have many supporters.[2] Who would complain on their behalf? Who would side with the Gypsies? How could Gypsies and Travellers respond to this attack themselves?

The answer to these questions serves to demonstrate the problem at hand. It is a problem of fairness and a question of balance. How do relatively small and (politically) powerless ethnic minority communities best represent the issues and problems they endure and get their own clear and representative messages across? Specifically, how can Gypsies and Travellers challenge the largely negative and hostile dominant discourses about them? There are no easy solutions of course and what is interesting in this case is that only hours after Howard's assault and battery an articulate and measured response, in the form of a press release from the G&TLRC, was sent out to the press and the media.[3] It stated, contrary to Howard's speech, that Gypsies and Travellers did believe in 'fair play too'. It is worth reading in full:

> We live in a modern Britain. We are proud to be part of a diverse and multicultural nation. We are proud to be Gypsies and Travellers.
>
> Too many councils, politicians and newspapers seem to think they don't have to play by the rules. Gypsies and Travellers are being discriminated against.
>
> Fair play means being honest and telling the truth, it means giving the weak and vulnerable a helping hand not 'stamping on' them.
>
> 90 per cent of planning applications by Gypsies and Travellers fail as opposed to 20 per cent from the settled community. In the past councils have failed to follow planning guidance and help Gypsies and Travellers find land they can buy.
>
> It's not fair that so many Gypsies and Travellers are homeless. It's not fair that many official sites are next to rubbish dumps and sewer works. It's not fair that our children can't stay in one place long enough to get a decent education. It's not fair that our community has a life expectancy 10 years less than average.
>
> But it's not fair either that some people in the settled community are inconvenienced by unauthorised encampments.
>
> We don't want knee jerk reactions. We want solutions that are fair for everyone. We need more choice, more legal sites, more dialogue and more understanding.[4]

This challenging and carefully constructed response received next to no attention across the range of media outlets in Britain. It was, in fact, ceremoniously ignored. This matter, we argue, is emblematic of a much wider legal, policy and academic malaise when it comes to Gypsies and Travellers in Britain; they are in many ways an 'invisible' minority.[5] How can such complex issues affecting these communities be resolved if they rarely get to sit at the discussion table, let alone be heard? Our aim in writing this book is to draw Gypsies and Travellers into the debates and discussions about them as communities, families, individuals. We try and ensure, as far as we can and in a balanced, fair and sensitive way, that their different points of view are written about and heard.

Other recent events

Aside from the last General Election, we can identify at least two other major national events in the UK that have recently illustrated the types of attitudes and responses that Gypsies and Travellers can incite: the burning of a Gypsy caravan effigy at a Firle Bonfire Society event in October 2003 and the murder of Irish Traveller Johnny Delaney in Liverpool in May 2003. Both of these events generated national attention and are again emblematic of the types of hatred that can be stirred up towards Gypsies and Travellers in this country, one with fatal and tragic consequences.

Burning trailers

In November 2003, the police arrested twelve people on suspicion of inciting racial hatred after Firle Bonfire Society in East Sussex torched an effigy of a caravan with a Gypsy family painted on the side. The registration plate on the caravan displayed P1 KEY and a message on the side stated 'Do You As You Likey Driveways Ltd – Guaranteed to Rip You Off'.[6] Once the controversial story broke, the Society quickly denied that the effigy was 'racist' and offered an apology to anyone who may have been offended, although it was also stated that the use of the caravan effigy was in response to alleged 'problems' the village had experienced with Travellers camping in the area in the summer of 2003. The Firle Bonfire Society website stated that: 'During the summer, a number of Travellers moved to privately owned farmland. It was some time before the landowner was able to reclaim the field. The tableau was a symbolic reminder of those events and called into question the way that the authorities dealt with the situation'.[7]

Indeed, Richard Gravett, Chairman of Firle Bonfire Society, also said to the BBC that, 'There was no racist slant towards anyone from the Travelling community. If anything, it's actually completely the other way. It is to try to make people sit up and listen and realise that these people obviously – as all of us do – need somewhere to live'.[8]

This interesting and rather novel interpretation of events from Gravett did not convince many people and the police acted swiftly under 'incitement to racial hatred' provisions in the Public Order Act 1986 and sent a report to the Crown Prosecution Service (CPS), and then forwarded relevant materials to the Director of Public Prosecutions for consideration. Superintendent Grenville Wilson was also quoted by the BBC as saying, 'We recognise the concerns being made across communities in East Sussex about events which happened at Firle. A full, open and thorough investigation is in the process of being carried out, which will uncover all the issues in the case.' [9]

The Commission for Racial Equality (CRE) also became involved and called for those implicated in the burning of the effigy to be brought to justice. Trevor Phillips, Chair of the CRE, put it bluntly:

> Gypsies and Travellers probably suffer the most discrimination in this country. This is clearly an example of incitement to racial hatred. You couldn't really get more provocative than this. The police have to take it seriously. If we are asked at the CRE, we will say this case should be pursued and the people involved should be punished – which can lead to seven years in prison. The idea that you can carry out an act like this and then apologise and get away with it, is exactly what produces a culture that says racism and discrimination and victimisation of people, because of what they are, is OK.[10]

However, in July 2004 the CPS advised Sussex Police that there should be no prosecutions for incitement to racial hatred or public order offences as a result of the bonfire event. The Director of Public Prosecutions, Ken McDonald QC, explained that:

> This was a complex and challenging case both legally and factually and I am entirely satisfied with the decision reached by the reviewing lawyer that there should be no prosecution. I quite understand the disquiet and repugnance of those who were offended by the burning of a caravan with effigies of people inside, including those of children, and the numberplate 'P1 KEY' on it, which they considered abusive

and insulting to travellers. The time taken to review the case indicates that these concerns were taken very seriously; all the evidence was reviewed thoroughly and advice was sought from independent counsel. But in order to prosecute there must be sufficient evidence for a realistic prospect of conviction and if the evidence is not there, no matter how disturbing or unpleasant the allegations may be, a case cannot go ahead.[11]

Responding to the CPS decision, the CRE simply stated that Firle Bonfire Society's actions were 'unacceptable' and it was glad that the police had investigated the matter. The CRE statement also made a more general point about how this incident came about – 'community tensions due to an unauthorised encampment' – and how more adequate site provision for Gypsies and Travellers was urgently needed.[12]

At the time of writing, Firle Bonfire Society, via its website, is still requesting donations towards the cost of legal fees for who it calls the 'Firle 12'.[13]

Justice for Johnny

On 8 May 2003, a fifteen-year-old Irish Traveller was kicked, stamped and beaten to death by two racists in Ellesmere Port. The name of this Irish Traveller was Johnny Delaney and he lived with his family at a local site in Liverpool.[14] The two older boys, Lewis McVeigh and Ricky Kearney, took a twisted kind of pride in what they did to Johnny. A woman who witnessed the attack was told by one of the boys just after they had killed Johnny that 'he deserved it, he's only a fucking gyppo'.[15]

At the court case, at Chester Crown Court, a number of witnesses, under oath, reported the racist anti-Traveller abuse that both McVeigh and Kearney had shouted before, during and immediately after the attack. One girl who witnessed the attack said in court that if she had to rate the kicks out of ten then they would rate as nine – they were delivered with huge force.[16] The Cheshire Police and the prosecution saw this case as one that had clear underlying racist intent: Christopher Vospa QC argued the attack was motivated by a racist hatred of Irish Travellers. However, the judge in the case, Justice Richards, dismissed this element and found the defendants guilty of manslaughter. They were later sentenced to four and a half years' imprisonment each, effectively two years if they met conditions of 'good behaviour'.

Reporting on the case, the locally based *Kirkby Times* rightly made a comparison to the murder of Stephen Lawrence in London in 1993.[17] Johnny wasn't Black but he was a Traveller, he did live on a caravan site, and he did have an identifiable Irish accent. Patrick Delaney, Johnny's father, speaking after the court case said:

> There is no justice here. They were kicking my son like a football. Are they going to let this happen to another Gypsy? Every Travelling person is going to be upset at this verdict. As far as we are concerned it was a racist attack. I have lost my son for life. This has left a big hole in our family. He was a very polite lad who never did anything wrong. He didn't deserve this.[18]

Also commenting on the manslaughter verdict, Trevor Phillips of the CRE stated that:

> There has been some measure of justice in this ruling, though it is extremely hard to see how this particular killing wasn't motivated in some way by racial prejudice. It would be most disturbing if the attack wasn't considered racially motivated because the victim wasn't black or Asian. The extreme levels of public hostility that exist in relation to Gypsies and Travellers would be met with outrage if it was targeted at any other racial group.[19]

The murder of Johnny Delaney and the events at the bonfire display in Firle suitably and sadly demonstrate that to be a Gypsy or Traveller in the UK is to be a kind of 'moving target'. Racists and bigots, fuelled by what they undoubtedly read within some sections of the press and what can be heard in the House of Commons, need little excuse to have a go at Gypsies and Travellers.

The aim of this book

'In gorgio (non-Gypsy) print, distorted views repeat themselves
... Plain facts are real illusions. On each side of these
reflections there is a vested interest in distortion'.[20]

The aim of this book is to try and tell a series of stories that are rarely heard concerning the Gypsies and Travellers of Britain. In doing this we pay close attention to the cautionary note issued above by Judith Okely and attempt to avoid distortion and its repetition wherever possible. The reflections we want to show aim to ring true and be revealing, not to perpetuate age-old stereotypes. The dominant messages about Gypsies and Travellers that are regularly aired – whether by politicians, councillors, residents' groups or newspaper columnists – are usually hostile, biased, aggressive and one sided.[21] Gypsies and Travellers, you would be forgiven for thinking, can do no right and are almost regarded as an affront to 'civilised' (meaning 'settled') society. The mere existence of such minority groups seems to cause politicians to froth at the mouth – Hansard bears witness to this – and newspaper editors to put them on the front page, headlines blazing about a 'Gypsy Invasion' or a 'Gipsy [sic] free-for-all'.[22] Indeed, regarding Hansard, Royce Turner has suggested that, 'The trawl through Hansard is revealing ... Gypsies are vilified ... the themes are familiar and repetitive ... the same words keep recurring ... filth, crime, excrement ... there are few words of sympathy'.[23]

The headlines all too often speak for themselves: families not 'playing fair' when it comes to planning regulations; the 'nuisance' to settled communities caused by 'illegal' roadside encampments; the environmental destruction generated by fly-tipping and the rubbish left by Gypsies after they leave a site; alleged non-payment of taxes; house-calling 'scams' involving the deception of older people and laying of poor quality driveways; benefit fraud; having too many children – the list is almost endless and the impression one is left with is that this is a 'shameless' community in need of some urgent ASBO-based (Anti-Social Behaviour Order) justice.[24] Indeed, public opinion does seem to lead in this direction as a Market and Opinion Research International (MORI) public-opinion poll conducted in 2003 found a third of people admitting a personal prejudice against Gypsies and Travellers. This is a level of prejudice matched only by that directed against asylum seekers. It is also worth bearing in mind that these are just the people admitting their prejudices and wearing them on their sleeves – the real figure, we suggest, is in fact a lot higher than just a third.[25]

There is, of course, another side to these headlines. This is a side that does not often make it to the front pages and is instead hidden away in the side columns if printed at all. It is also a story that does not sell newspapers or win votes. Our approach is to look at the situation, experiences and day-to-day realities of the Gypsy and Traveller population of Britain from a perspective that does not see them as a 'problem' or as a community to be demonised (nor, we stress, to be romanticised). Rather, we see the Gypsies and Travellers of Britain as an important, energetic and under-represented community that is a vital part of not just the history of Britain but also its progress towards being an inclusive multicultural society. We also suggest that Gypsy and Traveller nomadism needs to be seen within this context of debates on multiculturalism and cultural racism directed towards minorities such as Gypsies and Travellers: it is something that needs to be paid attention to within the British context. As George Monbiot has written, 'Envy is intimately connected with racism. Racists associate Jews with money and black people with sexual power, but our hatred of Gypsies may arise from a still deeper grievance, the envy of a people whose instinct for continual movement is frustrated by the constraints of the humdrum settled life'.[26]

In each of the following chapters we hope to challenge certain assumptions that are made about Gypsies and Travellers – whether these are concerned with sites, schools and civil rights or other areas of social life and British society. We attempt to demonstrate that the Gypsy and Traveller population of Britain is one that has much difference and diversity within it. It is clearly not a community but rather a series of distinct yet related communities. Gypsies and Travellers are not a homogeneous grouping although it is important to state that there are, at times, as many cultural, economic and political commonalities as there are differences, though we concede it is often convenient for everyone involved to focus on the differences only. It is evident that there is a mix of different ethnic groups to be included and the book endeavours to do justice to most of them, whether English Romani Gypsies, Welsh Gypsies, Irish Travellers, Scottish Gypsy/Travellers, New Travellers or Romanies from various parts of central and eastern Europe who have arrived in Britain as refugees. We marginally discuss other groups who might regard themselves as part of a wider Traveller population, such as Travelling Showpeople and Circus people, although we make clear in the book why such groups are, in a sense, outside of the remit of our project and why their story, to do it full justice, has been told in other books, reports, articles and volumes.

How the book is organised

The chapters are organised in a way that we hope reflects the main issues and concerns that appear to impact on the day-to-day lives of Gypsies and Travellers in Britain. Chapter 1 acts as an introduction to who the Gypsies and Travellers of Britain are and we look at the different groups that live in Britain today, their numbers and cultural make-up. Chapter 2 is concerned with more specific issues relating to the centrality of family life within the communities and how the family and social networks fit together around notions of 'Traveller identity'. Chapters 3, 4 and 5 are all concerned with aspects of Gypsy and Traveller land use and accommodation – whether they are roadside encampments, council sites, private sites or 'bricks and mortar' housing. Chapter 6 is a lengthy chapter and deals with the plethora of legal issues that concern and impact on the day-to-day lives of Gypsy and Traveller families. Chapters 7 and 8 examine health, education and social services issues, illustrating how such services have responded (or not responded) to the needs of Gypsy and Traveller communities in their areas. Chapter 9 looks at how the media in Britain have tended to portray and represent Gypsies and Travellers in words and pictures and Chapter 10 extends the reach of the book, in a contextual way, to see how European social policy and Roma/Gypsy and Traveller agendas are being played out in Britain. The chapter on planning and private sites was contributed by Dr Robert Home and the chapter on the media was written by Dr Rachel Morris. Both are acknowledged experts within these specialist areas and we are very grateful indeed to both of them for taking the time to offer these chapters.

CHAPTER ONE

Who are the Gypsies and Travellers of Britain?

Colin Clark

Introduction

The question of who the Roma [Gypsies] are is bound up with the question of what to call them, which also remains unresolved. Most names bestowed on them by indigenous Europeans reflect early misconceptions about where they came from. The European imagination ranged freely: among the places suggested were Atlantis and the Moon.[1]

The aim of this chapter is to provide an answer to what is still a very common question: 'Who are the Gypsies and Travellers of Britain?' To answer this question we begin by examining some of the definitions and 'labels' that have been applied to these communities as well as those that would appear to be self-definitions, generated from within the particular communities concerned. Importantly, we also give attention to the implications such sets of definitions and labels can have. From this base we proceed to briefly describe who the main groups in Britain are and some of the differences and similarities they have in terms of culture, identity, language and social structure. We begin to explore the contested issues of legal definitions that can impact on the communities and also what is normally the second most common question asked about Gypsies and Travellers in Britain: 'How many Gypsies and Travellers live in Britain?' The chapter closes by offering a European-focused overview of the debates on the origins, history and migration routes of those Gypsies and Travellers who live across the different parts of a now politically devolved British Isles.

Definitions and terminology

Despite the presence of different Gypsy and Traveller groups in Britain for at least 500 years, much confusion still appears to surround even the most basic of questions: 'Who are they?' We would suggest that one reason for this continued uncertainty is that the terms 'Gypsy' and 'Traveller' (and indeed, looking to Europe, 'Roma' and 'Sinti') are heavily contested and definitions are not politically neutral, either within or outside the communities directly concerned.[2] For the purposes of this book we largely draw on the often cited definitions employed by a Minority Rights Group report entitled *Roma/Gypsies: A European Minority* written by Professor J.-P. Liégeois and the Romani sociologist Nicolae Gheorghe in 1995.[3] These broad and inclusive definitions tend to refer to 'Gypsies' as ethnic groups formed by a diaspora of commercial and nomadic groups from India from the tenth century, and subsequent mixing with European and other groups; to 'Travellers' as predominantly indigenous European ethnic groups whose culture is characterised by self-employment, occupational fluidity and nomadism; and to 'Roma' broadly as European Romani-speaking groups. As Liégeois and Gheorghe state on page 6 of their influential report:

> *'Gypsy'* – 'Term used to denote ethnic groups formed by the dispersal of commercial, nomadic and other groups from within India from the tenth century, and their mixing with European and other groups during their Diaspora'.
>
> *'Traveller'* – 'A member of any of the (predominantly) indigenous European ethnic groups (*Woonwagenbewoners*, *Minceiri*, *Jenisch*, *Quinquis*, *Resende*, etc.) whose culture is characterized, inter-alia, by self-employment, occupational fluidity, and nomadism. These groups have been influenced, to a greater or lesser degree, by ethnic groups of (predominantly) Indian origin with a similar cultural base'.
>
> *'Roma/Rom'* – 'A broad term used in various ways, to signify: (a) Those ethnic groups (e.g. *Kalderash*, *Lovari, etc.*) who speak the '*Vlach*', '*Xoraxane*' or '*Rom*' varieties of the Romani language. (b) Any person identified by others as '*Tsigane*' in central and eastern Europe and Turkey, plus those outside the region of East European extraction. (c) Romani people in general'.

We now examine the different groups in Britain and how far they 'fit' with the broad definitions just mentioned.

Gypsy and Traveller groups in Britain today

In Britain today we can find examples of communities and families who would fit, in some manner, within these different collective groupings. We can also find other groups in Britain who do not fit under such banners but who would rightfully demand inclusion in any text seeking to discuss 'the Gypsies and Travellers of Britain': for example, New Travellers or Fairground Travellers (Showpeople). The crucial element to consider when thinking about definitions is whether or not the term applied or used is done so in a *self-ascriptive* manner or an *imposed* one, whether the term is Gypsy, Traveller, Gypsy and Traveller or Roma. This choice can be carried out self-ascriptively, as when Gypsies and Travellers may talk about 'our people', describing, in a Benedict Anderson way, an 'imagined community' of kith and kin who are part of a wider grouping living across different counties, borders, states and territories.[4] Terms and labels can also be imposed by non-Gypsies or Travellers in order to discuss or make laws about those they *think of* as being Gypsies or Travellers. Such important tussles are not abstract or just a question of semantics. They strike to the very heart of Gypsy and Traveller identity politics and can have, as we shall see later, social, cultural, economic and legal implications.

Debates on terminology can often seem arcane and confusing but both 'internal' (self-ascriptive) and 'external' (imposed) definitions can be related to other terms and ideas such as ethnicity, 'race', 'blood', occupation, language, culture, and/or nomadic tradition.[5] By embracing such a wide and holistic definition, we are able to cover a range of groups, such as Scottish Gypsy/Travellers, Welsh Gypsies, English Gypsies, Fairground Travellers, Roma, Circus Travellers, Boat-Dwellers and New Travellers. Importantly, and this needs to be underlined, any debate examining definitions of 'who Gypsies and Travellers really are' does not exclude those who are settled and/or those who are presently living in houses. To be sure, culturally, an ethnicity or ethnic identity is not somehow magically 'lost' or abandoned when a family settles into 'bricks and mortar': it continues and adapts to the new circumstances, and this is commonly accepted within the communities concerned. This is not to say that in the eyes of the law 'settled Gypsies' appears to be a legal misnomer (for example, in areas such as planning, education and health) and later chapters will address these issues more fully. Another important point to stress is that such groups are often linked together and related through intermarriage. Communities are not always as separate as they and others might wish for. Intermarriage between groups and families has been a reality for many years now and the often racialised 'divisions' that are placed around different communities ('English', 'Irish', 'Showmen', etc.) are often artificial and are about establishing cultural, economic and political boundaries rather than presenting a clear statement on mythologised 'racial blood-lines'.

Generalisations are almost always a bad idea and are usually presented in order to be argued down. This is true of most topics, issues, places and people and is equally true when talking and writing about Gypsies and Travellers. Nonetheless, some general statements and ideas are required to present a foundational base from which to work. Whereas it seems to be true that some groups, families and individuals will define themselves in *general terms* as 'Gypsies' (with the possible addition of Romani; this is especially true of English Gypsies), others will prefer the term 'Travellers'. It is important to be aware that the terms 'Gypsy' and 'Traveller' can *both* be perceived as pejorative depending on who you are speaking with and in what situation. Time, space and place are also important contexts in which to appreciate this question of usage. For example, in the early 1990s some Scottish Travellers (often referring to themselves as 'Travelling people' to non-Travellers) began to adopt and use, at least in a political sense, the term 'Gypsy/Traveller' in public dialogue so that they could distinguish themselves from mainly English New Travellers who were moving into the country at that time, often accompanied by a hostile press keen to reveal all about the 'Travellers' who attend 'raves' and take drugs. The label 'Scottish Gypsy/Traveller' lives on and is used by many within the community today as a self-definition to outsiders. Also, the often negative use and connotations of such labels and terms by majority society, via the media or at the level of national/local policy, has set a context in which certain individuals, families and groups are reluctant to be associated with the labels of 'Gypsy' and 'Traveller'. It can be a badge that is sometimes difficult to wear or a tick box that might be skipped over, even though proud of who and what you are. Nevertheless, 'Gypsy' and 'Traveller' are the two terms still commonly used by most groups in Britain to define themselves and these are the terms that are most commonly used throughout the book.

A New Traveller site in the early 1980s (photograph by Margaret Greenfields)

This book, where feasible, also draws on the experiences of all the different groups mentioned above. However, the book does not, in any great depth, address the situation and experiences of Travelling Showpeople, Circus Travellers or Boat-Dwellers. Although we do briefly discuss Showpeople below, accommodation laws apply to them in quite a different way, and the issues highlighted for Gypsies and Travellers are not therefore always relevant. With Circus Travellers, they certainly have problems of access to education due to their peripatetic life, especially for those children who travel the full twelve months of the year. In addition, many artistes and families are international and may experience exclusion on language and ethnic grounds. The nature of hostility or discrimination is therefore different to that experienced by Gypsies and Travellers in Britain. To be sure, their story is for other books to do justice to.[6]

It is clear then that Gypsies and Travellers in Britain do not form one homogeneous group. Some groups of Gypsies and Travellers are nomadic whilst others live in static trailers or mobile homes or in houses. Different groups can also, with some caution, be identified according to their traditional occupations and other preferences. More reliable, however, is to differentiate between groups according to their culture and where they traditionally stay within Britain. Language is also a differentiating factor between groups although the main issues surrounding language are how English is used and the differences of language and communication that exist between Gypsies, Travellers and settled society. To clarify then, in Britain we have:

- **English Romani Gypsies** (sometimes referred to as 'Romanichals') of England and south Wales. This is the largest group in Britain and families will often speak a mixture of English and Romani (Anglo-Romani) within the family and wider Gypsy community. Common family names include Lee, Smith, Cooper and Boswell and a number of families now live in houses. Precise data on numbers is unknown due to the lack of census information on Gypsy and Traveller populations in Britain. They are, it is said, descendants of Romanies (also, incorrectly, known as 'Egyptians') who came to England from the Continent in the sixteenth and seventeenth centuries. Like all Gypsy and Traveller communities, some intermarriage with non-Gypsies has taken place, but earlier customs and cultural practices are still preserved. In particular, different sorts of washing are kept separate, and often the possessions of the dead are burnt or otherwise destroyed.[7]
- **Welsh Gypsies** (sometimes referred to as 'Kalé', which means 'Black' in the Romani language and is used here to refer to the apparent darker skin of this community) of north Wales. These very few families are supposed to have migrated from the south-west of England to Wales in the seventeenth and eighteenth centuries. There is much debate regarding the actual existence, or otherwise, of this group. From the evidence available it appears to be a very small population who all live in houses in the north of Wales. Again, from the evidence, it appears that up until recently an inflected Romani (with endings changing for tense and case) was spoken by these families (the Woods family in particular).[8]
- **Irish Travellers** (sometimes referred to as 'Minceir' or 'Pavees') are a largely nomadic group from Ireland who speak a variety of English and Gammon/Shelta. Irish Travellers are a relatively small indigenous ethnic minority group who have been part of Irish society for many centuries. Their sense of common identity, their history, their nomadism and their own language sets them apart from who they call 'buffers' (non-Travellers) in contemporary Irish society. Common family names include McDonagh, Joyce,

Sweeney and Collins. Unlike Britain, Ireland did include Irish
Travellers in the last census (2002). According to the census
figures, there are well over 4,000 Traveller families in Ireland
today, making a total Traveller population of some 23,681 people.[9]
Like other Gypsy and Traveller populations, the Irish Traveller
community is a young and growing one; from the census we can
also see that 63 per cent of Irish Travellers are under the age of
twenty-five yet only 3.3 per cent of the population are over the age
of sixty-five. It is also a moving population, and not just within
Ireland. For example, Gmelch and Gmelch (1985) have noted the
cross-channel migration of Irish Travellers into Britain and also
into America.[10] They regard this process as a result of increasing
urbanisation and industrial change in Ireland back in the 1950s
and as a Traveller adaptation strategy to changing economic
circumstances.[11]

- **Scottish Gypsy/Travellers** (sometimes referred to as 'Nawkins' or
  'Nachins') are a largely nomadic group although like in England,
  Ireland and Wales many families are now living on established
  sites or in houses and many tend to travel during the summer
  months for work and holidays. Some families speak a 'Cant'
  language that has a range of dialects reflecting geographical
  location. The Cant has a large vocabulary of words which are
  derived from a variety of different sources. In the north-east of
  Scotland, the Cant tends to have more of a Gaelic structure whilst
  in the south, around the Borders, it is closer to the Anglo-Romani
  spoken by English Romanichals. Scottish Gypsy/Travellers have a
  rich history and a tradition of artistic endeavour and many ballads
  have been preserved from the Scottish tradition by Travellers from
  the likes of the Stewart and Robertson families, to name but two.
  Likewise, folk-storytellers such as Duncan Williamson, Stanley
  Robertson and Jimmy McBeath have written books which keep
  alive the history, values and traditions of Scottish Gypsy/
  Travellers. Common Traveller family names include Robertson,
  Faa, McDonald, Stewart and McPhee.[12]

- **New Travellers** (sometimes referred to as 'New Age Travellers') are
  a multi-ethnic, mixed-class community that largely emerged from
  the free-festival movement of the 1960s. The New Traveller
  population also includes individuals and families who took to life
  on the road during the 1980s when the harsh and restrictive social

policies of Thatcherism impacted on younger people and led to high rates of unemployment. Again, like most of the Gypsy and Traveller groups identified here, robust data on numbers is not collected; 'Tash' (Alan Lodge) has suggested numbers could be as low as 5,000 and as high as 50,000.[13] Those New Traveller families and individuals staying in Britain today tend to try and follow an 'alternative' or 'low impact' nomadic lifestyle and for some the lifestyle is through choice or birth whilst for others it is due to social or economic reasons. Many families have moved into mainland Europe to continue their nomadic way of life, especially after the 1994 Criminal Justice and Public Order Act was introduced.[14]

Other Gypsy and Traveller communities live in Britain as well, such as those Romanies from various parts of central and eastern Europe who arrived during the twentieth century. This includes Coppersmiths (*Kalderash*) whose grandparents came in the 1930s and Hungarian Romanies (*Romungro*) who came as refugees following the events of 1956.[15] More recent arrivals, in the last decade or so, from Romania, Poland, the former Yugoslavia, the Czech Republic and Slovakia have not been allowed to settle in the main, with only a few families and individuals having 'exceptional leave to remain' (as it used to be known until 2002 when it changed to 'humanitarian protection'). Most of the 4,000–5,000-plus Romanies who live throughout Britain are settled in houses and amongst some of the groups, such as the Coppersmiths, the Romani language is spoken in the home. An element of 'ethnic passing' occurs whereby Romanies may tell neighbours that they are another nationality, such as Greek, in order to avoid potential discrimination. Romani asylum seekers and refugees in Britain have their own quite unique needs, not least language issues.

Travelling Showpeople, it has been argued, are Britain's 'last lost tribe'.[16] They total some 21,000–25,000 people and, like Romanies, have their own language and culture. They also tend to marry within the extended group. Showpeople are commercial nomads who move from town to town during the fair season which lasts from February through to November.[17] During the height of the season it is not uncommon for some 250 fairs to be held each week across larger towns. Ancient charters dating from the Middle Ages give Showpeople the right to pitch their rides, shows and stalls in certain places at certain times. These often coincide with saints' days and feasts. For example, Stratford was granted a charter in 1196 and a statute protects this fair. It would take an Act of Parliament to stop the fair taking place on Stratford's streets. The fairs act as a fixed point in what is, by definition, a highly nomadic life. For Showpeople families, such as the Kemps, the Robinsons, the Noyces and the Clarks, they are a social as well as economic calendar. Life events, such as births, marriages and deaths, can all be related to dates of fairs in various parts of the country.

As with Gypsies, the Showpeople's way of life has long been seen as being out of date and redundant. The end of the fairs has been regularly predicted almost since they first started. In the mid-nineteenth century, the historian Thomas Frost argued that the fairs were becoming extinct due to the new attractions that the 'flatties' (settled people) were being entertained by: the music halls, zoological gardens and aquariums. He suggested that 'the last Showmen will soon be as great a curiosity as the dodo'.[18] It is clear, however, that the Showpeople in the twenty-first century have survived and continued to prosper. Some of the legislation affecting Gypsies in Britain has also affected Showpeople and vice versa. It was the Showpeople's resistance to the 1889 Movable Dwellings Bill that led to the creation of the Van Dwellers Association (VDA). The VDA was later to become known as the Showmen's Guild that today both represents and governs the Showpeople.[19] It has a membership of some 5,000 and almost all of these are men. Nearly all the fairs in Britain are run under the auspices of the guild. More recent legislation, such as the Caravan Sites Act of 1968, never applied to Showpeople (or Circus people). In theory, their situation in relation to the 1994 Criminal Justice and Public Order Act (CJPOA) is just as precarious as it is for Gypsies and New Travellers. Tradition and heritage are two common words used to justify, support and legitimise both the fairs and Showpeople themselves. With local authorities constantly closing down such events, the Showpeople require a solid defence to protect their livelihood and very way of life.

Clearly, the diverse and heterogeneous nature of Gypsy and Traveller communities reveals the difficulties inherent in any attempt at analysing 'their' situation as a whole. In the large and growing literature on Gypsies and Travellers in Britain there is an abundance of books, articles and reports which simply promote overgeneralisations and merely add to the stereotypes that they are usually seeking to challenge. Nevertheless, it is important that issues common to these groups (such as the discrimination they face) are recognised and addressed in order that progress can be made in policy and practice development across a number of areas.

The legal position

It is important to state that in the eyes of the law different Gypsy and Traveller groups in Britain are regarded, formally, as ethnic minority groups. Both English Gypsies (since 1988, *CRE* v. *Dutton*, on appeal) and Irish Travellers (since 2000, *Kiely and Others* v. *Allied Domecq and Others*) are formally recognised as such and have protection under race-relations legislation. Scottish Gypsy/Travellers, although accepted by the Scottish Parliament and Executive as an ethnic minority group vis-à-vis race-relations legislation, have no formal legal recognition as no test case has yet gone through the courts. However, whatever their legal status, a significant aspect of the exclusion endured by Gypsies and Travellers is the *substantive* denial of ethnic minority status and corresponding rights. This takes many forms and operates on a day-to-day basis for many families as we shall see throughout the book: they are frequently perceived by service providers, the public and politicians as being social 'drop-outs' or living within 'deviant sub-cultures' that actively reject sedentarist norms.[20] As we shall see, this view has clear historical roots.

A question of numbers

The process of *estimating* the numbers of Gypsies and Travellers in Britain is a problematic one. The task of accurately *counting* the numbers of Gypsies and Travellers in Britain is an even more difficult undertaking. Problems are rooted in the general difficulties associated with counting so-called 'hard to reach' ethnic minority groups and mobile communities. The often subjective criteria associated with the definition of Gypsies and Travellers, coupled with inadequate representation in formal censuses, and a reluctance (of some) to declare their identity (out of fear of discrimination), have led to few quality datasets being produced.[21] Nevertheless, various individuals and organisations have made genuine attempts at reaching semi-credible estimates based on a mixture of official and unofficial sources.

The CRE currently estimates the overall number of Gypsies and Travellers in Britain to be between 200,000 and 300,000. However, they acknowledge that this is very much an estimate and reflects the fact that ethnic monitoring of the Gypsy and Traveller population, outside of schools, does not happen.[22] Other groups, such as the G&TLRC, estimate some 200,000 Gypsies and Travellers living across Britain whilst the Gypsy Council puts the figure at closer to 300,000 (as of 2004).[23] Our own educated estimate would be around the 250,000 figure.

In terms of official sources, national censuses in Britain do not have categories for Gypsy and Traveller groups and this did not change for the last one conducted during 2001. It is likely that pressure will be exerted to ensure that the categories of Gypsy and Traveller are included for the 2011 exercise.[24] Formal statistics on Gypsies and Travellers in England, Scotland and Wales therefore mainly derive from a confusing mix of caravan, household and pitch counts (see 'Gypsy Sites Policy' section at the Office of the Deputy Prime Minister [ODPM] website).[25] In England caravan counts are carried out twice a year on council and private sites as well as so-called 'unauthorised sites'. The biannual Gypsy counts reveal that about one-third live on sites which lack planning permission and are referred to as 'unauthorised'. About 70 per cent are described as 'settled', i.e. likely to have lived on the site for some time and wishing to stay, and 30 per cent as 'transit', i.e. relatively mobile. The latest available Office of the Deputy Prime Minister figures at the time of writing are for July 2004 covering England only. According to these figures, there were 4,232 caravans on unauthorised sites, 5,964 caravans on council/local authority sites and 4,813 caravans on authorised private sites; that is some 15,009 caravans in total.[26]

The counting of Gypsies and Travellers in Scotland is a relatively new development. Prior to 1998 there had only been two official counts, one in 1969 and one in 1992, where it was estimated that there were 450 households and 540 households respectively.[27] The reliability of these two counts, particularly in terms of the methodology used, was questioned by a number of organisations in Scotland, including the well-respected Save the Children, which considered the true numbers to be much higher. Since 1998 biannual counts are carried out of Gypsies and Travellers living in caravans in Scotland but these counts do not include Showpeople, Circus Travellers, New Travellers or Gypsy/Travellers residing in housing for all or part of the year. Similarly, concerns have been expressed about the methodology used in the biannual counts and the accuracy of figures. The latest figures available, for July 2004, based on information produced by the Scottish Executive Central Research Unit, recorded a total of 259 households on council sites, 146 on privately owned sites and 178 using unauthorised locations: the total Gypsy/Traveller population was thus 583 households or approximately 1,960 people.[28]

The last caravan count in Wales by the then Department of the Environment (DoE) was taken in 1997. It is not known when the next one will take place or even if one will actually happen again. A total of 732 caravans were counted for the 1997 count. This figure included 217 caravans located on unauthorised sites, 502 on council sites and only thirteen on private sites. The previous count in 1990 recorded a total of 692 caravans.[29] Like the counts in Scotland, a number of organisations have questioned the counting methods. Save the Children and the School of Education at Cardiff University published a report in 1998, which identified far greater numbers of Gypsies and Travellers living in Wales, especially those under the age of eighteen. Based on a wide range of sources, the report suggests that there are at least 1,809 Gypsy and Traveller children in Wales.[30] This is more than double the figure the Welsh Office counted in 1997.

It is worth noting that the question of numbers is important to 'get right' for a number of reasons. In Scotland, for example, the numbers collected during these twice-yearly counts are used by the Executive to help determine and inform issues such as pitch targets and 'toleration policies' that are used in relation to 'unauthorised' sites. More broadly, as Romanies in central and eastern Europe have found, if Gypsies and Travellers are not 'counted' then they tend to 'disappear' from official government policies and discourses and their specific needs are simply not recognised or planned and budgeted for. Of course, with the issue of suspect counting methodologies and understandable Gypsy and Traveller mistrust of certain census requests, it is little wonder that to this day debates rage regarding the question of numbers.[31]

Having briefly explored who the populations are and the issue of their numbers it seems prudent to briefly examine what history can tell us about Gypsies and Travellers and their relationship to Britain and Europe. What are the origins of these different groups?

Origins, history and migrations

> That the fate of Roma in the Holocaust, and their plight in contemporary Europe have generated only marginal concern are only two manifestations of the fact that, outside of the academic world, little is understood about Gypsies generally … the average person's Romani associations are with the 'gypsy' of fictional literature [and] of [the] Hollywood movie.'[32]

Although the western European mistake of regarding Egypt as the 'home' of the Gypsies has long been discounted, the 'true' origins of this community of people continues to cause a great deal of debate and discussion. This issue of origins, like no other, has fuelled a series of often bitter and personalised exchanges both within and outside the academic community, especially in the pages of the *Journal of the Gypsy Lore Society*, (first established in 1888 and now called *Romani Studies*).[33] In more recent times these arguments and debates have been taken into other books and journal articles by leading scholars such as Ian Hancock, Leo Lucassen, Wim Willems and Anne-Marie Cottaar, Yaron Matras and Judith Okely, to name but a few.[34]

Okely, as well as the Dutch team of Lucassen, Willems and Cottaar, contends that the Indian origin thesis has served as a charter for accepting Gypsies as a genuine 'exotic' group. Drawing on a period of extended fieldwork with English Gypsies in south-east England, she argues that the origins question is largely irrelevant to Gypsies today. However, Matras, and others such as Hancock, point to the linguistic evidence to support their claims regarding the Indian heritage. In the context of this chapter, it is not our intention to add weight to one camp's arguments over the other. One thing that could be said with some certainty, however, is that the 'real Romani' debate dates back to when Gypsies were first recorded as 'arriving' in the British Isles, around the fifteenth/sixteenth century. The 'real' Romani is considered to be dark-haired with brown eyes whilst the 'pretended Egyptian' possesses lighter hair and blue eyes. Such 'darkness' is not a criterion or basis for membership though. Just like non-Gypsies,

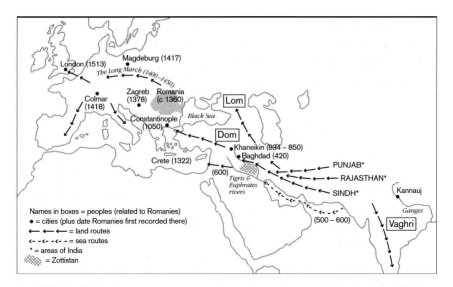

Map of possible migration routes from India to Asia, Africa and Europe from
Gypsies: from the Ganges to the Thames by Donald Kenrick

Gypsies have entertained ideas about 'pure-blooded' Gypsies, without the Indian linkage. Indeed, in many ways it is essential to draw upon such ideas in exchanges, work deals and trading insults between different families and groups in order to establish hierarchies, rank and privileges.[35] For both non-Gypsies and Gypsies, the 'real' Romanies are seen as a very distinct genetic group. 'Blood' here is used as an important metaphor for favoured and despised groups; depending on the context and interests of the labeller. For example, dark-skinned 'Gypsy Rose Lee' with her crystal ball and uncorrupted 'pure' Romani is for some the 'real thing', whilst the fair-skinned hawker with a strange dialect of pidgin or creolised Romani is *didikai* (half-caste, a rough Traveller), or, even worse, *mochadi* (unclean, ritually polluted). In the British Isles, it is the fabled Welsh Kalé (and the English Romani Gypsies) who are often accorded the status of 'real' Romanies, whilst the Irish Minceir (until the arrival of New [Age] Travellers at least) were considered the 'tinkers' and 'half-breeds'. These types of 'ethnic' contests and rivalries are not unique within the Gypsy and Traveller communities and they happen within and between most national and ethnic groupings to some degree.

Although the question of 'origins' is still heavily contested, it is now largely agreed that it was north-west India that formed the cradle of the Romani nation[36] (see p.23).

This much at least is accepted by the majority of scholars who have attempted to reconstruct the history of this people. Possibly they existed as a loose confederation of nomadic craftsmen and entertainers following a pattern similar to groups such as the Banjara and Sapera (Kalbelia) in modern India. Such a confederation formed during their stay in the Middle East. No contemporary accounts exist of the first Romanies to reach Persia but the poet Firdausi and other authors in the tenth century write of the arrival of Indian entertainers 500 years earlier.[37] Linguistic and other evidence suggests that the Romanies of Europe belong to groups who left India over 1,000 years ago.[38] They spent a comparatively short time in the Middle East. At no time did they move in a solid mass from East to West but their pattern of migration was probably similar to that of today with family groups moving at different speeds, according to local circumstances and opportunities for work.[39] The first families recorded in eastern Europe arrived from Asia Minor and earned their living as bootmakers and metalworkers. Eastern Europe has continued to have a large settled Romani population, usually called *Tsigani*, in contrast to western Europe where the word 'Gypsy' is synonymous with nomad. The first authenticated records of their presence in Britain are in 1505 for Scotland and 1514 for Lambeth in England.[40] However, since two ladies apparently dressed up as Romanies for a court masked ball in England as early as 1510 it is *possible* that 'real' Romanies had been in the country for some years before then.[41]

Roma/Gypsies: from India to Europe? [42]

The map shows movement of groups of Romanies from India through the Middle East, Asia-Minor, eastern Europe and western Europe. This 'path' is constructed from various historical records of a Romani presence in the various countries and from available linguistic data. It should also be noted, as indicated previously, that this 'route of diaspora' is contested by the likes of Judith Okely and Wim Willems.[43]

Across Europe, since the fourteenth and fifteenth centuries, Gypsies and Travellers have experienced periods of exclusion, containment and assimilation. Throughout their history, Gypsies have been labelled as criminals, aliens and trespassers (and a lot more besides) by the various nation states which have encountered them within their borders. Perhaps due to the hazardous times, small local villages and towns when first encountering these 'dark-skinned outsiders' reacted with fear, contempt and outright rejection. Despite their relatively small numbers and peaceful intentions, all and sundry – from peasants to princes – took it upon themselves to enact measures against the presence of Gypsies and Travellers in their locality.[44] The rejection of the various guilds and churches quickly translated into a national and transnational affair where the condemnation and banishment of Gypsies and Travellers was signed and sealed by royal decree.

All the present members of the European Union (EU) (including recent members from the central and eastern parts of Europe) at one time in their history have had anti-Gypsy policies on their statute books. The examples are many and brutal – such as the policies of Frederick William I, who, in 1725, condemned to death any Gypsy over the age of eighteen caught on Prussian territory.[45] Sanctions have ranged from deportation to corporal punishment, from hanging to organised state genocide. For example, in England the historical catalogue of the horrors and atrocities committed against Gypsies is extensive. In the sixteenth century, under Henry VIII, legislation was introduced whereby Gypsies (or 'Egyptians') could be (and were) imprisoned, executed or banished from the realm and have their property confiscated for no offence other than being *perceived* to be a Gypsy.[46]

Such treatment and acts of inhumanity are not confined to the vaults of history. In the twentieth century anti-Gypsy exclusion came in the extreme form of what Professor Ian Hancock has termed '*O Baro Porrajmos*' – 'The Great Devouring' or Gypsy Holocaust – carried out under the Nazis in Germany.[47] Bio-medical 'evidence' was produced to 'prove' that there was no other way to deal with the 'anti-socials'. From 1938 to late 1943, Gypsies living in Germany experienced house arrest, deportation to Poland, shootings and internment in camps such as Auschwitz-Birkenau.[48] Almost no eastern European Gypsy family was left unaffected by such actions. Given the limitations of present research data, most estimates range from 250,000 to 500,000 in terms of numbers killed during this period of European history.[49]

The history of the Gypsies is important to understand and be aware of. Such experiences have shaped their interactions and dealings with non-Gypsies, even those with an apparent sympathetic or humanist face. The real and continuing fear of a 'final solution', such as that attempted by the Nazis, means that British legislation, for example, the CJPOA is seen by many Gypsies as a form of 'ethnic cleansing' in itself; the criminalisation of a nomadic way of life. To the non-Gypsy reader this may seem extreme and a rather unrealistic perception and fear. However, this legislation, alongside recent events in the former Yugoslavia, suggests to Gypsies in Britain, and indeed Europe, that some countries are 'against' them in a variety of forms. Clearly, to a group that has endured a 'devouring' such as the Romanies, it is not unrealistic.

Strangely, the technocratic twentieth century has seen policies of exclusion and assimilation almost meet and coexist with one another. In Europe, the latter half of that century saw legal moves to outlaw various forms of anti-Gypsy restrictions and impositions, such as punishments, slavery and forced settlement. Humanists and liberals argued that Gypsies were now 'socially adaptable' and, through psycho-social processes of reintegration, could be transformed into 'useful citizens'.[50] The countries making up central and eastern Europe were by no means alone in searching out such policies. Most western European countries were also engaged in 'saving Gypsies from themselves'. The day-to-day lifestyle of Gypsies came to be regulated by the state, for example, the ability to stop, stay, travel and work in ways which fitted with their cultural norms and practices. As J.-P. Liégeois has noted, such assimilationist policies can be contradictory: whilst in most (if not all) EU countries there is a legal obligation for children to attend school, there is also legislation which limits the duration and location of stay in certain urban areas.[51] Education is not alone in this respect; Clark's work on New Travellers and social security in England and Scotland found similar contradictions in state policies regarding work and travel.[52]

Conclusion

This chapter has given a brief profile of the different groups which could be said to make up the present-day Gypsy and Traveller population of Britain. More detail on each group will reveal itself as the book progresses. As well as providing some facts and figures regarding Gypsy and Traveller numbers, we also reviewed the exclusion, containment and assimilation that has thus far marked their history. The question of origins was also briefly outlined and explored. As we have suggested, it is not just a question of looking at Gypsies and Travellers who are nomadic. In defining who is and who is not part of the Gypsy and Traveller population of Britain we have attempted to be as inclusive as possible. This is why we have also mentioned groups such as New Travellers and Travelling Showpeople and their place in Britain. We have also seen how the roots of prejudice against Gypsies and Travellers took hold in Europe and we have seen how a largely negative (and false) picture emerged. Gypsies are, in many ways, the perfect 'stranger' that the sociologist Simmel discussed: a type of stranger that can be made to fit as a scapegoat for any particular crisis. As Simmel notes, the stranger has certain defining characteristics, such as a strangeness of origin and not being an owner of land. He suggests:

> The Stranger is thus being discussed here, not in the sense often touched upon in the past, as the wanderer who comes today and goes tomorrow, but rather as the person *who comes today and stays tomorrow*. He is, so to speak, the potential wanderer … He is fixed within a spatial group, or within a group whose boundaries are similar to spatial boundaries. But his position in this group is determined, essentially, by the fact that he has not belonged to it from the beginning … *He is near and far at the same time.*[53] (author's emphasis)

Although using the Jewish community as his example in this essay, it could quite easily have been Gypsies and Travellers that Simmel was discussing.[54] They have 'wandered' and stayed in Britain and are now in a position, because of their culture, values, language and identity, of being 'near and far' from their settled neighbours. Those choosing a 'house with wheels on it' (a trailer) are considered outside normal 'moral boundaries' of the settled majority and therefore open to 'legitimate' forms of social and political injustice.[55]

CHAPTER TWO

Family, community and identity

Margaret Greenfields

Introduction

In this chapter we set out to explore the ways in which 'family' and 'community' are central to understanding the nature of Gypsy and Traveller identities. As we have stated in the book's main Introduction, no attempt is being made to fit all Travellers into one box and say that particular characteristics are (for example) 'what Irish/New/ Occupational Travellers do' or that 'x means someone must be an English Gypsy'. Given the differences both between and among differing travelling communities, and the complex nature of individuals and families, it is only possible to discuss certain concepts and behaviours and state that specific traits are more commonly found within *some* groups, or are widely acknowledged to exist amongst *all* Gypsies and Travellers. By definition, therefore, we can only provide a crude map of Gypsy and Traveller identities and characteristics and then strongly recommend that the reader expands their knowledge and understanding by talking to individual Gypsies and Travellers, who are, after all, the experts on their own lives.

However, while considering the nature of identity, family and community, we *might* tentatively draw conclusions that certain aspects of Gypsy and Traveller lifestyles arise as a logical response to nomadism (or previously being nomadic), while other elements of Gypsy and Traveller lifestyles and belief systems may be socio-cultural behaviours (e.g. membership of a particular group may involve acting in particular ways and sharing certain beliefs which identify individuals – both to 'insiders' and 'outsiders' – as members of that community) which in turn act as markers to indicate who a person is; their values; what they believe; and their relationships with other groups.[1] In other words, behaviours and cultural expectations may function as keys to a recognisable *identity*, possession of which marks someone out as a member of the Travelling community. In addition, identity is often closely bound up with a person's *ethnicity*,[2] a term which is often understood to incorporate not only behaviours and practices, but also individual and community genetic heritage, given the strong preference among some minority ethnic groups for marriages to take place between individuals from within the same community.

Identity and community social-control mechanisms

From the above discussion we can see that identity is both complex, and central, to an individual's sense of self and their understanding of their place in the world. The existence of cultural ideals, norms and behaviours, 'what a Gypsy or Traveller does, or does *not* do', often constitutes such a strong element of individual or group identity that the absence or presence of a particular constituent or the breaking of a code of behaviour may lead (in an individual's own eyes, or that of other group members), to a person's acculturation,[3] or deculturation[4] and thus the weakening of their Gypsy- or Traveller-specific identity. In some cases (as with most ethnic and social communities) flagrant breaches of expected behaviour may be severe enough to lead to an individual being 'punished' through internal social-control mechanisms, or in extreme cases expelled from their own community (at least on a temporary basis or until reparation is made).[5]

Generally, however, where an individual or family have offended against, or been 'shamed' by, other Gypsies or Travellers, 'avoidance'[6] techniques are used to minimise social disruption. This way of responding to internal tensions is so common among the Travelling communities that it can be said to be a social norm, a pattern of behaviour which is recognised and accepted as part of the culturally correct way of responding to difficulties, and as such may be identified as a marker, adherence to which indicates a person's knowledge and membership of the community.

Given the relatively small size of the Travelling communities, not only will other Gypsy or Traveller families rapidly become aware of the infringement of social rules which have led to such an 'avoidance' situation, but many families may also be related to (or in a relationship of social obligation with) another party to the dispute, in turn leading to expectations that they will behave in a particular manner, which at the very least may carry the potential for social distress or embarrassment. Thus by avoiding places and situations where members of the opposing family and their friends are likely to be present, not only does the person who has infringed social codes avoid the potential escalation of disputes between kin groups, but they may in some cases experience a form of self-imposed punishment combined with a public acknowledgement of their inappropriate behaviour, for example, when a Gypsy or Traveller feels the need to avoid much treasured social gatherings such as Appleby or Epsom to avoid contact with individuals or families with whom they are in dispute.

While internal control systems therefore generally function extremely well in ensuring that members of a community are aware of the 'correct way' of living as a Gypsy or Traveller, it is also worth stressing that an individual cannot be deprived of their ethnicity or their identity as a Gypsy or Traveller as a result of their breach of social rules. They may be seen to be behaving inappropriately, or be spoken of as acting more like a *gorje* than a Romani *chal* (for example), but someone who is born into a Travelling family will be regarded by their community as a Gypsy or Traveller for life, although (as we will see), depending upon context, a person might be spoken of as possessing 'more' or 'fewer' Traveller characteristics, and this may sometimes be put down to their degree of contact with non-Travellers, or a marriage to someone from a different community which may perhaps have influenced them to breach accepted codes of behaviour.

One identity or many?

Given that different Travelling groups (and indeed families) will vary in their practices and the centrality of specific beliefs and behaviours, we refer to 'identities' throughout this chapter, as an individual will hold multiple roles and beliefs throughout their life cycle. Thus a Traveller may identify themself as such, but also specify that they are a Romani Gypsy, an Irish/Scottish/Welsh Traveller or a Showman or woman, whilst at the same time performing[7] an identity as a mother, father, son, daughter, husband or wife *within* their own culture. Certain expectations and understandings will exist within the specific Traveller community, and also wider society, about the meaning of each role, as a person moves through their life cycle. Indeed, within every culture, understanding of appropriate behaviours for an individual will alter as, for example, they grow from child to spouse, to parent to elder.[8]

So a person can be identified as, for example, 'a Traveller who is a member of a particular family by birth and another family by marriage, the mother of A and B, grandmother of X, Y and Z and also someone who is a skilled singer, and specialist worker or trader'. In our example (let us call the lady Mrs M), she would have a set of expectations and understandings about how she behaves (in general) towards her relatives (both older and younger), how they act towards her and the mutual duties and obligations that individuals owe to each other, either out of common courtesy or because of close friendly relationships that exist between particular relatives.[9] A further set of relationships (which are qualitatively different from those created by marriage or birth) might also exist between Mrs M and the families she travelled with, both as a child and since her marriage, and she will also have a role as an in-law to her married children's spouses and relatives (although in practice these in-laws might also be Mrs M's cousins).

So, while Mrs M may be related by blood as well as marriage or through ties of friendship to a number of her families, her identity as a relative or friend will still vary in different contexts as, for example, someone will usually expect to be able to ask for greater help with child care from a parent or sister than they would from a cousin. Similarly, as Mrs M becomes older and perhaps less able to manage certain chores for herself, while she might see old childhood friends and relatives on an almost daily basis, she would probably expect to receive most practical help from her daughters or daughters-in-law rather than from more 'distant' relatives. In addition Mrs M may still have her own set of responsibilities which result from her role as a daughter or daughter-in-law, for example, needing to support her own older kin, or ensure that graves are tended regularly.

Identity is therefore a combination of 'given' characteristics (being male, and a Traveller) and 'earned' or 'ascribed' factors (father, brother, good provider, horseman). As an individual 'performs' the behaviours which are culturally ascribed to each of those roles, they will internalise those actions and reinforce them as a key part of that identity. For example, 'a good mother' will usually be a description of a woman who cares for her children in a manner which is recognised as 'correct' and worthy of praise within her particular culture. Thus, acting in a particular manner means that a people will say of a woman 'she is a good mother' and in turn, she will incorporate this culturally defined concept of herself as 'a good mother' into her *identity*.

Positive and negative aspects of 'identity'

We can therefore see that membership of a community can enable someone to have positive feelings about themself and their actions and can allow them to celebrate their cultural identity within a strongly supportive environment. Equally, a sense of identity that results from membership of a group or community can be a double-edged sword, as social-control mechanisms initiated from within that community (for example, 'shaming' someone who does not conform to the behaviour expected by the group) can diminish a person's sense of identity and lead instead to feelings of grief, or a sense that they are letting down their family or other members of the community.

A strong sense of identity, reinforced by the support of a community, can, however, strengthen an individual's political and social position and enable them to achieve positive outcomes which they might not have felt within their grasp if they had remained isolated and unaware of the solidarity of their individual and wider community. For example, the growth of 'Gypsy politics' over the past four decades and the exciting initiatives represented by the (UK) Gypsy and Traveller Law Reform Coalition (launched in 2003) which brought together a broad coalition of Romani Gypsy, Irish, Scottish and New Travellers to campaign for social inclusion for all Travelling groups, could not have come about without the increased confidence of Travellers and their awareness of the need to transcend differences to raise awareness and improve conditions for members of the diverse communities.

However, it is worth noting that alongside the growth of identity politics, and the associated higher profile of individuals and communities who may in the past have sought to diminish their 'otherness' or (particularly for house-dwelling Travellers or individuals who have perhaps gained prestige through academic or industrial success) hide their origins from members of wider society; the increased recognition of anti-Traveller racism casts a dark shadow. Accordingly, acknowledging a Gypsy or Traveller identity (a source of pride and strength in many circumstances), may place individuals and communities at risk of discrimination or violence if faced by groups which are hostile to their specific culture or ethnicity.

Whilst we explore the issues of anti-Traveller racism elsewhere in this book (Chapters 6 and 9), in late 2003, not only did the Chair of the CRE note that the level of discrimination experienced by Travellers in the UK was still 'like the (American) Deep South for black people in the 1950s',[10] but also a major public-opinion poll carried out by MORI for the pressure group Stonewall[11] found that 35 per cent of respondents admitted to hostile and racist attitudes towards Gypsies and Travellers, a higher percentage than reported feeling the same emotions towards asylum seekers and refugees (34 per cent), members of ethnic groups other than their own (18 per cent), or gay and lesbian people (17 per cent). In the light of these grim statistics, the critical importance of family and community practices in enabling Travellers to retain a sense of security and identity becomes starkly and uncompromisingly clear.

Accordingly, in the remainder of this chapter we set out to consider (often broadly, but where appropriate, through the use of concrete, culture-specific examples) a range of issues that are of focal importance to Traveller culture, the making of community identities and the nature of family.

Marriage, partnership and the transmission of culture

As we have discussed in Chapter 1, there are many Travelling communities in the UK. Apart from New Travellers, who tend to cohabit rather than go through a formal marriage ceremony,[12] new family units are generally formed within the communities through the celebration of a wedding. Very often the marriage will take place in a church with which the family has longstanding connections, and it is not uncommon to find that several generations of a family may have been married at that location, and indeed other relatives may be buried in the churchyard (see 'The end of life and respect for the deceased').

Weddings are a time for immense celebration, both of the young couple's future life, and also of the joining of families and the hope for future generations. Typically wedding parties will continue over several days and usually involve large numbers of relatives and friends travelling to join in the celebrations. Sadly, and once again symptomatic

Wedding of Gwendolyn and
Cyril Lyneham (courtesy of
Sam Wilson)

of the misunderstandings that typify the relationships between
Gypsies and Travellers and sedentary society, gatherings of Travellers
from a wide area are often causes of complaint and fear for *gorje* house-
dwellers who fail to appreciate that Travellers bring their homes when
they come together for community celebrations, instead of moving into
a hotel with some suitcases for a few days, which would be the
equivalent for a house-dweller attending a similar event. Even more
problematic for the family hosting the wedding are the strict
regulations that usually apply at private or local authority sites, which
mean that relatives are often unable to pull onto the site with their
trailers or the host family may be in breach of planning permission
(see Chapter 4). In this way, traditional wedding (and christening or
funeral) gatherings can sometimes lead to additional stress and fear of
conflict with authorities for the communities who are coming together
in celebration (or mourning). Overwhelmingly, however, immense
efforts will be made by Travellers to gather together for weddings, and
resultant difficulties are generally overcome amid the community
festivities.

Within the Romani Irish and Scottish Traveller communities,
marriage tends to take place at a young age, often while the bride and
groom are in their late teens. Marriage is regarded as being for life, and
the level of divorce or separation is exceptionally low among
traditional Gypsies and Travellers. When couples are experiencing
difficulties in their relationship, other family members or someone
with moral authority (for example, a priest where the family are
Catholics) will usually make strenuous attempts to bring about a
reconciliation or to assist the couple in dealing with the problems
within the family.

Under Church Army guidance, two Gypsy brothers marry two Gypsy sisters,
Burley, New Forest, c.1922 (courtesy of Len Smith)

The Church Army persuaded many Gypsies to marry formally. Here three
couples leave Bransgore Church, New Forest, after a joint ceremony, c.1920
(courtesy of Len Smith)

Couples will often have known each other for most of their lives before agreeing to marry, and it is not uncommon for cousins to wed, or for two sisters to marry a set of brothers or relatives (perhaps cousins) of a brother-in-law. Given the close-knit and relatively small size of the traditional Travelling communities, it is unsurprising that the majority of families are related to each other in some way through blood or marriage ties. In general, Gypsies or Travellers will marry someone of the same ethnicity as themselves, although increasingly, intermarriage is beginning to occur, for example, between Romani Gypsies and Irish Travellers or Scottish Gypsy/Travellers. In addition, in some cases New Travellers who have been 'on the road' for a long period of time (or who are perhaps second-generation Travellers), who have become familiar with and are respected by traditional Gypsies and Travellers, are 'marrying in' to the other communities, although the New Travellers, despite their nomadic practices, will still be perceived of as a *gorje*, just like any other non-Gypsy or Traveller who has 'married in' to a traditional community.

In general, given the importance of family and community to Gypsies and Travellers, a non-Traveller spouse (in our experience usually a wife) would be expected to move to live with their Gypsy or Traveller relatives to learn the cultural practices and social codes of their new family and to ensure that any children born to the couple are raised in a culturally appropriate manner.

Although 'mixed marriages' are gradually becoming more common among the younger generations of Gypsies and Travellers, and may in turn bring about changes in cultural practices and sets of family connections that can strengthen both communities, marriage between Gypsies and Travellers of different ethnicities may be greeted with caution or disapproval by older travelling people who may believe that a wedding to someone whose background and family are well known and who is a member of the same community offers more stability and cultural continuity. Where the spouse is from a non-Gypsy or Traveller background, given the need for the new partner to learn the ways of the Travelling community (and perhaps to overcome their own expectations and limited knowledge about Gypsies and Travellers), the transition to a stable family unit may sometimes be quite slow, as the newcomer will need to learn a different set of skills and values, and may sometimes find that it is difficult for them to be accepted. As their knowledge of the culture increases and particularly as children are born to the couple, the integration of the non-Gypsy or Traveller spouse will become more complete as they are then the parent of Gypsy and Traveller children. Despite acceptance by the community, however, it is our experience that (even, for example, when a couple may have been married for thirty years) the *gorje* spouse will usually make clear that they are not an 'ethnic' Traveller, as they can never fully attain the status of a person who has been born and brought up as a member of the community, any more (for example) than a White English convert to Hinduism (however devout) can be culturally identical to someone who is South Asian Hindu by birth.

The cultural advantages therefore of relatively early marriage to someone from a 'known' family are that the spouses come from the same community, know the ways of the family they are marrying into, and have often had many years of contact with both their future husband or wife (perhaps through knowing the sisters or brothers of the person they will marry) and their in-laws. The young couple will often have met while stopping at the same roadside halt, on authorised sites, or at social events such as weddings, christenings or the big horse fairs at Appleby or Stow. For the parents of the bride or groom, knowing the family their daughter or son is marrying into usually provides security and confidence about their child's future welfare, and in addition creates new relationship ties between families that may be of use when working together, gaining access to pitches, communally purchasing land for a site, or generally simply strengthening the ties of the community. It has also been drawn to our attention that with increasing independence for young people, (although this has always been so to some extent) some Gypsies or Travellers are choosing partners from families that are *not* on the 'approved list' which can result in tensions that last for many years.

The degree of knowledge that Gypsies and Travellers have about other members of the community (although privacy is also valued and gossip about neighbours and family members discouraged) means that information is available to the prospective bride and groom and their wider kin about the family into which they are marrying, their new relatives' abilities as providers, strength of family connections, wealth, reputation and standing within the community. By marrying within the same ethnic community, transmission of cultural values and knowledge of traditional practices are also assured, allowing children to feel confident in their heritage, although inevitably, over time, cultures change as a result of contact with a range of individuals and institutions and the impact of developments in the wider world.

In contrast to 'traditional' Gypsy and Travelling communities, many New Travellers enter into a nomadic lifestyle after commencing a relationship with a partner who is already 'on the road', often as a result of the couple meeting while attending a festival or fair where the nomadic partner was working (for example, as site crew).[13] However, indications exist that the longer an individual remains travelling, the greater the likelihood of second or subsequent partnerships taking place with someone with a similar nomadic history,[14] so, for example, someone may leave a house to partner with a New Traveller, remain nomadic when the relationship ends, and then re-partner with an individual who has been travelling for a number of years. Given that we are now seeing second- and even young third-generation New Travellers, it is unsurprising that networks of family connections are beginning to develop between families who have travelled for perhaps twenty-plus years.[15] Although evidence is limited, indications exist that among those New Traveller families that have remained nomadic for considerable lengths of time, young adults who grew up Travelling are demonstrating a preference for partnering with other New Travellers who have been 'on the road' for their entire lives. Accordingly, over time it may be that kin networks between certain sets of New Travellers continue to develop, and grow to mirror the relationship patterns that are common to traditional Gypsies and Travellers, with the same benefits accruing from inter-community partnerships (for example, social cohesion, transmission of culture, knowledge of family background), as are noted among traditional Travelling communities.

For New Travellers, partnership formation is generally less formalised than among other Travelling communities and tends to crystallise into cohabitation rather than marriage. While cohabiting relationships may be of long standing (and often result in the birth of children), New Travellers, in common with many younger non-Travellers, do not generally consider that marriage is an essential part of a close relationship, and therefore both relationship formation and ending tend to be seen as a personal matter rather than a community issue.[16] Although formal marriage is relatively unusual, some couples may make a personal commitment through undergoing a public or private ceremony, for example, a 'hand-fasting',[17] before their friends and members of their community, or private exchange of promises. Where children are born to a couple, regardless of whether the parents separate, strong community expectations exist among New Travellers that both parents will participate in their children's upbringing and share responsibility for their well-being.[18]

Reputation and collective responsibility within the Travelling communities

Reputation amongst Gypsies and Travellers (both traditional and 'New') is of primary importance in determining the level of respect owed to individuals (and their extended families) and can even make the difference between a person achieving marriage to their preferred partner or having the opportunity to participate in successful trading activities. If a person has a 'bad reputation' or is regarded as behaving in a non-Gypsy or Traveller-like way (for example, by cheating on a deal with another community member, having given one's word as to the worth or value of an object and having reached an agreement over sale; or by leaving their spouse for another partner) then the shame of their behaviour will not only damage them as an individual, but also (particularly in 'traditional' communities) reflect upon their family. As touched upon above, kinship obligations are taken extremely seriously by Gypsies and Travellers and 'word' will travel fast about a person to be avoided, or who has broken the moral contract.[19] Similarly, within Romani and Scottish/Irish Traveller communities someone who is regarded (for example) as being a very 'traditional person', generous, or a good provider for their family, will be regarded with the respect that is due to them, and in turn their family's honour will be enhanced as well as their personal reputation and social and cultural capital.[20]

In this way, the reputation of an individual will impact upon their network of relatives and friends, so that family members share a moral responsibility for the reputation and actions of their kin. Among New Traveller communities, although no formal notion of collective responsibility exists for a family member's aberrant behaviour, research indicates that friends, relatives and other site residents will often seek to exert some form of social control over an individual who is perceived to be breaking the moral contract. This is particularly noteworthy where a parent (perhaps a separated father) is perceived to be failing in their responsibilities towards a child, in which case social sanctions will usually be applied until they conform to the expectations of their community.[21]

Given the importance of reputation, and the tendency towards shared responsibility for the behaviour of close family members, it is therefore understandable (among traditional Gypsies and Travellers) that parents will wish their sons and daughters to marry into 'a good family', one, for example, where high moral standards are kept (see 'Gender relationships' below), and where both partners share a mutual agreement about their obligations to the wider family and their role within the community.

Gender relationships

The discussion below focuses predominantly on gender roles within the Romani, Irish and Scottish Traveller communities. Among New Travellers gender roles tend to be fluid and no clear expectations exist over which partner will take primary responsibility for raising children, undertaking manual work, or occupying the role of primary breadwinner and 'head of the household'. It is not unusual to find men caring for young children while their partners participate in paid employment, male lone parents, or female mechanics, within the New Traveller communities. Generally, responsibility for domestic duties and employment patterns depends upon an individually negotiated agreement made between the parties to a relationship, with the couple's roles depending to a large extent on the skills and opportunities available to each partner.[22]

However, within the traditional Travelling communities, men and women occupy distinct roles. A couple do not regard themselves as being in competition, but part of a mutually complementary relationship, with men being primarily responsible for supporting their family financially and practically – for example, through making connections with other relatives so that employment opportunities exist – and women taking overall responsibility for the home and children. Certain aspects of life – for example, matters relating to pregnancy, personal care for elders and teaching appropriate household and hygiene skills to daughters – are very much the role of women, and it would be inappropriate and cause offence to both men and women if a man were to intervene in these matters. Similarly, a man will take care of his sons' training in employment skills, negotiate over finances, deal with land purchase (although the land will usually be formally registered in the name of his wife), matters of family reputation and practical issues such as vehicle repairs and employment opportunities. While a woman will generally take a lesser part in public discussions about these matters, doubtless in private the couple will be equally involved in decision-making and debate, as Traveller women are as strong and confident in their roles as are their men.

In public, however, women are expected, and willing, to appear to be subservient to men, although much joking to the opposite sometimes occurs. At social gatherings, weddings, funerals, etc., men and women will *always* split into their separate gender groups.

When working with Gypsy and Traveller families, health issues, education of children and matters pertaining to home life will generally be discussed with the woman of the household,[23] with consultations on the 'outside world' (financial issues, etc.) remaining the realm of her husband. This is not to say that men are not interested or involved with their children's upbringing, or that women do not participate in financial decision-making, however, as given that both children and the elders remain central to Gypsy and Traveller community life, any individual who failed to consider and take account of the needs of the wider family would be held to be in breach of fundamental social codes. In essence, they would be perceived to be behaving in a manner that diminished their identity as a Gypsy or Traveller, possibly becoming 'gorjified', a scathing term which delineates 'Traveller-appropriate' ways of living from the behaviours of *gorje*, who (in our experience) are not uncommonly criticised for placing their elderly relatives in 'homes' and their children in day care from a very young age, instead of ensuring that these vulnerable (and valued) members of the community remain with their family.

When considering gender relationships, it is important to be aware that 'rules' pertaining to hygiene within the home and of the individual are closely bound up with morality, in a manner which is similar to that found amongst orthodox Jewish households. A great amount has been written about the concepts of cleanliness and pollution (in both the moral and physical sense) among Romani Travellers,[24] although over time, and within individual families, some practices have altered or fallen into disuse. Despite variations in how strictly these rules of *mochadi* are interpreted – for example, Travellers in houses and static mobile homes will not generally be able, or may not wish, to have the structures adapted to follow traditional notions of where hygiene facilities are placed – it can be argued that knowledge of *mochadi* is a form of cultural boundary, providing a guide about who and what are included into, or rejected from, Traveller society. Even among families who do not outwardly appear particularly traditional, rules about behaviour between generations, how and when hands should be washed, the handling of food, cleaning implements and items pertaining to the family animals, will generally be firmly adhered to.

Among traditional Gypsies and Travellers there is a strong observance of strict moral codes governing the relationships between men and women. Young women are expected to be chaste before marriage and families will 'watch out' for their relatives to ensure that gossip will not adhere to young people about their behaviour. With the close-knit family structure, presence of relatives during social interactions, and knowledge of that community is vital to the Traveller way of life, traditional values remain central to the upbringing and behaviour of both men and women. Generally, persons of the opposite gender (unless they are very closely related) must not be alone together, and discussions on matters pertaining to sexuality and reproduction are highly inappropriate between men and women, particularly those of different generations. Concerns about sex education at school, and about youngsters mixing with teenagers with different cultural beliefs pertaining to sexuality, gender roles and drug use are often cited as reasons for disliking sending children to secondary school as discussions about, and exposure to, these issues, are contrary to the values and cultures of traditional travelling communities. Lone parenthood is very rarely found among traditional Gypsies and Travellers, and where this does occur, is almost always as a result of the (unusual but very slowly increasing) separation of a married couple. Within traditional communities, an unmarried woman with a child would always require the presence of family members (and particularly a close male relative) to ensure social integration and the protection of her reputation.

The expanding family

Children are exceptionally important to traditional Gypsies and Travellers, and generally a young couple will start their family within a short while of being married. Accordingly, many young couples will be parents in their late teens or early twenties. Among New Travellers it is not uncommon for a young woman to have her first child with one partner, and then (as is common among many settled communities where relationships start at an early age) for the relationship to break down while the child(ren) is(are) young. In such cases, if the woman remains travelling as a lone parent, the family will often be reconstituted as she forms a relationship with another Traveller partner. In some cases, lone parent New Travellers move into settled housing and cease their nomadic lifestyles. Lone parenthood is no barrier to subsequent re-partnership among New Travellers, but is far more rarely found among traditional Travelling communities, where a woman may find it difficult to overcome the degree of social isolation and stigma, unless she is fully supported by her family. Generally speaking, traditional Gypsy and Traveller families have a slightly larger number of children than are found among *gorje* communities, often having three or four children. Irish Travellers in particular may have larger families (five or six children are not uncommon), for reasons connected with culture or religious practices. New Travellers also frequently appear to have a slightly higher than usual number of children, although this may be related to personal family choice (including decisions over contraceptive use) rather than well-defined cultural reasons.

Although Gypsy and Traveller children are primarily the responsibility of their parents, grandparents, immediate relatives and the wider community will all be involved in the upbringing of children and watching out for their well-being. This pattern is repeated across all of the Traveller communities (including New Travellers) as where certain families and individuals tend to travel together, or where possible live in close proximity, the children will have been known to other members of the community for their entire lives and thus a sense of collective responsibility for their care will exist. Gypsies and Travellers will generally stress the importance of children being raised within the whole community as a way of ensuring that young people are educated in appropriate cultural practices, as well as developing a clear sense of their social and ethnic identity.

While we consider health matters further in Chapter 7, health workers with Gypsies and traditional Travellers who wish to discuss such issues as contraception and pregnancy must always ensure that advice is presented in a culturally appropriate manner and generally (although less so among younger couples) would need to see the woman on her own, or with a female relative. Pregnancy and childbirth are largely a female preserve among Gypsies and Travellers, and the pregnancy (and subsequent delivery and aftercare) will generally not be discussed in mixed company, particularly where older people are present. It would be highly unusual for a pregnant woman to wear clothes which reveal her 'bump', and health information booklets that show photographs of semi-naked couples or nude pregnant women have been subjected to considerable criticism among Gypsies and traditional Travellers as using inappropriate imagery.

Generally Gypsy and Traveller fathers will stay with their partner during some of her labour but will not be present at the actual birth, where she will usually be attended by her mother and close female relatives. Although increasingly some young fathers will stay with their wife for the delivery (which where possible will usually take place at a hospital both for safety and to avoid pollution of the trailer or home – see above), the breach of gender-appropriate relationships that this entails may be greeted with disapproval within more traditional families, particularly by older kin. Among New Travellers in contrast, not only will the father be expected to be present at a birth and take a full role during the pregnancy and delivery, but other close friends from a site or Travelling group (both male and female) may be present or very close at hand during the birth. While traditional Travellers will generally favour a hospital delivery as noted above, (although women will usually seek a discharge from hospital within a few hours to return to the care of their relatives who will undertake cooking, cleaning, domestic chores and care of the mother and child for some weeks), New Travellers tend to prefer wherever possible to opt for a home delivery with a community midwife.

For all Travelling communities, however, the birth of a child is a great social and family event. While New Travellers may sometimes practise a public naming ceremony, some time after a child's birth, (perhaps at a ritually important gathering such as the summer Solstice celebrations at Stonehenge), traditional travelling communities will generally mark the child's entrance into the world with a large family christening, which will often involve a gathering of Gypsies and Travellers from a great distance, in a similar manner to that found at weddings. Among some very traditional travelling families, before a newly delivered woman takes up her domestic responsibilities and role within the community, she may be expected to be 'churched'. Churching involves attendance at a religious ceremony where the priest or vicar blesses and gives thanks for the safe delivery of the baby. Traditionally, churching lifts the state of ritual uncleanliness (*mochadi*) associated with childbirth. Similar ritual cleansing and thanksgiving after birth are practised by many other cultures, for example, orthodox Jewish communities.

The end of life and respect for the deceased

We have noted above the fundamental importance of the elderly to Gypsy and Traveller families, and the way in which respect and responsibility for their care rests both with their immediate kin and the community as a whole. When an elderly person reaches the end of their life (or when tragically a younger person or a child dies), their death is felt exceptionally strongly and in effect diminishes the community as a whole. The members of the travelling community to which the deceased person belonged will join together to offer their respect and support to the bereaved family (with word of the loss travelling remarkably rapidly across the country or beyond), and relatives and friends will often travel hundreds of miles to 'sit up' with the bereaved family and attend the funeral the next day.

Funerals are generally rather lavish events and may involve many people attending at the graveside and following the procession to the deceased's final place of rest. In areas with large Gypsy or Traveller populations it is not unusual to see an entire section of a cemetery which can be identified as belonging to members of the community by the sumptuous gravestones (perhaps showing horses or other associated symbols, or a photograph of the departed relative) and immaculately tended flowers and plants. A strong tradition of visiting the deceased is found among all of the traditional Travelling communities and it would be contrary to custom (and a source of some shame) if the grave was not well looked after. Generally families will visit their deceased relative on the anniversary of the death, at holidays such as Christmas and Easter and on a very regular basis. If close relatives are unable to attend as a result of Travelling away from the area, then other family members will be expected to tend the grave in their absence. Amongst Irish Traveller families the deceased person is often buried 'at home' in Ireland and family members will travel back from the UK to visit their grave on anniversaries and other major occasions, although 'locally' based relatives will tend the grave between their visits.

When a family member dies, where possible, a family will leave the place of the death, as the memories associated with the loss are so painful. A family will typically go off travelling for a considerable length of time during the mourning period or may sell the land where the deceased person was living at the time of their death. This cultural practice of leaving the site of the bereavement may cause particular hardship if the family wish to sell an authorised site which they owned and due to planning restrictions they are unable to purchase an alternative piece of land to live upon. After a death, the majority of personal belongings of the deceased (such as clothes) will be destroyed and their trailer may be sold or broken up, as other Travellers would not wish to live there.

At the time of the burial, most families will place photographs of the deceased person (perhaps pictured with close family members) in the coffin, as well as a quantity of the deceased's jewellery.

Immense respect is paid to the memory of the deceased relative, for example, through the display of photographs of grandparents and other more distant relatives and regular attendance at their grave, and their name and memory will also generally be preserved through the practice of naming successive generations after their ancestors (the use of 'family names'). However, where a 'family name' is 'reused' following a birth this will usually be qualified by referring to someone through their family connections, which is often necessary when so many names are the same. For example, 'Carrie's Alby', or 'Uncle Tubby's Henry'. This manner of 'identifying an individual', will be carried on for a number of years until that person becomes sufficiently identifiable in other ways.

Despite the above discussion, at the loss of an immediate relative, the pain of bereavement is so great within the exceptionally close-knit

A beautifully tended traditional Romani grave (with thanks to the family members for permitting use of this picture) (photograph by Margaret Greenfields)

Gypsy and Traveller communities that many bereaved families will put photographs of the deceased away, on the basis that it is too difficult to look at them, at least for a lengthy period of time. It is a fairly widespread custom (amongst Romani Gypsy families) that after the first few days of mourning, the deceased is very rarely, if ever, referred to by name again. If occasion does arise, then the name is often accompanied by other words, such as 'bless-ed', for example: 'blessed Ruby'. Even neutral names such as 'Dad' may be treated in the same manner, for example: 'me poor blessed Dad' and often, again, followed by a comment such as 'God love him', sometimes repeated by others who are participating in the conversation, for example, 'aye, God love his memory'. People who 'wish' on their departed, for example, 'on me poor dead Dad', will usually be 'scolded' for so doing. Equally, probably the worst that can ever be said to someone is, for example, 'go dig up your dead'. As a footnote to the above discussion, information

Floral tributes for Alice (May) Ayres, September 2003
(courtesy of Sam Wilson)

received from members of Gypsy and Traveller communities indicates
that bereaved relatives may often enter into a period of lengthy
depression following a loss, or 'never get over it' as the immense
impact of a death within a close-knit community where family
members often see each other on a daily basis throughout their entire
lives has profound psycho-social ramifications for relatives who have
outlived their loved one. (See Chapter 7 on health for further
information on the extent of depression amongst Gypsy and Traveller
community members.)

Religious practices

Religion is extremely important to Gypsies and Travellers, and
religious observance tends to be far higher than among the settled
population. Throughout the world Gypsies and Travellers tend to take
on the religious practices of the wider community in which they live,
and we therefore find that (for example) in eastern European countries
many Roma are practising Muslims and this religious adherence will
be continued if they are in the UK. Among Gypsies and British
Travellers (Irish, Scottish and Welsh) the predominant religion is
Christianity. Although a fairly high percentage of Travellers (most

particularly Irish Travellers) are Roman Catholic, some families are members of the Church of England. Levels of church attendance vary, as among the sedentary population, but in general the majority of Christian Gypsy and Traveller families attend church at Christmas and Easter, and a high proportion will be far more regular in their religious observances, perhaps attending church on a weekly basis. For many families, longstanding connections exist with a particular church, and, in such situations, rituals such as weddings, funerals and christenings will generally take place at that location.

In addition to membership of longstanding Christian denominations, there is a large and increasing membership of the Evangelical Gypsy Churches (Born Again Christians) both in Britain and abroad. The Born Again Christian Churches (for example, the Light and Life Movement) often hold large tented rallies at which many Travellers will attend from across the country. Many New Travellers adhere devoutly to forms of paganism, such as Wicca or Earth magic, preferring to practise their faith in the outdoors, and particularly at sacred sites such as Stonehenge or Glastonbury Tor. Paganism is not organised religion in the sense of Christianity or other world faiths, but a clear set of moral codes underpin the beliefs of practitioners, and a cycle of festivals exists, celebrating the seasons of the year and the elements such as air, water, fire and earth.

Although not all Gypsies and Travellers are members of a faith group (or in the case of New Travellers and Roma Gypsies may not be Christian), priests, vicars and pastors often have a longstanding knowledge of the Travelling families in their area (or where they typically halt), and these religious leaders may therefore sometimes be able to act as a bridge between statutory authorities and families in need of support, that is, by negotiating with local authorities or writing supportive letters or character references where evictions are threatened or planning applications are being made.

Employment

Gypsy and Traveller women traditionally regard their role in creating a family home as fundamental to their identity, and indeed the importance of a caring role cannot be over-emphasised, yet increasingly more women are participating in the formalised labour market (particularly where a family are resident at a secure site, or are housed) as women's opportunities for employment expand. Gypsy and Traveller women have always worked to help to support their families, but in general (and the ideal for most traditional families) it has been that the man is the main provider for the household. In the past, when families tended to be more mobile, and greater opportunities for casual trading or fieldwork existed, women usually participated in harvesting and similar work, or individual or small group trading (for example, 'knocking' for scrap, selling items made by family members, etc.). However, with the shift in employment patterns across society, and the decline of traditional occupations, we are now seeing a change in Gypsy and Traveller women's working practices, as young women in particular (mainly those who are living at an authorised site or in a house), are beginning to undertake training in skills that can be used to provide a regular income for the family (for example, young women attending hairdressing courses, obtaining shop work, cleaning jobs or returning to education to learn IT, etc.). The fundamental change in women's employment therefore (for those with the security to take advantage of such opportunities) appears to involve moving away from working within the family group, into the role of employee – a position that men appear more reluctant to undertake, generally preferring to work for themselves or with other relatives. The majority of young women, however, still tend to marry young and remain at home with their children, although increasingly girls are likely to discuss their ambitions to go to work or learn new skills once their children are in school or pre-school education. It is therefore possible that in future years, as more young women move towards paid employment (both prior to, and after marriage) or possibly defer marriage and childbearing in favour of work opportunities in the way found among *gorje* communities, discourse on gender equality, education and employment opportunities may become more common among Gypsies and Travellers. If this shift in attitude and practice does continue as anticipated, it will inevitably impact on traditional lifestyles, and the Travelling communities (as well as employers and education providers) will need to consider ways to avoid men becoming marginalised or their role within the family diminishing as women begin to identify new opportunities within a changing economy and society.

For Gypsy and Traveller men, the necessity of earning a living which will enable them to support their families, and the stress on education (and we do not here necessarily mean in the academic sense) which is relevant to their lives and culture, is often driven by different emphases and needs than are found among settled communities. Educational skills have historically often been of limited importance for Gypsies and Travellers and culturally there is still a strong drive for males (in particular) to learn relevant practical skills and move towards adulthood through participating in employment opportunities. Typically boys will work alongside their fathers and male relatives from a fairly young age, learning a trade, and becoming socialised into male patterns of employment and culturally appropriate behaviour. While 'hands-on' education, in the company of relatives who will ensure that a child learns a skill in a safe environment, is both a socio-cultural practice and a practical response to living within a skills-based community, some Gypsy and Traveller families find themselves in conflict with statutory authorities over this issue. While fifty years ago, learning through working alongside adult relatives would not have been regarded as unusual in *gorje* society,[25] changing notions of what are 'appropriate' and 'inappropriate' responsibilities for children and young people, and the increased emphasis on attendance at school for set periods of time, may on occasion lead Travelling families into conflict with education authorities or social services departments whose values and concepts are at odds with the notion of education for membership of community and adult life.

Although increased numbers of Gypsy and Traveller children are now accessing and remaining in school-based education (see Chapter 8), it is still common for young people to leave school (or diminish their attendance as they move towards adult status) from the time they transfer to secondary school (see concerns over attendance at mixed-sex schools, p.42). While it is a logical decision for many young people within the Travelling communities to leave education at this stage, particularly if they see their peer group engaging in employment or are experiencing isolation or discrimination in school, their opportunities to obtain qualifications or skills, which may be necessary for them in the future as society continues to change rapidly, are diminished.

While younger Gypsy and Traveller men who are in contact with the Traveller Education Service (TES) (see Chapter 8) or Connexions services may be able to access opportunities to train in trades that are relevant to their lifestyle and preferred patterns of employment (for

example, taking qualifications in building skills or tree surgery), a very
real risk exists that in years to come, as society becomes more
mechanised and controlled, Gypsy and Traveller men will be
increasingly marginalised and hampered by lack of formalised training
qualifications and the demands that traders and craftsmen are IT
literate and, in some form, registered and certified. Accordingly, older
Gypsy and Traveller men, or those whose educational prospects have
been damaged by constant eviction or the necessity (practical or
cultural) of early school-leaving, are at particular risk of social
exclusion, an issue which is currently the subject of much debate
among education services who are attempting to find innovative ways
to engage with Travelling communities in a culturally appropriate
manner.[26]

Overwhelmingly, unless patterns of eviction, ill health or lack of
employment possibilities lead to reliance on benefits, Gypsy and
Traveller men support their families by engaging in some form of
'trading', for example, selling carpets and sofas at markets; dealing in
scrap metal; importing cars or Christmas trees, etc.; or skilled activity
such as gardening and tree surgery, or horse-breeding/trading.
Typically, family members will work together when the job in hand
requires a number of men, but individuals' skill bases also mean that
father-son combinations, or two brothers or cousins, may equally be
engaged in small-scale contract work, where possible following a
regular circuit and carrying out work for particular clients. The
strengths of family connections and the importance of assisting kin
means that it is always possible to recruit other relatives if extra labour
is required for a job, or if an opportunity arises that may benefit a
number of family members. In such cases the benefits of membership
of a strong kin network are clear.

As noted above, a tendency exists for children to participate in
employment opportunities with their relatives as they become
physically capable of playing a role in the family business. Although
many children attend school (particularly up until secondary level),
when the family is travelling for employment purposes or during
holidays, young people will often work alongside their parents,
learning the family trade or skill. So, for example, while both genders
might perhaps undertake pea- or apple-picking (where families still
follow these rapidly diminishing opportunities) boys are likely to
participate in market trading, gardening or 'scrapping', while girls may

Trojan the horse and young New Travellers at a Friends, Family and Travellers Woodland Skills course in Dorset, 1998 (photograph by Margaret Greenfields)

perhaps spend the winter holidays making holly wreaths (a typically female occupation) with their mothers and female relatives. New Traveller children and young people may sometimes assist their parents with fieldwork (for example, daffodil-picking in the spring) but will also learn occupations such as vehicle scrapping and woodcrafts, catering and circus skills, etc., which can be utilised at festivals over the summer months.

Although considered in more detail in Chapter 8 on education, it is important to note that where families have obtained authorised sites, or moved into houses, there is a slow but much welcomed increase in young Gypsies and Travellers remaining in education and beginning to obtain professional qualifications such as social work, law and research degrees, or training as professional photographers, Gypsy Liaison Officers, etc. Where Gypsies and Travellers have been able to utilise educational opportunities, we are beginning to see clear trends indicative of the supposition that these newly opening opportunities are being used to benefit both the individual and their wider community.

Community relationships among Gypsies and Travellers

While in this chapter we have attempted a general introduction to family practices[27] among the Travelling communities, we feel that it is important to acknowledge that considerable differences may exist between different 'types' of traditional Traveller (e.g. English Gypsies, Scottish Gypsy/Travellers, Irish Travellers, etc.). Not only may there be variations in interpretation of hygiene and social codes, or in types of favoured employment, but, unsurprisingly, as a result of their community and individual history, various groups of Gypsies and Travellers may have different expectations and understandings of how best to engage with members of the settled community. A key area of internal conflict that arises between some Gypsies and Travellers (as well as between Travellers and the settled population) concerns responsibility for maintenance of site environment (i.e. cleaning up of rubbish after leaving an unauthorised roadside site or a field where they have been able to halt, or ensuring that transit sites are left in a fit state for the next person who pulls on), and the reactions from the settled population to such issues. While conflicts over 'standards' may in some cases be down to individual family or group issues, or result from variations in cultural or employment practices (e.g. commercial waste resulting from employment activities such as tarmacing and car scrapping) or the speed and hostility with which an eviction occurs, as noted in the 2004 Institute for Public Policy Research[28] report: 'while all Travellers are blamed for tipping, the majority of Traveller households are as dismayed by tipping activities as the majority of the settled community'. The fact that the activities of a minority of Gypsies and Travellers can lead to increased hostility towards the majority of community members may, in turn, enhance tensions between different 'types' of Travellers, for example, where one ethnic or social group is perceived as giving the entire community a bad reputation. A particular case in point concerns the political and media concentration on New Travellers as a perceived danger to society during the passage through Parliament of the 1994 CJPOA. Given that the Act has had a profound effect on every Travelling community in Britain (see Chapter 3), and that considerable internal community debate has taken place on the use of the term 'Traveller' to describe 'non-ethnic' nomadic communities, for some period of time, it was not uncommon to find traditional Travellers and Gypsies disassociating themselves firmly from New Travellers who were often seen as rootless individuals who had temporarily become nomadic, and then as a result of their poor behaviour brought about far-reaching legal changes with profound impacts for families who could not simply return to living in a house if public policy became too harsh.

Further differences may sometimes occur between Gypsy and Traveller communities due to high-profile sites, which may have a bad reputation as a result of the behaviour of certain residents, or the preference for inhabitants to ensure that any vacant plots are only allocated to members of their own ethnic community through the active discouragement of 'outsiders'. The tensions over shortage of sites (see Chapters 3 and 4) can therefore sometimes lead to increasing differentiation between the various communities (and resultant insularity), as only limited interaction occurs between various 'types' of Travelling communities. In addition, as a practical response to the shortage of sites, some Gypsies and Travellers (often 'long-distance' and without local connections to an area which would enable them to identify a more suitable place) pull in at supermarket car parks or playing fields. Accordingly, as a result of their location, these unauthorised transit sites receive great (and overwhelmingly hostile) publicity. Similarly, where a large number of families are travelling together (perhaps for employment purposes or to attend a wedding or funeral) their presence at one place may lead to increased difficulties over sanitary and rubbish disposal, or there may on occasion be inter-family disputes which can flare up and may spill out into the wider community, in turn leading to increased anti-Traveller racism.

As with all communities (whether defined by residence in a particular town, or by ethnicity, religion, gender or age), inevitably some members of the Travelling communities will on occasion behave in a manner that is problematic to both their own people and the wider sedentary population. Unfortunately, when there is significant pressure over sites, land usage and the level of discrimination and bad publicity that Travellers commonly experience, it is human nature that individuals will have a tendency to express the opinion that 'it's not Travellers like X, it's Travellers of Y ethnicity who behave in this manner'. Accordingly a perceived hierarchy of 'acceptable Travelling communities' may be said to exist in the minds of the media, the public and, to some extent, of Gypsies and Travellers themselves. While the G&TLRC has been instrumental in bringing together

Travelling people from a range of ethnicities and backgrounds in the recognition that the structural disadvantages experienced by the communities are identical, it can generally be said that Gypsies and Travellers tend to prefer to live within communities who share their own ethnicity.

Relationships between the different Travelling communities should not, however, be assumed to be marked by negative attitudes towards each other. Individual families may have close friendships, or perhaps live on sites with Gypsies and Travellers from other communities, indeed over the years we are seeing more intermarriage (for example, between Irish Travellers and English Gypsies or New and Scottish Travellers). These relationships have often arisen as a result of families meeting at the horse fairs or through being resident on the same authorised sites. With new relationships developing between the communities, variations in some cultural practices (for example, methods of cooking, hygiene maintenance rules, etc.) will often take place and indeed employment activities may alter as a result of the new kin-groupings which can develop. Of no less importance, knowledge of other Travelling groups and understanding of particular community practices can gradually develop, along with an increased tolerance towards living among Gypsies and Travellers with a different ethnic and cultural background. However, given the close-knit nature of Gypsy and Traveller society and the importance of kin networks, in general, sites (unless they are local authority owned and residents have no say over who obtains a pitch) and Travelling groups will usually consist of members of one particular ethnic or cultural background.

CHAPTER THREE

Stopping places

Margaret Greenfields

Photograph of Roma (provided from Alan Dearling's private collection)

Introduction

In this chapter we set out to provide an overview of Gypsies and Travellers' land use and the social and legal changes which have led to the current crisis in accommodation, which means that approximately one-third of the total Traveller population (estimated to comprise between 120,000 and 160,000 people) lives at unauthorised roadside encampments.[1]

In Chapters 3 and 4 we look in more depth at the Government's role in driving land-use policy, provision (or not) of local authority sites, and the extreme difficulties faced by Travellers who seek to obtain a licence for a 'private Gypsy site'. However, in order to understand the fundamentally negative impact of designated land use on Travellers, and the ways in which planning regulations increase the difficulties faced by families who seek to live a 'traditional' lifestyle, either remaining permanently nomadic, or residing in trailers on a fixed site while Travelling seasonally, it is important to explore the way in which regulated access to sites and the closure of traditional stopping places have, over the past sixty years, consistently constrained the options open to Travellers, leading to many families being effectively forced to move into houses and abandon their preferred way of life.[2]

Controlled and constrained

The history of Britain's land-ownership struggles over many centuries has been well documented by historians and political theorists, and indeed the theme of Traveller rights in the UK is simply another strand of this tale. While the British (and particularly the English) have a reputation as a law-abiding and somewhat politically passive nation, it is worth noting that much of the 'secret history' of Britain involves the profound repression of the working classes and the attempt to subdue 'anti-social behaviour' or activities which are perceived as being in opposition to the well-being of the sedentary, conforming, majority population.[3] (See also Chapters 5 and 6 for discussions on the way in which the law is used to control Travellers' activities.)

In the Introduction we have touched on the ways in which stereotypes, myths and common perceptions of 'Gypsy wildness' and 'danger' to the law-abiding public are linked to the dominant paradigm of respectability and connection to a specific locality, and it is clear that the struggles for freedom of movement, access to land and property rights experienced by the dispossessed poor and 'vagrants' of Britain bear more than a passing resemblance to the anti-Traveller legislation passed in Britain over many centuries.[4] Whilst historically, many laws were expressly aimed at minimising the number of 'wandering masterless men'[5] of native origin who might provide an incendiary flame to the already tension-ridden country following years of poor harvests, population growth and the dangerous increase in disaffection amongst returning servicemen who often found that their families had fallen into extreme poverty and homelessness during their absence at the wars, Gypsies and Travellers were subject to even more draconian punishments than 'home-grown' vagrants.[6]

Mayall (1995) lists twenty-nine pieces of legislation passed in England and Wales between 1530 and 1908 that directly impinged on Travellers seeking to live a nomadic way of life. A summary of some key statutes (Table 3.1) reveals that while *all* persons without a fixed abode were liable to swingeing penalties, aimed at enforcing settlement of a potentially seditious population, for Gypsies and other Travellers the focus of state policy initially involved attempts to cleanse Britain of 'outlandish people callynge themselves Egyptians' by use of powers of deportation and the death penalty. Over time, as Mayall notes, the thrust of legislation altered, in recognition of the fact that it would prove difficult to expel either the English-born children of Gypsies who had intermarried with indigenous Travellers or formerly sedentary populations who had become nomadic through choice or necessity. Accordingly, from the late sixteenth century onwards, the objective of statutory provisions relating to persons of no fixed abode become explicitly slanted towards settlement and enforced assimilation into the sedentary community.

As is demonstrated by Table 3.1, even when the death penalty and expulsion from Britain ceased to be used as common punishments for Travelling people, the assumption of criminality (most specifically vagabondage which was punishable by imprisonment in the stocks or a house of correction, or both) equating to lack of a settled lifestyle persisted. Thus even mid- to late nineteenth-century legislation aimed to 'tidy up' the rural environment and ensure that Travellers were as far as possible kept away from the sedentary population.

While current UK policy is clearly less *explicitly* racist and proscriptive towards nomadic lifestyles,[7] to frame this debate on land use and access to sites, it is important to retain an awareness of historical legislative responses to Travellers in order to fully understand the continuity of assimilationist policies that in many ways are still adhered to assiduously in twenty-first-century Britain. (See particularly Chapter 5 on movement into housing). It is also relevant to note that throughout the past century, a plethora of other 'general application' enactments have impacted on Travellers' traditional way of life, creating a pressure to 'settle' and adopt sedentary cultural and social practices. For example, statutes which were not explicitly aimed at Travellers still incorporated clauses that

Table 3.1 Summary of legislation pertaining to Travellers' nomadic lifestyles, England, 1530–1894

YEAR	TITLE OF ACT	KEY PROVISIONS
1530	An Act concerning outlandish people calling themselves Egyptians	Lists the 'frauds of certain outlandish people calling themselves Egyptians'. Prescribes imprisonment, forfeiture of belongings and banishment of all Gypsies from England and Wales. Proportion of goods seized from Travellers to be kept by person who took possession of such items.
1547	An Act for the punishment of vagabonds	Statute directed at 'wandering persons'. Punishments to include branding and enslavement.
1554	An Act for the punishment of certain persons calling themselves Egyptians	Gypsies forbidden to enter the realm. Persons assisting in bringing Gypsies into the country fined 40 shillings, those Gypsies entering the realm liable to death penalty after one month. If a Gypsy already in England stayed for twenty days they forfeited their goods, after forty days, they were liable to death penalty. Exemptions if the Traveller went 'into service'.
1562	An Act for further punishment of vagabonds calling themselves Egyptians	Extended the punishments of 1554 to those persons travelling with Gypsies. If travelling 'disguised' with Gypsies for one month, liable to the death penalty. Exemptions for children under fourteen. People born in England not required to leave the country.
1597 (subsequently re-enacted 1743)	An Act for the punishment of rogues, vagabonds and sturdy beggars and Justices Commitment Act	Declared 'all tinkers wandering abroad and all persons not felons [those liable to death penalty] wandering and pretending to be Egyptians or counterfeit Egyptians' as rogues and vagabonds.
1822	Turnpike Roads Act	Forty-shilling fine for Gypsies camping on the side of a Turnpike road (from 1835, any highway).
1835	Highways Act	
1889 and 1894	Local Government Acts	County Councils permitted to make local (bye) laws against vagrancy and to regulate village greens and open areas.

The Doe family on Epsom Downs in 1908 (courtesy of Grant Doe)

asserted: control on 'nuisances in tents and vans' (Housing of the Working Classes Act 1885); compulsory education of Traveller children (Children Act 1908); regulation of employment (Children and Young Persons Act 1933); and sanitary facilities within accommodation (Public Health Act 1936).[8] Indeed, the subsidiary impacts of public-health legislation can still be a fundamental cause of conflict between some planning authorities and Travellers. We are aware, for example, of several disputes occurring over the 'appropriate' location of sanitation facilities, which some local authorities interpret as requiring an internal location *within* trailers rather than the culturally appropriate free-standing external units required by strict *mochadi* rules (see further Chapter 2).

Discreet coexistence

By the late nineteenth century, despite the increased statutory controls which ensured that Travelling people were constrained in their choice of stopping place (both in order to avoid prosecution for camping at roadsides or on village greens and to escape the over-vigilance of social reformers keen to enquire into their living conditions), the fact that green lanes and other traditional 'atchin tans' were still reasonably freely available meant that Gypsies and Travellers could follow a circuit of seasonal employment (for example, calling on known customers or undertaking field labour for farmers), and yet remain relatively invisible from potentially hostile settled populations. To a large extent, therefore, members of the sedentary community accepted the fact that Travellers were present within their society (even if only on an occasional basis), and indeed that families would follow specific travelling circuits and offer useful services while in the locality. In essence, a relationship of benign interdependence existed between settled and Travelling populations for a considerable period of time.

While this was not to say that Travellers did not experience discrimination, or that they were always the most welcomed of visitors,[9] the need for seasonal land labour and other particular skills of Gypsies and Travellers, when coupled with the (middle- and upper-class) interest in the developing 'science' of anthropology, and the romantic notion of the 'Gypsy wanderer', ensured that members of the nomadic community were increasingly tolerated as a necessary (or perhaps picturesque) presence at the margins of society albeit still seen as individuals in need of 'conversion' to the rules of morality and Christian behaviour.[10]

Thus despite, or perhaps because of, the coexisting paradigm of Travellers as 'romantic heathens' and occasional sources of labour who disappeared when no longer wanted, as long as Travellers took care not to halt on the highway or on open land controlled by a county council opposed to their presence, for a considerable number of years it was possible to lead a nomadic life reasonably discreetly and untroubled by the law. Travellers dwelling on green lanes and other traditional stopping places were generally tolerated and considered a part of the sustainable cycle of rural life, often returning to a particular site on an annual basis over many decades. Indeed, it is still possible to meet with older Gypsies and Travellers in England who can recount being born at or near to a site where their grandparents and other earlier generations had halted on an annual basis for work-related purposes, or while en route to employment opportunities. Sadly, many of these sites are now banked and ditched to stop Travellers' use of the

Gypsy families stopping in Birkby Brow Wood (a traditional stopping place), 1959 (from *Gypsies & Travellers in their own words*, courtesy of the Leeds Traveller Education Service)

land or have been sold for development as car parks and housing estates.[11]

This pattern of Travelling on specific 'circuits' and stopping at recognised traditional sites continued largely unabated until the huge social dislocation caused by the outbreak of the Second World War in 1939. With the commencement of hostilities and the need for intensive labour (both on the land and elsewhere) Gypsies were actively encouraged to become further immersed into the mainstream population, often taking up the opportunity to work on the land on a semi-permanent basis or, in the case of women, being recruited to factory and munitions work.[12] In addition, young men with well-developed practical skills were actively sought by the recruiting authorities and found themselves forcibly enlisted to work in the mining industries or to fight in the British army. The transition from trailer to barracks could be shockingly rapid: one elderly gentleman – who at the time of writing was fighting his local authority for the right to obtain planning permission to stay on land he and his family had purchased – recounted that he had 'been picking cabbages one day and was in uniform the next'. Many Travellers became renowned for their skills as snipers, scouts and night-time fighters and were decorated for their bravery in action both in the First and Second World Wars.[13] The lack of literacy skills, which would prove so problematic for later generations were, in wartime circumstances, no barrier to recognition as experts in particular fields, and Gypsies' specialised skills could be put to extremely good use. One of only four private soldiers *ever* to win a Victoria Cross was a Romani, Private Jack Cunningham. Indeed, the gentleman quoted above achieved significant recognition as a 'runner' and was awarded the Distinguished Service Medal for his part in the Second World War hostilities.

In the immediate post-war era, while Britain, a country devastated by six years of bombing and loss of life, was attempting to rebuild a severely damaged infrastructure, Gypsies were welcomed within the majority of communities as possessing much-needed practical work skills and also as having suffered the experiences common to all returning service men and their families who had survived the war.[14] Indeed, it has been noted that for a period of some years '[Gypsies] were able to live at peace with their house-dwelling neighbours',[15] assisted by a spirit of growing tolerance in the late 1940s and early 1950s, and the fact that in a country where many individuals were living in shanty accommodation, prefabricated homes and squatted former army camps,[16] caravan dwellers no longer appeared to be such an anomaly.[17] Thus, for perhaps the only time in modern British history, house-dwellers did not classify caravans as 'makeshift, transient eyesores; either temporary holiday accommodation or evidence of inadequate municipal housing programmes'[18] and, by extension, their occupants as undesirable or transient. Gypsies and Travellers had finally (albeit temporarily) moved from the status of feared pariahs to (semi-)integrated citizens and were recognised as such by the wider community.

Post-war industrialisation and the land squeeze

In the immediate post-war period, times were good for many Gypsies and Travellers. Their specialist skills were greatly in demand and the relatively affordable price of land offered some families the opportunity to buy or rent large enough plots to set up a home base, often in a locality where longstanding family connections existed. Although in many ways this era represented an anomaly in British

Travellers' history, virtually for the first time substantial numbers of families were able to settle and put down roots in an area, which in turn enabled them to plan for the future and set up businesses or develop trading connections that could be passed on to future generations. For example, we are aware of several families who built up large fortunes from scrap dealing and recycling activities commenced during this era. With greater acceptance of Gypsies and Travellers among the sedentary population, children accessing schooling and the opportunity to retain a stable winter base, some indications also exist of increased intermarriage between Travellers and the settled population, and that some families (in contrast to the constrained moves that took place within the next decade) voluntarily settled into housed accommodation while retaining the habit of travelling during the spring and summer months.[19] It is during this period of time that many members of the large Gypsy communities in Kent, Hampshire and Somerset began to move from a fully nomadic life to one of relative stability and economic well-being as a direct result of greater land access (see Chapter 5 for a further discussion on 'housed Travellers').

However, for those families who were unable to afford or obtain a site, or who did not want to cease a fully nomadic life, opportunities for traditional Travelling patterns were in decline.[20] The increased industrialisation and rapid movement of the post-war population into urban conurbations meant that Travellers seeking scrap and tarmacing work needed sites within easy reach of their 'customers'. Accordingly, Travellers too began to move towards cities and towns and often met with hostile reactions from the local population or authorities. In many ways, this was a return to the situation of the early nineteenth century when the expansion in Victorian town planning had meant that Travellers were pushed to the edges of built-up areas in an attempt to 'tidy up' desirable locations where properties were being developed for sale.[21] We have already noted that a range of public-health and planning legislation, which possessed the potential to impinge on nomadic peoples, was already on the statute books. Increasingly, from the early 1950s onwards, these and other laws such as the subsequent Scrap Metal Dealers Act 1964, which required a dealer to re-register in every authority where they were 'totting' (see Glossary), were used to harass Travellers and to move them on. While a few trailers parked up discreetly in a green lane or traditional rural stopping place may have been ignored, a group of caravans on a bomb site or next to a roadside in a busy town centre were far more likely to attract the attention of the local police force or council officials,[22] with the consequence that families and groups of Travellers became embroiled in a cycle of rapid repeat eviction. With the post-war emphasis on rebuilding the nation (development of urban and rural areas, social-welfare reform and reindustrialisation), the move towards a modernised (and paternalistic) society meant that nomadic Travellers were increasingly perceived as an unwelcome anachronism.[23]

To add further to the difficulties faced by unsited Travellers, a series of Road Traffic and Highway Acts in the 1950s re-enacted the proscription against stopping at the roadside, and the decline of traditional agricultural methods, brought about by the use of pesticides and mechanised harvesting, meant that employment-related sites were increasingly inaccessible to nomadic families, creating a situation where Travellers were simultaneously finding it harder to stop and to find work. At the same time, the development of zoned planning regulations and the pressure to build new housing exacerbated the situation so that even green lanes and traditional stopping places became harder to access.

The combination of the above elements led to increasing numbers of Travellers being forced to stop at the few remaining traditional 'atchin tans' or yards for longer periods of time, and in the process inevitably becoming more visible and subject to pressure to leave from the sedentary population. While in Chapter 5 we explore the movement of Travellers into housing that arose in part from these constraints, it is important to note that this was the era of mass evictions of large numbers of Travellers who had initially gathered at winter sites and then remained at the same location, often throughout the year, through lack of alternative options. The situation was particularly noticeable in the south-east of England, which had long been noted as possessing the largest Gypsy and Traveller population in the country, attracted in part by the availability of hop-picking and harvest work, and also the proximity to London. Over many years an enormous community of Travellers had developed clear connections to Kent and Surrey, and while it was abundantly obvious that simply telling them that no sites were available would not lead to their packing up and leaving, many families found that officials greeted them with this casually callous attitude, and then were aggrieved when Travellers settled down in encampments and shanty towns in wood and marshland or continued to squeeze together in overcrowded yards, rather than leave the area where they had been born, worked, married and buried their dead for many generations. The resultant overcrowding and poor quality sanitation and water supply at Belvedere and Erith Marshes, Darenth Woods and similar locations soon became a cause of scandal among local authority and public-health officials, with horror being expressed at such unhygienic living conditions in the post-war era. However, despite this widespread condemnation, little attention was paid to the concerns of the residents of these sites who, while obviously wanting better facilities, equally wished to live among their own communities and follow their traditional cultural and social practices.[24]

With a failure by officials to improve conditions and a clear policy of clearance of sites and 'encouragement' for Travellers to become housed, the struggle for civil rights, provision of appropriate accommodation and self-determination became manifest.[25] It was to prove to be a grossly uneven match, with Gypsies and Travellers vastly outweighed by the legislative and social power brought to bear upon them.

> Police stood by at Tuesday's eviction, but the remaining caravanners, grumbling quietly, made no real attempt to stop the move. Huddled up in shawls and raincoats against the rain, they stood by their vans, or by their piles of belongings, saying they had nowhere else to go ... Where a few weeks ago the common had been strewn with lines of washing, and children and puppies played together around the cooking fires, the lines of painted vans on the roadway, leaving heavy tracks in the mud, made a desolate sight.

Kentish Express, March 1959, quoted in Evans (2004: 81)

Throughout the entire 1950s, the struggle over accommodation remained high on the agenda of both Travellers and local councillors who were worried about both voters' opposition to Gypsy sites and maximising their revenue through selling off land for development. Local authorities were resolute on doing away with the 'Gypsy Problem'[26] (often compulsorily purchasing freehold land from Travellers who had obtained a plot on longstanding sites such as Belvedere Marshes, and then attempting to force landowners to move onto a leasehold pitch on local authority sites) and understandably, Travellers were equally determined not to leave traditional 'atchin tans' without ensuring that they had access to another site. While owners or long leaseholders of pitches were in some cases offered alternative accommodation (often on the basis of access to a pitch when suitable land was identified), for those families who had squatted on the marshes the situation was even worse. They were to be driven away from the area, forcibly moved over the district border if necessary and then left to their own devices. A press release from Dartford Rural Council[27] sums up the prevailing attitude of local councillors across the South-East: 'our responsibility is to put them out on the highway. The Council is faced with difficult planning problems'.

In certain cases (notably Erith and Belvedere Marshes) lengthy struggles over the future of site inhabitants managed to delay the inevitable evictions for several months or years, but ultimately (in the case of Belvedere Marshes the demise hastened by the disastrous floods of 1953[28]), the brief era of peaceful coexistence between Travellers and settled communities was at an end. In a few short years the largest and best-known stopping places in the South-East were all cleared and steps taken to ensure that they could not be reoccupied. However, the destruction of Corke's Meadow, Belvedere and Erith Marshes, and the evictions of over 200 men, women and children from Darenth Woods,[29] did not go unremarked. The sight of families being thrown onto the roadside, shanty towns being demolished and well-publicised bitter confrontations over evictions led to national debate and the slow public recognition of the appalling plight of Gypsies and Travellers in Britain.[30]

Meanwhile, whilst politicians largely remained blind to (or chose not to see) the destruction wreaked upon Travelling communities by rapid changes in legislation and lifestyles of the settled majority, the tireless Norman Dodds, Labour MP for Dartford elected in 1945, waged what was virtually a one-man war against political apathy and disregard of Travellers' human rights. Dodds commenced his campaign by targeting his own party while they were in government, badgering away relentlessly at ministers for health and housing, and then, following the return to power of the Conservatives in 1951, turning his attention first to Harold Macmillan[31] (who eventually and somewhat reluctantly agreed to a pilot survey of numbers of Gypsies in Kent in 1962) and subsequently (when the Labour Party once again formed a government) Richard Crossman, Minister for Local Government,[32] who initiated a national survey of Gypsy and Traveller numbers, the findings of which assisted in convincing the Government of the need for a national policy on accommodation (see Chapter 4 for a fuller discussion on government and local authority accommodation policies).

Throughout his parliamentary career, Dodds never gave up on his demands for a network of sites across the country, educational opportunities for Gypsy children and a comprehensive statistical survey of the number and accommodation situation of Travellers in England and Wales,[33] and was indefatigable in his support of Travellers, going so far as to move into a trailer and join families awaiting eviction in Darenth Woods, until he was injuncted from the area by an increasingly beleaguered Dartford Rural Council who were bemused and irritated by his relentless insistence on involving the media in every twist and turn of the battle. Dodds was a genuine crusader who cared deeply about the plight of Traveller families who had often fought, or lost relatives, in the war, but who at the end of hostilities were hounded from pillar to post and, in some cases (following compulsory purchase orders made to enable building redevelopment), were evicted from land they had owned and lived on for many years. Not only was Dodds MP for an area with a large Gypsy population, but he had witnessed first hand the situation of evicted and harassed Traveller families living in the shanty towns of the Thames Marshes within his own constituency.

Dodds campaigned for years, working with a network of authors such as Brian Vesey-Fitzgerald,[34] a few far-sighted local government officers, a number of clergy (including William Larmour of the London City Mission) and academics. The National Council for Civil Liberties (NCCL)[35] played its part too by monitoring the cycle of evictions and repressive local authority actions[36] and by ensuring that records were kept of potential and actual breaches of human rights. However, despite the growing attention to the 'Gypsy problem', the opposition (particularly rural district council associations and planners) was vocal and powerful.[37] Indeed, things were, if possible, destined to become even worse for Gypsies and Travellers before the law was reviewed and a humane (if badly flawed) solution devised.

Probably the lowest point for Travellers in the immediate post-war period came about with the enactment of the Caravan Sites and Control of Development Act of 1960. This piece of legislation was predominantly aimed at limiting the increasing numbers of non-

Travellers who were moving into caravans as a result of the housing shortages of the 1950s, but in practice it affected many families who had bought their own land and felt they were safe from threat of eviction. The 1960 Act empowered local authorities to control the unlicensed development of caravan sites and to prohibit encampment on commons. Whilst authorities were able to issue site licences and provide new sites for Gypsies, in practice, not only were few such sites set up, but those which were, frequently faced such an extraordinary degree of hostility from local (housed) residents that councillors were loath to make use of their newly acquired powers. In the main, however, the unequivocal consequence of the 1960 statute was to bring about the closure of many sites used by Travellers on either a long-term or short-term (transit) basis.[38] Even those Travellers who had purchased land some years prior to the Act were required to prove 'established use' of the land as a caravan site in order to obtain a licence, and this was fraught with difficulties for many families as written evidence may have been unavailable, locals unwilling to provide support, or the claim overturned in the face of unproven contradictory assertions by those opposed to their presence in the neighbourhood.[39] Ultimately, all Travellers became subject to the 'universalistic and inflexible law of the dominant house-dwelling society'.[40] Even if a family were able to establish historical use (or moved onto a newly opened site) the regulations pertaining to site licences strictly controlled the mode of living, number of caravans and activities that could be carried out at a particular location. Moreover, for those families (and farmers or landowners who had allowed Travellers to remain on their land other than for a short period of time as specified within the Act[41]) who were unable to obtain planning permission (a prerequisite to obtaining a licence unless 'established user' could be shown), a series of swingeing fines led to the occupants being forced onto the roads once more.

Thus, by the mid-1960s Gypsies were facing an increasingly untenable situation, unable to stop at traditional halting places, often incapable of accessing a secure site, and subject to evictions and prosecutions for remaining at unlicensed locations. These were the years that saw up to 300 people living on the side of the A2 in Kent for months, ejected from longstanding sites and forced to live within feet of a major road carrying heavy lorries after a series of cat-and-mouse evictions that pushed them from one parish to another.

the A2 was a very dangerous place at the time, there was a lorry came down with a load of board on and it came off and smashed three trailers, it broke them all down, there were holes in the side that you could walk through ... it was dangerous. Used to get people come through of a night throwing, hollering and shouting, they'd throw bricks and stones, whatever they had in the motor at the time.

Joe Ripley quoted in Evans (2004)

I remember the days when we were stopping along Badgers Mount when we was taken to the court just for sawing off a limb of a tree and my dad was took to the court for just pulling his vehicle up on the verge. I mean he couldn't leave it in the middle of the road because another lorry could come along, or a car and smash it to bits, so he had to pull it somewhere.

Bill Smith quoted in Evans (2004)

In desperate reaction to the relentless use of the law to harass them from their traditional lifestyle, increasing numbers of Travellers reluctantly sought to be rehoused into local authority (council) accommodation (despite their frequently expressed distress at having to give up their way of life), where they had to face the hostility of their settled neighbours who often feared and resented their presence. As we will explore further in Chapter 5, for many families, moving into housing was a 'last resort' leading to significant emotional, psychological and practical difficulties. Yet not all families were able to obtain settled accommodation, as some authorities refused to consider them for housing,[42] limiting their options still further.

Despite the power in the 1960 Act to provide local authority sites, it was obvious that, at county and district level, no political will existed to alleviate the plight of Gypsies and Travellers. The situation had reached deadlock and as the pressure mounted from outraged local voters, regional and national newspapers and the ever-persistent Norman Dodds, it was quite clear that government action was required to ensure that local authorities took steps to provide accommodation for Gypsies and Travellers in their area. As noted above, in 1962 Macmillan had reluctantly agreed that a survey of Gypsy numbers was required. Dr Charles Hill (Minister for Housing and Local Government) issued Circular 6/62 urging local authorities to undertake a count of all Gypsies in their areas and to consider providing sites, based upon a statistical analysis of need. Gradually a (very) slow trickle of sites was provided by local authorities, and a number of individuals (including

Norman Dodds and the novelist Barbara Cartland) braved the wrath of their neighbours to open up private site facilities for Gypsies. Finally, Dodds's persistence paid off, and in 1965 the new Labour administration agreed that a national survey of Travellers' geographical distribution and social and economic needs was urgently required.

The first Gypsy census[43] was carried out in March 1965 and the disturbing findings of this study formed the basis of subsequent legislation and policy initiatives. Although it has been estimated that only 75 per cent of 'Gypsies and other Travellers' were actually included in the survey, for the first time, adequate information had been obtained which ensured that the Government could no longer ignore a situation that was becoming a national scandal. Sixty per cent of families were found to have travelled in the year prior to the census, and for the majority of Travellers, movement had been enforced by the necessity of obtaining a site, or to escape local authority and police harassment and eviction. Very few children had been able to access education, as the constant round of eviction had profoundly disrupted their schooling (a situation which, as we shall see, still continues today), and only one-third of families had access to on-site water. Despite the provision in the 1960 Caravan Sites and Control of Development Act for local authorities to set up 'Gypsy caravan sites', only twelve local authorities had actually acted on this power. It was quite clear that action needed to be taken to improve the situation of Travellers if Britain wished to be seen as a modern democracy.

The newly formed Gypsy Council seized the opportunity afforded by the publication of the 1965 survey to raise the profile of their campaign for sites, and the combination of their tactical lobbying and the felicitous advent of Eric Lubbock's Private Member's Bill, which aimed to regulate the bad practice of some owners of private mobile home sites, afforded an opportunity for the Government to take decisive action.[44] Part II of the Caravan Sites Act 1968 was tacked onto Lubbock's Bill in exchange for government support, which ensured that the provisions would pass into law with minimal opposition. In theory, a new era was about to commence for Travellers.

The partial solution

Part II of the 1968 Caravan Sites Act (the section which deals with Gypsy site provision) came into force on 1 April 1970. The relevant sections of the Act were designed to impose a statutory framework on the hitherto piecemeal provision of accommodation for Gypsies and Travellers. As we will demonstrate in Chapter 4 ('The planning system and the accommodation needs of Gypsies'), while perhaps regarded as being of limited importance during the drafting of the Act, one of the most important aspects of this piece of legislation involved the definition used to classify who would or would not be permitted access to 'Gypsy sites'. While, as we have seen, 'counterfeit Egyptians' (or those who were not ethnically Romani but 'wandered abroad') were subject to severe penalties in the sixteenth century, in the main, the term 'Gypsy' has been used to refer to a specific group of people of distinct racial descent. Under the 1968 Act, 'Gypsies' were redefined as 'persons of nomadic habit of life, whatever their race or origin', although this definition explicitly excluded Showmen and Circus performers.

Thus, since 1970, under planning law (both statute and judge-made precedent), people who travelled for economic purposes could be classed as Gypsies and be eligible to apply for a pitch regardless of their family background or ethnicity, yet people of Romani ancestry who had moved into a house and subsequently sought to obtain access to a site, could be deemed not to be 'Gypsies' under the Act. With the retrospective reading-in of this definition of 'Gypsies' into the 1960 Caravan Sites and Control of Development Act (see above), applications for private Gypsy site licences also became dependent upon the owner's travelling habits, creating a paradox that has been the subject of intense debate and some ill feeling amongst Romanies ever since, who understandably often resent the idea that under certain laws, their ethnicity can be 'removed' simply because they do not adhere to the sedentary population's preconceptions of what a Gypsy 'does' (see further Chapter 4 for a fuller discussion on planning requirements).

Aside from the redefinition of 'Gypsies', the three key sections of the statute which impacted on Travellers (all of which at the time of implementation of the Act were regarded as being of far greater immediate importance than the definition of a 'gypsy' [sic]) were as follows:

- **Section 6** London borough and county councils were under a duty to provide accommodation for 'Gypsies' 'residing in, or resorting to' their area. London boroughs, however, (based on the dual assumption of greater land pressure and lower numbers of Travellers residing in or visiting cities), were only *required* to provide fifteen pitches per local authority.
- **Section 9** empowered the Secretary of State to direct recalcitrant local authorities to provide sites, with the 'direction' enforceable by a writ of *mandamus* [or legal order to a local authority official to carry out their public duties].
- **Sections 10 and 11** enabled a local authority, which believed that it had provided enough sites for 'Gypsies', to apply for a 'designation order'. Where such an order was granted by the Secretary of State, it became a criminal offence for any Traveller to park their caravan anywhere within that authority, other than on a vacant pitch at an official Gypsy caravan site.

As anticipated, the Act was passed with a broadly cross-party consensus; in part because the 'stick' provisions (the power of the Secretary of State to order sites to be set up) were to a large extent offset by the 'carrot' of local authorities' ability to apply for 'designation'. While theoretically, 'designation' should only have been permitted when a local authority could demonstrate that adequate pitches existed in the locality for all local Gypsy families as well as Travellers who might be passing through the area or who needed access to a pitch in order to visit relatives, in practice, designation status was sought whenever a local authority considered that it had provided the minimum number of sites which the Department of the Environment might accept.

Once designation had been achieved (a process which was commenced in 1972 when a number of authorities announced that they had met their target of provision of adequate sites and were duly awarded with the coveted status) any Traveller who halted within the named area could be (and usually were) served with a summons within a matter of days if not hours, ensuring that they rapidly moved on to avoid the threat of criminal prosecution. If the Act had been implemented as designed, rapid eviction or the requirement that Travellers disperse to avoid prosecution could be seen as harsh (and in today's terms an infringement of human rights) but at least it could be

A local authority site in Scotland (photograph by Felicity Greenfields)

argued that families had a choice of available halting places. In actual fact, it has been said that the provisions were used in a similar manner to the 'Pass Laws and apartheid once operating in South Africa'.[45]

Apart from the recalcitrance of local authorities, many of which remained bitterly opposed to the provision of Gypsy sites, the main difficulty with ensuring that adequate sites were provided was the mechanism used for deciding how many pitches were required in each local authority. Based upon the methodology of the 1965 'census' each local authority was required to carry out a crude count of Gypsy caravans and, from this operation, to calculate the number of Gypsies and Travellers in its area who would require access to sites. The count was (somewhat problematically) to be carried out by local authority employees on two dates per year, one in the summer and one in the winter. This biannual count (which has been subjected to significant criticism both because of the 'snap-shot' methodology and the implicit benefit which accrues to a local authority which 'under-counts' Travellers in its area)[46] is still used today, despite the subsequent abolition of the duty to provide local authority sites (see further below).

While it is fair to say that *some* local authorities did carry out their duties conscientiously (unlike the many which would simply ask the relevant council official to drive along main roads and see how many caravans they could easily identify, or those who simply counted

unauthorised sites about which a housed resident had complained)
and sought to ensure that sites made available roughly coincided with
the level of need among the community, in general councils carried
out their new duties with extreme reluctance, often citing difficulties
in identifying suitable locations for sites or the expense of provision of
such facilities. Indeed the duty to provide sites was so poorly received
that, following the 1976 review of the effectiveness of the Act[47]
(published as the 'Cripps Report'), the Local Government Act of 1980
introduced 100 per cent central government grants payable to local
authorities to meet the cost of setting up public sites. Despite these
further incentives (available between 1980 and 1994), many local
authorities opted either to set up sites at highly undesirable locations
such as abutting sewage works or by motorways, or failed to provide
adequate (or any) public pitches, preferring to simply move families
on repeatedly until they left the area. It is noteworthy, too, that
although such incentive schemes failed significantly to improve the
situation of Travellers, successive Secretaries of State only exercised
their power to require authorities to set up sites on five occasions,[48]
each time following judicial review brought by families desperate to
obtain a pitch within the area of a non-complying authority. Overall,
regardless of whether or not an area was 'designated', the factors that
tended to define the level of travelling populations in any given area
were local authority policies, attitudes to site provision, and
'toleration'[49] of nomadic people within the locality.

Even where local sites were provided by councils, tension could
also exist among the travelling communities as a result of the pressure
created by struggling to obtain a pitch. The general shortfall in site
provision, even among 'good' authorities, led to competition between
Travellers to be seen as 'local', in the hope that they would be able to
proceed up the waiting list at a more rapid rate than individuals
simply moving into the area. With a growing population and no
requirement for a local authority to take account of the increased
numbers of Travellers in a locality once 'designation' had been
achieved, a large percentage of the Traveller population were unable to
obtain a site (see further Chapter 4) and thus were forced to either seek
accommodation in housing (Chapter 5), or continually move from
place to place, often away from their local area, in an attempt to avoid
repeated evictions.[50]

We discuss life on public sites and the reasons why families may prefer to apply for their own private site licence in Chapter 4, but it is worth briefly noting that where Travellers were able to obtain a pitch on a local authority site, although they were free from the constant round of evictions and harassment, life could still be far from ideal. While *some* council sites were (and are) extremely well run and offered a suitable and happy environment for families, many sites were built to the lowest possible specifications with extremely small pitches, surrounded by barbed wire and high walls in a manner more suitable to a prison, and often forbade working vehicles to be placed near to accommodation, leaving tools and plant vulnerable to theft from intruders.[51]

Moreover, anomalies in the law meant that no security of tenure existed for residents of local authority sites, for example, it was extremely easy to evict a person from a site as they held their pitch by licence rather than under a tenancy akin to that enjoyed by council house tenants.[52] Pitch costs were often exorbitant and could include the compulsory purchase of electricity (at an inflated cost) payable to the local authority or company who managed the site; family groups were frequently required to separate through lack of pitches or as a result of individual plots being dotted around a large site; and intra-group disputes (for example, between Irish Travellers and English Gypsies or feuding families from the same ethnic group) placed on the same site by authorities who consider all Travellers to be culturally and socially the same, led (and still lead) to particularly conflictual situations in some areas.[53] In addition, the complex rules for deciding who is and is not a Gypsy (in planning and site-access terms) means that an individual's cultural heritage could be ignored in favour of debate on their pattern of employment and lifestyle, and thus potentially someone of impeccable Romani origin could be denied access to a site and co-residence with their relatives, because they were not considered to follow a 'nomadic way of life' but were perceived as travelling merely for occasional employment-related reasons or to attend at certain social gatherings.

Regardless of the problems inherent in individual local authorities' interpretation of the Act (outlined above), the period of time during which the Caravan Sites Act 1968 operated (1970–94) is now widely regarded as an 'era of consensus', in that central government gave a lead (however grudgingly followed) to the notion that Travellers were no longer to be seen simply as a 'problem' but as individuals, who in common with other members of society were in need of accommodation. Whilst it is clear that the 1968 Act did not operate fully in the manner intended, there is plentiful evidence that it had a positive impact on site provision, reducing unauthorised encampments from 80 per cent to 30 per cent of park-ups over the relevant years[54] despite the quadrupling of Gypsy caravan numbers counted between 1965 and 1994, and significantly increasing the proportion of young Travellers who were able to access education.[55]

Alongside the slow development of public sites during these years, a slow but steady increase in private-site provision may also be noted. We have recorded above the ways in which the 1960 Caravan Sites and Control of Development Act created a regime that made it substantially harder to obtain permission for a private caravan site. However, for some individuals who could overcome the almost universal local hostility to such applications *and* fulfil the stringent conditions necessary to obtain a licence for a Gypsy caravan site, the opportunity to provide themselves and other members of their community with a secure place to live presented an escape from the trap of ceaseless eviction, and concomitant health and education difficulties faced by unsited Travellers.

Although Travellers often anecdotally report that they would prefer to live on a private site than a local authority facility, it is important to be aware that private sites vary considerably. In some cases private sites opened during this period of time were only for small groups (perhaps a single family or two or three siblings and their parents), while other sites (often owned and managed by Travellers) obtained permission for the provision of pitches for a larger number of families.

With regard to 'Gypsy'-owned facilities, while on the one hand members of the community might have an instinctive preference for living on sites designed and owned by other Travellers, where rules on working vehicles and animals might be regarded as being more attuned to their community lifestyle, on the other hand, difficulties of a type similar to those found on council sites could also arise. Not only could conflicts between neighbours occur (perhaps over children's behaviour or allocation of pitches) or disputes arise over the cost of plots and utilities, but owners would often (in the circumstances of shortage of sites this is generally seen as being quite justified by other Travellers) 'pick and choose' site residents, favouring their own family members and associated kin-group over strangers or Travellers without close ties to the area. Thus even where private sites were developed during the years in which the 1968 Act operated, the overall impact on Travellers' accommodation needs was often less dramatic than the statistics would indicate, given the natural growth in the population. In 1979 (the earliest date for which statistics are available) we see that 1,194 caravans were stationed on private sites; by January 1994, this had increased to 3,271, an increase from 14 per cent to 25 per cent of caravans included in the biannual count.[56] However, given the estimated population growth over these years, and that many 'next generation' Travellers may have reluctantly opted to move into housing rather than be exposed to roadside life,[57] the apparently large increase in pitch provision over these years still signally failed to meet the shortfall in pitches required to accommodate all those families who would prefer to live on an authorised site.

Although we turn to the issues of government policies on site provision (and indeed the process of applying for a private site licence) in the succeeding chapter, at this stage of the discussion it is enough to bear in mind that the issue of access to both private and public (local authority) sites remained an increasingly vexed locus of dissatisfaction even throughout the 'years of consensus'.

The end of the era of consensus and return to the roadside

Given that the Caravan Sites Act 1968 provided only a partial solution to the accommodation needs of Travellers, it would be sensible to assume that steps would have been taken by the Government to ensure that local authorities were required to meet their obligations to provide accommodation and that private site licences would become easier to obtain in order to ease the pressure on existing pitch provision. Contrary to common sense, however, in 1992 (at the beginning of the fourth term in office of the Conservative administration), a review of the Caravan Sites Act 1968 was announced, being introduced under the flagship statement that, '[the Act] has become an open-ended commitment to provide sites, which inevitably leads to a drain on the taxpayer's money and undermines gypsies' [sic] to provide for themselves'.[58] Thus, although the review was timed in such a manner that it appeared to be a response to the political and media outrage at the number of 'raves' and other events organised in conjunction with New Travellers (who were presented as an increasingly out-of-control and dangerous minority at this time),[59] the language used clearly indicated that fiscal considerations, perhaps allied with an attempt to utilise popular prejudice against Travellers for political gain, were the primary motivation behind the reassessment of the essentially successful legislation.

The consultation paper on the Caravan Sites Act 1968 issued by the Government received an astounding number of responses (over 1,400, of which approximately 1,000 were officially recognised as drafted in a manner that enabled them to be accepted as 'responses', with the remainder being rejected at this first stage[60]) from Gypsies, Travellers, local authorities and organisations working with the Travelling communities. Although the overwhelming reaction to the proposals that would subsequently form part of the Criminal Justice and Public Order Act (CJPOA) 1994 was negative, with the Department of the Environment's own analysis of responses referring to the common perception that 'the proposals represent an attack on basic human rights and are designed to stop [Travellers] travelling for good ... the phrase "ethnic cleansing" was used by several respondents',[61] the Government characteristically pushed ahead with the change of legislation, despite the vocal opposition of Liberal Democrats, the Labour Party, Gypsies and Travellers and, perhaps surprisingly, the majority of local authorities.[62]

The key proposals in the CJPOA 1994 which, on its introduction as a Bill included the majority of the measures proposed in the consultation paper of 1992, included the following:

- The repeal of Sections 6–12 of the 1968 CSA – in essence a return to the pre-1968 provisions, where local authorities had no duty to provide Gypsy sites including the abolition of the 100 per cent grant provision for the provision of local authority sites (CJPOA, s80).
- Police powers to evict Travellers where two or more people are 'trespassing' on land, who are there with the common purpose of residing on the land, *and* that reasonable steps have been taken by or on behalf of the occupier to ask them to leave. In order for the police to give a 'direction' to leave, the 'trespassers' must have six or more vehicles present with them. As each towing vehicle and trailer is counted individually, this means that no more than two families each towing one caravan and one non-towing vehicle can

be present at the same site, or the group is at risk of breaching this provision. Moreover, we are aware (anecdotally) of cases where directions to leave have been given by including a visiting midwife's car in the vehicle count. Finally, 'damage' must have been caused to the land (which can be as little as removing a fence or boulders to enter land or crushing grass as Travellers drive onto a field) or the 'trespassers' have used threatening, insulting or abusive words or behaviour towards the occupier, his family, an employee or agent. Where Travellers receive a 'direction' to leave given by the police, but fail to leave the land as soon as is reasonably practicable, or they re-enter the land within three months of being told to go, they can be convicted of an imprisonable offence or receive a large fine (under current scales up to £2,500) (s61, CJPOA).

- Local authority powers to evict Travellers from roadsides, unoccupied land, or land that was not occupied with the owner's consent. Where the persons 'residing in a vehicle or vehicles within the Authority's area' fail to leave the land as soon as is practicable and remove their vehicles, they can be convicted and subject to a heavy fine (s77, CJPOA).
- Police powers to 'seize' and remove vehicles from a site where Travellers have failed to leave, or have returned to, the land, subject to the direction within the three-month time limit (s62, CJPOA).

The awesome array of powers that exists to be used against Travellers has, therefore, since the implementation of the Act in November 1994 created a situation where, technically, the only places where someone can legally park their trailers and vehicles are as follows:

- A piece of land owned by the Traveller that has planning permission for a Gypsy caravan site (see Chapter 4).
- Land owned by a third party (local authority or private individual/company) with planning permission, laid out as a caravan site, where a site licence exists and the owner has agreed that the Traveller can park.
- Any piece of land (not necessarily a caravan site) where planning permission or a site licence are not required for an agricultural or forestry worker to stay in a caravan for a period of time, and the landowner has given permission for the Traveller to stay on the

land. (Time scales for staying on farm/forestry land are usually quite short, often around twenty-eight days.)

- 'Established Land User' (very hard to obtain), where it can be proved that one or more caravans have remained continuously on the piece of land for more than ten years and no planning enforcement notices have been served (see above about Control of Development Act 1960 and further, Chapter 4). Where it can be proved that caravans have been present for that length of time, the landowner can apply for a Certificate of Lawful Established Use and Development, which acts in the same manner as receiving a grant of full planning permission.[63]

In all other circumstances, camping is *potentially* illegal, a situation that crystallises once the 'unauthorised camper' receives a direction to move ('Go Notices' as they are often colloquially known) and they become in breach of the CJPOA through failure to leave or to raise a defence to their failure to so do. (With regard to 'defences' to ss61 and 77 of the CJPOA: in some circumstances, mechanical breakdown of a towing vehicle or ill health of someone on the site may be considered adequate grounds for not leaving the site immediately.)

In addition to the draconian powers outlined above, other powers which can be used to force Travellers to move on are provided under the Civil Procedure Rules (CPR) Part 55 (civil law eviction proceedings) which may be invoked by a landowner or a person with 'an interest' in the land in question. A Part 55 application for a possession notice must be made using the specific forms, and should usually be brought to the County Court, rather than an immediate application to the High Court. Once a possession notice is obtained, the landowner/applicant can apply for a warrant (County Court) or Writ of Possession (High Court) for the land. Unlike the CJPOA procedures which are against *specific individuals given a direction to leave*, proceedings under Part 55 mean that any person on the land at the time the bailiffs arrive to carry out the eviction must leave, even if they have not entered the land until after the persons present at the time the possession notice was obtained have already moved on. However, civil proceedings under Part 55 do have the advantage of (usually) taking effect at a somewhat slower rate than CJPOA proceedings, as the occupants must receive notice that the possession proceedings will take place at least two days before the court hearing,

By-laws can increase the difficulty of following a Travelling life (photograph by Felicity Greenfields)

with the eviction usually timetabled for some days later. In contrast, CJPOA proceedings often set a date for compliance which is as short as twenty-four hours, or in the case of police directions, may be even less.

Finally, to add to the misery of unsited Travellers, or those who are in transit, the long-established Highways Act powers (with the current version, being the Highways Act 1980), which have been used to harass Gypsies for many years, enable the local highway authorities to bring proceedings where there is an 'obstruction of the Highway', or failing all else, local authorities may resort to local bylaws, or common law powers, of 'self-help' which can be used by all landowners, and permit the use of 'reasonable force' to remove trespassers. The use of common law powers (which we have noted are finding a resurgence of favour among some large supermarket chains) generally involves serving a notice on the site and giving perhaps twenty-four hours' notice before the arrival of bailiffs who may claim to 'specialise' in the removal of Travellers and Gypsies, although it is arguable whether such claims of expertise are in breach of the amended Race Relations Act (RRA) 2000.

When we consider the impact of the CJPOA, and ways in which it intersects with pre-existing powers of eviction, it becomes abundantly clear that the implementation of the new regime imposed a fundamentally more oppressive control over Travellers' movement than had existed in Britain for many centuries. Little wonder, then, that for many Travellers and Gypsies, the question of whether it would be possible to remain nomadic in the UK or whether their way of life was doomed to extinction was of paramount concern in the mid-1990s.

The CJPOA in practice

From November 1994, those Travellers who demonstrated the audacity to wish to continue moving from place to place, despite the newly imposed legislation, were immediately put in a perilous legal situation, unless they were fortunate enough to have access to a prearranged travelling circuit that permitted them to stop on relatives' land, authorised sites, employment-related park-ups or 'transit sites' provided by some local authorities.

Of these alternatives (many of which were completely unavailable to a considerable number of families), transit sites were probably the most disliked option, not only because of their generally appalling quality of provision, unsuitable locations, unusable or vandalised sanitary equipment, perhaps only one or two filthy taps between fifteen pitches, muddy paths and damaged hard-standing, but also because of the complete lack of knowledge or choice over who else would be resident on the site. Niner (2003) found that a number of respondents to her survey were concerned that transit sites could be used by people masquerading as Gypsies or Travellers, or individuals seeking anonymity for less than credible reasons:

> Whoever would come on them? People hiding from the police could just use it as a stopover. I wouldn't feel safe on them anyway, because you don't know who's going to move on to transit sites beside you really, or who is there before you get there. 'Cos anyone could be on it, like perverts, murderers or anything. Like we don't know all the Travellers, we can't say they are all Travellers.'[64]

Despite the commonly rehearsed objections to transit sites, following the implementation of the CJPOA competition was fierce to obtain a pitch anywhere, rather than be exposed to the risk of constant eviction. A number of families contemplated moving to Ireland or the Continent to avoid the CJPOA; others with intense reluctance put their names down for 'bricks and mortar' accommodation, knowing full well that they were unlikely to obtain a secure pitch on an authorised site, or be able to raise the money to purchase their own land and apply for planning permission. For the rest of the Traveller population (including those young people who were beginning to form their own households and knew that on marriage they would have to leave a site where the rest of the family lived as there were no pitches available to them), it was simply a case of waiting for the storm to break.

The first recorded prosecution under the CJPOA took place in February 1995,[65] a bare three months past the implementation date. However, it is likely that a number of other families had been moved on under the legislation at an earlier stage. As predicted by opponents of the Act, in the February 1995 case the two Irish Traveller families who were given twenty-four hours' notice to leave their site simply moved onto the roadside at a location very close to their previous encampment. It was to be the beginning of the cycle of evictions and enforced movement which outstripped the events of the late 1950s and early 1960s, when families had been pushed from pillar to post by a diverse range of local authorities.

Not only were families who were subject to the draconian CJPOA at significant risk of disrupted medical care (see Chapter 7) and loss of education (Chapter 8) but, for the first time, they were exposed to fast-track legal proceedings that left them exhausted from constant movement and in some cases unable to complete essential vehicle repairs or even prepare food for their children before being required to move on yet again.

Traveller (West Country circuit): yeah we were parked up at Edge, got evicted from Edge and we went to a place over Arlingham way, Frampton – beautiful site – parked there the night, in the morning the landowner was there with machinery to pull us off while we were out getting [the] other vehicles. So we moved from there and down to Arlingham and we only got the night there and were moved in the morning. Down to Arlingham, the farmers were up threatening to muck spread us while we were there unless we weren't gone, we got about two and a half days there we had – we upped and moved by the Sunday 'cos they were threatening to bring in the Ministry of Transport and all their gear to test all our rigs which would be a pain so we moved in the middle of the night about five o'clock in the morning, went back to get the rest of the rigs and the farmer and police were down there, 'you can't stop here, you've got to go' [but] half the site's inside and half the site's

on the road, so we go, move. There's not a lot we can do, so we get
trailed [by police] onto the A38 and turned right. If we turn left
we're impounded, so we turn right and end up going to Sharpness.
Come back to get the other motors we'd left before the Ministry
turned up at two o'clock and there were riot police and everyone
there, and we couldn't go anywhere and I had me home and me
bus inside on the site and the cars and everything outside.

MG: so you're stuck basically.

Traveller: we're stuck, we haven't got enough drivers and if you leave
anything there, they're gonna impound it before you can come
back.

MG: so what – are you having to move the trailers along, come back get
some more vehicles and relay up the road?

Traveller: well it ended up we got drivers, people who'd never driven
before, giving them crash courses so they drive big things, stick
them in the convoy in the middle and keep going.

> (Interview undertaken in summer 1998 pertaining to events of the
> previous four weeks)

Completely understandably, families who were served with a
'direction' to move (whether by the police or the local authority)
tended not to wait until they were prosecuted but, from the earliest
days of the Act, decided that the easiest response to receiving a 'go
notice' was to pack up and move on as rapidly as possible. Although
local authority policies varied considerably, with some councils
willing to allow a longer time period for compliance with a 'direction',
no guarantees were made that on return to a particular locality the
attitude towards Travellers would not have hardened as a result of
political agendas or in response to the presence of a particular group of
Travellers who had littered or behaved in a manner that caused ill-
feeling to all other Travellers passing through. As the Gypsy Council
noted: 'The councils and the newspapers notice where there is a mess
and fail to comment where there is no mess ... even if a group of
families behave impeccably. ... they will *still* be evicted'.[66]

A further difficulty encountered by Travellers in the early years of
the CJPOA was that, in tandem with the passage of the new legislation,
pre-existing government circulars that encouraged 'tolerance' towards
unauthorised and unofficial private sites where no viable alternatives
existed were abolished. In place of this guidance (produced in part as
sugar to coat the bitter pill of the CJPOA), two new circulars were

issued, one (Circular 18/94) that asked local authorities to consider 'toleration' of unofficial roadside sites where they 'cause no nuisance' and the other (Circular 1/94 – returned to in some depth in Chapter 4) that dealt with planning issues and proposed that local authorities develop a policy on Gypsy sites in their area and provide a 'level playing field' for Travellers who sought planning permission for a private site. For families who simply could not afford to purchase land and apply for a site licence, 1/94 was of no interest or help, and 18/94 was frequently ignored or wilfully misinterpreted by local authorities.

To this complex picture of state-sponsored oppression and inadequately enforced 'guidance' must be added, too, the additional factor of increased numbers of homeless Traveller families, brought about by the repeal of the local authority duty to provide caravan sites. Although some authorities have continued to operate sites, or even (in rare cases) open new ones, the repeal of the Caravan Sites Act (CSA) 1968 enabled local authorities to close pre-existing public sites. Inevitably, some councils enthusiastically took advantage of this opportunity, offering site residents the Hobson's Choice of either moving into housing or returning to living on the roadside to face the full rigours of the CJPOA.

Kenrick and Clark (1999: 110) note that when Sussex County Council closed one of their public authority sites and rehoused the resident families into conventional accommodation, within a very short period 70 per cent of the families had returned to roadside life as a result of their inability to settle (and see further Chapter 5).

Between the years 1995 and 2002, government figures (Niner 2002) demonstrate that, as a result of closure of public sites, a net loss of 596 pitches had occurred, an average of seventy-six plots disappearing each year. Moreover, no evidence exists to support the supposition that Travellers would be able to provide their own sites at a rate that would compensate for the loss of the statutory duty to provide pitches.[67] Accordingly, the past decade has seen greater numbers of families either 'settling' into housing, leaving the country to travel abroad[68] or seeking to purchase land on which to live.

Although a number of small-scale research projects have been carried out into the impact of the CJPOA on Travellers,[69] mainly exploring the ways in which health and education suffer as a result of rapid repeat eviction, only one major national study has been commissioned by the Government, and this explored the prevalence of the use of police powers to 'direct' Travellers to leave a site rather than the overall effect of the legislation. In the Home Office review (Bucke and James 1998), while it was found that use of s61 provisions varied considerably, and depended upon the policy of local police forces, in general the picture which emerged was one of groups of Travellers being 'chased ... from one bit of land to another bit of land, to another bit of land to another bit of land ... you just chase them around' (Bucke and James 1998: 15), a finding that concurred with Webster's (1995) research for the Children's Society which identified higher rates of mobility, often within a fairly small area, as resulting from frequent eviction. Moreover, this latter study also noted that where many small sites were evicted in quick succession, Travellers tended to group together into larger bands on fewer sites, leading in turn to higher rates of public anxiety over their presence, and a further round of evictions.

By the late 1990s, an increasing number of respected voices (over and above those groups who worked exclusively with Gypsy and Traveller communities) were being raised in objection to the appalling condition of unsited Travellers. The Chartered Institute of Environmental Health condemned the CJPOA as creating a 'merry-go-round of evictions. ... [which is] financially wasteful and environmentally damaging'.[70] Liberty (formerly NCCL) responded in uncompromising terms[71] to claims by the Government that the Act was only designed for use with 'a troublesome minority of Travellers' rather than a deliberate attempt at suppressing a legitimate way of life. A tacit understanding of the futility and harshness of simply 'recycling' Travellers was reached by a number of local authorities and police forces to the extent that after a fairly short time period where some local authorities enthusiastically made use of their increased powers, the Act was not being implemented as ferociously as had been initially feared.[72] Nonetheless, local policies varied so considerably that some counties became virtually 'Traveller-free' zones while others were regarded as safer options, and accordingly found that their population increased, which in turn could create greater pressure on sites, or potential for tensions within the local Traveller communities.

In Chapter 4 we explore further the government response to the self-evident failure of the 1994 legislation and the range of policy initiatives and guidance documents that have been launched in the past few years. While at the time of writing a major government review of Gypsy policy is underway within the Office of the Deputy Prime

Minister,[73] until such time as firm decisions are taken on future policy directions, for an increased number of distressed Traveller families (including those who fail to obtain planning permission for private sites) there is quite simply nowhere to go other than back to the roadside. For many Gypsies and Travellers it is as if the reforms of 1968 had never occurred.

CHAPTER FOUR

The planning system and the accommodation needs of Gypsies

Robert Home

The numbers of Gypsies and Travellers are disproportionately small compared to the public resources expended in controlling and regulating them. There is abundant evidence from researchers of a serious shortage of sites,[1] and the closure over the past ten years of many council pitches and sites has not been compensated for by the increase in private site provision. Gypsies are seeking licensed long-stay pitches because the Travelling way of life is being made so difficult, and their home life and patterns of work and travel are becoming shaped less by their own preferences than in response to the legal constraints imposed by law and the state.

The search for land and security can take many years and involve a succession of battles with the planning authority, at considerable cost to both sides, and with uncertain outcomes. The local authority can deploy a formidable armoury of weapons: refusal of planning permission, enforcement, contravention and temporary stop notices, magistrate's court prosecution for breach of planning or site licence control and High Court injunctions in extreme cases. The Gypsies and Travellers may have to negotiate a succession of enforcement notices, applications for planning permission or variation to conditions, court appearances and appeals. The process involves tactical manoeuvring by both sides, with the occupiers trying to achieve security and improve living conditions, and the council usually seeking to prevent the creation of new residential use rights in the countryside, or at least to circumscribe such rights as tightly as possible. The central government inspectors who determine appeals have to balance the needs of Gypsies and Travellers against countryside protection policies and local residents' 'third party' objections.

The first part of this chapter discusses the general effect of planning, while the second part explores practical aspects of getting planning permission for private sites.

Part I Legislative changes

The key recent laws affecting the accommodation needs of Gypsies and Travellers have been the Caravan Sites Acts 1960 and 1968, and the Criminal Justice and Public Order Act 1994. The preceding era of relatively unconstrained nomadism ended with the Second World War, and also with the creation of the planning control system in 1947. The Caravan Sites Act 1960 brought caravans under closer control, and had the effect of reducing the number of places where Gypsies and Travellers could legally stop, while giving local authorities a compensatory discretionary power to establish sites for them.

The Caravan Sites Act 1968 (Part II), responding to the continuing difficulties that Gypsies and Travellers faced, imposed a statutory duty upon local authorities to provide adequate accommodation for Gypsies and Travellers residing in or resorting to their area. It also empowered the Secretary of State to make designation orders for areas where he was satisfied that there was adequate accommodation, or on grounds of expediency. Designation, which gave local authorities additional powers to remove unlawful encampments, was intended as a carrot to encourage a more positive approach, but was much criticised by the Gypsies and Travellers as a form of *apartheid* or separate treatment. Following the 1968 Act a succession of reports and circulars urged local authorities to increase site provision, and by 2000 nearly half of Gypsy and Traveller caravans were on council sites, developed with central government capital grant support.

Meanwhile a growing public intolerance of Gypsies and Travellers was reflected in a range of new legislation. The Planning and Compensation Act 1991, for instance, strengthened local-government enforcement powers against breaches of planning control, some of which were targeted specifically at Gypsies and Travellers, even when occupying land which they owned.

The Criminal Justice and Public Order Act 1994 remains the major piece of legislation governing relations between the state and Gypsies and Travellers. It made unauthorised encampment on land without the owner's consent a criminal offence (although not applying to owner-

Mid-1980s Dublin Travellers' Education and Development Group
(courtesy of Margaret Greenfields)

occupied land, which was subject to enforcement controls). It also abolished the duty on local authorities to provide accommodation, resulting in a gradual phasing out of government grants to provide sites, and the closing of many sites by councils. As a result of the Act's approach, the public and policy debates have until recently been conducted in negative terms, concerned with issues of criminalisation, public order and anti-social behaviour, rather than with those of accommodation needs, equality and rights. Large sums of public money have been spent on legal action against Gypsies and Travellers by police and local authorities: research by the Traveller Law Research Unit at Cardiff University estimated that each unauthorised caravan costs landowners (public and private) an average of about £3,000 a year.[2]

Since 2003, after ten years of a deteriorating situation, and under pressure from the Gypsy and Traveller Law Reform Coalition, the Government has been reviewing law and policy in the area. A Home Office draft consultation paper urged local authorities to take a more 'pro-active' approach, advocating a balanced local strategy at 'sub-regional' level and a reassessment of existing provision, using a Best Value approach, reviewing policy and delivery over a five-year cycle.[3] The Institute for Public Policy Research produced an influential report,[4] and, under pressure from the Gypsy and Traveller Law Reform Coalition,[5] a policy review was initiated in 2004, including a revision of government planning guidance. The CRE became involved, and a parliamentary committee examined the issue and reported in November 2004.[6] The Housing Act 2004 required local authorities to include Gypsies and Travellers in their local housing needs assessments, and some have commissioned specific studies (for example, Cambridgeshire local authorities, whose approach to needs assessment has been endorsed by the Traveller Law Reform Coalition). At the time of going to press a revision of Circular 1/94 was imminent.

Types of site

Authorised accommodation for Gypsies and Travellers can come from various sources: council sites (new, or through the expansion or intensification of existing sites), private sites with planning permission, movement into conventional housing, and movement onto non-Gypsy caravan sites and mobile home parks.

England currently has about 300 council Gypsy and Traveller sites, providing about 5,000 pitches. (The official counts show about 6,000 pitches, but overstate the numbers actually in use, which have fallen since the 1994 Act abolished the statutory duty to provide.) New council sites were not being provided since the end of the statutory duty. About 95 per cent of the pitches are classed as residential, but many Gypsies and Travellers reject them because of overcrowding, constant changes of neighbours, police interventions, unsanitary conditions, etc.

The number of private authorised sites has grown, and now accommodates a third of total caravans in England, usually following many battles over planning permission. The number of unsuccessful planning applications for private sites suggests that many more

A family-owned private site. Utility buildings and lurcher (photograph by
Margaret Greenfields)

Gypsies would like to live at authorised sites than are currently
allowed. While council sites were mostly built with central
government grants, private sites have been funded by the Gypsies
themselves, including the costs of getting planning permission.

Central government has since 1979 required 'Gypsy caravans'
(distinguished from other types of caravan or mobile home) to be
counted every six months by local authorities, using three categories
(council authorised, private authorised and unauthorised). The first
official count in 1979 recorded some 8,000 caravans in England, and
this rose to about 14,000 by 2004, of which about a quarter were still
on unauthorised sites. The 14,000 figure probably corresponds to
about 10,000 families, or 40,000 individuals, while estimates of total
Gypsy and Traveller population (including those settled) have been as
high as 300,000. University of Birmingham research estimated the
need for caravan pitches in England to be for 1,000–2,000 more
residential, and 2,000–2,500 more transit or stopping places.[7]

Government policy guidance also distinguishes three types of
caravan site: long-stay or permanent residential sites, transit sites and
emergency stopping places. The distinction that is sometimes made,

between 'settled' Gypsies and Travellers needing residential pitches, and those resorting to an area for a short period, and so apparently needing only transit accommodation, is hard to maintain in practice: many families travel around a cluster of counties or districts, and may be classified everywhere as 'passing through', but want and need a settled base, which could be in any of the areas where they travel.

Even if every Gypsy and Traveller family in the country had their own long-stay residential or 'settled' base, there would still be a need for transit sites for those who are travelling, particularly in the summer months from April to October. Successive official reports have identified a need for a national or regional network of such sites, but there has been little consensus on how they should be provided and what facilities offered, and at present there are about 300 council transit pitches (and perhaps 200 private). Existing transit sites are often unsatisfactory for various reasons,[8] and the general shortfall of pitches has meant that transit sites tend to become occupied as long-stay. Since the Anti-Social Behaviour Act 2003 increased their powers, the police can direct Gypsies and Travellers illegally encamped to transit sites, but only where these are available.

The regulation of caravans

Gypsies and Travellers wanting planning permission for their accommodation are limited to caravan sites, the argument being that, if they want to live in a house, then they should buy or rent like anyone else. Caravans have been subject to a special regulatory regime since the Caravan Sites and Control of Development Act 1960, which was primarily intended to control holiday camping and prevent the growth of unsightly caravan sites in rural areas. As well as the requirement for planning permission, the Act introduced site licensing, and model standards were issued by central government, covering such matters as density, distance between caravans, hard-standings, car parking, and recreational space.[9]

The Caravan Sites Act 1968 (s13) enlarged the definition of a caravan to include a twin-unit caravan up to 1,200 square feet in area (which would be a substantial mobile home big enough for a family). While mobile homes have their own legislation (conferring security of tenure on mobile home parks), the statutory definition does not distinguish between caravans and mobile homes. Since the planning system expects Gypsies and Travellers to be nomadic, their sites, even if long-stay, should include some provision for touring caravans or trailers, and applicants often want to have both mobile homes and caravans on the same site.

Gypsies in the planning system

The planning system of land-use control has 'proved a crucial blow to the traditional, if hazardous, life which modern Gypsies had carved out for themselves'.[10] Since the 1994 Act the responsibility for site provision has shifted from the state to the private sector (the Gypsies themselves). As put by the 1992 consultation paper which preceded it:

> People who wish to adopt a nomadic existence should be free to do so, provided they live within the law in the same way as their fellow citizens ... Travellers, like other citizens, should seek to provide their own accommodation seeking planning permission where necessary, like anyone else.[11]

In its view, 'gypsies [sic] enjoy a privileged position in the planning system' (presumably because they have a special policy regime).

Nowhere in law or policy are Gypsies expected or encouraged to settle down, although in practice they may be put under pressure to do so (for instance when council sites are refurbished they may be put in council housing). The closest to such a policy is the development control policy note on caravan sites after the 1968 Act:

> the first need is to provide an adequate number of properly equipped sites on which the Gypsies can live in decent conditions and where they can be encouraged to settle down and send their children to school ... Their need, unlike that of the settled population, is for caravan sites, not houses. Eventually, of course, they may move into houses, but the majority are not yet fitted or willing to do so.[12]

Current case law means that a decision to settle on land and cease the nomadic habit of life may forfeit the legal status of 'gypsy'.

Gypsies and Travellers have gradually, and only reluctantly, been accorded special policy consideration. Since the law changed in 1990, the planning system has become 'plan-led', decisions being based primarily upon the policies in the development plan rather than 'other material considerations'. Central government has for years been urging local authorities to devise specific policies for Gypsy sites in their local plans, but allows substantial discretion in how they word them.[13] As a result, the development control system allows wide variations and inconsistencies of approach, operating on a case-by-case basis. The balance that has to be struck is between protecting the rural character of the countryside (and other planning considerations) and the accommodation needs of a small minority group.

Central government advises local authorities in the form of circulars (literally circular letters to chief executives). The number of circulars issued on the subject over the years reflects the state's perplexity over how to deal with the 'gypsy problem': a quick count throws up 6/62, 26/66, 49/68, 38/70, 59/72, 28/77, 57/78, 8/81, 1/94 and 18/94.[14] For some seventeen years the key circular was 28/77, but with the coming of the Criminal Justice Act 1994 this was revised as 1/94,[15], with 18/94 dealing with unauthorised encampment. A recent review of 1/94 proposes changes more of tone than substance, since there is no legislative change, and certainly no restoration of a statutory duty upon local authorities to provide sites.

Only a minority of local authorities seem to have formulated specific planning policies for Gypsies and Travellers.[16] Circular 1/94 urges the use of 'criterion-based' local policies, and these typically include: closeness to facilities and services, minimal impact on amenities, acceptable vehicular access, potential for screening or landscaping, capable of being serviced, not located in protected areas and minimal impact upon environment or countryside. The planning system places great emphasis upon countryside protection, and even a mild encouragement for self-help sites meets often virulent resistance from local authorities and residents.

Most private Gypsy and Traveller sites have to win planning permission on appeal. An analysis of appeal decisions found the main considerations at appeal to be: special need, Green Belt, effect on landscape and highway safety. Appeal success rates vary at regional and county levels, and the numbers of appeals reveal strong demand in the South-east, eastern, South-west and West Midlands regions. Some 1,200 unauthorised private sites in the country are currently subject to council enforcement action.

Race, equality and human rights

The statutory definition of a 'gypsy' specifically excludes a racial element, and the courts have been reluctant to hear Romani arguments in case law, but the CRE, recognising the extent of discrimination experienced, has recently focused on the failure of public bodies to meet their race equality obligations to Gypsies and Travellers in such critical functions as planning, site provision and management, eviction and housing. Various resolutions of European bodies have referred to the 'special responsibility' of local and regional authorities towards Gypsies and other Travellers.[17]

Increasingly human rights issues have been introduced. The judge in the Wealden case (1996) stressed the importance of considerations of 'common humanity, none of which can properly be ignored when dealing with one of the most fundamental human needs, the need for shelter with at least a modicum of security'. (A subsequent case – Kerrier[18] – applied the same arguments to enforcement.) Article 8 of the European Convention on Human Rights (incorporated into UK law by the Human Rights Act 1998) protects the right to respect for family life and home without interference by a public authority, except as necessary in a democratic society in the public interest (which includes protection of health, the environment, or the rights and freedoms of others). Local planning authorities are now obliged to consider the human-rights implications of their decisions.

The key case to be taken to the European Court of Human Rights was that of *Buckley* v. *UK* (1996),[19] in which the planning system was found to override Article 8 rights, but the later *Chapman* case[20] offered some assistance to Gypsies and Travellers, finding that measures affecting the stationing of the caravan had an impact upon their ability to maintain their ethnic identity and to lead a private and family life in accordance with that tradition.[21]

Part II

Finding land for a site and getting planning permission is not easy, mainly because of restrictive planning policies. Some 13 per cent of England is covered by restrictive Green Belt policies and generally these should be avoided (although it may be possible to get permission, especially if there is a severe shortage of accommodation in the area). Councils are urged in Circular 1/94 to identify land that is suitable, but in practice hardly any have done so. Land can often be found through local connections and estate agents, usually 'accommodation land' (which relates to agricultural rather than residential use). Sometimes a site may have a residential history (such as the foundations of a demolished dwelling), but once the use has ceased it is difficult to persuade the planners to reinstate it. Nevertheless, the existence of development (sheds, hard-standings, septic tanks, farm buildings) may be part of the argument for getting permission. A use that has existed for ten years undisturbed (four years for operational development) may be able to claim established use rights under a Certificate of Lawful Use or Development, but in practice the case may be difficult and expensive to prove, requiring sworn affidavits and documentation such as past utility bills.

An application for planning permission is made on forms provided by the local authority (each authority usually has their own forms, although the content is largely the same). As well as the form the following needs to be supplied: a certificate of ownership, the planning fee (probably £265 for a change of use application), and plans. These plans would usually be a 1: 2500 scale plan showing the location of the site, and a 1: 500 plan of the layout of the site. If any structures are proposed (for example, sheds or day rooms), some councils require further drawings (plans and elevations). A letter can accompany the application, clarifying particularly the grounds for claiming Gypsy and Traveller status (effectively a short life history, setting out the Travelling pattern of life and its employment connection). Some local authorities have special forms asking detailed (and sometimes unnecessarily intrusive) questions to clarify the applicant's status.

Sometimes there may be site-specific aspects that need to be addressed, such as highway matters, drainage and, increasingly in recent years, flood risk. For specialist consultants to prepare such assessments can be expensive, and the applicant has to pay for them.

The description of the development for which permission is sought requires careful wording. A caravan site, because caravans are movable structures, is held to be a material change of use of the land. The associated operational development, such as hard-standings for caravans and vehicles, roads and drainage arrangements (such as septic tanks), is usually a requirement of any site licence under the Caravan Sites Act 1960, and as such is regarded as permitted development (not needing a specific permission). Unfortunately the site licence can only be granted after the planning permission, so planning authorities usually expect the application to include these as 'ancillary' or 'associated' development. A typical description would be as a 'long-stay caravan site for x gypsy'[22] families, indicating the number of caravans or mobile homes, and listing the associated development (for example, modified access, septic tank and hard-standings).

Proving Gypsy and Traveller status

The applicant has to prove status to be considered against any local plan policy for Gypsy and Traveller sites. The statutory definition s16 of the 1968 Caravan Sites Act has been much amended in case law, and cases continue to come before the courts. The latest preferred definition in the consultation document on Circular 1/94 is as follows:

> a person or persons who have a traditional cultural preference for living in caravans and who either pursue a nomadic habit of life or have pursued such a habit but have ceased travelling, whether permanently or temporarily, because of the educational needs of their dependant children, or ill-health, old-age, or caring responsibilities (whether of themselves, their dependants living with them, or the widows and widowers of such dependants), but does not include members of an organised group of travelling showmen, or of persons engaged in travelling circuses, travelling together as such.

The judges have amended the statutory definition, sometimes adding yet another hurdle to be overcome by anyone wishing to claim Gypsy and Traveller status. New Age Travellers were effectively excluded from the definition by the South Hams or Gibb case (1993). Judicial interpretation has imposed increasing restrictions upon the definition, making it more difficult to get planning permission, while challenges under human-rights law have had limited success. The growing number of applications for private Gypsy and Traveller sites raised the possibility that someone could gain a valuable benefit from a public authority in the form of a planning permission to live in the countryside, even in the Green Belt, thus enjoying a 'privileged' position relative to members of the 'settled' community. With the rising price of housing land, this benefit could be substantial, and the loophole significant enough to be felt worth challenging by local authorities.

The frustration felt by pro-Gypsy and Traveller groups at this negative development of case law has been expressed thus: 'tortuous intellectual wrangling to which the state and the courts have had to resort in their pursuit of pointless categorising'.[23] It creates a real Catch-22 situation: government policy recognises that Gypsies and Travellers need somewhere to live, but in practice, if they intend long-stay 'settled' accommodation on land which they own, they risk forfeiting their legal status and (presumably) being forced back on the road, to a way of life which is increasingly difficult to lead and potentially being criminalised. As the case law grows, usually to the disbenefit of the Gypsies and Travellers, they find their lifestyle caught in a daunting bureaucratic and legalistic net, yet persist in seeking a way forward.

The need for accommodation

The accommodation needs of Gypsies and Travellers are slowly being officially acknowledged as representing a specialised form of housing need. Central government policy guidance urged local authorities to recognise the housing needs of specific groups, including 'the homeless and travellers and occupiers of mobile homes and houseboats'.[24] Local authorities have been undertaking local housing needs assessment for some time, and the Housing Act 2004 introduced a specific requirement to include 'gypsies [sic]', drawing upon consultations with Gypsy and Traveller organisations, a common evidence base (drawing mainly, but not exclusively, upon the statistical data in the six-monthly counts), figures on unauthorised encampments (and the status of existing authorised sites, such as temporary or personal conditions), and the outcome of applications and appeals.

There appear to be no statistics on the numbers of Gypsies accommodated in conventional housing, or on 'non-gypsy' caravan sites or mobile home parks, but many do not stay long: the courts have recognised the 'deep cultural aversion to bricks and mortar accommodation' in relation to planning appeals.[25]

The statutory definition of a homeless person includes someone whose accommodation is a 'moveable structure, vehicle or vessel, designed or adapted for living in', caravan, houseboat or other mobile structure and who has no place where they are entitled or permitted to put it and live on it (s172[2][b] of the 1996 Housing Act). In the key *Awua*[26] case (not a Gypsy) the accommodation provided to a homeless applicant need be neither permanent nor settled, and should be a 'lifeline of last resort' rather than a device 'to make inroads into the waiting list'. Under the Homelessness Code of Practice the local authority has no statutory duty to provide equivalent accommodation (since the Criminal Justice and Public Order Act 1994), and Gypsy applicants are considered on the same basis as any other applicant. Given the pressure on sites, it is unlikely that a council pitch will be available, and therefore some other form of housing may be offered, and advice if nothing is available.

Paragraph 12 of 1/94 requires development plans to include a quantitative assessment of need. As measured by the unauthorised caravans in the official six-monthly counts, the county or unitary authorities with the greatest need for Gypsy and Traveller accommodation in 2002 were: Essex, Hampshire, Cambridgeshire, Kent, Northamptonshire, Bedfordshire, Hertfordshire, Worcestershire, Thurrock and Warwickshire.

The planning decision and appeals

Once the application has been accepted as valid by the council (and the council often raises queries, perhaps more in Gypsy and Traveller cases than others), then a decision should be given by law within eight weeks. The application will normally be put before the council's planning committee, and, even though the planning officers may recommend approval, councillors usually prefer to refuse, because they believe that is what the electorate want. The decision could be to grant planning permission (with or without conditions), but in Gypsy and Traveller cases this is rare (Williams found that over 90 per cent of applications for Gypsy sites were refused by the local authority, by contrast with about 80 per cent of all applications for development).[27]

On refusal of planning permission, or service of an enforcement notice, there is a right of appeal to the Planning Inspectorate (based in Bristol), who will then decide the appeal on behalf of the Minister, as if the application had been made to him in the first place. Over 90 per cent of appeals are decided by an inspector, but a small number may be referred to the Minister, in which instance the inspector hears the case and writes a report with a recommendation, which the Minister (or the civil servant dealing with it on his or her behalf) may accept or reject. The success rate at appeals is about a third, ranging from about

40 per cent in the 1980s, when central government policy generally favoured the developer, but falling to about 28 per cent in the 1990s, as law and policy towards Gypsies became less tolerant. Where the council has failed to include a specific policy, it may have difficulty at appeal, and indeed may be at risk of having costs awarded against it.

An appeal must be made within six months of the decision (date of the refusal or date of the enforcement notice), and these dates are strictly enforced. There is a choice of procedure, between an exchange of so-called 'written representations' (which most appeals follow, being the quickest and cheapest, but not most suitable for Gypsy and Traveller cases), informal hearing and public local inquiry (the most costly, usually involving barristers, with formal proofs of evidence subject to cross-examination and re-examination). Some councils may opt for public inquiries, knowing that their financial resources are stronger than those of the appellant.

Following the site visit, hearing or inquiry, the decision on an appeal comes in the form of a letter, which is usually issued within a month, setting out the inspector's decision, his or her findings of fact and the reasoning behind it. In exceptional circumstances there may be a further appeal to the High Court on a point of law; while these are generally rare, they have become more common in Gypsy cases, as the issues have become more contentious.

About a third of Gypsy and Traveller appeals succeed, and research on the main issues considered has identified the following:

a) Special need.
b) Green Belt and countryside. An estimated 97 per cent of Gypsy cases are sites in rural areas, but not all countryside is Green Belt (which at present comprises some 13 per cent of the land area of England).
c) Effect on landscape.
d) Highway safety.[28]

Conditions

When planning permission is obtained, whether from the council or on appeal, it will usually be subject to conditions, which in Gypsy cases typically include the following:

a) Restriction to 'gypsies [*sic*]' as statutorily defined. Sometimes this is a personal restriction, although government advice generally discourages their use; in the past perhaps half of 'gypsy' permissions on appeal were subject to personal conditions, and, if the land was sold, the new owner/occupier would have to prove their Gypsy status.

b) Restrictions on the number and type of caravans. Usually one mobile home and one tourer per family would be appropriate, but this may vary according to need and the physical capacity of the site.

c) Landscaping/screening, usually of the boundaries of the site where open to public view.

d) Prohibition of business activity, except the overnight parking of one lorry per family (not a heavy goods vehicle, for which a separate licence would be required).

e) Temporary consent for a limited period. Government circular advice on the use of temporary permissions generally discourages them, especially when money needs to be spent on the site; for example, an expensive landscaping requirement would not be justified if the permission was only temporary.

Once permission is granted, a caravan site licence is the next requirement, which is issued by the council's environmental health officers. This will also be subject to conditions, usually based upon model standards produced by central government, but is a much less painful process than that of getting planning permission.

Enforcement

Councils have wide powers to act against unauthorised sites, and the usual approach is through the enforcement notice procedure, starting with a requisition for information. The enforcement notice itself, served on all persons with an interest in the land, follows a set format, identifying the breach of control, the measures that are required for compliance, the reasons why the council considered it 'expedient' to take action, the period of compliance, and the date when the notice takes effect. There is a right of appeal, which unfortunately Gypsies sometimes do not use (perhaps because they do not understand the procedure, or do not believe they can win), and in such a case the same procedural rules apply as on a planning appeal.

The grounds of appeal against an enforcement notice are laid down in law. In practice the common ones in 'gypsy cases' are grounds (a) (that planning permission should be granted) and (g) (that insufficient period of time has been given). If ground (a) is used, then a double planning fee has to be paid (one to the Inspectorate, the other to the council); if a planning application has already been made, the double fee does not have to be paid.

An enforcement notice applies to the land, not the person who is served with it. A common mistake is to believe that by selling the land on, the notice is cancelled, but this is not the case, and a subsequent owner may find himself taken to court over a notice that predated his buying the land. Councils are not obliged to take action against breaches of control, and indeed sometimes may choose to 'tolerate' a site, although central government does not favour the approach.

Someone breaching an enforcement notice can be prosecuted by the council, and the fines can be heavy (up to £20,000 or a daily fine). In practice, where there is a continuing shortage of sites in the area, the courts may be reluctant to impose heavy fines, but this cannot be relied upon. Ultimately, someone in breach of an enforcement notice may find themselves sent to prison for contempt of court, and stay there until they apologise (or 'purge their contempt').

Some councils, frustrated by the perceived ineffectiveness of the enforcement process, resort to the more drastic and expensive remedy of applying for an injunction in the High Court, which can be done even before a site is occupied (based upon their suspicion that something is about to happen). Such an injunction may be taken out against 'persons unknown'.

Conclusions

The state, usually through the land-use planning system, has expended significant resources to control and manage the 'gypsy problem': by central government through capital funding, policy reviews and changes in the law, and planning appeal decisions; by the judicial system through individual cases and appeals, and interpretations of the law; and by local authorities through working parties and enforcement action on individual sites. The costs of the system to both sides are high, in time, resources and stress-related health problems. There has often been an inconsistency of approach, with both central and local government vacillating between repressive or preventative measures and a more permissive policy.

Over the past forty years the planning issues and concerns around accommodation for Gypsies and Travellers have not changed much, and have included resistance to site provision from the settled community, especially in countryside locations, and calls for transit sites or emergency stopping places. More long-stay sites are needed, for which the main source of supply will be private sites, and this requires a more positive approach by local planning authorities than has been evident hitherto. Local-needs assessment may help identify the shortages, but in reality any Gypsy with no authorised stopping place is in need, and a local-needs assessment at local or even county level is likely to be less helpful than one carried out at a regional level, preferably by independent researchers. Local planning policies based upon criteria often appear to have been devised to frustrate applications, and this has to change before the situation can improve. Local authorities should monitor more closely planning applications and breaches of planning control associated with private Gypsy and Traveller sites, and assess the impact of their policies.

A 'best value' approach is overdue, comparing the costs (both direct and indirect) of dealing with unauthorised Gypsy and Traveller encampments with the possible costs and benefits of a more proactive approach to site provision. The planning system in the UK works on a case-by-case basis, with a wide degree of discretion afforded to the local authority, within a framework of central government policy. Such a system can involve what might seem an excessive attention to site-specific and minor detail, and has to balance protection of the rural character of the countryside (and other planning considerations) against the undoubted accommodation needs of a small minority group. The contested position of Gypsies and Travellers derives from a number of factors: the settled community's general antipathy towards them, the perceived inconsistency of the nomad seeking a settled base, the difficulties of incorporating caravans (essentially movable property) under land-use regulation, and the reluctance of the planning system to accord a special exemption from countryside protection policy for a minority group. A case-based land-management approach requires Gypsies and Travellers to negotiate their land and housing rights site by site, and often family by family. Few council sites exceed fifteen pitches, and most private self-help sites are smaller, so inevitably the planning system has to deal with small-scale sites. The main responsibility for negotiating with the planning system falls to the immediate or extended family group in relation to its particular plot of land.

The key event in achieving land-use rights and secure accommodation for Gypsies and Travellers is not the purchase of the land, but the grant of planning permission. Once uncertainty over the right to stay has been resolved, usually at considerable cost and delay, then the owner-occupiers can invest in facilities within the licensing requirements for caravan sites. Conditions restricting the planning permission may need to be removed or varied, incrementally adding property rights in recognition of changed circumstances, usually against the continuing resistance of the local council. Because of its concern with countryside protection, the council may oppose more permanent structures, resisting not only the replacement of a caravan with a permanent dwelling-house or bungalow, but even lesser structures such as amenity/toilet blocks. So, although improved security and living conditions may be negotiated with the planning system step by step, that progression is usually contested, and the case-by-case basis of the system allows wide variations and inconsistencies of approach, with central government policy on the subject often ambivalent.

CHAPTER FIVE

Bricks and mortar accommodation: Travellers in houses

Margaret Greenfields

Introduction

We have discussed in earlier chapters some of the reasons why Gypsies and Travellers have moved into housing, and why in particular areas they have formed large 'settled' communities. Although in the main, Travellers have resorted to 'bricks and mortar' accommodation as a result of planning restrictions and shortages of sites which have occurred over many decades, this does not explain fully the size of the housed population who have Gypsy and Traveller origins, and why, in some areas Travellers are able to live contentedly in conventional housing, while continuing to travel seasonally.[1] More importantly, while living in a house can be quite frankly a form of torture for families who have been forcibly settled, for other Gypsies and Travellers, resort to housing does *not* mean losing their community identity or feeling that they have to hide their ethnic origins.

Very little research has been undertaken with Travellers living in housing,[2] and that which has been carried out has tended to focus on the immense difficulties faced by families when they first move from trailers and/or other 'traditional' accommodation into bricks and mortar buildings. For many Travellers, the transition from living among a close-knit community to experiencing the social isolation of dwelling within four walls (which in most urban situations may mean that unknown neighbours reside beside, above and below them) can be profound and traumatic. The situation is often exacerbated by the fact that many newly housed Travellers may, for the first time in their lives, now reside miles away from their friends and family and (not infrequently) they find themselves exposed to racist abuse or fear when their ethnic origins become apparent to their new neighbours.

Not only do families have to come to terms with living among potentially hostile neighbours, but the limited research evidence (and anecdotal information gathered from community workers and Travellers[3] themselves) indicates that Travellers often find it quite difficult to adjust to the necessity of paying rent and water bills from low incomes, or allowing for regular bills as opposed to purchasing calor gas and fuel as and when they are needed. Consequently, budgeting problems frequently arise for newly housed Travellers and some families can find themselves in debt for the first time in their lives.

Balanced against the negative aspects of moving into housing (on which more below), we find that some families report welcoming 'the hot running water' or 'not having to go outside in all weather'.[4] For the majority of first-generation housed Travellers, however, even where they successfully make the transition to living in conventional accommodation and appreciate the convenience of 'bricks and mortar', living in a house can be 'lonely when you close the door at night' or 'isolated' unless you are surrounded by a network of family and friends. So how *do* they and their families come to terms with such a profound change in their traditional lifestyle?

In the rest of this chapter we explore Gypsies' and Travellers' relationship with, and attitude towards, living in houses, and consider how the community can retain its strengths and individuality despite living in a manner which is very different from the conventional image of travelling people.

Nineteenth-century housed Travellers

Although Travellers tend to be invisible in historical analyses of housing need (unless they are included within 'homelessness' or 'poverty' statistics), it is possible to find traces of their movement in and out of housing. Often evidence is anecdotal and scanty. For example, one co-author's grandmother (who was born in the 1880s) had a close friend – a Romani Gypsy lady – whose family lived in rented rooms in London in the winter while they worked as costermongers and hawkers, and who then joined up with other relatives and travelled out of town to work for some seven months of the year. Histories of inner-city London (most particularly those which focus on indices of poverty) also offer some tantalising glimpses of the existence of a 'settled' or at the very least semi-sedentary Traveller population since at least the early nineteenth century. Booth (1902)[5] in his perambulations through Notting Dale (a district currently known as Notting Hill), an area which today still houses families with Gypsy and Traveller origins as well as the notorious Westway Traveller site,[6] observed that 'gypsy [sic] blood is very evident amongst the children in the schools and noticeable even in the streets'. Travellers had been recorded as halting in wagons and tents in Notting Dale since the mid-1700s, with some families subsequently moving into rooming houses during the expansion of the area in the middle of the nineteenth century. By the time of Booth's great survey of poverty in the capital, a considerable number of Travellers were engaged in labouring and trading work associated with the growth of the city and had utilised the opportunity of sending their children to the local boarding school to provide them with at least a rudimentary education.[7] Nor is the Notting Hill area alone in boasting long-term housed populations of Travellers. Wandsworth and Bethnal Green were reported as being 'Metropolitan Gypsyries' by Borrow in 1874[8] and throughout the nineteenth and early twentieth centuries there are persistent reports of Gypsies and other Travellers moving in and out of housing as a result of urban employment opportunities coupled with evictions which meant it was impractical to remain encamped for more than a few months on open spaces within the boundaries of the ever-encroaching metropolis.[9] Evidence from the 1881 and 1891 censuses[10] provides us with further information on the existence of houses across the country (although predominantly in cities) where the majority of the tenants are 'Gipsey [sic] pedlars' or 'Gipsey hawkers'. What is particularly fascinating, is that in some cases we see a close coexistence of 'Gipsey tents' and houses with Gypsy and Traveller occupants who share the same name,[11] enabling us to trace the ways in which community structures and family relationships transcended the move into conventional accommodation.

By the early twentieth century, certain urban areas (e.g. parishes within Manchester, Black Patch [Handsworth] in Birmingham, and Battersea and Finsbury Park in London) are noted as having 'a Gypsy connection', in which an 'oral tradition is overwhelming'[12] often despite the lack of clear documentary evidence. Extrapolating from oral history and fragmentary references to traditional stopping places that had become overwhelmed by the spread of the inner city, it is likely that families with a reason to remain in the city, either for employment opportunities or as a result of family tragedy, simply moved into available (cheap) housing within a few yards of their former campsites.

White (1986: 55) refers to 'Liza Harmer, a flower seller who died in Campbell Road in 1919 [who] came from a travelling family who had settled ... by the early 1870s. Her father. ... had been murdered in the country for the bag of gold coins he kept about him' while other Traveller families known to live in the notorious Campbell Bunk area included 'The Stevensons [who were] street sellers ... who had accumulated sufficient capital by the 1930s to hire out barrows and later still open a coal shop in the road' (1986: 55). Descendants of these, and other Gypsy families, were noted as working in a variety of traditional occupations such as cane-chair repairers, knife-grinders and mat salesmen in north London up until just after the Second World War. Despite their lengthy period of settlement, evidence exists that members of these families still annually attended Barnet Fair (the nearest horse fair to north London) and spoke at least some Romani in private, thus demonstrating a clear continuity of culture, and awareness of their Gypsy identity although in occupation, accommodation and indeed brushes with the law, they were indistinguishable from all the other denizens of Campbell Road. Indications therefore exist that over time, as particular localities (often only a few roads in an area) became known as places where Gypsies and Travellers lived, other members of the community who required accommodation in the city sought rooms, or moved to live with family connections until such time as they either returned to travelling, or became semi-permanently settled. Thus from references to settled Travellers in Finsbury Park and the Black Patch area of Handsworth,[13] a picture begins to emerge of the ways in which such families adapted their behaviours to urban life and in some cases married city-dwellers from non-Traveller backgrounds, leading to greater integration into the sedentary community which surrounded them.

Housing as a response to inadequate site provision

While movement into housing in the nineteenth century can be predominantly seen as a *choice* made by Gypsies and Travellers who in some cases appear to have treated settlement as simply a phase of

Disused pitches on a run-down local authority site. Existing residents have to
live near to closed pitches (such as the one pictured) which have been used
for fly-tipping by people who drive in off the road through the 'ungated'
entrance and dispose of their rubbish at night
(photograph by Frank Blackmore)

life to be experienced between times spent Travelling, the increasingly
oppressive legal regimes of the twentieth century (see Chapter 3)
meant that many families were forced into public-sector
accommodation as a result of 'settlement policies' (see below) or to
avoid the constant harassment experienced by those with no legal
place to stop.

In this book we return on a number of occasions to the vexed issue
of shortage of sites. We would argue that the predominant reason for
Gypsies and Travellers moving into housing over the past fifty years is
this specific issue. As discussed extensively elsewhere in this text,
unsited Travellers experience social exclusion on a wide range of
indices (particularly in terms of health and education). However, a
considerable number of residents of public sites also suffer from
preventable health problems as a result of the unacceptable quality of
facilities provided to them. Not only are a substantial proportion of local
authority sites in a poor condition, perhaps vandalised, badly
maintained or suffering from problems with water supplies or vermin,[14]
but the location of such sites, often in polluted or unhealthy

environments,[15] inevitably increases the likelihood of residents experiencing ill health.

> they [the children] had constant bad health ... all the time infections at that place – up and down going to the doctor all the time for the pills – and the rats, I'd be distracted trying to keep the trailer clean, filthy they were, and scared of nothing. I've seen them [vermin] peering in the window at us, so that I dropped the baby's bottle with the shock that first night. Every day I'd use a bottle of Dettol a day to try to keep them away but still they'd dirty outside by the trailer and get into the [utility] shed. Filthy, it were disgusting.
>
> (Traveller woman whose family left an authorised council site
> interviewed by MG 2002)

In such circumstances it is unsurprising that some families apply for housing as a way of improving their living conditions. Disability or chronic illness can also result in the decision to move into conventional accommodation, even where a family has managed to access a fairly good quality site. Kenrick and Clark (1999: 31) give an example of health needs that led to a family requesting housing to enable them to take care of a child who required an operation on his brain. The limited space available on pitches, particularly if a family resides in a trailer rather than a mobile home (structures that generally have to be paid for and provided by the pitch resident, requiring that they spend upwards of £7,000 to accommodate themselves), can create real hardship where the family is large, or where significant health difficulties exist that require access to equipment or mobility aids. Indeed Niner (2003: 56) found that 51 per cent of local housing authorities that gave reasons for Travellers moving into housing cited medical needs as the primary reason for accommodation requests.

Perhaps surprisingly, given the national shortfall in pitches and the inherent difficulties of either travelling or living on a site where a family member is disabled or severely ill, 44 per cent of authorities surveyed by Niner (2003) claimed that no Gypsy or Traveller families were on the waiting list for social housing, 29 per cent said that fewer than five families required conventional accommodation and only 2 per cent of authorities reported in excess of twenty families requesting housing. It is telling, however, that Niner notes:

> it is apparent that many local authorities keep no records of Gypsies and other Travellers in rented housing even where they maintain

ethnic records and [they] are generally blind to this aspect of ethnic minority housing. Many authorities were unable to provide accurate information and unable or unwilling to guess ... some respondents noted on their questionnaires that rehousing of Gypsies and other Travellers is so rare that they simply had no experience to draw upon.

Niner (2003: 55)

Given that Kenrick and Clark (1999: 33), on the basis of their knowledge of statistics and published family trees, estimate that perhaps half of every generation of Romani Gypsies has moved into housing during the twentieth century, there is a clear discrepancy between official administrative statistics and actual practice.

Travellers and homelessness legislation

Aside from those Travellers who already reside on an authorised site but who for some reason wish to move into housing, the other single largest pool of Traveller applicants for 'bricks and mortar' accommodation are individuals who are technically homeless, in that they have nowhere to legally station their caravan. Although local authorities have a duty (s172[2][b] Housing Act 1996) to provide accommodation for Travellers in the above circumstances, the Homelessness Code of Practice does not require that the accommodation is culturally suitable, or equivalent to the accommodation a family or 'vulnerable person' may have occupied prior to becoming homeless. Thus, despite acknowledging that 'many Travelling families will not wish to settle in conventional housing', the Code of Practice states that 'travelers [sic] should be considered on the same basis as any other applicant'.[16] While to some extent the harshness of this guidance has been ameliorated by recent case law which clarifies that a Gypsy or Traveller with a 'cultural aversion to bricks and mortar'[17] ought to be offered a pitch rather than housing where it is possible to do so (and that to fail to offer a pitch where such provisions exist may be in breach of the right to respect for home and family life under Article 8 of the European Convention on Human Rights [ECHR]) no statutory duty exists that requires the local authority to guarantee access to a site for the homeless person.

A homeless Traveller is therefore in a Catch-22 situation in terms of attempting to access culturally suitable accommodation. Although local authority homelessness strategies should include consideration of the accommodation needs of *all* members of the local community, and moreover under the Race Relations (Amendment) Act 2000 there is a specific requirement to promote equality of opportunity for people of all ethnicities, Lord Avebury's 2003 survey[18] of the homelessness policies of 157 local authorities found that 72 per cent of councils had failed to consult with or take note of the needs of Gypsies and Travellers. By dint of such a breach, Gypsies and Travellers are ignored when accommodation policies are drawn up, meaning that additional sites are not provided,[19] and the pressure on access to plots continues. Despite judicial and policy pronouncements that homeless Travellers should be offered pitches if possible, if none exist and no requirement is imposed which ensures local authorities acknowledge the shortage of sites for homeless families, then inevitably Travellers are forced into accepting conventional housing if they are recognised as being in priority need of accommodation.

But the situation for Travellers who register for social housing is not as simple as informing a housing officer that they have nowhere to park and will accept a house if one is offered. Further hurdles must still be negotiated, in respect of the requirement of a 'local connection', before an applicant can be assessed as being 'in need'.[20] In order to be counted as having a 'local connection' (defined as close relatives living in the area or at least six months' residence in the locality), documentary proof of residence is often required, creating significant problems for families who may have literacy problems or who have tended to move on prior to eviction and thus only hold evidence of possession orders or CJPOA notices which refer to them as 'persons unknown'. However, despite the rigid standards of proof required within local authority interpretations of homelessness law, a legislative acknowledgement exists that some people may not be able to show a close connection to any one area. Thus long-distance or highly mobile Travellers who have been repeatedly evicted and moved across county or borough boundaries should *technically* be able to be considered for accommodation within the terms of this exception. In practice, however, some local authorities insist that Travellers return to the area where they were formerly camped and then make an application from that locality. Where families have experienced a series of rapid evictions that push them across numerous authority boundaries, it can be so difficult to show residence in any one area that it may simply be easier to move on to an

Owner-occupied bungalows in a 'Gypsy area' of a town with a large Romani
population (photograph by Margaret Greenfields)

area where greater 'toleration' of unauthorised encampments exists,
and then reapply for accommodation, or simply give up the idea of
obtaining access to housing. Given the virtual impossibility of a
Traveller being offered a pitch on a site, even when they are accepted
as homeless, we can see the way in which homelessness law has
driven further nails into the coffin of the 1968 Act and diminished the
concept of appropriate accommodation for Travellers despite the lip
service paid to their preferences in the Homelessness Code of Practice.

Compounds, camps and the transition to housing

As we have indicated above, some Travellers have lived in housing for
several generations, adapting their lifestyles and employment
practices until they are integrated into the surrounding populations.
For example, it has been estimated that in some parts of Kent (e.g.
some villages near Canterbury, Orpington, St. Mary Cray and Bromley)
as many as 50 per cent of the local population are of Gypsy and
Traveller origins.[21] While historically these families were forced to
move into housing as a result of eviction and resettlement policies,
over time their descendants have become as much part of the

community as any other local family. While long-settled Gypsies and Travellers generally retain a clear awareness of their relationships to certain families and can trace their lineage both through tradition and parish records,[22] their networks are as likely to involve sedentary 'non-Traveller' kin and friends, as people who share their ethnic origins. Similarly, it is not uncommon to find descendants of settled Travellers working in a wide range of occupations in localities where their presence is statistically significant.

What is noticeable, however, is the fact that housed Travellers (and the descendants of first-generation settled Travellers) are often to be found living in fairly tight-knit communities which are geographically close to former traditional stopping places.[23] In many cases families who were evicted from their old sites by compulsory purchase between the 1930s and 1960s were offered prefabricated or conventional brick-built housing in lieu of an alternative site. In some cases, Travellers report that the transition from trailer or *vardo* to a secure tenancy with access to modern services was welcome; a reaction that was particularly found where networks of related families were offered property in immediate proximity to each other, with room to keep a touring caravan or work vehicle outside. In other words, provision of accommodation which was essentially suitable for the needs of the occupants and which enabled them to recreate their former lives whilst providing them with security and access to employment and education opportunities.

> When we moved off the Belvedere Marsh, after the war they moved us to a place called Dashwood Farm ... it wasn't very far from the Marsh, just across the fields and it was a place where the soldiers used to be in the war, huts everywhere. They were lovely huts, absolutely beautiful, as clean as a whistle ... they were all wood and we lived in them for several years until we moved into houses. I had some lovely years on there ... the floorboards were as white as snow and we had electric light for the first time in our lives ... that was nice.
>
> Betsy Stanley's memoirs (2002: 48)

Some Travellers, however, did not find the transition so pleasant. Len Smith (2004)[24] recounts the way in which Gypsies and Travellers in the New Forest were in 1926 confined first to 'compounds', outside of which it was unlawful to camp, and entry to which was restricted by the use of 'permits' and then, in the immediate post-Second World War era, were transported to former army camps in a move that mirrors the one narrated by Betsy Stanley (above). While similar processes were underway in both areas (hastened in Kent by the drive to build houses on valuable land and the disastrous floods of the early 1950s), in Hampshire a more sinister process was underway. In the New Forest, a conscious process of 'purging'[25] the area of Gypsies commenced, hand-picking potential tenants from among the younger, more widely travelled men who may have seen service in the war, who had in many cases obtained paid employment from the Forestry Commission and who were considered most likely to accept movement first into huts and then housing. The process of persuasion (initially), followed by force, was based upon an explicit policy for the:

> reclamation of character and education ... the object being that as soon as the children's behaviour and morals improved and their bodies and clothes became clean ... when the gypsies [sic] learned the ordinary mode of life. ... they would then graduate to Council houses.
> New Forest Rural District Council 'The Baker Report', 1947, cited in
> Smith (2004: 112)

By the early 1960s, despite some (perhaps unexpected) opposition to the plans from the New Forest Parish Councils Association which favoured the provision of transit sites, better quality compounds and access to housing for those families who particularly desired such accommodation, the pressure to forcibly house Gypsies was being actively implemented. Smith (2004) recounts that some New Forest families who had access to finances purchased small plots of land on which to live (although as we have seen in Chapter 3 they were soon to become bound by the requirements of the 1960 Caravan Sites and Control of Development Act), and others moved into self-provided bungalows,[26] while a tiny proportion went 'back on the road' on a permanent basis. The remainder of the compound residents were required to make the transition to 'camps' or directly into council housing. The last few families who had refused to leave the New Forest 'compounds' were forcibly evicted and provided with housing some considerable distance away from their relatives and friends with whom they had shared a site for many years.

Communities in houses

The fact that the New Forest Traveller communities were in some cases deliberately dispersed into housing with the intent of assimilating the community into the 'mainstream' population is a particularly damning indictment of the (then current) local authority policies. We have discussed in Chapter 2 the importance of family to Gypsy and Traveller culture and the ways in which community intersects with the economic and social networks that are fundamental to Travellers' way of life. By separating extended family units not only does social disruption occur (for example, child care, practical and emotional support) but chances for employment may diminish through loss of contact with employers and partners in business ventures. It is through such attenuation of community that social exclusion may increase.

Despite the fact that local authority policies favoured assimilation at this time (an attitude which indeed continued throughout much of the 1960s and 1970s), it is too simplistic to conclude that family and community disruption were an inevitable correlation of movement into housing. Even where local authorities were willing to attempt to keep former residents of sites or extended family members within a single locality, the shortage of public housing stock (both in the 1960s and more particularly since the right-to-buy initiatives of the Thatcher Government) meant that with the best will in the world it was not always possible to place eligible families in close proximity. While some families might find themselves living in the same road or housing estate as other Travellers, this was often a hit-and-miss affair given the fact that accommodation was provided on a 'points' or 'need' basis rather than depending on affiliation and community ties. Inevitably, in some cases families in conflict might find themselves living uncomfortably close to people with whom they would never willingly have shared a site. Conversely, the strengths of the community also empowered families to make their own decisions over housing exchanges, meaning that some families were able to come to mutually beneficial arrangements which permitted them to swap a conveniently sized property with other Travellers and find themselves once again living among their own kin.

Whilst local authorities are not generally renowned for their cultural sensitivity or willingness to meet the needs and desires of local residents, what has become clear from the limited data that exists on Travellers in housing is that particular housing estates (as well as areas of privately owned homes) in counties and boroughs throughout Britain are well known to local residents as 'Gypsy' or 'Traveller

areas',[27] either because of local authority policies of offering
accommodation on particular estates, or as families make a conscious
effort to live near to other members of their community.

> when the houses [almost entirely bungalows] up here come up for sale,
> well there's a lot of people want to have one. You hear from family
> about it, they don't bring in the sellers [estate agents], 'cos you want to
> know who's coming in to the roads. Sometimes if someone [non-
> Traveller] sees one up for sale and they think about it, well they know
> where they are coming and they want to live among Travellers, and if
> they don't know, well someone will soon tell them and they won't buy
> unless they like the life. Course there are some *gorjes* round here, the
> old lady next to my auntie's bungalow she and her husband – rest his
> soul – they lived here ever so long but they are part of us now, he [the
> neighbour's husband] came and sat up when my uncle died and they
> have the china in the front room too.
>
> Romani lady discussing the road where many of her family live in
> bungalows (Interviewed by MG 2004)

The above quotation casts an interesting insight into the way in which
localities can take on a particular 'Traveller' character, to the extent
that members of the settled (non-Traveller) population moving into the
neighbourhood would to some degree need to assimilate into Gypsy
and Traveller culture to feel comfortable or accepted as integrated
members of the area. The elderly couple referred to above not only
were aware of, and welcomed to participate in, cultural behaviours
(such as 'sitting up' prior to a funeral, see Chapter 2) but over time,
through long association with their Traveller neighbours, they also
acquired certain 'Gypsy' traits such as collecting Crown Derby china.
The comment that properties (in this case owner-occupied) would also
usually exchange hands within the community, indicates too that
protective mechanisms may exist to ensure that neighbours are either
familiar with, and sympathetic to, Traveller lifestyles or most
commonly are family members who are moving to be nearer their
relatives. Fascinatingly, it would appear, too, that *gorjes* who might
perhaps have expressed an interest in property in the locality without
knowing of the existence of a vibrant Traveller community would also
be advised 'through the grape-vine' of the ethnic make-up of the
neighbourhood enabling them to make an informed decision as to
whether to put in an offer to buy, and in the process, indicate their
cultural familiarity and sympathy (or ambiguous relationship) with
the community.

'Traveller' houses

We have mentioned above that where possible Gypsies and Travellers will often live in clustered communities where they can recreate as near a proximity to site life as is possible in housing. Not only will such communities often live near to former traditional stopping places (for example a well-known 'Gypsy' area in Southampton borders a number of 'atchin tans' which are no longer available as a result of planning regulations or the restrictions of roadworks and urban development), but in many cases bungalows have been purposely built by Gypsy and Traveller families who have purchased the land surrounding their former camping grounds. As noted above, when asked to discuss their preferred form of housing (although bearing in mind that the majority of Gypsies and Travellers cite as their first preference for accommodation small, purpose-designed single-family sites where they can occupy static mobile homes – Niner 2003), many Travellers will consider that a bungalow provides a good alternative to living in a trailer. We therefore find that Gypsies and Travellers who have the finances to purchase property will almost overwhelmingly opt to buy a bungalow with enough hard-standing to park up a touring caravan and perhaps keep a horse and sulky (light two-wheeled, one-person horse-drawn carriage).

The 'Gypsy area' in Southampton provides a classic example of Traveller-friendly accommodation. A walk down the street will reveal neat rows of bungalows, many with caravans parked outside, some with stables and sheds and the majority of such bungalows displaying gleaming crystal and china in the front windows. Another characteristic sign of Gypsy or Traveller occupancy is the presence of low stone walls with wagon wheels or models of horses' heads adorning the brickwork or gate posts. Evidence of cultural markers and a pride in their heritage is readily available to identify who lives within these smartly painted homes. Moreover, a considerable amount of daily life takes place outside of the buildings, and many Travellers will be seen driving along the street, acknowledging their friends, or standing and talking to their neighbours and relatives outside their homes. Children and young people are known by the entire neighbourhood who retain a level of responsibility for the well-being and safety of the youngsters and an awareness of their activities and friendships.

In this way, the semi-communal life that is such a part of living on site is reproduced within the setting of peri-urban development, often on the fringes of a large town. Similarly, when the 'travelling season' begins in the spring, many multigenerational families will leave their homes together, perhaps beginning the circuit working at the same location and then separating into small groups for work purposes, and meeting up again at the horse fairs or for specific employment reasons. Where some members of the family need to remain at home (perhaps because they are elderly, due to give birth or in poor health, or families with school-age children decide that the mother and children will meet up with the men of the family at the end of the school term) the sense of security and support which is available within the street community ensures that family structures remain intact and individuals do not become isolated or endangered by the absence of their relatives. We can thus see that where the right conditions exist to enable the community to ensure that networks, culture and social behaviours remain intact, it is possible for some Travellers to make the transition into housing in a positive manner.

Group housing

One factor that is critically important when considering why some Gypsies and Travellers are willing or happy to live in conventional accommodation is the issue of the design of housing and the suitability of accommodation for the needs of community members. Where Gypsies and Travellers are required or 'encouraged' to live in multi-storey or even terraced properties, the design of the accommodation they are offered has generally been imposed in a top-down manner that precludes the mixture of work/living space and keeping of animals and touring caravans next to the family's main accommodation. Not only are houses of more than one storey often psychologically unsuitable for Travellers who have spent their lives in trailers, but when families are expected to disrupt their entire method of household organisation, it is unsurprising that a high percentage of moves into housing break down in a fairly short time.[28]

One option that has been experimented with in the Republic of Ireland[29] and more recently on a pilot basis in Northern Ireland, is 'Group housing'. In Ireland, this option is now considered as a perfectly normal aspect of provision of accommodation for Travellers and is routinely provided alongside the development of permanent and transit sites. Group housing is residential housing developments with additional aspects and amenities that have been designed in consultation with Travellers with the intention that they should provide long-term accommodation for families and those who are too elderly or ill to travel. Group housing is local authority property, available for rent by individuals who are eligible for social housing, and consists of small groups of bungalows with adjacent space for lorries, work vehicles and touring trailers. It is fairly standard to find that such schemes include communal facilities such as a community centre, play area, secure work tool spaces, animal grazing and stables. In this way, the preferences and needs of the community can be accommodated by the local authority in a manner that is only self-provided in certain areas of mainland Britain such as in the 'Gypsy area' of Southampton and some suburbs of Leicester and, moreover, is only available to those families who have the financial resources and personal contacts which enable them to purchase a bungalow in a Gypsy or Traveller enclave. Niner reports that a number of Gypsies and Travellers whom she interviewed were aware of the existence of group housing schemes in Ireland and that such a possibility, if it existed in Britain, would be 'generally popular' (2003: 164). Although a number of Niner's interviewees expressed concerns that they would 'feel trapped' (2003: 166) if living in a bungalow even if they were amongst their own community and resident on a purpose-designed site, it is interesting to note that the key issues of social isolation, fear of discrimination and insecurity faced by many housed Travellers would often be alleviated.

Social housing

We have explored earlier why many Travellers move into social housing,[30] and commented on the high number of placements that break down fairly rapidly. Niner (2003) reports that local authorities in her survey provided the following reasons for the ending of tenancies:

- Inability to settle into housing: 79 per cent
- Problems with neighbours: 54 per cent
- Isolation from family and friends: 37 per cent
- Desire to move to a caravan site: 33 per cent
- Budgeting problems/rent arrears: 28 per cent

Although the categories may at first sight appear fairly distinct, an inability to settle into housing may easily result from a combination of difficulties such as having to deal with a constant round of bills, or adjust to living in a flat with the constant noise of neighbours. There is plentiful evidence that moving into a house or flat can cause great tension and unhappiness for some Travellers, and anecdotally it is reported that family tensions associated with 'bricks and mortar' accommodation can in some cases lead to marital breakdown.

> when the second baby was due she put her name down for a council house and I just couldn't stick it in an house ... I was staying there on and off but I just fekken hated it while I was there, now you know what I mean, it just was arguments an all.
>
> Irish Traveller (interviewed by MG 2002)

The man's marriage broke down within three months of taking up a council tenancy. The mother and children remained in the house for a further few months while the father lived in the touring caravan on a variety of suburban car parks and lay-bys, experiencing rapid repeat evictions. The family (who at the time of interview had three children) gave up their tenancy and after eighteen months on the road in both England and Ireland obtained a pitch on an authorised private site.

While New Travellers might be expected to tolerate the move into housing rather better than Gypsies and other Travellers who have *never* lived in 'bricks and mortar', after a number of years living as part of a community and travelling on a full-time basis, they appear to experience similar emotional and practical difficulties to other Travellers when first attempting to settle. It is particularly striking that Travellers of all 'types' report that isolation and loneliness are often the hardest aspects to bear of living in a house (Greenfields 2002).

> it was awful, just really awful we hated it, the kids were bored and they had no one to play with, they couldn't go outside, they couldn't run around and it was a nightmare and I will not do that again until I'm physically incapable of living like this ... I was in this bloody house all that winter on my own ... come four o'clock you're in a house on your own with the children ... the isolation and the cold, we had gas central heating but I'm used to a wood burner and so we were cold, and bills ... so it was basically schooling [for seven-year-old daughter] but then I found out she's actually not behind in any – she came out nearly top in her SATs tests.
>
> New Traveller (interviewed by MG 2001)
> – at time of interview living at an unauthorised site

Despite the very real distress reported by these Travellers in having to adjust to a very different lifestyle involving (perhaps) living in a flat, dealing with a constant round of bills and being socially isolated from culture and family, housing can be tolerated in the interests of keeping children in school or accessing medical care. However, interviewees often recount that 'problems with neighbours' are the final straw that leads them to give up a tenancy and face the problems of living on the roadside.

The seemingly bland category of 'neighbour troubles' can, however, hide a range of problems – from simple cultural misunderstandings and perhaps fear (Niner 2003) pertaining to visitors staying in a trailer parked on a house driveway whilst seeing relatives, to objections to large, perhaps noisy, gatherings to celebrate a wedding or christening, or the spreading of malicious gossip about families spending a great deal of time in their gardens, perhaps sitting with an open fire.

Information received from community groups working with housed Travellers in Manchester and Birmingham would also indicate that Gypsies and Travellers tend to be over-represented as recipients of Anti-Social Behaviour Orders (ASBOs)[31] (see Chapter 6) and evictions from local authority housing following neighbours' complaints about noise, visitors and 'inappropriate' use of accommodation such as living only in the lower floors of a two-storey house, or using touring trailers for sleeping purposes.[32] It is likely that the 'visibility' of Gypsies and Travellers in houses makes them both vulnerable to 'policing' and racist control mechanisms as well as easy targets for scapegoating by dissatisfied residents of poor quality housing estates.

On a far more vicious level, 18 per cent of Niner's respondents reported that Gypsies and Travellers who left tenancies did so because of racist harassment. While we deal with the issue of discrimination, media treatment of Travellers, race-relations legislation and the CRE's initiatives elsewhere in this book, it is worth reiterating the fact that 35 per cent of respondents to a survey on discriminatory attitudes reported that they felt negative towards Gypsies and Travellers,[33] and that considerable hostility to the concept of Gypsy and Traveller sites in the locality (subsequently admitted by participants to be an over-reaction caused by fear, and experience of unauthorised encampments) was noted in a Scottish study.[34] Tragically, an unacceptable number of non-Travellers follow up these racist attitudes by resorting to physical or psychological harassment, aimed at forcing

Travellers to leave their houses. Kenrick and Clark (1999: 31) cite a typical case of harassment experienced by a family who suffered continual complaints from *gorje* neighbours, based on allegations of littering, barking dogs and responsibility for any thefts or burglaries that took place in the neighbourhood. Ultimately the family in question were evicted for 'anti-social behaviour' and denied the opportunity for rehousing.

A more extreme (but sadly not uncommon) example of such abuse was recounted during a planning application by a Romani family who were seeking to obtain a licence for a private site.

> They pushed dog dirt through the letter box, sprayed dirty words on our house, threw a brick through the house window and smeared muck [faeces] in the van and the tourer ... when we went away travelling we come back and the house'd been burgled and messed on, all our lovely things. We – I – was that scared I couldn't go back in, so we spent as long away as we could but we had to go back sometimes, I was so scared, they swore and shouted at me and the kids in the street ... the police did what they could, they put a watch, a camera [on the house] but it still happened, we reported it but they couldn't be there all the time. We left there, went out on the road for a bit, meant taking [the children] out of school but we couldn't take no more.
>
> Interview by MG, November 2003

The lady quoted above subsequently had a nervous breakdown, leading to the loss of her employment and the receipt of lengthy medical treatment. Although she recovered from her ill health when the family managed to access a pitch on an authorised site where they lived among their relatives, at the time of interview she still became highly distressed recalling the family's experience of trying to 'settle' at a village within five miles of where they had all been born.

While harassment at this level is very much the end of the continuum of negative experiences faced by Travellers in housing, perhaps the most common depressing effect of settlement on Travellers is the loss of a sense of freedom, with many families stating that even if they have made the transition to 'bricks and mortar' quite well, they experience a sense of being 'trapped', unable to simply pull off and go elsewhere without arranging for rent and bills to be paid or perhaps notifying a housing authority of their intent to travel.[35] This particular aspect of settlement, although theoretically one that is shared by Travellers living on authorised public sites, has been touched upon in some studies,[36] leading to a tentative conclusion that the psychological concept of being *able* to easily go off travelling when desired may sometimes be as important as the actual amount of time spent travelling. In support of this theory, some limited evidence exists that indicates that, for a substantial number of families, their travelling circuit has decreased, as has the length of time spent away from their home base (whether this is a house or an authorised site).[37]

Regardless of the amount of time spent 'out' and away from housing, it is incontrovertible that significant numbers of Travellers who move into conventional accommodation experience claustrophobia, depression and mental health problems as a result of the abrupt transition to unsuitable and potentially hostile environments.[38] Anecdotally, we are aware that there appears to be a disproportionate use of anti-depressants and, in some cases, a worryingly high suicide and sudden death rate amongst older, never previously housed Gypsies and Travellers who have perhaps moved into accommodation as a result of age, ill health or caring responsibilities. Similarly, as noted by O'Dwyer (1997) and supported by information received from social and community workers engaged with Gypsy and Traveller families,[39] breakdown in child-caring mechanisms, a slow but worrying increase in drug abuse amongst the younger generation and family separation leading to child protection concerns[40] may result from a combination of disrupted community support following movement into houses, greater contact with mainstream youth culture and lack of information and access to appropriate health and social services support. All of these alarming trends appear to be mitigated where families reside in a 'Gypsy or Traveller area' where substantial community networks exist, in some cases involving considerable to-ing and fro-ing between residents of houses and nearby authorised sites.

Finally, even where Gypsies and Travellers live in relatively close proximity to family members (both in social housing and owner-occupied homes) but not in an identified 'Gypsy or Traveller area' where the majority of residents are of the same ethnicity, a number of interviewees have reported that they 'keep quiet' about being Gypsies or Travellers or 'keep who we are to ourselves'. These comments are commonly reported even when families may be extremely well networked and integrated into their community (perhaps working in shops, factories or even offices alongside non-Traveller neighbours whose children and grandchildren attend at the same schools and social clubs). This expectation of prejudice from the settled community, and a belief in the necessity of discretion, may therefore work on an insidious level to reinforce a sense of being an 'outsider', even where families have very long-term connections to an area. As one gentleman in a relatively large market town in the west of England told us: 'you'd never know it but maybe a third of people in this town have Gypsy backgrounds, we all know who we are, but we don't make a song and dance about it, because you might not want the whole town knowing who's who'.

How many Travellers are in housing and where do they live?

Given the difficulty in identifying the size of the Traveller population in the UK (see earlier discussions on absence from census figures and local authority monitoring mechanisms as well as some individuals' decision to 'hide' their ethnicity), we are only able to make a rough estimate of the extent of the population. It has been calculated that the entire population is in the region of 300,000 individuals,[41] although that figure does not necessarily include second- or third-generation housed families who may have intermarried with the non-Traveller population. Accordingly the true figure for families with Gypsy and Traveller origins may be far higher, especially in areas where Travellers represent the largest minority ethnic community or have a long history of resort to the area. In time, the newly initiated ethnic-monitoring records kept by educational establishments will enable us to gain a more accurate picture of the true size of the Gypsy and Traveller population (although by definition this will exclude children who are 'out of school' or who decline to self-identify within official statistics). For the present, however, our calculations on this matter must to some extent be 'guesstimates'.

Given that we can identify the numbers of Gypsies and Travellers on authorised and unauthorised sites with at least some degree of accuracy using ODPM biannual counts, it is probably reasonable to assume that around 200,000 Travellers live in housing across the UK.

So where are Gypsy and Traveller areas? While it is likely that 'visible' Traveller heritage will only be noted by the observant or knowledgeable (for example, other Gypsies and Travellers), in some areas, a large percentage of the local population show clear signs of their cultural and ethnic heritage. Still other towns and localities are well known for possessing substantial settled Traveller communities. In this final section of the chapter we have listed a few such areas in England.

Birmingham

We have discussed above the Romani population who have lived in the Black Patch area for the past 100 years. A fairly substantial Irish Traveller population are also known to reside in Birmingham.

Blackpool, Preston, Wigan, York, Newcastle, Middlesbrough and Doncaster

All towns and cities with substantial housed Gypsy and Traveller populations, which in each locality have been estimated to include 'hundreds' of families. Doncaster (anecdotally) has a population of around 5,000 Gypsies and Travellers, claimed by some to be the largest Gypsy and Traveller population in the North. It has been suggested by community workers in the north-east of England that the housed Traveller population could well be in the region of 60,000–70,000 people.

The Forest of Dean

The Forest of Dean has a highly visible Gypsy and Traveller population. It is claimed by some locals that around one in three residents of the majority of towns and villages in the area are of Romani descent.

'Gypsy Towns' – North/North Midlands

We are told that Darlington and Newark are known locally as 'Gypsy towns' because of the large size of their Traveller populations. Newark in particular is noted for the number of authorised sites in the locality, and it is popularly supposed that for every Traveller living on an authorised site, there are perhaps five persons resident in housing.

Hampshire and Buckinghamshire

Both Hampshire and Buckinghamshire have long-established Romani Gypsy communities and smaller Irish Traveller populations. Although precise figures are difficult to calculate, anecdotal evidence suggests that Buckinghamshire (particularly Amersham) may be home to around 600 families and Hampshire a substantially larger population. At the time of writing the national charity Shelter[42] (following the identification of need through outreach work) are currently developing a project to support Gypsies and Travellers who are moving into 'bricks and mortar' accommodation as a result of site shortages and health or education needs.

Kent

Certain areas of Kent are renowned for their Traveller population. A number of villages surrounding Canterbury are calculated as having in the region of 25–50 per cent Traveller residents. Such limited ethnic-monitoring statistics as are available from schools (see above) confirm that some schools in Gravesend, Cranbrook and Paddock Wood have approximately 20 per cent Traveller pupils. Maidstone has a large and visible Traveller population and a particular locality within Mitcham was popularly known as 'Redskin Village' in the 1950s and 1960s due to the highly visible Romani Gypsy population. At the launch of the Bridge Housing Association on 20 February 1998 it was announced that over 1,000 people with Traveller origins lived in the social housing in the Cray Valley area (close to the former Belvedere Marsh sites closed in the early 1950s).

Leeds

In 2005 GATE (Gypsy and Traveller Exchange Project) undertook a baseline census of the city's Traveller populations with the support of the local authority and the Race Equality Council. A rough estimate had been made that around 700 families in housing were known to project workers but in practice only 199 families chose to participate in the study, of which 58 per cent were resident in social housing. The full report is available for download, free of charge at <http://www.travellersinleeds.co.uk/travellers/downloads/Baseline

Census.pdf>. GATE carries out similar work to that described under the Manchester Irish Traveller Project.

Leicester

Certain estates and areas within Leicester City have cohesive Gypsy and Traveller populations who are deeply connected to the residents of sites in the locality.

London

The London Boroughs of Battersea, Brent, Haringey, Croydon, Ealing, Camden and Greenwich are all known to have longstanding housed Gypsy and Traveller communities, although it would appear that community members tend to be fairly dispersed across the boroughs as a result of accommodation shortages. Occasional small estates or blocks may have a noticeable Traveller population, as, for example, in certain areas of Haringey. The Irish Traveller Movement supports families throughout London from its offices in Brent, an area with a fairly large Irish population. We are aware of the existence of housed Romani families in boroughs that border Kent and the South-East (e.g. Greenwich, Croydon and Mitcham). Generally, these populations are found living in localities near to traditional halting sites which would have been used by those en route to work in Kent.

Manchester

Manchester has a substantial housed Irish Traveller population. In the late 1990s, the Traveller Education Service was supporting over 350 children who were newly 'settled'. The Irish Traveller Project supports families in both the Cheetham Hill and Levenshulme areas, providing advice and support on a range of issues such as accommodation, provision of counselling, liaising with education authorities, dealing with social services, supporting families through court processes and providing social and sporting opportunities for young Travellers.

Somerset

In common with the counties of Dorset, Devon, Gloucestershire, Cornwall and Herefordshire whose local authority websites make mention of the substantial Gypsy and Traveller populations in their areas, Somerset is known to be home to a large settled Gypsy population. It is believed that between 25 per cent and 40 per cent of the residents of a mid-Somerset medium-sized market town are of Romani Gypsy origins. Certain villages (one of which is home to a traditional horse fair) are also known to have well-networked Traveller communities living in the immediate vicinity.

Southampton/South Coast

As has been noted above, Southampton has a longstanding and extremely cohesive Gypsy and Traveller population who are predominantly of Romani origin. An extremely well-connected and politically active Gypsy 'elder' estimates (based on his own knowledge and family connections) a housed population in the region of 20,000 Romanies living in the 'coastal block' of Chichester, Portsmouth, Southampton, Bournemouth and Poole (and nearby Dorchester and Christchurch). He further calculates that Gypsies resident in the New Forest area probably account for around 3,000 members of the community.

Doubtless many other deeply embedded Gypsy and Traveller communities exist throughout Britain. We would be pleased to receive further information from readers on the size, visibility and cultural pride of Gypsies and Travellers in their neighbourhood.

CHAPTER SIX

Gypsies, Travellers and legal matters

Margaret Greenfields

Police roadblocks used to stop New Travellers reaching a site in Wiltshire in 1986. The Travellers were later arrested and/or dispersed and moved across the county line (photograph by Margaret Greenfields)

Introduction

In this chapter we consider the often problematic area of Travellers' engagement with the law and legal processes. As we demonstrate in other sections of this book, the relationship between organs of the state and members of the Travelling communities can often be fraught with difficulties, not only as a result of inherently discriminatory legal regimes (see, for example, the discrepancy in planning outcomes and the ease with which Gypsies and Travellers can become criminalised as a result of breach of planning regulations or not having a place to legally stop), but also due to institutional racism[1] and the inequitable operation of regimes and regulations which in themselves may be benign, but which often cause significant hardship to Gypsies and Travellers as a result of either professional ignorance of their impacts[2] or, more sinisterly, overt racism.

Historically, Gypsies and Travellers have always laboured under the burden of popular and unjust associations with criminality,[3] a construct which it has been argued owes much to the idea of lack of rootedness within a given settled locality[4] and the perceived threat to the sedentary identity that has been adopted by every non-nomadic community regardless of residents' ethnic or social background. A great deal of print has been expended on writing about the constructed discourse around the perceived threat to settled society of 'dangerous classes' and 'masterless men'[5] (see earlier chapters) and when an 'alien' community are seen as travelling about in groups and halting temporarily in self-contained encampments at the edge of an established settlement, not only may their presence act as an invitation for opportunistic petty crime (after all, it is likely to be blamed on the 'strangers' rather than the known person, even if residents know full well that the man around the corner has 'light fingers' and in other circumstances would be the first person to be regarded with suspicion); but even where no increase in criminality occurs, rumour and fear are almost certain to increase and gain credence in the retelling.

The patterns of movement of Gypsies and Travellers – mysterious comings and goings (from the viewpoint of sedentary populations) – and the lack of accordance with the norms of embedded settled communities often enhances the sense of concern or mistrust felt by house-dwellers who have experienced generations of quasi-myth and prejudicial visual and literary constructions of the Gypsy identity and who, in consequence, are likely to place the blame for any local wrongdoing firmly at the caravan door of members of the community. We shall see later in this book the way in which media reports are often used to whip up hysteria and hatred against Gypsies and Travellers, but, at this stage, suffice it to say that the rather ugly and virtually universal human characteristic of suspicion of 'the people over the hill'[6] and the notion that one can identify a potential criminal by their obvious 'otherness' (which might depend on physical appearance, mode of performing particular actions, accent, etc.) are magnified remarkably when one contemplates the treatment of,[7] and attitudes towards, nomadic people across many centuries.

And then, too, as with *any* community, regardless of ethnicity, sedentary or nomadic habit, age, gender or other characteristics, there will always be a small proportion of individuals who behave in an anti-social or criminal manner. Unfortunately, if such a person is a member of the Gypsy or Traveller community, the inherently racist constructions of Gypsy and Traveller identities lead to public accusations of the 'characteristics' of the community or the abusive accusations that 'they are like that and can't be trusted'. In this way, racist stereotypes and suspicion are exacerbated and the cycle of prejudice continues.

Within the remainder of this chapter we therefore explore the ways in which Gypsies and Travellers may experience legal engagements, whether in the negative sense of 'falling foul' of the law or in terms of good practice, such as the innovative police-training scheme 'Pride Not Prejudice' initiated by the Derbyshire Gypsy Liaison Group[8] which won the Queen's Golden Jubilee Award in 2003 in respect of its community-relations activities,[9] and we consider the research evidence which, whilst limited in quantity, reveals significant inequalities in treatment, disproportionate levels of dissatisfaction amongst Gypsies and Travellers, poor communication between service providers and clients and, most strikingly of all, a virtually complete absence of cultural awareness amongst professionals working within legal and statutory frameworks.

The CJPOA 1994 and enforcement-related cases

To a large extent, we have considered the impacts of the CJPOA in Chapters 3 and 4. However, it is worth reiterating within this section of the text the capacity for criminalisation of Gypsies and Travellers which is inherent within the legislation, and the profoundly traumatic and long-lasting impacts of evictions from Gypsy- and Traveller-owned land that may result in not only the loss of family possessions and home but also potentially the entire sum paid for the site when the cost of eviction is reclaimed against the landowners.

We have dealt elsewhere with the way in which a Gypsy or Traveller can obtain a criminal conviction for failing to leave land (unauthorised encampments) when directed to so do, and without reasonable excuse (ss61, 62, 77, 79, etc. CJPOA and the Anti-Social Behaviour Act 2003 which creates a criminal offence where a Traveller,

Strategic Director:	Please ask for: Mr D. Clark Direct Line: (01322) 343955 Direct Fax: (01322) 343209 E-mail: DX: 31908 Your Ref: - Our Ref: DC/ 06 /2004. Date: 21 / 06 /2004.

Dear Traveller

UNAUTHORISED PLACING OF CARAVANS AND VEHICLES ON LAND AT:

Barn End Lane junction with Goss Hill, Dartford, Kent.

....

Contrary to the CRIMINAL JUSTICE AND PUBLIC ORDER ACT 1994 SECTION 77

You are on land without the permission of the owner. The Council has the power under the above Act to serve a Direction on you to leave the land by a certain date and time.

There may be good reasons why the Council should allow you longer to stay on the land. If this is the case, please answer the questions on the attached questionnaire and take it to the Civic Centre (next to Dartford Railway Station) within the next 24 hours.

For assistance in completing these forms please contact North West Kent Racial Equality Council on 01322 287251 or The Citizens Advice Bureau on 01322 224686.

If you do not provide information or fail to give reasons for your stay on this land, the Council will, in accordance with its powers issue you a Direction to leave this land.

The Direction will confirm the date and time that you are required to leave and will take into account any relevant information that you have provided.

Yours sincerely

> *Copies of these documents were served by*
> *me on the occupants of all caravans sited*
> *at the above named venue at 1600..hrs*
> *On..21ˢᵗ June.2004*
>
> *Signed.........DClly........*
> *Print name...David Clark.:*

Robert Penny
Regeneration Manager.

An example of a typical 'go notice' under the CJPOA 1994 (courtesy of Margaret Greenfields) knowing that a direction to leave land exists, fails to so do, or returns within three months). Perhaps even more devastating are the cases where families have applied for retrospective planning permission for a site (see Chapter 4 for further information) and failed in their application, often after a long-drawn-out legal battle that may have exhausted their entire financial resources.

When an individual or family are found to be in breach of planning regulations a local planning authority may issue an enforcement notice that specifies the breach of regulation and what the owner of the land is required to do. In the case of Gypsy- and Traveller-owned sites, quite simply the owners are usually required to cease living on the site, remove any structures thereon and return the land to the condition it was in prior to any changes undertaken.[10] A right of appeal exists against the issue of an enforcement notice and, at this stage, many Gypsy and Traveller families find themselves faced by large legal bills if they are unable to access assistance from the Legal Services Commission to pay the often extensive costs of a court battle. Inevitably, therefore, a balancing act must take place, wherein the owners of the land decide whether to incur the stress and expense of legal action on the chance of winning their case; make the hard decision to sell their land to another person who might be willing to risk the undecided planning matters, move off their land to face the merry-go-round of attempting to access an authorised site, or go back onto the roadside with all the hardship that entails.

In a number of highly publicised cases, Gypsies and Travellers have sought to either defend their home by barricading themselves onto their land (for example, the first Woodside eviction[11] and the Bulkington Fields case[12] where the 150 people living on that site initially won a stay of eviction when bailiffs and police were confronted by residents forming a human barrier behind a network of ditches and burning blockades), or, as in the case of Twin Oaks, attempted to negotiate a 'land-swap'[13] up until the moment of eviction.[14]

Tragically, Gypsies and Travellers are at greatest risk of both physical injury and financial loss when planning enforcement proceeds to physical eviction. Increasingly, local authorities are resorting to the use of 'specialist' firms of bailiffs who advertise themselves in terms similar to the following:

Police action during an eviction in Birmingham in the 1960s (from *Gypsies & Travellers in their own words*, courtesy of the Leeds Traveller Education Service)

> We can organise evictions, with as much manpower that is needed with minimal fuss and disruption ... We use the legal remedies available to landowners to move the illegal campsites with support from our own fully skilled and professional staff and the Police are often only required to ensure that the eviction is undertaken without the gypsies [*sic*] causing a breach of the peace ... We are highly skilled in the eviction of travellers and Gypsies and normally undertake the eviction process in the early hours of the morning.
>
> <http://www.hatwelservices.co.uk/3063.html>

The deliberate tactic of moving in for evictions in the early hours of the morning (often around 3 or 4 a.m.) when families are asleep is appallingly reminiscent of current scenes of Roma persecution in eastern Europe,[15] the demolition of the squatter settlements in developing countries[16] or even more alarmingly, when one considers the eyewitness accounts of families being hounded from their beds in their nightclothes, surrounded by large numbers of bailiffs supported by police (who may be in riot gear) who often cordon off an area to stop residents moving on or off the site, or media personnel attending

Evicted from Halton Moor – an 'unofficial' camp – 1985 (from *Gypsies & Travellers in their own words*, courtesy of the Leeds Traveller Education Service)

at the scene of a highly publicised eviction, of events in mainland Europe in the 1930s and 1940s.

A not untypical experience for families facing forcible eviction from their own land (and one that has been historically common to families who have experienced roadside evictions) is the destruction (either wilful or as a result of wanton carelessness) of their home and treasured personal possessions and the impounding of vehicles. Even more seriously, in the past (although mercifully far rarer at the time of writing), we have been aware of many pre-planned large-scale evictions from unauthorised encampments where state agencies have removed children into the care of social services[17] (see below), and animals have been taken away by animal-welfare agencies or the police. In some cases, dogs have been destroyed in these circumstances or injured or killed when trailers and vehicles have been towed off sites.[18] In one horrendous and well-publicised incident in Enfield in 1998 a six-year-old child was killed when he was run over by a vehicle whilst attempting to hide during an eviction.[19]

Although, as noted above, the tendency to remove children from their parents when eviction occurs appears (anecdotally) to be far rarer than in the past, we understand that threats are still made at times in a (usually highly successful) attempt to 'persuade' families that it is better to leave a site 'voluntarily' than to wait until eviction occurs.[20] As recently as 2004 we understand that the families who had failed to leave their own land at Paynes Lane in Essex as a result of having nowhere else to go, were threatened with being imprisoned and their children removed into care if they did not comply with a court order obtained by Epping Forest District Council.[21]

Even when families are not put under threat of this kind, local authorities in possession of a court order pertaining to enforcement possess draconian 'direct action' powers to compel compliance with an enforcement notice, including claiming their costs for returning a site to its former condition (e.g. removing structures and hard-standing, etc.) and putting a charge on the land if that fee is not met.[22] Indeed, when the Bulkington site was evicted, the local authority presented the landowners with a huge bill and similar events have occurred following the traumatic evictions at Meadowlands and Twin Oaks sites.

Families subject to enforced evictions under the draconian British planning laws are therefore exposed not only to incalculable risks to their family (in the sense of long-term emotional, psychological and financial impacts), but can also face convictions for obstruction or in some cases assault (either alleged against them, or when they are victims of assault) when seeking to intervene if violence is being threatened to their relatives under the guise of removal from land.

In one well-publicised case in 2005, a wheelchair-bound elderly lady in exceptionally poor health was forced to witness the destruction of her home around her, including the crushing of her special electric wheelchair and orthopaedic bed by a mechanical digger. When this lady collapsed as a result of the trauma, an ambulance was not permitted to enter the site to take her to hospital and the paramedics had to walk across the fields to tend to her. Meanwhile, an elderly man suffering from cancer and diabetes was thrown to the ground and handcuffed, despite his willingness to leave the site. These disgraceful spectacles are becoming more common as a result of the conflict over land use and the minimal success rate of families in obtaining planning permission. Inevitably, faced with such evidence of unnecessary violence and intimidation, families and supporters of Gypsies and Travellers are likely to become involved in conflictual situations, and the barriers to successful dialogue will increase, feeding suspicion and fear and maximising the risk of criminalisation of law-abiding families.

At the time of writing, the Council of Europe Office of the Commissioner for Human Rights had just issued a report on their November 2004 visit to the UK wherein significant attention is paid to the circumstances of Gypsies and Travellers and the plight of families who are unable to access authorised sites.[23] Whilst noting the recent policy changes introduced by the ODPM (e.g. Housing Act accommodation needs assessments and the policy review underway at the time of writing), the Commissioner was unequivocal in noting the hardships caused by the current regime.

> Access to accommodation would appear to present the greatest difficulty and give rise to the most contention ... this life-style evidently requires sites for Gypsies to settle on, both permanently and temporarily. Recent legislative changes have made this increasingly difficult, resulting in an increasing number of illegal settlements and an inevitable rise in social friction ... Local authorities are expected, but not obliged, to conduct an assessment of the accommodation needs of Gypsies and Travellers in the area and to identify land suitable for settlement. This switch in policy has, however, singularly failed to meet their needs. Few local authorities have conducted needs assessments, or identified appropriate land ... in the absence of purchasable land in more suitable areas and owing to lack of space in the remaining local authority sites, Gypsies are all too often faced with little choice but to purchase where they can and settle there – illegally if need be ... The evident failure of the current system, and the tensions that have resulted plead strongly in favour of a return to the earlier statutory obligation on local authorities to provide caravan sites. This will enable the local council to identify areas that satisfy the needs of Gypsies and Travellers and the reasonable concerns of local residents, thus reducing the potential for conflict and satisfying the right of Gypsies and Travellers to housing.
>
> CommDH(2005)6 8/6/05 paras 144–8
> <http://www.statewatch.org/news/2005/jun/coe-uk-report.pdf>

We can but hope that the Committee of Ministers and the Parliamentary Assembly in Strasbourg responsible for overseeing human rights issues in Europe will continue to monitor the situation and bring appropriate pressure to bear on the British Government to adequately resolve a morally untenable state of affairs.

The ruling from the ECHR published 8 June 2005[24] which condemned the Greek Government for breach of Article 16 of the European Social Charter (which guarantees protection of family life and accommodation for all EU citizens), on the basis of 'insufficient number of stopping places for Roma who choose to follow an itinerant lifestyle or who are forced to do so; and the systematic eviction of Roma from sites or dwellings unlawfully occupied by them' (at paragraph 1 of the ECHR report) is likely to strengthen the case against local authorities in Britain who continue to forcibly evict Gypsies and Travellers in the manner outlined above. Moreover, this judgment may potentially enable victims of such actions to apply for damages against both local and central government for breach of human rights. We await further developments from Europe with interest.

Social services departments and the Children Act 1989

We have touched above on the way in which social services child protection officers may become involved in eviction proceedings. Although the complex area of child protection and the grounds for obtaining an emergency protection or care order for a child are mainly outside of the remit of this chapter,[25] we consider it important to refer to the very limited research that has been undertaken on Gypsy and Traveller families and the ways in which community members may come into contact (and potentially conflict) with social workers.

Historically, Gypsies and Travellers have had significant reason to express concerns over the way in which mainstream society has viewed traditional Travelling and child-rearing behaviours. Despite the fact that community life revolves around 'the family' and parents are renowned for being devoted to their children, a long and shameful history exists (both in the UK[26] and far more commonly abroad[27]) of removing Gypsy and Traveller children from their parents and families. The grounds given for commencing child protection proceedings are often 'neglect' or 'endangerment' when in fact a child has merely been participating in cultural or employment practices common to their community; that concerns exist about their parents' ability to provide a stable home as a result of frequent evictions, or that children have attended school infrequently and parents are perceived as deliberately avoiding the requirements of the Education Act.[28]

Sarah Cemlyn is the only academic in the UK who has consistently written on Gypsy and Traveller families' engagements with social services departments and the way in which the essentially assimilationist state policies within Britain are interwoven with access to services that can potentially mitigate the worst hardships of lack of adequate site provision and culturally appropriate services. Much of her work stems from her ground-breaking 1998 survey of social services departments and their policies and provisions for Gypsy and Traveller children and families,[29] wherein she sought to obtain a clear national picture of the state of services provided to the Travelling communities and the tensions in relationships and roles of both social workers and service recipients.

As we have demonstrated repeatedly throughout this text, Gypsies and Travellers are often socially excluded in many areas of life, and, as a result of the hardships of state-imposed instability, are frequently unable to access services that are essentially designed for, and geared to, a sedentary population with access to information and knowledge of local provision. Accordingly, for many Gypsies and Travellers, their sole contact with social services departments, which by their nature offer a wide range of services that can assist vulnerable individuals in a range of circumstances (e.g. the elderly, disabled, mentally ill, homeless, etc.), are confined to situations where a family is either facing eviction and enquiries are being carried out as to whether their personal circumstances required a delay in such action or the greatly dreaded child-protection interventions referred to above.

Cemlyn's study of service provision found that only a small minority of local authorities who responded to the survey referred to engaging actively with Gypsy and Traveller communities, and the majority of these noted that their policies related explicitly to evictions under the CJPOA. Only just under half of the sample were able to record any information pertaining to the size or ethnicity of communities in their areas, and, unsurprisingly, generally these were social services departments in localities where large numbers of Gypsies or Travellers resided. Overwhelmingly, information was sourced from the biannual caravan counts when attempting to assess the size of communities in an authority, rather than stemming from personal contacts with community members.

The key aspect of the research explored the way in which the Children Act 1989 (the main piece of legislation pertaining to both 'private'[30] and 'public'[31] family law) was (or could be) used to assist Gypsy and Traveller families by ensuring that they had access to services for children 'in need' or those who are disabled. Of particular interest was the way in which s17 of the Children Act could be potentially utilised to support children who in the terms of the Act are unable to 'achieve or maintain a reasonable standard of health and development' and are thus 'in need'.

Section 17 of the Children Act is an extremely valuable tool in the armoury of service providers and advocates for the community given that incontrovertible evidence exists on the negative impacts on Gypsy and Traveller children of poor access to sites, inappropriate services and inequality of opportunity – all elements that in themselves can support a finding that a child is failing to achieve or maintain a 'reasonable standard' of health and development. Indeed, the impacts of repeated or traumatic eviction on children are often reported to lead to long-term emotional suffering, insecurity and psychological damage, despite the best efforts of their families to protect children from harm. Furthermore, as has been discussed elsewhere in this book, the transition from trailer to housing which may occur if a family cannot find suitable accommodation can cause untold upheaval that in itself may damage a child's development and health, in part perhaps through witnessing the trauma experienced by parents and carers. The phrasing of s17 and the wide variety of services (and even financial support) that can be provided under the auspices of this section of the Act can therefore assist in mitigating some of the worst aspects of institutionalised neglect of Gypsy and Traveller families.

Despite the potential for using s17 of the Children Act, Cemlyn found that only limited numbers of social services departments were utilising this section of the legislation and those that were, tended to make use of the provisions to provide pre-school or day-care provision for children within their locality. A further (small group) of authorities provided social services of a practical nature for Gypsies and Travellers, generally access to laundry facilities or water. A small number of social services departments reported that they had contact with families over child-protection matters or had 'accommodated' children – provided voluntary care where a parent was unable to look after a child for any reason. (It is important to note that in some cases 'accommodation' is agreed by parents to avoid social services departments seeking a care order.[32] However, it may also relate to situations where a parent is ill and a child is looked after by foster carers until other relatives can be contacted or the parent is fit enough to take over their parenting role again.) Over a third of respondent authorities were unable to provide information on Gypsy and Traveller contact with social services departments and this may relate either to lack of adequate record-keeping, or, (as is more likely), a community sense of independence and reluctance to approach an authority for assistance, even where they may be entitled to access support services which could alleviate difficulties.

Key findings pertaining to the relationship between Gypsies, Travellers and social workers related to community members viewing the services with fear and suspicion, particularly in relation to a perceived threat to remove children into care, or make negative appraisals of child-rearing patterns, or 'judge' families for allowing young people to work alongside their parents in the home or when practising a trade. Responses from social workers echoed these findings, with a number of professionals appearing to indicate that they believed Gypsies and Travellers actively rejected offers of services or support that might be forthcoming from 'authorities'. Whilst it is true that a strong tradition of self-help and extended family support may well lead Gypsies and Travellers to conclude that they are able to care for their own families adequately without resorting to social services assistance, by assuming 'they look after their own' we can see clear elements of institutional racism, an assumption that mainstream society does not need to actively work with communities to provide appropriate support where it is desired, in a manner that is acceptable to the recipients. The limited extent of community consultation that Cemlyn identified within the study tends to bear out the contention that many departments (at least at the time the research was undertaken) were reluctant to engage with Gypsies and Travellers in a manner that would be regarded as essential when working with any other minority ethnic community.

In seeking to explore barriers to engagement with Gypsy and Traveller families, Cemlyn identified that social workers frequently attributed their lack of contact to misunderstandings and ignorance of cultural matters and 'fear' of entering onto sites: 'I think most people –

not just social workers – have preconceived ideas about Travellers ... that [they] pose some kind of threat – it's about prejudice and discrimination and they have a fixed image' (quotation from agency worker, in Cemlyn 1998: 28).

Other core assumptions that can disrupt successful working with community members are the perceptions of professionals that it is 'simply not worth bothering' to provide support or intervention, as Gypsies and Travellers' lifestyle precludes effective support. In other words, that it isn't the responsibility of social services departments to get involved with families, unless they are required to engage in child protection matters.

Whilst this somewhat gloomy picture was mitigated to some extent by examples of good practice in certain localities (for example, in the provision of a specialist Travellers Development Officer to promote policy development and involvement in multi disciplinary assessment forums to provide support services for families on unauthorised encampments), overwhelmingly the study pointed to Gypsy and Traveller issues as representing a very low priority for the majority of social services departments and a culture of prejudice, fear and misunderstanding rife amongst professionals who may come into contact with the communities.

As Cemlyn's research was undertaken prior to the implementation of the Race Relations (Amendment) Act 2000 and the Human Rights Act 1998, and thus took place at a time when local authority awareness of legal duties and responsibilities towards Gypsies and Travellers was less pronounced, it is to be hoped that in recent years service delivery and awareness of the needs of Travelling communities has improved, although anecdotal evidence has so far failed to indicate many changes in working practice amongst social services departments.

The author of this chapter spent several years working with families (of a broad range of ethnicities) involved with social services departments over child protection issues. During the course of her work as a policy officer, she encountered a number of Gypsy and Traveller families who had either unwittingly come to the attention of social services; or in some cases had actively sought assistance to support their families when a relative had become involved with drug use or other behaviours that meant that it had proved necessary for parents or relatives to move away from their traditional self-reliance and seek outside help. Some examples of not untypical cases encountered in practice may illustrate the fact that institutional racism and lack of understanding of community values continue to impact on service delivery and good relationships between social workers and travelling communities.

Although all cases must of necessity remain confidential, it would appear that between the late 1990s and 2004, little had changed with regard to the degree of prejudice experienced by Gypsies and Travellers attempting to access services. In one particular case a young person who had become involved with undesirable companions on the estate where the family had been housed had begun to disappear from home for days at a time, failing to notify their family of their movements. On seeking help to deal with the young person's behaviour and suspected drug use the family were turned away on two occasions on the grounds that 'X is a Traveller – of course they will get up and go – she'll come back some time' (despite the fact that the young person was only fourteen), and when the father became understandably irate at this response, he was then recorded as being potentially violent, which might account for the young person's disappearance. No effort was made to discover the degree of literacy present within the family and when letters went unanswered and appointments unattended the family were written off as uncooperative and enquiries made as to their parenting of other children in the household. Fortunately in this case we were able to intervene and provide support and advocacy, but how often do families fail to access appropriate services or become inaccurately labelled by professionals as a result of lack of knowledge or concern over their difficulties?

A further example which had appallingly tragic consequences concerned a separated couple (one from a Travelling family and the other from a *gorje* household). As a result of alcohol and drug abuse, the parents separated and the young mother was awarded residence (custody) of the young children, despite known substance abuse and alcohol problems within her birth family and her family's known hostility and racism towards her former partner and his Gypsy relatives. After a series of social services interventions, it was considered that the mother was unable to care adequately for the children and the father (by now clear of drugs) and his thoroughly respectable family who had their own authorised site applied for residence of the children. At hearings, the social workers involved in the case and the children's guardian, who was ordered to prepare a report for the court on what would be in the best interests of the children, repeated a number of statements that bore extremely limited connections to Gypsy and Traveller child-rearing behaviours and announced that they felt the children should not live on a site as they might miss school as a result of Travelling, might engage in inappropriate working practices when older or might fail to grow up with a clear understanding of their sedentary family's background. After a long-drawn-out series of court cases, the children were eventually placed with their paternal grandparents to grow up surrounded by their family yet retaining contact with their maternal relatives, but not before several attempts were made at rehabilitation to the mother and her parents, resulting in the police removing the children because of neglect and the death of the youngest baby in circumstances that may have been related to the substances taken by the mother during her pregnancy.

Whilst these are dramatic examples of situations where social workers' lack of knowledge (or even perhaps prejudice) has potentially harmed rather than helped children at risk of abuse, what limited evidence exists from research indicates that such cases may be more common than is thought, providing adequate grounds for continued hostility, cynicism and suspicion from Gypsies and Travellers who come into contact with social services departments.

Research carried out in the late 1990s explored in greater depth the impacts of engagement with family law processes for New Travellers who were separated from the child's other parent. This study,[33] which found that New Travellers shared similarities of attitude with Gypsies and traditional Travellers towards use of the family court system – for example, all communities considering that parenting matters were (or should be) outside the rule of law and that it would be highly inappropriate to apply for a legal ruling over the upbringing and residence of children – concentrated on the minority of cases where New Travellers had become involved in legal proceedings, considering the variations between voluntary (respondent initiated proceedings) and coerced (taken to court by another party) participation in a range of family law situations. An interesting overlap occurred with the cases undertaken on behalf of Gypsies and traditional Travellers, with the researcher (MG) only finding a tiny percentage of examples where parents in dispute both came from Travelling communities. In the earlier study, in the vast majority of cases, New Travellers were challenged in their parenting and upbringing by a sedentary former partner who objected to a child being raised on a site, with objections to residence mirroring those used when Gypsies and traditional Travellers were taken to court over their parenting. In several cases, social services involvement resulted from objections made by the former partner and, once again, issues of education, site safety and the perceived dangers of 'nomadism' were key elements in legal arguments and court reports.

Perhaps the most important finding in this study related to the use of prohibited steps orders[34] during the interim period before a final decision was made as to whether a child could live with a Traveller parent or if a sedentary former partner, or indeed foster parents, should provide an alternative home. Despite the fact that prohibited steps orders were, at the time of the study, only ordered in 10 per cent of all family law cases, within the sample group such an order was made in 30 per cent of legal proceedings, in each case specifying that the child should reside with the parent in a house; essentially leading to enforced settlement of the Traveller parent. The study reiterated Cemlyn's (1998) findings on most professionals' lack of awareness of Travelling communities and fear of entering onto sites. New Traveller respondents' complaints pertaining to the presentation of their lifestyle in court reports were (following retrospective analysis and comparison between the diverse communities) found to be remarkably similar to those outlined by Gypsies and traditional Travellers. In approximately two-thirds of cases examined, concerns were raised by court welfare officers and social workers with regard to a child's attendance at school. Indeed, in a number of cases, steps were taken to monitor that a parent was resident in a house and the child attended school regularly prior to a final residence order being made or closure of a social services case. Quite apart from the enforced move into housing which such orders brought about, and associated hardship caused by the inability to travel for work-related purposes, New Travellers (those within the sample had been nomadic for an average of ten to twelve years) reported psychological and emotional impacts of residence in settled housing (including prejudice from neighbours and children being bullied at school) which bears marked similarities to the difficulties encountered so frequently by Gypsies and Travellers who are forced to move into housing as a result of lack of access to sites.

The final study we are aware of that touches upon Gypsies' and Travellers' engagements with social services departments (Power 2004, at Chapter 3[35]) emphasises the destabilising effects of frequent evictions, enforced settlement and subsequent loss of the extended-family support network on Irish Traveller families. The lack of sensitivity of social workers in engaging with community members, and the understandable tendency for families to seek to 'move on' when intrusive social-work interventions occur, leads to a pathologisation of Travellers by professionals. Social workers frequently fail to undertake adequate supporting work and are often likely to seek to impose a coercive regime that leads to conflicts between family members and the police (see below). In Power's report, which includes a significant amount of interview data from young Irish Travellers, many respondents are bitter about the ways in which social services involvement in a family may coincide with loss of contact with community members (and subsequent internal community control and support) as the assimilation process is exacerbated by policing and monitoring regimes imposed upon a family by culturally unaware (and perhaps unwittingly cruel) 'authorities': 'my two sisters were taken into foster care ... for maybe eight years and ... when my mother died the Social Services wouldn't let them attend the funeral' (Power, 2004: 49).

Good practice in social services and voluntary-sector agencies

In some areas of the UK, however, the situation may be slightly more enlightened. Stewart and Kilfeather (1999)[36] report on a community initiative in Northern Ireland where practitioners actively engage in outreach work, including provision of services to unauthorised sites; direct social work with Travellers, including provision of information and advice on a range of services; and the provision of training for Travellers resident in the area. A further important strand of the project is the provision of anti-racism awareness training within the local community and ongoing needs assessments for families who access their services.

A further innovative good-practice model in use in the Republic of Ireland has led to the development of a specialist fostering service in cases where children are unable to remain with their parents or immediate family.[37] In these upsetting circumstances (usually associated with child-protection cases), an initiative has been developed to ensure that Traveller children are not simply torn away from their community and culture and placed with settled people to be assimilated into sedentary life, but are provided with either a short- or long-term home amongst their own community and wider family members. The background to the project arose from findings that Traveller children were significantly over-represented amongst children 'in care'[38] with their risk of being placed in substitute care four times that of other children. Over 90 per cent of Traveller children placed into care in Ireland spent significantly longer periods in public care than other children and tended to be placed either in residential units or with settled foster carers without specialist knowledge of their communities, leading to loss of contact with their families and culture and the risk of assimilation. In common with many other children leaving care around the world, Traveller children who had experienced state care tended to find it difficult to readjust to either independent living or to return to their own communities and often became involved in cycles of depression, criminality and substance abuse. The severe impacts on these children led to the setting up of a specialist fostering service where social workers could work in partnership with members of the Travelling community to provide extended family care. Although the scheme is still subject to evaluation, it is at least a positive step forward and demonstrates the ways in which social workers can work closely with community members to deliver services that support and empower Gypsies and Travellers even in the most difficult of situations.

Within mainland Britain, as noted elsewhere, some authorities have been beacons of good practice for a number of years (e.g. London Borough of Haringey who operate the only established team of statutory social workers dedicated to working with Travellers), and still more are slowly changing their practices, driven by an enhanced awareness of Gypsy and Traveller culture and the fact that agencies such as the Irish Traveller Movement, G&TLRC, Derbyshire Gypsy Liaison Group, Leeds GATE and Manchester Irish Community Care are actively engaged in referral, advocacy, monitoring of local authorities and, in some cases, direct project delivery.

Where the most dramatic changes have come about, however, appears to be in the increasing numbers of local-level community projects where staff advocate for, and work with, Gypsies and Travellers to ensure access to services (including in some cases directly delivered support services) and provide information on community and cultural practices to service providers. Within Manchester, the Travellers Project that operates under the auspices of Irish Community Care is particularly active in supporting young homeless Travellers at risk on the streets and in providing services in a culturally appropriate, non-judgemental manner. Similar projects are offered in London (Irish Traveller Movement and Brent Irish Advisory Service), Cambridgeshire (the Ormiston Trust Travellers Initiative), Cardiff (where the Cardiff Gypsy Sites Group has provided services for more than twenty years) and in west Kent (where the Bromley Gypsy and Traveller Community Project actively engages in outreach and social care work). Leeds GATE, whose staff consists mainly of Gypsies and Travellers, reports similar successes in engaging with community members and in supporting families who would be loath to come into direct contact with social services staff, but who are comfortable enough to engage with staff members who can assist in liaison with statutory authorities.

Despite the sterling efforts of such agencies, attempts to access services (in particular discretionary social services or benefits grants to assist with purchasing essentials housed people tend to take for granted) may often be particularly difficult for Gypsies and Travellers whose levels of mobility or literacy skills may lead to applicants being passed between departments in the hope they will move on and leave an area, or for those families who may be moving into a house or have lost everything in a trailer fire, whose requirements are regarded as unreasonable by services not used to dealing with people in such situations. The support available from specialist service providers, church groups and small charities such as the Travellers Aid Trust[39] has often proved invaluable for Travelling families when social services are either unable or unwilling to help in times of need,[40] yet it is clear that reliance on voluntary-sector agencies to provide the staples of life is completely inappropriate if a duty exists to assess and support *all* families equally where criteria are met for service provision.

Despite this somewhat 'patchy' picture, recent information initiatives that are bringing about changes in the perceptions of and service delivery to Gypsies and Travellers are the increased profile (and

Travelling community awareness) of statutory duties owed to them by a range of authorities. Much of the praise for raising awareness of legislative procedures and responsibilities must be given to the variety of local projects engaged with community members, as well as the ground-breaking work of certain lawyers who tirelessly challenge the decisions of statutory bodies if they feel that race equality legislation and Human Rights Act duties are not being adequately considered when decisions are taken. The CRE's far-ranging review of the impact of the implementation of the 2002 statutory race equality duty on Gypsies and Travellers and the launch of their Strategy for Gypsies and Travellers 2004–7[41] are further enhancing awareness of expectations of agencies and of the fact that no longer can authorities continue to treat community members as second-class citizens to be offered scraps from the table of mainstream society.

Discrimination and the RRAs

As noted elsewhere in this text, both English Gypsies (Romanies) and Irish Travellers (although not as yet Scottish Gypsy/Travellers) are ethnic minorities[42] within the terms of the RRAs (1976 and 2000) and as such are technically protected from discrimination and ill treatment resulting from their membership of an ethnic group. In practice, as any person who has read this far will have clearly grasped, the legislation not only provides an imperfect protection for Gypsies and Travellers, but is often more honoured in the breach than in the observance, with signs stating 'No Travellers' still encountered fairly frequently on the doors of pubs, launderettes and other public facilities and numerous anecdotal reports of Gypsies and Travellers being refused work opportunities once potential employers realise they live on a site or are a member of the travelling communities.

A loophole in the law leaves broadcasts and newsprint outside of the remit of the RRA (despite the fact that authors and publishers of articles that incite racial hatred can be prosecuted by the police under the Public Order Act 1986), enabling the quite disgraceful coverage of Gypsy and Traveller matters in local and national press to continue largely unabated, despite the concerted efforts of media monitors and individuals who strenuously complain to the Press Complaints Commission. Although the subject of media coverage of Gypsies and Travellers is discussed in another chapter in this book, it is worth quoting from the report by the Commissioner for Human Rights on the level of hostile abuse regularly unleashed against community members:

> to judge by the levels of invective that can regularly be read in the national press, Gypsies would appear to be the last ethnic minority in respect of which openly racist views can still be acceptably expressed. I was truly amazed by some of the headlines, articles and editorials that were shown to me. Such reporting would appear to be symptomatic of a widespread and seemingly growing distrust of Gypsies resulting in their discrimination in a broad range of areas.
> Office of the Human Rights Commissioner/CoE report, June 2005, p.43

Despite the lack of protection from media harassment, a wide variety of other forms of discrimination and victimisation are illegal under the RRA (including segregation and discrimination in the provision of services such as education, employment and health care).[43] An example of the way in which the legislation can be used to enforce equal treatment comes from a 1999 case brought by the CRE on behalf of two Gypsy women,[44] when a local authority refused to hire them a hall for a wedding reception unless stringent conditions were in place. The local authority were found to be in breach of the RRA, and the police force who had advised of public-order concerns if the party was to take place was censured although not found in breach of the Act, as they had acted as advisers rather than taking the primary decision with regard to the hire of the venue.

Whilst the situation above is a 'classic' case of prosecution for direct discrimination against Gypsies and Travellers, what is less well known (although it is to be hoped the CRE's efforts to heighten public awareness will bear fruit) is that since the RRA was amended in 2000 a positive obligation exists on public bodies (including the police, local authorities, education and health authorities) 'to promote equality of opportunity and good relations between persons of different racial groups' (RRA 1976 (as amended) s71) when carrying out all their functions. A key aspect of this piece of legislation is the requirement for all bodies to prepare and publish a race-equality scheme that takes account of the impact of policies on race equality and to consult with people likely to be affected by such policies (RRA 1976 (Statutory Duties) Order 2001 SI No 3438). Facilities now exist for ensuring that public bodies actively pursue these duties in a proactive manner to ensure that opportunities for discrimination are minimised.

Perhaps unsurprisingly in the light of earlier discussions in this book, many agencies and individuals are both ignorant of the 'ethnic status' of Gypsies and Travellers and equally cavalier in their attitudes towards inclusion and consultation with members of the communities. Morris and Clements[45] (2002), when undertaking their survey of the costs of eviction and site provision, reported that many local authority officers 'show a lack of awareness that many Travelling people could be considered members of minority ethnic groups' (2002: 91) and, moreover, demonstrated 'attitudes clearly not compliant with the spirit and letter of the RRA'. The positive duty under the Act clearly presents a significant dilemma to those authorities who routinely evict unauthorised encampments, or social services departments and health authorities who fail to engage fully with service users from Travelling communities. Although the CRE scrutiny project currently underway focuses mainly on accommodation issues (including access to information on planning procedures for Gypsies and Travellers who may be contemplating purchasing land and the role of the police and other agencies in evaluating the impacts of eviction policies) the overall CRE strategy document[46] includes a far wider range of issues (e.g. active consultation with community members, addressing racist attitudes amongst the public at large, ensuring equality of access to services and benefits, etc.) which will prove of benefit to those challenging unlawful discrimination, as well as assisting public bodies in developing greater awareness of their role and duties in enhancing community relations. Finally, we may be entering a time where Gypsies and Travellers will no longer be able to be excluded from everyday society on the grounds that they are 'hard to reach' and thus a hidden problem or a 'totally unjustified burden on local council taxpayers, robbing them of services which could otherwise be provided'.[47]

Policing

The subject of policing of Gypsies and Travellers could in itself occupy an entire chapter. However, other than the relatively recent work on policing and governance undertaken by James (2005), James and Barton (2003) and Cowan and Lomax (2003),[48] limited academic research exists on this topic, given the tendency for many Travelling people to resignedly accept the fact that for their entire lives they have been moved on by the police, treated as second-class citizens or verbally and physically abused. Narratives by older Gypsies and Travellers frequently report incidents where having just halted for the night they would be visited by the police and verbally and sometimes physically assaulted or their fires kicked over, spoiling food put on to feed the family after a hard day's work.

> You can't win with the law, we used to move about eight o'clock of night in the winter, they'd make you ... when you got out of his beat you'd be in another beat and there was a copper waiting for you there to drive you onto another beat ... that's how it was ... they'd kick the fire over, throw the grub off from the fire ... you may be cooking your meal in the pot ... hanging on a kettle frame and they'd kick it off the kettle frame they would. That would be your meal for the day and that would be gone ... this time I'm talking about was through the war so all food was on ration and hard to find.
>
> Evans (2004: 46)

Although over time methods of enforcing movement might have become slightly more subtle (or at least regulated), Gypsies and Travellers in the late 1990s could recite similar experiences of being forced to move whilst hungry children cried for dinner, not being allowed to stop to heat a bottle for a baby or put a child down to sleep whilst being escorted to the county line.

> the babbies were hungry and they kept us going on – moving an' all up the motorway ... we needed to stop to put the water on and feed them, they were that hungry and crying but we was told if we stopped they'd take the trailers, arrest the men – they'd keep us going for hours and more would come and take us out of [X county] and keep us going but one gavver was good when we was stopped near to the [petrol] station with them all round us just laughing they was – we were told not to all get out but we was to stop for a short bit, just a few minutes – he went and brought sandwiches back for the babbies, said he had some [children] at home hisself and wouldn't like it at all but the others they didn't care.
>
> Traveller (interviewed by MG 1999)

Quite apart from the cruelties of harsh policing at times of eviction, many Gypsies and Travellers report the sense of suspicion with which they are treated whenever they come into contact with police forces, with many officers' attitudes mirroring those of mainstream society, compounded by their contact with Travelling people in times of high conflict such as evictions, when dialogue may often be virtually non-existent and tempers are likely to be raised.[49] Common complaints from Gypsies and Travellers include frequently being stopped by police officers and asked to show their papers every time they are seen in working vehicles, even when they are well-established residents of a local area, or being turned away if they attempt to report an attack on their site by drunks or vigilantes. Similarly, many individuals recount experiences of having their vehicles stopped and being asked to produce receipts for every item in their home or to account for where they obtained working tools. These reports have been too frequently received over far too many years to doubt that this is still a fairly common occurrence, as are the complaints that some officers behave in a racist or abusive manner or disregard conventions when undertaking a raid or eviction, for example, men appearing to search trailers during the night, walking in and turning over property even when young women are asleep in a caravan.

We are also aware of the tendency for some police forces to criminalise and label entire communities on the basis of suspicion that Travelling people must be involved whenever an allegation of receiving stolen property is made, or a car or caravan has disappeared in the locality. Even if with some justification a particular person is being sought on a site, a disturbing tendency exists in certain areas for the property and home of unrelated individuals to be searched and entire Traveller sites raided, often undertaken by large groups of police, sometimes with dogs or even with helicopters hovering overhead, and frequently involving the entire site being sealed off at the road so children cannot be taken to school. These bad practices (thankfully – see below – gradually being addressed by more enlightened policing and community involvement in police liaison and cultural awareness training) inevitably add to tensions and a sense that Gypsies and Travellers are deliberately scapegoated by police forces who exist merely to serve the needs of settled people.

Significant disquiet has also been expressed over the responsibility of the police and the CPS in their investigatory and prosecution role with regard to two horrific incidents that occurred in 2003. Although the police recorded the brutal killing of Johnny Delaney (a fifteen-year-old Irish Traveller boy from Liverpool who was kicked and beaten to death by a group of teenagers who made racist comments as they attacked him[50] including shouting he was 'only a ... Gypsy') as a racist assault, at his trial the assailants were merely convicted of manslaughter despite the evidence of a number of witnesses who had tried to intervene in the attack. Even though individual officers and the Cheshire Police were praised by the family of Johnny Delaney for their support and the way in which they investigated the crime, a number of comparisons have been drawn between the variation in outcome, sentencing and the degree of publicity attracted by Johnny's death and that of Stephen Lawrence, another young boy who was murdered in a racist attack in 1993.[51] At the conclusion of the trial of Johnny Delaney's killers, the Chair of the CRE (see above) was concerned enough to express the view that:

> There has been some measure of justice in this ruling, though it is extremely hard to see how this particular killing wasn't motivated in some way by racial prejudice. It would be most disturbing if the attack wasn't considered racially motivated because the victim wasn't black or Asian. The extreme levels of public hostility that exist in relation to Gypsies and Travellers would be met with outrage if it was targeted at any other racial group.
> (See report at <http://www.travellersinleeds.co.uk/_information/delaney.html>)

The notorious Firle village bonfire party incident in November 2003, in which an effigy of a trailer (complete with a painted numberplate – P1 KEY – and cardboard figures of children inside) was burnt, caused ripples throughout not only the Travelling communities[52] but amongst all people who were concerned that images of minority ethnic people could be torched amidst a mood of high glee. Despite claims by the organisers that they were simply following an old Sussex tradition of demonstrating their abhorrence of disliked people or groups by setting light to a symbolic image, the particular resonance of torching a caravan complete with 'children' inside caused cold shivers to run down the spines of many who had witnessed the devastation of caravan fires which are known to claim many lives amongst Travelling people each year. The perception of a thinly veiled threat was impossible to ignore for those who have for years known that arson as well as accident has caused the most horrific deaths of Gypsies and Travellers in a matter of moments. As was immediately noted by the many horrified individuals and community groups around the UK who protested strongly at the burning of the image, it is unimaginable in the present climate that other minority communities could be subjected to such ritualised conflagrations without attention being drawn to the organisers of the unacceptable nature of the 'entertainment' and, moreover, without immediate charges brought against them on the grounds that their actions could constitute an incitement to racial hatred, a crime under the Public Order Act 1986.

The person who first made an official complaint about the incident (themself of Romani ancestry) was subjected to anonymous threats and abuse and an almost medieval mood of intolerance against 'strangers' and fear swept the quiet village where the incident had taken place. Of more concern to those who were monitoring the role of the police and the CPS was the lack of seriousness with which this incident was taken when it first occurred. Following a heated campaign to raise consciousness about the seriousness of the issue (including interventions by the CRE) and the discrepancy in response to that which would have been expected if other minority communities were subjected to such behaviour, the police (reluctantly it is rumoured amongst some activists) charged twelve members of the Firle Bonfire Society with incitement to racial hatred. The saga meandered on, with the firework society issuing a belated apology for their actions and the original complainant refusing to make a statement to the police in the hopes that the village could 'move on'[53] as the media furore gradually died down and her family could return to their previously peaceful existence. Eventually, some nine months after the incident, the CPS decided not to prosecute the firework society members on the grounds of 'insufficient evidence'[54] although in some quarters doubts still remain as to whether the decision would have been the same had other ethnic minority communities been targeted in such a manner.[55]

These incidents are not recounted to indicate that all contacts with the police and legal systems are negative or that Gypsies and Travellers always consider themselves 'forgotten' by the law, but simply to underline the tendency for Travelling people to historically have had a 'rough deal' from the criminal justice system. In a piece of research underway in Cambridgeshire at the time of writing,[56] specific questions were asked as to whether respondents had experienced racism or harassment, whether they had ever reported such incidents to the police, and if not, why not. Emerging findings indicate that not only had almost all respondents experienced some form of racism (ranging from bricks thrown at trailers to abusive comments or physical assault), but that almost nobody would consider reporting such an incident unless it was extremely serious (e.g. threats to burn down a house where Travellers were living, repeated vandalism and graffiti to property or threats made to children) as (i) it was taken as being a hazard of Travelling life; and (ii) while individual officers were spoken of as being fair, in general it was considered a waste of time to report such events. The negativity pertaining to police responses to victimisation confirms what activists have known for a long time: that far higher rates of racist incidents are experienced by Gypsies and Travellers than are ever officially reported; that overall the sense of community self-help and 'dealing' with problems alone remains strong; and that the perception of being outside of 'the system' implies that involvement with officialdom will bring greater hazards than benefits.

> The way we do live is pretty much – well you don't get in contact with the police, and you don't because it's a taboo thing and you just do not do it which in some circumstances can get quite bad
>
> (Traveller interviewed by MG, summer 1999)

Whilst it is quite clear from the above discussions that some officers do abuse their position and harass Gypsies and Travellers or fail to deal responsibly with incidents where families are victims of crime, it would be unjust to fail to refer to the excellent relationships that can and do exist in some areas, the situations where individual police officers treat Travelling people with the same degree of respect as they would afford to anyone else resident in their locality, and the increasing evidence of good practice and willingness to learn amongst police forces that take their RRA duties seriously. The implementation of the positive duty to promote equality and to implement an audit of policy and practice has, for some police forces, proved a breath of fresh air, enabling them to examine their own practices and to develop innovative ways of working with the community to redress the years of mutual suspicion and acknowledged institutional racism that has blighted police and community relationships.

Some particularly noteworthy projects (and we will be delighted to hear of others) include initiatives such as the Pride Not Prejudice[57] (PNP) Conference, the brainchild of an innovative partnership working

The second Pride Not Prejudice Conference – senior police officers with
Richard O'Neill and Helen Jones of Leeds Gypsy & Travellers Exchange
(courtesy of Richard O'Neill)

project started by the Derbyshire Gypsy Liaison Group and Sergeant
John Coxhead of Derbyshire Police, which set out to provide a forum
for discussion of community policing and to establish networks of
communication and information on Gypsy and Traveller culture and
equality issues for police officers, as well as empowering community
members with knowledge of their rights with regard to the law and
expected police responses to complaints.

The first PNP Conference held in Derbyshire in 2004 was
financially supported by the Home Office and attracted the largest
group of Gypsies and Travellers who had ever gathered together for a
community policing event, leading to 'frank and free' discussion
between community members and officers from over twenty-five
forces who attended the conference.

The outstanding success of the 2004 conference was followed up
by an even larger gathering in Cheshire in 2005 – dedicated to the
memory of Johnny Delaney and attended by his father who spoke

movingly and supportively on the role of the police in investigating his son's brutal killing. The second conference attracted even greater public attention and the presence of police officers from a diverse range of forces from across the country. Indeed a third conference is being planned for 2006 and we understand that great competition exists from local forces wishing to host such an event.

As already noted, the county of Cambridgeshire, which is at the forefront of many innovative projects, retains a policy unit and liaison group consisting of police, health, education and local authority staff who work with the Gypsy and Traveller communities in the area (generally acknowledged to be the largest in the UK) and is the home to the Ormiston Trust Traveller Project which has funded a number of critically important advice and advocacy schemes as well as commissioning research into the needs of travelling people across the county. A major community-policing initiative led in 2004 to the production of a superb CD (*Del Gavvers Pukker-Cheerus*) by the Gypsy Media Company, funded jointly by the Home Office and Cambridgeshire Constabulary, in which Jake Bowers (one of the UK's few Romani journalists) and activists (including members of the G&TLRC, Derbyshire Gypsy Liaison Group, Irish Traveller Movement and National Romani Rights Association) spoke with Gypsies and Travellers and senior police officers about legal rights, dealing with racism and the role of the police. On the CD a number of community members who had made complaints about racist incidents detailed their experiences of working with the police and recounted the outcomes, including successful prosecutions of racists and interventions to protect their families at school and in the community. The success of the CD and the culturally appropriate manner in which it was produced are a model of good practice and deserve to be widely disseminated and indeed mirrored elsewhere across the UK.

The Metropolitan Police have also rightly been recognised as undertaking cutting-edge work in race equality and community good practice, working closely with Cliff Codona who, during his family's epic battle (sadly finally lost after a six-year legal fight) to retain their site at Woodside,[58] has tirelessly engaged in a range of community-relations and policing projects across south-east England. Mr Codona, who is the Chair of the Metropolitan Police Gypsy and Traveller Group, has undertaken cultural training for a substantial number of police officers in the London area and has worked closely with Acting

Inspector Nick Williams of the Metropolitan Police to devise a series of leaflets and training materials on equality matters, as well as encouraging more Gypsies and Travellers to join the police, or to openly acknowledge their ethnic heritage if they are already members of the force.[59]

The development of these schemes is greatly to be applauded, but further work is still needed to build trust between Travelling people and agents of the courts and enforcement agencies, in particular to address the (anecdotal, as no adequate statistics are retained, but well-attested by support workers)[60] over-representation of Gypsies and Travellers in prison populations and the inequitable treatment at committal proceedings, including refusal of bail when on criminal charges. In the remainder of this chapter we therefore explore what limited research evidence exists to support our beliefs that at all levels of the criminal justice system Gypsies and Travellers are subjected to institutional racism and hardship.

Anti-social behaviour and controlling legislation

At the time of writing, one of the major debates concerning the way in which the legal system is being used to criminalise Gypsies and Travellers concerns the use of ASBOs, a form of civil restraining order incorporated into British law under the Crime and Disorder Act 1998 and amended by the Anti-Social Behaviour Act 2004. Initially designed to 'protect the public from behaviour that causes or is likely to cause harassment, alarm or distress',[61] an order contains certain conditions that prohibit the recipient from undertaking certain actions or entering particular areas. These orders, which may be applied for by a range of bodies including police forces, local authorities and registered social landlords, were designed to deal with individuals or families who essentially harass and terrorise neighbourhoods with violent, aggressive behaviour or who continually create a nuisance by non-stop partying, swearing or behaving abusively to local residents. They are perceived as 'community-based orders' that enable local people to monitor breaches and to gather evidence to assist with an application for an order. Breach of an order once made is a criminal offence that can result in huge fines or imprisonment and also the loss of a home (for example) when the offender is resident in rented accommodation.

In theory, therefore, they are perfectly designed to support people who are having their lives made a misery by the sort of persistent anti-social behaviour that nobody should have to put up with in their local area.[62] However, since the implementation of the Act, the use of ASBOs has increased exponentially,[63] and civil-liberties activists are extremely concerned that orders are being sought to 'gentrify' areas (for example, to appease the middle classes who object to the sight of beggars in their locality) and increasingly to suppress the young, the poor, the vulnerable and those who are not members of a particular form of sedentary society[64] – in other words, people like Gypsies and Travellers who, as we have repeatedly demonstrated, are subject to victimisation and prejudice in many localities where they reside.

Although no clear evidence existed until recently (see below) on the targeting of ASBOs against Gypsy and Traveller families,[65] data indicates that the orders are generally used against large or 'problem' families, often resident in social housing on estates.[66] As we have discussed elsewhere in this book, Gypsies and Travellers who are unable to find sites are frequently accommodated by local authorities in 'sink' housing estates, often have greater than average numbers of children, a tendency to experience visits from large numbers of relatives *and* to some extent continue a pattern of visiting and socialising outdoors or in groups – all patterns that fit the 'classic' examples of behaviour cited as associated with the application for an ASBO. Given the role of the surrounding neighbourhood in gathering evidence and making complaints about 'problem neighbours' and the discriminatory and racist behaviour so frequently cited by Gypsies and Travellers when they are required to move into housing, it comes as little surprise to find that community workers can recount a stream of stories about threats to obtain ASBOs or actual orders made against Travelling people.

Anecdotally, the first two ASBOs issued in a large northern city in the UK were both ordered against Irish Traveller families, with specific objections made to visits from extended families, children being 'out of school', noise and the 'behaviour' of young people and their relatives and friends. The number of reports we have received from agencies working with housed Travellers and Gypsies on the ways in which ASBOs can be used to criminalise and victimise members of these communities who are following behaviours that would be culturally appropriate on a site are too striking to dismiss as mere rumour. Moreover, we are further advised that where a group of children from a particular estate is generally acknowledged to be creating a nuisance, it is often the young person from the Travelling background who is perceived as a 'ringleader' or whose parents are presented as not supporting the authorities in controlling their behaviour.

Whilst a generalised suspicion therefore exists that housed Gypsies and Travellers may be unduly over-represented in ASBO terms, in June 2005, the dramatic attempt by Wakefield Council to issue a blanket ASBO covering five well-known stopping places produced clear evidence that for many people Gypsies and Travellers are by definition 'anti-social' and in need of control.[67] In the trial scheme (subsequently halted following legal advice that an incorrect section of the Act had been used when interpreting the power to issue orders to anyone stopping on the areas 'plagued by illegal encampments' and, moreover, that targeting Gypsies and Travellers in this way would potentially be in breach of the RRAs[68]) any person who sought to camp would have been within a police-enforced exclusion zone and likely to receive a criminal conviction if they failed to leave immediately. Despite opposition from the local authority, the police refused to cooperate with the planned orders, forcing Wakefield Council to rethink their scheme. Whilst on this occasion the attempt to use ASBOs in a discriminatory manner failed, it is of great concern that a number of local authorities were reported to be watching the Wakefield initiative avidly, hoping to take similar action themselves.

In this book we have explored a great deal of material about the attitudes towards Gypsies and Travellers expressed by much of mainstream society and it is now perhaps time to consider two of the main allegations that are frequently levelled against members of the Travelling communities. The claims that Gypsies and Travellers are 'lawless' or consider themselves 'above the law'[69] make frequent headlines, with particular note paid to the setting up of unauthorised encampments, allegations that income and council tax are not paid, the swindling of customers and, above all, the issue of littering.

We have dealt extensively elsewhere with the reasons why Gypsies and Travellers buy land and then apply for retrospective planning permission. While this is clearly outside of the strict regulations that govern provision of sites, we are adamant that for the overwhelming majority of families this is quite simply the only way in which they can provide themselves with a home and respite from eviction or insecure accommodation, given the appalling state of Britain's planning laws and the lack of local authority provided sites. In a bid to end the use of this 'self-help' method of accommodation, the Government has recently passed legislation that includes the facility for issuing a 'temporary stop notice' which forbids any other caravans to be placed on an unauthorised development – a tool that explicitly impacts on families who hope to move onto a site – after the order is issued. One saving grace in this piece of legislation is the fact that concerns exist not to fall foul of the general duty under the RRA and human rights legislation by discriminating too excessively against travelling people. Thus, although additional works (or indeed siting of caravans) can be barred from taking place at a newly formed site, it is illegal to demand that a home is removed from a site or water and electricity supplies disconnected until such time as enforcement action is taken. Moreover, local authorities are reminded that they have a responsibility to ensure that minimum health, hygiene and public health standards are maintained on the site even when a temporary stop notice is in force.[70] Thus, when coupled with the increasing public awareness of accommodation needs and the Housing Act duties to assess site provision within a local area, the stop-notice provisions go some way to ensuring that counter-arguments exist to the notion that Travelling people blatantly breach planning regulations for motives of personal gain. The minimal standards that will be permitted to prevail on newly set up sites seeking retrospective planning permission are but the basic human right to access simple services until such time as the case is subject to full review.

The topics of payment of council and income tax, which excite so much concern and slander amongst those opposed to Gypsy and Traveller sites, is reliant upon rather more anecdotal evidence given the lack of official statistics to support our suppositions. However it is our contention, based upon knowledge of many site residents over a number of years, that the overwhelming majority of Gypsies and Travellers do indeed pay such taxes as are required. For families resident on roadside unauthorised encampments, who are moved on frequently, no facilities exist to pay council tax as they are but temporary residents. However, in some locations where arrangements exist, residents of 'tolerated' sites pay a sum of money to the local authority for the supply of basic sanitary facilities and collection of litter. We are unaware of any widespread cases of residents of 'unauthorised developments' failing to pay council tax where local authorities have entered into an agreement to collect the sum owed and to provide services in return. Cases of non-payment of council tax where a site resident is registered or receiving services are doubtless no greater than amongst the sedentary population.

Income tax payments are for Gypsies and Travellers as much a personal matter as for any member of the settled community; the sole difference between most traditionally 'employed' people and many Travelling communities is that people travelling for economic purposes are likely to accept cash payments in a mutually acceptable arrangement between customer and service provider. As with any community, some individuals may pay the Inland Revenue service less than it is owed, but *unlike* any other member of society, a Gypsy or Traveller who is applying for planning permission for land is likely to be asked to hand over evidence of their taxable income and accounts to justify permitting them to establish a stable home. The increasingly common habit of local authorities demanding that applicants for a site can demonstrate that they travel for economic purposes[71] and prove this to the court by production of accounts would not only appear grossly discriminatory and potentially racist, but would also tend to run counter to the allegation that tax is never paid. Indeed, many Gypsies and Travellers run highly successful businesses and employ accountants in an identical manner to other small traders.

The preponderance of self-employed tradespeople amongst Travelling communities inevitably leads to allegations of 'fiddling' the books or overcharging customers for shoddy work, but such statements are also alleged about all manual workers and tradesmen[72] whose income and expenditure varies on a weekly basis and who are not subject to the rigorous control exerted by employees subject to PAYE. Finally, it is worth remembering that untold numbers of Gypsies and Travellers resident in houses and on authorised sites are employed in a variety of jobs in the mainstream economy. For these individuals, the potential for tax evasion is no greater than for the overwhelming majority of UK citizens.

The debate around the costs of cleaning up after unauthorised encampments quite understandably concerns many residents of local areas.[73] In fact, the majority of Gypsies and Travellers are themselves as disgusted and enraged about the behaviour of a minority of community members as any settled person and, in particular, are appalled at the way the anti-social behaviour of a minority can lead to entire Travelling communities being 'tarred with the same brush'.[74] To some extent when considering the issue of litter it can be argued that local authorities should actively take responsibility for providing skips or make arrangements for site residents to have rubbish collected on a weekly basis, a situation that would give no excuse to the minority of families who do despoil an area and that would ensure that those responsible are identified, whilst the majority of residents of well behaved and maintained sites are duly commended. In some localities, in exchange for 'toleration' of a site for a specific time, site residents will enter into a 'bond' or make a payment to local authorities for litter collection and provision of water and sanitary facilities,[75] however, all too commonly, no such arrangements are made, with councils declining to assist with keeping unauthorised encampments clean or to accept payment for services on the grounds that acknowledging need and entering into a contract provides Gypsies and Travellers with 'status' as temporary residents of the area. Inevitably, the unwillingness of local authorities to enter into dialogue or provide rubbish collection greatly exacerbates the costs of clean-up after unauthorised encampments are moved on (see Morris and Clements 2002 for a lengthy discussion on the costs of unauthorised encampments and local authority responses and responsibilities).

Although it is widely acknowledged that residents of unauthorised encampments, and in particular those whose are moved on hastily, may find it difficult to dispose of their rubbish as efficiently as individuals with access to skips and bin collections (and in the case of those experiencing yet another forcible eviction may not feel particularly inclined to take great care ensuring the site is left tidy); it is important to reiterate that adequate discussion and arrangements between site residents and local authorities can mitigate much of the expense and nuisance of cleaning up sites once residents have moved on. Work-related debris in particular (e.g. tree-cuttings, scrap metal, etc.) can add to the mess and anger once a site has ended its life cycle, and it is these particular types of rubbish that are often the source of the most bitter complaints.

Whilst considerable controversy exists over the allegations of fly-tipping by Gypsies and Travellers,[76] there is much anecdotal evidence to indicate that not all of the work-related rubbish is the responsibility of former residents: 'The stereotyping actually encourages fly-tipping, because the fly-tippers know that they have only to tip near a Gypsy encampment to ensure that the Gypsies take the blame and that there is no proper investigation into the crime' (Professor Thomas Acton cited in Crawley 2004: 35).

Indeed, while local authorities are in some cases willing to acknowledge that unscrupulous people will take advantage of a site to dispose of their unwanted rubbish without paying for commercial disposal,[77] it would present an unbalanced picture if we did not acknowledge that in some cases Gypsies and Travellers involved in building and gardening work did at times leave rubbish from their income-generating activities. It has been pointed out (personal communication) that one way of resolving this particular problem is to ensure that Gypsies and Travellers working in an area are allowed to access council tips; many of which will not accept employment-related waste, leaving Travelling workers to dispose of green waste from coppicing and garden work, scrap-metal remnants and stripped wire wherever they can, regardless of environmental damage, given the impossibility of taking the debris away with them when they move on. One solution to this difficulty (personal communication; Helen Jones of Leeds GATE) is for local authorities to provide residents of unauthorised encampments with information on their nearest disposal arrangements for work-related rubbish and to make sure that managers of refuse-disposal facilities will accept such waste. Typical waste-recycling plant regulations that exacerbate the difficulties of trade disposal are as follows:

On entry to either of the rubbish tips, you will be asked what type(s) of waste you wish to dispose of. You are asked this so that you can be advised which bay to take the waste to and to separate out anything that can be recycled. You may also be asked for proof of address. This is to ensure that only residents of the borough of Walsall use the facilities. Examples of suitable proof of address include: a driving licence, council tax bill or utility bill.

You may be refused access to the sites if the operator suspects you are disposing of trade waste.

Height restrictions: There is a height restriction barrier at both of the rubbish tips which prevents access to vehicles of greater height than 6 feet 6 inches / 1.98 metres. This is to prevent trade waste being disposed of at these sites. Domestic vehicles (not vans) greater than 6 feet 6 inches / 1.98 metres are allowed to access the Fryers Road site

only, on Wednesdays between 5.00 p.m. and 6.00 p.m. Permission
must be obtained in advance.

<http://www.walsall.gov.uk/environment/civicamenity.asp>

Whilst not wishing to downplay the damage caused by wanton waste
disposal and fly-tipping, it becomes clear that with some form of
negotiation from both 'sides' and acknowledgement of the material
difficulties faced by mobile service providers, the worst impacts and
negative publicity faced by Gypsies and Travellers might potentially
be alleviated, ensuring that 'blame' is apportioned, the true 'villains of
the piece' are identified and the majority of law-abiding responsible
Gypsies and Travellers are treated with the respect to which they are
due, and that individual local authority officers are willing to accord
to them in private discourse.

The courts and the criminal justice system

In this final section of the chapter we turn to the situation where
Gypsies and Travellers come before the courts, perhaps merely as a
result of the hazards of living a traditional lifestyle or simply, as with
any other community, because an individual may have become
involved in law-breaking and crime. As we have seen, increased risks
of criminalisation tend to occur for Gypsies and Travellers regardless
of their living situation, and in many cases this is directly related to
discrimination and social exclusion. Although it is outside of the remit
of this chapter to discuss why 'risk-taking' and criminal behaviours
may potentially attract some young people,[78] anecdotal evidence from
community workers and family members indicates that some young
Gypsies and Travellers (particularly those who are 'out of school' or
living in poor quality social housing) may be especially 'at risk' of
obtaining a criminal record. Regardless of why Travelling people (of
whatever age) may come to the attention of the police or youth
offending teams, both anecdotal reports and the extremely limited
academic research into this area indicate that Gypsies and Travellers
may be significantly disadvantaged in their contacts with the criminal
justice system.

In considering this proposition we are once again considerably
hampered by the fact that very little clear data exists on the numbers of
Gypsies and Travellers who have been prosecuted or indeed
imprisoned for criminal offences. The lack of an adequate ethnic-

monitoring system which identifies Gypsies and Travellers as defendants in criminal cases means that to a large extent we must rely on narrative, small-scale studies and project reports. However, such data as does exist strongly indicates that institutional racism and legal systems that are essentially designed to deal with sedentary populations often lead to Travelling people being treated in an unfair and discriminatory manner in legal engagements.

Pizani-Williams's 1998 study of Gypsies' and Travellers' experience of the criminal justice process[79] focused predominantly on the role of Pre-Sentence Reports (PSRs) prepared by the Probation Service to assist magistrates and judges in selecting an appropriate sentence. Her research was limited in the sense of being undertaken in only one county (Kent), but involved not only a consideration of the role of the Probation Service, but also an exploration of statistics on outcomes for defendants known to come from a Gypsy or Traveller background. In addition, a series of interviews was carried out with community members and officials involved in the legal process. Key findings from the study indicated that where offences were not serious enough to lead to imprisonment (e.g. motoring offences, petty theft, etc.), probation officers tended to recommend community-service sentences for Travelling people rather than probation, based on the assumption that Gypsies and Travellers would be more likely to complete a service order than to comply with reporting requirements. (Consider here the assumptions outlined in the study of family-court interventions where Greenfields [2002] found that it was assumed that Travellers would fail to meet conditions unless orders restricting movement were imposed.) Inevitably, employment opportunities that required that the offender travelled for work were minimised during such time as a community sentence was imposed.

Although protocols surrounding PSRs are designed to limit the possibility of ethnic stereotyping or pejorative statements pertaining to ethnicity, Pizani-Williams found that in a number of cases officers had failed to understand the intrinsic message within statutory guidance on report-writing. The removal of all (or almost all) statements that related to an individual's lifestyle could sometimes be counter-productive for defendants, given that evidence of experience of victimisation or racism should be presented to the court. However, 'such minimal reference to the defendant's personal circumstances [meant that] the documents ... were completely sanitised and virtually worthless as an aid to the sentencing process' (Pizani-Williams 1998: 19).

Whilst the age range of defendants varied considerably, the study supported the proposition discussed above that some police officers harass Gypsies and Travellers by continually targeting them and believe that they are likely to have behaved in a criminal manner:

> the number of cautions previously received also suggested ... they were likely to be prosecuted earlier in their criminal careers than non-Travellers ... wide variations in the number of times the respondents had been stopped and searched during the previous year but several Travellers said they had lost count due to the frequency and one claimed to have been subjected to a strip-search on the roadside.
>
> Pizani-Williams (1998: 19)

Indeed a number of respondents to the survey reported being stopped on a daily basis by the police, subjected to racist abuse by officers or even (not uncommonly) physically attacked with injuries put down to 'resisting arrest'.

Once a Gypsy or Traveller had been arrested for an offence, respondents reported a widespread sense that the police, courts and local solicitors colluded throughout the prosecution process. A particularly alarming finding was that 52 per cent of respondents had never been cautioned for a previous offence prior to arrest, indicating that a tendency may have existed to immediately proceed to prosecution where the defendant was known or believed to be a Gypsy or Traveller. (An alternative explanation is of course that first-time offenders were arrested for more serious crimes than non-Gypsies or Travellers but this is not borne out by Pizani-Williams's data.)

The survey of magistrates' court cases revealed an over-representation of adult Gypsies or Travellers and that defendants of these ethnicities received differential treatment, with just under 60 per cent of Travelling people receiving a 'restrictive sentence' (e.g. community as opposed to probation) in relation to 35 per cent of 'others' (Pizani-Williams 1998: 21).

The type of crimes committed by Gypsies and Travellers in this study were particularly interesting, reflecting our own understanding of community patterns and opportunities. Although, as may perhaps be expected, car crimes (e.g. driving without a licence, tax, etc.) were represented in statistical categories, these offences were often related in some way to the difficulties of accessing transport when living on a low income or in a rural area, for example, a woman requiring hospital treatment for cancer, driving her son's car while not insured to attend for appointments; an unemployed man who could not afford road tax, etc. Of particular interest was the fact that certain offences were *not* encountered amongst the community, namely: fraud, forgery and, most strikingly, sexual offences. Incidents of theft, burglary and handling stolen goods were found in equal proportions amongst both Gypsies and Travellers and *gorje* (non-Traveller) populations, although, as we have seen, with a tendency for the groups to be sentenced in a different manner, often following advice provided in PSRs.

Court clerks and magistrates appeared to share agreement over the preferability of sentencing Gypsies and Travellers at first hearing, based on the belief that defendants might not attend for an adjourned case. A similar set of racist or stereotypical assumptions were considered to underpin a tendency for 'minor motoring' offences to be met with a fine on the basis that Travelling people 'have access to more money than they claim and will always pay a fine (often after a committal [to prison] warrant has been issued) rather than risk imprisonment' (Pizani-Williams 1998: 23), and further, that a number of court officials were suspicious that 'Travellers use different names for dubious reasons, either to avoid a severe sentence based on previous convictions or their connections with other local Travellers' (Pizani-Williams 1998: 23).

Finally, and of critical importance, whilst young Gypsies and Travellers are less commonly represented in Pizani-Williams's set of statistics than older members of the community (which she interprets as possibly relating to a strong family ethos controlling potentially 'delinquent behaviour' and the early transition to employment and thus adult responsibilities),[80] as age increases, differential rates of arrest and prosecution were noted between Gypsies, Travellers and 'mainstream' community residents in Kent.

Within this set of findings we can therefore see a reprise of the consistent themes of 'professional' suspicion, control, institut-ionalised racism and lack of understanding of community and cultural issues. The key policy recommendations that Pizani-Williams identifies within her report appear little different from those of Cemlyn's (1998) study of social workers and Greenfields's (2002) work with court welfare officers and solicitors in that all of the researchers clearly identify the need for identification of cultural requirements of community members, enhanced (and compulsory) training for professionals, greater use of advocacy and community involvement in training and clear monitoring and research into professional activities. It is to be hoped that with the implementation of the RRA 2000 and greater awareness of the 'general duty', coupled with the upsurge in community involvement with service providers, we will begin to see long-overdue changes.

One final piece of research must be given due precedence when considering the situation of Gypsies and Travellers in the criminal justice system. Anecdotal evidence has long asserted that Irish Travellers are over-represented in criminal justice statistics, have a far greater likelihood of receiving a custodial sentence when arrested for a criminal offence and in many ways are victims of both 'anti-Traveller' and 'anti-Irish' racism. Power (2004) devotes a highly important chapter of the *Room to Roam* report to Irish Travellers, policing and criminal justice. The relevant section of the report found that policing of the communities is still widely perceived as related to public-order issues, for example, in the circumstances where a large number of relatives have gathered to bury a family member, and that communication is often very poor between police, Travellers and the wider community even when diversity training explicitly includes information on Gypsies and Travellers.

Although evidence exists that the police are gradually taking steps to work in an inclusive manner with community members (see above about Pride Not Prejudice and the spin-off 'Moving Forward' project[81]), significant work still needs to be undertaken, not least in reassuring community members that contact with the police (for example, when reporting that one has been a victim of crime) will not lead to the targeting of a family or community or unleash investigations which may significantly harm the complainant; and in changing police culture, which is often 'ill-prepared to engage with the idea of Irish ethnicity not to mention that of Irish Travellers' (Power 2004: 80).

Irish Travellers' reports of their experience of policing are sadly generally negative, with young people reporting (for example) 'loads of beatings off police' (Power 2004: 82). Even when Traveller liaison officers exist within a police force (indicating that a clear attempt is being made to work proactively with the community), Power (2004: 81) reports that the post is often only filled reluctantly, with one police interviewee reiterating that 'anti-Traveller prejudice prevalent in society generally is amplified in the police by the very nature of policing' (2004: 82–4). Significant difficulties can also occur at even the most basic level, for example, in training officers to recognise that Travellers can be the victims of racism, and that racist crime is not just a 'black and white issue'. Other alarming findings concern the willingness of some police officers to 'air their prejudices ... they will be quite happy to say "Yeah I don't like Travellers – can't stand them, because they are all thieves and will always have a story"' (police sergeant quoted in Power 2004: 83). Despite the shocking level of prejudice that some interviewees reported, it must not be forgotten that overall, the culture of policing is going through a tremendous period of change with post-Macpherson[82] amendments to policy and practice. In the past few years we have seen a sea change in attitudes with the development of partnership working between Gypsies, Travellers and police officers and a willingness amongst many forces to look beyond their traditional law-enforcement role and to consider the ways in which they can fulfil their role of *serving* all members of the community with whom they come into contact.

The role of community-delivered diversity training cannot therefore be emphasised enough in terms of training police officers in their responsibilities to all members of the community and encouraging a sense of 'ownership' of the force by Travellers and Gypsies as well as sedentary populations. Power highlighted key areas where sensitive policing and cultural awareness can change attitudes amongst both Travellers and individual police officers, noting, for example, the preventative and educational work undertaken with young offenders by some community officers. However, in his critique of policing, Power refers to the seemingly intractable difficulties inherent in shifting from a notion of 'intelligence led policing' which frequently led to the targeting of Travellers following public reports of 'suspicious, Gypsy looking people', to concentrating on those already in the criminal justice system and thus failing to engage with youths who may potentially be 'at risk' of criminality.

Whilst there are clear difficulties in adopting this approach, the increase in diversity awareness and police outreach work with schools and youth agencies is still a positive move forward. When coupled with the earlier identification of children 'at risk' (brought about by the interdepartmental government review of children's and young

people's services that led to the Every Child Matters initiative[83]) and
the cutting-edge partnership between Gypsies, Travellers and police
underway in the PNP project (see above) we believe that too great a
cynicism over developments in police–community relationships is a
mistaken response to slow but welcome changes in the history of
policing of Travelling people.

Apart from his work on policing, Power also undertook an
exploration of Irish Travellers' experiences of sentencing and
imprisonment. In many ways Power's findings mirrored those of
Pizani-Williams, despite a six-year gap between the two pieces of
research. Power, however, had the advantage of being able to access
data from a wider range of sources and geographical locations when
reviewing the situation of Travellers and the criminal justice system,
with particular attention being paid (within primary research) to
outcomes where young people enter the court system within two
major cities in Britain.

Although the same difficulties in monitoring actual statistics exist
for both the 1998 and 2004 studies, Power reports that a study in
Newark[84] highlighted Irish Travellers' over-representation in prison,
finding that police officers tended to target Travellers for mainly
vehicular crimes, holding them overnight until bail conditions could
be imposed (which is not usual practice for motoring offences). Where
Travellers were unable to claim unconditional bail (a difficulty
without a fixed address) the likelihood of remand into custody
remained strong. Similarly, research carried out by the National
Association for the Care and Resettlement of Offenders (cited in Power
2004: 87) found that a disproportionate number of Irish Travellers (38
per cent of all 'White' admissions to Feltham Young Offenders
Institution) were remanded into custody from London courts, a
particularly shocking statistic when one considers that Irish Traveller
ethnicity is not routinely recorded in criminal justice statistics.

In original qualitative work undertaken for the 2004 study (findings
published in full as a separate paper in 2003[85]), Power outlined the
results of a series of interviews and focus groups with criminal justice
professionals (probation and prison officers and voluntary sector staff)
on attitudes towards, and support for, Irish Travellers in the penal
system. Although Power referred to specific anti-Irish racism and the
sense of cultural isolation experienced by Irish Travellers within
prison, the focus of his 2003 paper (in common with the Pizani-

Williams study) was mainly upon the impact of PSRs in criminal justice outcomes. As a result of increased awareness of institutional racism and in the light of post-Macpherson investigations and the implementation of the RRA 2000, formalised bureaucratic arrangements have been put in place to monitor all PSRs and ensure that they do not have a disproportionate impact on Black and Minority Ethnic (BME) defendants. Unfortunately, and once again indicating the lack of awareness of Gypsy and Traveller ethnicity, it would appear that such monitoring is not always routinely applied to Travelling people, partly, it would seem, because of their invisibility in terms of ethnic monitoring categories.

In a review of research studies on PSRs and Irish defendants, Power records that not only are individuals of Irish origin more likely to be incarcerated than any other major ethnic group in Britain, but that a substantial number of PSRs contained 'information considered irrelevant' or 'likely to be harmful to the individual and to trigger prejudice'.[86] When a defendant is both Irish and of Traveller ethnicity the impact appears far more profound, with frequent negative or '"non-affirmative" comments on the transient nature of the particular subject', with the additional implication that lack of a custodial outcome may lead to the defendant absconding. Power notes that within PSRs, 'to be Irish, have nomadic or transient tendencies or to be presumed to have these predilections was construed negatively by PSR writers' (2003: 258).

Focus groups held with criminal justice professionals added additional weight to the 'paper review' of PSRs, with some participants recording comments that indicated an awareness of both a general prejudice within the criminal justice system towards Travellers and the techniques some colleagues used to ensure that the court was receiving a coded message on the inherent untrustworthiness of defendants as a result of their ethnicity:

> I've seen people's [Irish Travellers] referred to in such a way that it is clear they are derisory ... I mean, people who for example have lived in settled addresses for ten years and their [nomadic] origins were being discussed ... there is no need to whatsoever.
>
> You would definitely get a lot [of Irish Travellers] serving short custodial sentences where really they should have had a community sentence but because of the perceived lifestyle dangers they would not be considered in the first place.

> If you read the report you would know the hidden message that this
> person is a Traveller and that they're a bit dodgy.
>
> (Focus-group participants quoted in Power 2003: 93)

Further key findings from the study included the by now familiar observation (from a plethora of studies into service delivery on diverse levels) that many professionals are unaware of Traveller cultural issues and carry into their work attitudes that are the result of their own training and previous experiences, leading in many cases to an inability or unwillingness to 'think outside of the box'. In some cases, the conflict between forward thinking and politically aware officers and colleagues who are reluctant to change or challenge practices can lead to moral and ethical dilemmas over the production of PSRs and how best to present evidence in court, a situation that can be particularly acute when a defendant is seeking to 'hide' their ethnicity in an attempt to avoid experiencing the result of negative stereotypes and assumptions (Power 2003: 251).

Yet the picture Power paints is not entirely negative, and he cites examples of good practice which demonstrate that, in common with many police forces, senior personnel are generally supportive of equality issues. Indeed his study demonstrates that a number of probation and prison officers are contemplating their role and professional practices in the light of increased knowledge of institutional racism and the complex relationships that exist between perceptions of offending, defendants' experiences of social exclusion and available intervention strategies. The role of community advocates and voluntary-sector agencies is once again foregrounded in Power's conclusions, with his proposal that probation services, youth offending teams and prison services should work closely with partners who have expertise on Traveller matters to ensure that PSRs are produced with the active cooperation of community members and knowledgeable parties.

Finally, and in recognition of the often unacknowledged prison experience of Gypsies and Travellers, Power (in his 2004 study) turns his attention to the particular difficulties faced by members of this community, who as we have demonstrated tend to be disproportionately represented (albeit as a 'hidden' minority) in prison populations. Some prisons are beginning to provide support for Irish Travellers, in recognition that community members share a distinct culture and may need special support within jail, but overall no official distinction is drawn between Travellers and other 'White' prisoners. Heavens[87] (2003, cited Power 2004: 96) reported that there is virtually no understanding of Traveller culture and ethnicity by prison staff and 'very little knowledge' of Irish Travellers provided in prison-service training, concluding that 'this is an issue for the Prison service as a whole'. Although reports on White minority communities in prison tend to focus on the Irish community per se, finding that anti-Irish racism, intimidation and abuse are rife in some establishments (Power 2004: 97), specific difficulties appear to face Irish Traveller prisoners, with some officers perceiving that they 'make it hard for themselves' by deliberately challenging the system. Power posits that this assumption (which we note is similar to the attitudes of some teachers who consider Gypsy and Traveller pupils particularly disruptive; see further Chapter 8 on education) is a misunderstanding of the way in which Traveller culture engages with discrimination, and a lack of knowledge of 'how the prison system works'. Young Irish Travellers in particular may be perceived as threatening or high risk and potentially be remanded to unsuitable locations such as Category A prisons, placing them at immense risk of harm. Where incarceration leads to intense mental strain (see earlier references within this text to mental health issues when Gypsies and Travellers are isolated or forcibly settled), the risk of suicide is clearly enhanced. Other factors that impact disproportionately on Gypsy and Traveller prisoners include illiteracy and lack of understanding about rules and regulations (which may lead to additional 'charges' and a lengthening of a prison sentence) and an inability to keep in contact with family members who are nomadic and thus unable to know when or if they can attend for a visit, and who often do not have the literacy skills to keep in touch by letter. With isolation this intense it is not surprising that Irish Traveller prisoners are often prone to mental ill health and may be included within the high statistics for suicide amongst 'Irish' prisoners (see Heavens 2003.)

Indications also exist (Power: 2004: 99–100) that the 'revolving door' syndrome, whereby former prisoners are unable to obtain a job and thus return to a cycle of criminality and imprisonment, impacts particularly harshly on Travelling people, as after-prison support (including support in accessing employment, literacy skills and drug rehabilitation, etc.) is predominantly designed with a sedentary

Police (with media in attendance) instructing Travellers they cannot continue along a public highway in Wiltshire on pain of arrest. Roadblocks stopped the Travellers from moving forwards or returning the way they had come. Many people were subsequently arrested and their vehicles impounded, 1986 (photograph by Margaret Greenfields)

population in mind, leading to a 'forgotten minority' becoming even more marginalised if they have survived the prison experience. It is therefore likely that Gypsies and Travellers in prison are amongst the most socially disadvantaged of an already marginalised population. Ironically, therefore, individuals who have experienced deprivation for much of their lives once again receive the least support to come to terms with their situation both within prison, and during a potentially rehabilitative period, through the simple expedient of the state 'forgetting' their ethnicity and needs and simply focusing on their 'criminality'. It would appear that both institutional racism and structural barriers need to be addressed if inequalities are to be eradicated and Gypsies and Travellers treated as equal citizens before the law.

Conclusion

In this review of Gypsies, Travellers and the legal system we have explored a range of situations where Travelling people may come into contact with 'professionals' and the courts. In re-reading what we have written, perhaps the most striking aspect is the continuity of findings, regardless of the subject under consideration. The findings from a review of a range of reports make for stark reading, leading to the inescapable conclusion that consulting with Travelling communities, ensuring that targeted service for Gypsies and Travellers are embedded within all service provision, and race-equality policies and training are in place (and adequately monitored) is the barest minimum which is required to ensure equality of access and treatment for community members. The commitment to combating both overt and covert discrimination against Travelling populations must become more than a philosophical stance adopted by a few 'aware' individuals if we are to bring about a real change in delivery of services and ensure that *justice* in the purest sense is delivered to community members. To bring about true partnership working and the empowerment of Gypsies and Travellers (and their input into a range of services), all agents of the state and constituent parts of the legal system must work with community members to break down communication barriers and develop a sense of stake-holding and co-ownership of statutory service provision. In particular it is to be hoped that a range of policy developments which acknowledge the fundamental impact that inadequate accommodation provision has had on the history of social integration of Gypsies and Travellers will coalesce into new forms of partnership working. Ensuring that the voices of community members are heard will not only enhance access to equity and justice in legal and social care settings, but also enrich the quality of life of both sedentary and travelling populations.

CHAPTER SEVEN

Travellers' health

Margaret Greenfields

Introduction

In this chapter we explore the issues of access to health care and the specific medical needs of Gypsies and Travellers. While it is self-evident that unsited Travellers, as a direct result of their difficulties in obtaining both preventative health care and medical treatment, experience far greater health inequalities than the majority of the settled population, it is also true that members of the community living at authorised sites, or in housing, are still over-represented in terms of preventable ill health, premature death and disability. In this section of the book we therefore present a summary of the key factors affecting Travellers' well-being and identify a range of 'good practice' initiatives aimed at increasing access to treatment and diminishing premature morbidity and mortality among the diverse communities.

The principle of access to primary care services

Those of us who live in a house would usually expect to register with a family doctor (GP) as soon as we move into an area. Given that registration with a GP is the key that enables access to many preventative health services as well as standard treatments for common ailments (e.g. chest infections and bad backs) it is a core principle of the National Health Service (NHS) that every member of the British public is entitled to be registered with a doctor and to receive medical treatment free at source.

In the past few years there has been something of crisis in primary health care in some parts of the country, in that elderly GPs are retiring, family doctors are more likely to be attracted to localities where their pay is greater, and there are quite simply not enough doctors to accept all the patients who require registration in certain inner city areas.[1] However, regardless of these difficulties, in principle, members of the public who are resident in Britain have an absolute entitlement to receive medical services. In an emergency a patient can request 'immediate and necessary' treatment from any GP, and if they will require treatment or access to a doctor for longer than fourteen days they can be registered as a 'temporary patient'. In theory, at the end of a three-month temporary registration period a patient is then entitled to be registered as a permanent patient. A 'temporary patient' can be referred to hospital or other services, but until or unless they are registered on a permanent basis they cannot receive a medical card or have their medical records transferred to the new surgery. Generally speaking, temporary registrations are a holding mechanism to ensure that basic medical services are provided to individuals who may just have entered an area, or who are on holiday and require access to treatment. A GP can refuse to take any patient on as a permanent patient without providing a reason for a refusal, although their decision to refuse registration should be reasonable and certainly may not breach race- or sex-discrimination legislation. A common reason for refusal to accept a patient on a permanent basis is that a surgery has too many patients on the books to provide an adequate level of service. This particular problem is increasingly found in inner-city areas where many elderly single-handed GPs are retiring from practice and their patients have been dispersed to other surgeries. More alarmingly, however, most particularly since the advent of new NHS contracts and where GPs are fund-holders for their own practices, there is an increasing trend for doctors to refuse to accept patients who they regard as expensive or time-consuming to treat (for example, elderly patients or those with ailments that require multiple referrals or out-of-hours call-outs). Similarly, given that certain aspects of GP budgets are topped up on a payment by results basis (e.g. number of children receiving immunisations), there is a considerable disincentive to accept patients who are unlikely to complete courses of treatment or attend for screening.[2]

Despite the difficulties which may be faced by many Gypsies and Travellers in accessing primary health-care services (see below), particularly where GPs are rigidly avoiding any potential negative impact on their targets, contacts within the National Association of Health Workers with Travellers (NAHWT)[3] have advised us that the new GP contracts and other changes within funding regimes can work in a flexible and innovative manner where medical staff are committed to providing services to 'hard to reach' groups and individuals. GPs are now able to opt out of providing anything other than core basic services, (including, no longer providing vaccinations or other 'targeted' provision),[4] although where practices opt for the 'no-frills' service, primary care trusts are under an obligation to find alternative providers, or alternatively practices may receive extra funding for providing 'enhanced services'. Anecdotally (personal communication) we are aware of at least two practices who are amending their contracts by offering 'enhanced services' to the large number of Gypsy and Traveller families who make use of their facilities.[5] An 'enhanced service' contract enables families to access a wide variety of health treatment and preventative care through registration with a team of health and social-care staff who work to address inequalities in health. Even prior to the implementation of the new GP contracts, some practices had opted to provide personal medical service (PMS) contracts[6] in order to develop local solutions tailored to the needs of their populations and to escape the rigidity of the national GP contract. A particular example of using PMS contracts to provide services for Gypsies and Travellers comes from Herefordshire where the innovative and highly successful Traveller Health Project was developed to provide mobile GP services to Gypsies and Travellers living in and passing through the locality.[7]

Although subsequent to the initiation of the new GP contract, practices are still able to offer PMSs, which remain as a separate locally negotiated contract option, at the time of writing it is expected that those service providers currently offering PMSs will gradually move towards 'enhanced service' contracts as certain financial and practical benefits may accrue to surgeries by transferring over to the new contract. Where 'Traveller-friendly' or specialist medical services are currently in existence no negative impacts should accrue to service users as a result of contract changes, but where the challenge exists is in convincing more GPs to accept highly mobile Gypsies and Travellers onto their 'books' as patients.

For those Travellers unable to obtain medical care or to register with a GP, the local family health services authority (in some areas the primary care trust) have the power and duty to ensure that a patient who applies to them for help is 'allocated' to a GP and their medical needs are met. Theoretically, therefore, any Gypsy or Traveller, whether they are in transit through an area, living at a roadside camp, resident on an authorised site or settled in a house, should have identical access to primary health care to every other member of the community. The practice, however (as we demonstrate below), is often very different, with many Travellers experiencing considerable difficulties in obtaining primary health services.

Environmental risks for unsited Travellers

To fully understand the impact on Travellers' quality of life of poor quality access to health care, it is important to think about what sort of conditions are faced by Travellers on unauthorised sites and to contemplate the insidious effects of long-term residence at such locations, interspersed with cycles of eviction. Moreover, even where Travellers do manage to access secure sites or to settle into housing, the effects of residence within a poor quality (typically roadside) environment over a period of many years may still leave a legacy of damaged health or untreated conditions that can lead to premature mortality or long-term morbidity.

In general, unsited Travellers living at insecure or dangerous roadside sites are immediately at far higher risk of poor health than housed or securely sited members of the Traveller community, who in their *own* turn often experience poorer health than non-Traveller populations.[8] A literature review on health needs noted that Travellers are 'arguably the most socially excluded group in society' with health outcomes and status significantly poorer than that found in the lowest socio-economic group in the UK population.[9] Not only are the conditions at roadside sites often appalling and lacking in basic amenities,[10] but their locations, typically near to busy roads, canals that may be the source of water-borne contamination,[11] or vermin-ridden areas blighted by fly-tipping, significantly increase the risk of viral and bacterial diseases that can spread rapidly, partly because of the close living conditions of families who may often be unable to allow children outside to play safely. Nelligan (1993: 11)[12] reports that:

> in addition to illnesses any population are exposed to, Travellers are particularly at risk from diseases corresponding to their environment, e.g. respiratory illnesses, enteric infections such as dysentery, skin disorders such as impetigo, infectious diseases such as Hepatitis A and

B. These illnesses are mainly due to poor sanitation and lack of water supply and **not** to a low level of awareness of cleanliness by Travellers.

(emphasis in original)

Not only can families at roadside sites be at risk of poisoning from over-exposure to lead in the air and soil,[13] but fire hazards have also been noted as a cause of considerable concern for those families living at unauthorised locations[14] where water may be unavailable, ground surfaces are uneven and trailers are parked in close proximity to each other: all factors that increase the risk of fire and its rapid spread throughout a site. Beach (1999) in a pilot study in Cardiff found that accidental injury rates amongst Traveller children were far higher than amongst settled children, even where the control group lived in conditions of deprivation which meant that their accommodation was likely to be unsafe.[15] Similarly, the risk of road-traffic injury or death is a very real threat to children and the elderly or disabled within Traveller communities. Nelligan (1993) recorded that one child death in her area resulted from a family living next to a main road, and the authors of this book have direct knowledge of injuries and fatalities occurring to children and vulnerable adults in similar circumstances.

Whilst many health disadvantages could be minimised by access to authorised sites and a network of safe, appropriately serviced transit sites for highly mobile families, it is self-evident that unsited Travellers, whether permanently located within a small area or passing through a locality, require adequate access to primary health services to enable treatment of minor injuries, referrals for medical investigations and treatment, and equality of access to preventative care. In the light of our knowledge of environmental hazards and their impact on Travellers' well-being, and despite the Department of Health's stated priorities for narrowing the health gap between socio-economic groups,[16] it therefore seems somewhat contradictory, to say the least, that Gypsies and Travellers should still be experiencing difficulties in registering with a GP who could meet their basic health-care needs. So what exactly *are* the barriers to ensuring equality of access to care?

Registration difficulties

We have outlined above the duties of GPs with regard to new patients in their area. However, the right of a doctor to refuse to accept an applicant has been shown to be disproportionately used when Travellers apply to become a patient.[17] For those families who are resident on an unauthorised site, unless they are likely to remain within the immediate locality and can therefore travel fairly easily to their local doctor, it is often more practical to register as a temporary patient, as by the time records have been transferred to the new surgery, the family may well have moved on voluntarily (or have *been* moved on) to another county. However, where a close connection exists to a specific locality, and the family spends their time orbiting around a particular village, or they have a pitch on an authorised site, there is no good reason why they should not be registered as permanent patients with a local GP. Research evidence,[18] supported by frequent anecdotal reports, indicates, however, that substantial numbers of Travellers, in all forms of accommodation, have difficulties in registering as a patient.

Feder (1989)[19] found that 10 per cent of GPs in east London refused to accept Travellers onto their lists based on blatantly racist principles, and a 1996 report from Save the Children (Scotland)[20] reported that a third of Traveller women had difficulties registering with a GP, most often being given reasons that were clearly discriminatory. Where they had managed to register with a practice, reports were made that some GPs refused to attend on site or did so only if provided with a police escort. The 1998 Cardiff Gypsy Sites Group (CGSG) annual report noted approvingly that in the year of publication an improvement in GP registration had occurred as a result of new referral and liaison arrangements between the CGSG and health-care providers. In a previous report they had identified that some families 'were unable to establish continuity in health care because local GPs will not accept them for permanent registration'.[21]

Anecdotal information supplied to the authors included: GP receptionists stating that lists were full and no new patients were being taken on (although Travellers using a 'care-of' address in the immediate vicinity were advised that vacancies existed when they telephoned the surgery); Travellers being informed that doctors could not attend at the site (although it was known they would make house calls); and the not-uncommon situation of residents of unauthorised private sites (land purchased and then retrospective planning permission sought) being unable to access a GP in the neighbourhood.

In 2002 one of the co-authors of this text was present when a resident of an unauthorised private site sought to register her child at a GP's surgery in a village where a high-profile 'anti-Traveller site' campaign was being orchestrated. The mother and child were told to move away from the counter, that they could not come into the surgery as they were not patients and, moreover, no registration vacancies existed. On remonstrating with the receptionist both the Traveller and the author were asked to leave the premises immediately. We later discovered from a sympathetic village resident that doctors were being advised that their patients would transfer to a different surgery if they accepted Travellers from the new site. Fortunately, another primary-care practice in the village had no qualms over registering Traveller patients.

Anecdotally, too, even when they have access to an authorised site or housed accommodation, some Gypsies and Travellers are refused access to primary health care other than on an emergency basis, precisely because they are seen as 'difficult' patients who may fail to comply with immunisation programmes, thus having an adverse effect on GP targets for take-up of child preventative health services. (GP contracts under the NHS and Community Care Act 1990 impose a financial penalty on practices where doctors fail to achieve a high percentage of infant immunisation and pre-school booster acceptance[22] unless PMS or basic 'no-frills' contracts have been negotiated – see above.) Similarly, amongst some practitioners, preconceptions exist that (particularly among the older generation) Traveller women will not accept cervical or breast-cancer screening, which is also subject to monitoring to ensure GPs reach their targets.[23]

Given that Traveller populations tend to have larger than average families,[24] and since Traveller women have been demonstrated to experience significant difficulties in accessing ante- and post-natal care as a result of enforced movement[25] (see below under 'Pregnancy and women's health'), children are inevitably at risk of health inequalities from birth and should accordingly be given the highest priority in terms of ensuring their access to primary medical attention. Inequalities and preventable ill health are likely to increase exponentially throughout the lifetime of Travellers where families are denied access to primary health care, exacerbating the risks of premature morbidity or mortality associated with instability of accommodation, injury, poor environment and other lifestyle factors and behaviours (e.g. diet and smoking, see below).

Gypsies and Travellers often therefore find themselves in a Catch-22 situation, unable to obtain adequate health care, which means they become potentially higher-risk patients with more long-term difficulties which can prove expensive for fund-holding GPs to treat, in turn minimising a family's likelihood of being accepted onto a surgery's books. While this coldly logical attitude may make sense from a health economics point of view, the human cost is incalculable, and morally totally at odds with the philosophy of the NHS.

In such ways, Travellers have been indirectly affected by health legislation such as the NHS and Community Care Act 1990. Although, as we have noted, in some areas flexible services exist, or patients can approach the local health authority and demand that they are allocated a GP, in practice, Travellers are unlikely to avail themselves of this right, because either they do not know about the powers of the health authority (or how to contact them), or are lacking in the necessary literacy skills required to enter into such a bureaucratic maze and consider that the whole process could take so long and be so difficult that they are likely to have moved on to another location or, if resident on a site, have found a friendlier local surgery. Indeed, the problems associated with accessing primary medical services are so great, in the authors' experience, many Travellers who are passing through an area (or who may perhaps be waiting to see if they receive planning permission for a self-provided private site) remain registered with a 'known' GP in an area to which they commonly return, or make use of a 'care-of' address by pretending that they live at a relative's site or house. Such practices are not new. A 1986 study on Travellers' access to primary care found that 19 per cent of their sample had to travel at least five miles to see their doctor, with around 5 per cent going over twenty miles to see their registered GP.[26]

Hospital services/accident & emergency (casualty) departments and 'walk-in' centre use

Given the inherent difficulties in accessing adequate primary care it is unsurprising that many Travellers make use of hospital emergency services in lieu of GP registration. Pahl and Vaile (1986) report that while in many cases children require hospital treatment for lacerations, burns and scalds suffered while resident at poor quality or environmentally unsuitable unauthorised sites, in other cases, families will need to attend at a hospital for treatment that could have been adequately diagnosed and tended at a local surgery. Although families are likely to experience lengthy delays prior to seeing a doctor in a hospital setting, anecdotally, Travellers will often report greater trust in emergency-service provision than in local GPs, considering that they will receive more thorough treatment as a result of the array of technological equipment and facilities available in a large medical facility.[27] Moreover, not only does attendance at a hospital forestall the difficulties of attempting to make an appointment at a surgery, the risk of encountering potentially hostile reception staff[28] or avoid a subsequent journey to hospital should a doctor feel a referral is necessary, but the 'drop-in' nature of accident and emergency (A&E) departments means that Travellers will not be turned away regardless of the time of day or night. A further advantage to hospital attendance is that extended family members can often wait with the patient to provide support[29] (which is sometimes regarded with disapproval or difficult when there is limited available space at small GP practices).

While hospital staff may sometimes be less than enthusiastic to see Travelling families at A&E departments for relatively minor medical treatment (and indeed, a potential exists for conflict and misunderstandings over practical, cultural and communication issues as well as resulting from guidance on child protection matters which places a duty on medical staff to notify social services departments when a child is seen on a number of occasions at a casualty department), in health authorities with enlightened practice cultures, contact with Travelling families at general hospitals can lead to a referral to a specialist Traveller health visitor who can facilitate access to a range of services and support.[30]

The development of NHS walk-in centres[31] (currently only available in certain areas) has also provided a further source of easily accessed treatment for Gypsies and Travellers, as these facilities offer a range of advice and basic treatments for patients who are not registered elsewhere. We understand from health professionals that Travelling people are increasingly making use of these services as they become aware of their availability.

While emergency treatment at a hospital A&E department or walk-in centre may often prove convenient for a Traveller with urgent one-off medical needs, where an individual or family requires ongoing treatment   or   attendance   for   a   series   of   diagnostic   tests   or appointments, the lack of flexibility inherent in medical systems devised to serve a sedentary population often proves problematic. Not only is it virtually impossible for a family residing at an unauthorised site to know whether they will have been evicted prior to (or even on) their next booked appointment, meaning that they may either miss appointments or be marked down as 'non-attending' and consequently refused an alternative date, but also, critically important test results or urgent 'recalls' may fail to reach a patient as a result of frequent movement or the lack of postal deliveries to roadside sites. Webster (1995) found that cycles of eviction had a significantly detrimental effect on Travellers' ability to attend for medical treatment or follow-up hospital care, not least because families might become confused over dates while dealing with the urgent necessity of finding a new site. Even if a family are able to remain in the locality while awaiting a follow-up appointment, the lack of postal deliveries to unauthorised sites (and in some cases communal letter-boxes at authorised sites) means that letters may go astray or be misdirected if a number of residents at an authorised site have the same surname.

A number of studies also report that Travellers' 'different concept of time'[32] and unfamiliarity with diaries and calendars may mean that families exposed to conflicting time demands or multifactorial difficulties may fail to notify a hospital that they cannot attend an appointment, or they may simply arrive at a different time or date to their arranged appointment and expect to be seen. Where literacy problems also exist the opportunity for culture clashes or conflict is inevitably multiplied and may lead to overworked (or even prejudiced) nursing or medical staff assuming that health maintenance is of low importance among Traveller communities.

Further commonly reported areas of dispute involve the preferred tendency for Gypsy and Traveller families to attend for appointments in a family group which, while having the advantage of providing support to the family member in need of medical care, can be interpreted as threatening or confusing by health services staff.[33] Additional problems can occur where family health records are dispersed between different hospitals or GP practices and the person in need of care is reluctant to reiterate a history, or is frustrated at the need to repeat information which has been given to a number of different practitioners. Particular risks of health workers 'missing' key data can occur when a patient cannot recall to whom they have provided information, assumes that records have been passed onto their current care provider or simply cannot recall in which of numerous locations or dates they suffered from a particular ailment or attack of a chronic condition.

Specialist Traveller health visitors report too[34] that some Travellers (fairly logically) assume that a medical appointment booked for one family member can present an opportunity for other family members to discuss their health issues. Inevitably, health services staff in formal settings may find this assumption at odds with their own understanding and expectation of the role of medical service provision.

We explore further below (under 'Some examples of good practice') how the use of certain basic techniques or health authority provision of outreach services can minimise some difficulties associated with access to and provision of health services for highly mobile and socially excluded Traveller communities.

Pregnancy and women's health

We mentioned above that Traveller women without access to secure sites are particularly at risk during pregnancy and childbirth. There is overwhelming evidence that lack of available sites, residence in a poor quality environment and frequent movement caused by eviction during pregnancy has a detrimental effect on both maternal and child health.[35] In addition Traveller women's use of family planning, developmental screening of neonates and toddlers, immunisation and antenatal care is particularly low when compared with the profile of the sedentary population.[36] A higher proportion of babies born to unsited Travellers are of low birth weight[37] than is common amongst the whole population, some evidence exists for an increased number of congenital abnormalities and inherited disorders when compared to sedentary populations,[38] and, particularly alarmingly, stillbirths, perinatal and infant mortality rates are significantly inflated amongst highly mobile or insecurely sited Traveller populations.[39] We submit that this appalling indictment of the state of maternal and child health amongst some Traveller communities is (despite the dedication of individual staff and outstanding health initiatives available in some areas) in many cases directly attributable to inadequate access to sites, and discriminatory and inappropriate service delivery.

Over and above the personal tragedy of loss of a child, and the subsequent impact on whole family well-being after such a death, the significance of inflated child mortality figures[40] amongst a particular minority community is profound when we take account of the fact that infant mortality rates are internationally monitored as an indicator of a nation's health status. In the UK, the Office for National Statistics records all child deaths and correlates the figures by socio-economic status, ethnicity, parental age, biological status and a range of other factors.[41] Quality of environmental surroundings, access to good quality ante- and post-natal health care, and poverty are particularly implicated in infant mortality rates[42] with families in the lowest socio-economic class twice as likely to suffer the loss of a baby as those in the highest class.[43] It is therefore unsurprising that Travellers without access to a secure site, or whose environment is poor, are at greater risk of stillbirth and perinatal death.

We have noted above the difficulties of accessing adequate screening facilities for families who experience inequality of access to GP services or who find that medical facilities are culturally unsuitable (or even discriminatory) in their approach to Travellers. In the absence of suitable outreach services (including targeted, sensitive information materials), and in particular where there is a shortage of female doctors or conveniently timed (and culturally accessible) 'drop-in' clinics, Traveller women may be less likely to engage with preventative health programmes such as cervical and breast screening. The enhanced risk of delayed screening or treatment for gynaecological and other cancers exponentially increases the likelihood of mortality resulting from preventative or curable diseases, as well as exposing Gypsy and Traveller women to increased morbidity resulting from treatable gynaecological conditions.[44]

Although census categories (which are the ethnic-monitoring tool most commonly used by statutory authorities) do not include Gypsy and Traveller as an explicit category, limiting our ability to monitor the full extent of health inequalities experienced by Travellers, one of the starkest examples of the disparities in health outcomes concerns the findings from the Confidential Enquiries into Maternal Deaths in the United Kingdom 1997–9. In the report *Why Mothers Die: 1997–1999*,[45] which provides a detailed analysis of the mercifully low number of deaths directly related or attributable to pregnancy (including maternal deaths within a few months of parturition), it is specifically noted that Traveller women from traditional communities (although

New Travellers are also recorded as being at increased risk) are statistically at greater risk of maternal mortality than any other community in the UK. Of the six Traveller women whose deaths were investigated by the enquiry: 'three women died from Direct causes all associated with major substandard care, and two were Late deaths also associated with substandard care. One woman had an Indirect death where the quality of care was difficult to judge' (NICE/SEHD/ DHSSPSNI, 2001, p41 and appendix 1).[46]

It is shocking to contemplate that Traveller women and children in the early days of the twenty-first century are still dying needlessly in the UK in a land where childbirth has never before been so safe.

A healthy life?

We separated out women's health for specific comment (predominantly because research and health targets have often focused on this area of public health and epidemiology) yet it is critically important to be aware that Travellers as a social group (both those who are 'ethnically' Gypsies or Travellers and New Travellers) suffer from disproportionately worse health than the majority of society. The majority of research has focused on 'traditional' or 'ethnic' Gypsies and Travellers, but some research has been carried out with New Travellers,[47] which, whilst highly controversial in some of the more extreme claims pertaining to drug use and sexually transmitted diseases, found that environmental factors are virtually as likely to cause increased morbidity as amongst other Travelling groups. Although when contemplating the health of New Travellers it is necessary to remember that we are looking at a community where a reasonably high proportion of the population has lived in housing and grown up with access to mainstream health services in their early years, it is unarguable that years of dwelling on poor quality sites and intermittent opportunities to achieve good quality preventative health care will have a significantly detrimental impact on long-term community health. Whilst New Traveller children are perhaps as likely to experience decreased quality of health across their lifespan as are young people from more traditional Travelling communities, increased knowledge of health services and patients' rights, coupled with a generally higher literacy rate amongst parents, may well mitigate some of the harsher impacts of nomadic life. To date we are unaware of any specialist studies that explore the longitudinal impact of a nomadic life on the health of New Travellers or indeed whether life expectancy is lowered or morbidity rates increased amongst this community.

We would, however, expect to see similar rates of injury (particularly spinal) and environmental-related illness amongst all Gypsy and Traveller populations, particularly where heavy manual work is implicated in disability rates which in turn may lead to long-term employment difficulties or problems in undertaking the heavy physical tasks associated with travelling (e.g. transporting water, heavy tools or plant or hitching trailers). In our experience, a large proportion of Gypsy and Traveller men report 'back problems' which can sometimes limit their mobility or employment opportunities and may lead to occasional reliance on other site members when working or undertaking daily practical chores. Unsurprisingly, the older the informant the more likely they are to suffer from skeletal problems and arthritis or pain at the site of old injuries. The poor quality condition of ground on many unauthorised and transit sites (for example, where trailers or vehicles have to be bumped across rutted land or broken hard-standing may lead to the risk of stumbling on a site) undoubtedly increases the risk of pain and further injury for people afflicted with such conditions.

Although research into the life expectancy and causes of death amongst British Gypsies and Travellers is extremely limited, findings from Ireland demonstrate that the life expectancy of Travellers is far lower than amongst members of the sedentary population.[48] Shockingly, Irish Traveller women were found to live on average twelve years less than women in the general population, and men had a decreased life expectancy of ten years. Anecdotal reports (e.g. surveys carried out jointly by a housing association and 'Help the Aged' cited in Bromley Gypsy Traveller Project, annual report 1996) indicate that British Gypsies and Travellers consider themselves 'elderly at fifty', a finding that contradicts current trends in self-image amongst sedentary communities where people generally expect to enjoy a relatively long and healthy retirement and accordingly plan for their future in anticipation of a number of years of 'freedom' from responsibility once they have finished their working life. The Leeds Gypsy and Traveller Baseline Census (2005)[49] appears to support the Bromley findings, showing a demonstrable demographic inconsistency between older Gypsies and Travellers (over-sixties accounted for 2.3 per cent of the Traveller community compared with 19.9 per cent of the sedentary population) and mainstream populations.

Power (2004: 37) notes that in focus groups carried out on sites in Britain for a health-related qualitative study of Travellers' life experiences,[50] only four out of ninety participants were over the age of sixty-four. Whilst it could be argued that this finding merely indicates that older people were less likely to participate in the research than those with a different age profile, it is worth remarking that the authors of the current text have generally noted that older people (in their seventies and over) are less commonly found amongst Gypsy and Traveller communities than in the whole population. Census data from Ireland indicates that only 3.3 per cent of Irish Travellers are over the age of sixty-five years[51] compared to 11 per cent of the overall population, and it is likely that similar patterns of mortality exist across the UK, although the absence of Gypsies and Travellers as a distinct ethnic group within British census statistics means that no directly comparable data is available.

Causes of premature mortality and morbidity amongst Gypsy and Traveller communities

We have noted above that Traveller mothers and babies are disproportionately at risk of premature mortality potentially resulting from poor access to medical care, antenatal screening, birth complications and (possibly) eviction in the immediate post-natal period. However, assuming that the average Traveller child, even one without access to a secure site, survives until adulthood in good health (a fact that testifies to parental determination and care despite frequent inequality of access to health services), what non-environmental health problems are commonly implicated in premature mortality?

Although once again we are dependant upon a series of essentially localised studies for information on common Traveller health problems, findings from a range of studies (and anecdotal reports from the communities themselves) are demonstrably coherent in identifying the following causes of morbidity and premature mortality amongst Traveller communities: cardiovascular disease,[52] chronic renal and urinary-tract infections,[53] cancer,[54] asthma,[55] diabetes,[56] arthritis[57] and smoking-exacerbated/related diseases such as chronic upper respiratory-tract infections and chronic emphysema.

While, to some extent, conditions such as asthma, arthritis, diabetes and renal problems may be said to 'run in families' (and hence are likely to be more common where families are often multiply related through marriage) and moreover are likely to be exacerbated by poor environmental conditions, significant concerns exist amongst health workers and many Travellers themselves that lifestyle factors must bear the blame for at least a percentage of premature deaths or long-term illnesses.

Diet and exercise

The Men's Health Forum publication *On the Road to Better Health for Travelling Men* (2003)[58] explicitly refers to the pressures inherent in leading a travelling life in modern-day Britain. Not only are Travellers (whether accommodated on secure sites or living at roadside locations) less likely to be able to take regular physical exercise than in the days when they were responsible for caring for horses, 'calling' and 'hawking' door to door or undertaking fieldwork, but the necessity of long-distance driving for work purposes (or to find a safe place to halt), shortage of work and fear of harassment if a family pulls off the road for a night, inevitably increase the risk of depression and stress-related illnesses, and indeed risk-taking behaviours such as excessive drinking or smoking.

A number of researchers and health workers[59] refer to the fact that the traditional diet enjoyed by Travellers in the past has become culturally eroded and that families are today less likely to eat as healthily as when freshly harvested vegetables, newly caught game (e.g. rabbit, pheasant, etc.) and daily cooked (and low-fat) stews formed the majority of a family's dietary intake. With the advent of convenience food, or simply a reduction in access to good quality and affordable ingredients,[60] Travellers may find that they are nutritionally compromised (with families being at increased risk if they are living in poverty or dependent on benefits as a result of poor health or limited work opportunities), increasing their risk of dietary-related illnesses such as diabetes. Ironically, obesity is often associated with poor quality diet, and the risk is greatly increased when a fat-rich (e.g. large amount of fried foods), high-sugar diet is combined with decreased

Richard O'Neill, Founder of National Men's Health Week, at the launch in
2002 with Minister Hazel Blears (courtesy of Richard O'Neill)

opportunities for exercise. Crout (1987b) refers to the negative impact
on Travellers' health of becoming 'trailer bound' as a result of
'decreased mobility ... due to the loss of traditional professions' and
noted that obesity and depression were becoming more common
amongst the Travelling families she cared for as a health visitor during
the late 1980s.

The risk of cardiovascular disease, stroke and high blood pressure
are also exponentially increased if individuals are both overweight
and experiencing stress and it is therefore unsurprising, if tragic, that
so many Travellers continue to die prematurely from preventable
diseases, a warning repeated in the Men's Health Forum publication
(2003): 'On the Road to Better Health for Travelling Men'.

Smoking and drinking

A number of studies[61] have found that Travellers are highly likely to
smoke cigarettes, with decline in smoking habits less pronounced than
amongst other populations. In part, the stress of Travelling lifestyles

may contribute to this habit, as well as a general cultural acceptance of smoking amongst both sexes. The limited literacy of some of the Traveller community, often coupled with inadequate access to health-promotion information and smoking-cessation support, may account in part for the slow decline in smoking amongst Gypsies and Travellers. We have noted above that communication difficulties frequently exist between Travellers and medical staff, and, where this occurs, not only may health-promotion information be presented in a culturally inappropriate manner, but the impression of being 'told what to do' by staff who often have no knowledge of the realities of life for Travellers may lead to advice being discounted, misunderstood or regarded with suspicion as simply propaganda in a climate where smoking is decreasingly tolerated.

Even when Travellers are fully aware of the risks inherent in smoking, in common with many individuals from a range of communities,[62] the immediate 'benefits' of smoking (e.g. sense of well-being or stress reduction, having a 'time out' from immediate work and domestic strains to enjoy a cigarette, 'fitting in' with friends and relatives who also smoke) may mean that the perceived long-term gains from stopping smoking (longer life, better health, less expense) are seen as too intangible to warrant the effort and loss of 'pleasure' obtained through smoking. In addition, some Travellers report a fatalistic attitude to health, feeling that if someone is going to become ill or die, this will happen regardless of whether they smoke, or, indeed, that the damage may already be done by previous smoking habits so what is the point of giving up a pleasure when health is already impaired? Moreover, if an individual has seen friends and relatives smoke throughout their lives without evident long-term health impacts, it may be difficult to convince them that 'smoking kills'.

Regardless of why the smoking-cessation message has failed to reach, or has been rejected by, many Travellers, it would appear self-evident that the habit is implicated in the high rates of asthma, cancer, cardiovascular disease and chronic bronchitis and emphysema that many members of the community report they or close family members have experienced.

Although less information is available on the drinking habits of Gypsies and Travellers,[63] Crout (1987b) and the Men's Health Forum (2003) both refer to the tendency of Traveller men who are experiencing stress to drink more than the safe number of units of alcohol a week. Indeed, increased use of alcohol amongst minority ethnic communities who are marginalised or socially excluded is a widely recognised phenomenon, identified amongst Native Americans, Australian Aboriginals and Maori populations,[64] whose status is in many cases comparable to that of Gypsies and Travellers in the UK.

Again, as is common to members of the wider (sedentary) community, cultural and recreational/social practices have a significant impact on individual Travellers' drinking habits, but in any situation where alcohol forms a major drug of recreation or is widely accepted as a response to stressful or difficult circumstances, care needs to be taken that alcohol consumption does not exceed safe limits, information on 'safe drinking' is available in culturally acceptable and suitable formats and that use of alcohol does not exacerbate pre-existing conditions or increase the likelihood of premature mortality or morbidity.

Drugs and depression

Depression amongst Travellers, most particularly those who are resident in housing (see Chapter 5) as a result of an inability to obtain a pitch on an authorised site, or when families are subject to repeated eviction from roadside locations, has been noted by a number of researchers.[65] Interestingly (although perhaps somewhat obviously), one Irish study reports that levels of depression and stress amongst women fall significantly when families are able to obtain access to secure, culturally suitable accommodation.[66] In the experience of the authors, it is not at all uncommon for Traveller women to be prescribed anti-depressants by GPs when they attend reporting problems with 'nerves', which are often related to their accommodation difficulties.

Whilst in the correct context suitably prescribed anti-depressants undoubtedly do have a place in the treatment of depression and other psychiatric illnesses, some concern *must* exist over the numbers of Travellers with whom we have personally met who report long-term anti-depressant use. Not only is the risk of physical or psychological dependence upon anti-depressants well documented,[67] but where treatment may be inadequately monitored as a result of frequent movement of patients, or where the potential exists for inappropriate administration of the drug through lack of patient information, poor literacy skills or in some cases 'self-diagnosis' where friends share a prescription for anti-depressants where similar symptoms are reported by more than one person, then the possibility exists for significant harm to occur to Travellers who are taking such medication. Although to our knowledge no research has yet been undertaken into untreated depression and anxiety amongst the Traveller community, we are also anecdotally aware of a number of cases of suicide amongst Gypsies and Travellers who have moved into housing and have become isolated from their community. The implications are sobering.

Other forms of substance abuse amongst the Gypsy and Traveller communities are as yet relatively uncommon, but a disturbing trend has been noted by some activists and health workers of young people becoming involved with the use of illegal drugs. In the main, addiction to drugs such as heroin and crack cocaine has spread as a direct result of contact with substance abuse while living on housing estates or in close proximity to settled housing or while attending at social events and schools where drug use may be commonplace. For Travellers (in common with many socially excluded non-Travellers) problematic drug use appears to be directly related to issues of poverty, depression and a sense of hopelessness with life.

A recent (2004) CD/video launch by Jake Bowers and Barrie Taylor of the Gypsy Media Company[68] highlights the impact of drug use and addiction on families where a member has become a substance abuser and notes that one of the main difficulties has been lack of information and knowledge within traditional Traveller cultures of drug awareness and the signs and symptoms of problematic use. The producers report that Gypsies and Travellers who do become addicted to drugs are not only less likely to 'kick addiction', but are also more likely to meet an early death as a result of heroin use. Alarmingly, and somewhat against the trend of drug use amongst the sedentary (*gorje*) population, it is not only young people who are becoming involved with multi-substance abuse (e.g. alcohol, heroin, crack cocaine, cannabis) but in some cases men in their thirties are also coming into initial contact with a range of drugs and taking a variety of substances simultaneously, thus enhancing the likelihood of premature death, addiction and severe psychological problems.

Taylor reports that in many ways the substance-abuse problems that members of the Travelling community are beginning to encounter mirror the experience of the sedentary *gorje* communities in the 1960s, with a wide range of drugs becoming increasingly available and present within Travelling populations, despite the fact that Travellers are still generally reluctant to discuss the issue or recognise that for some young people (or residents of particular localities) recreational drug use is both acceptable and may in some cases lead into problematic and habit-forming drug use. The difficulty of accessing culturally suitable detoxification and support programmes (particularly when a family is unsited), and indeed the tradition of Travellers 'looking after their own', as well as a sense of shame when a family member becomes addicted to drugs, may also create barriers that militate against problematic substance users obtaining appropriate care to assist them to stop using drugs and deal with underlying difficulties in their lives.

Dental and eye care

Although the final health issues we wish to explore in this chapter are not life-threatening, and have not in the main received significant research interest, it is also noteworthy that members of Travelling communities have been recorded as likely to experience poor dental and optical care, potentially leading to conditions that impact on a sense of 'wellness' and quality of life or, in the case of untreated eye defects, permanent disability.

As with a range of other medical conditions, the effects of frequent movement and lack of contact with health services inevitably impact on Travellers' ability to access opticians and dentists. The decline in NHS dentists has been widely recognised across Britain,[69] and even where a family has access to a secure site or other accommodation, it may prove problematic to register with a dental surgery and obtain affordable care. For individuals who are highly mobile, and particularly if they are unable to afford to pay private dental fees, the costs of routine treatment may prove prohibitive, leading to neglect of oral health until such time as serious difficulties have accrued.[70] A survey of dental health amongst Travellers in Hertfordshire[71] carried out in 1996, found that 'Travellers in the study had a high level of unmet need, low dental registration and very little use of preventative services ... there is inequity of dental health and dental service use with more disadvantage being experienced by Travellers on unauthorised and transit sites'. In the experience of health workers and planning consultants who routinely enquire as to the health needs of clients, little has changed in the intervening years since this study was undertaken. Often children are unable to receive preventative or orthodontic care leading to a high rate of cavities, tooth loss and subsequent long-term dental and oral-health problems in adulthood. In severe cases, not only may individuals suffer from extreme self-consciousness as a result of untreated dental problems and the appearance of their teeth and jaw shape, but teeth may be removed on an emergency basis to provide alleviation from pain or to help with speech or eating difficulties. Once again, the impact of a sometimes inadequate diet, or a tendency *not* to limit children's intake of sweets and sweetened drinks, inevitably has an effect on oral health amongst Travelling communities. However, the predominant factor in the typically poor dental health experienced by Gypsies and Travellers remains (as always) lack of access to suitable facilities and clear information provided in an accessible format.

Although we are not aware of any research that considers access to optical care amongst Travelling communities, it is likely that the factors noted above have a significant impact on access to regular eye-care screening. Given the prevalence of diabetes amongst the Gypsy and Traveller communities it is critically important that regular opticians' appointments are available to members of the communities, as eye 'checks' often reveal health problems before other symptoms are noted. The side effects of diabetes can include blindness and therefore it would appear self-evident that Gypsies and Travellers are perhaps more at risk of poor eyesight than many other communities who are more able to access regular optical care.

In the experience of the authors, few Gypsies and Travellers wear glasses and although it is unclear whether this is due to a cultural reluctance to attend an optician (as suggested by one report)[72] coupled with a fatalistic acceptance of possibly inheritable[73] eye conditions, or relates purely to lack of access to services and accessible information on the importance of regular eye tests, the fact remains that many individuals are at risk of developing blindness (e.g. through glaucoma or diabetes) or poor eyesight that may severely limit their daily activities, as well as potentially placing them in breach of the law through driving with uncorrected vision. If an individual is found to have a serious visual impairment, not only may unsited Travellers experience difficulties in remaining in one place for long enough to receive treatment (e.g. hospital appointments, etc.), but even on authorised sites, the presence of equipment and vehicles, or rutted or poor quality hard-standing, inevitably creates an environment where partially sighted individuals are at increased risk of falls or accidental injury (see above on environmental factors). Finally, for children with uncorrected visual impairments, school work (where they have access to an educational establishment) as well as other daily activities can be considerably more difficult, leading to increased disillusionment with learning processes, problems with concentration or the risk of rebuke from teachers for 'not taking notice'.

Some examples of good practice in Traveller health care

Throughout this chapter we have consistently suggested that the key to provision of good quality and culturally appropriate services for Gypsies and Travellers is to work in partnership with members of the community, and to ensure that facilities offered can be *accessed* by Travellers.

We have therefore included some examples of good practice undertaken by various health teams in Britain:

- Specialist health workers, usually a health visitor who is able to ensure continuity of care for Travellers in a relatively large area by working across boundaries, and with the ability to refer patients for services, even if they are located in a different PCT. See below on NAHWT.
- Health-worker intervention with local GP practices to ensure that Travellers are able to register for primary health care. Development of links with specific GP practices who are flexible enough to meet Travellers' needs (see below on Herefordshire Traveller Health Project).
- Sure Start: several areas with Sure Start schemes[74] have now made sure that Travellers are included within service delivery and are ensuring adequate provision of extra services for under four-year-olds through the process of actively seeking views of Gypsy and Traveller parents in those localities.

- Flexible service delivery, for example, same-day appointments and drop-in clinics (see also above on walk-in NHS clinics).
- Cultural-awareness training for health staff (including receptionists) to reduce discrimination and prejudice and minimise 'assumptions', for example, that a patient will be resident at a particular location in a few days' time, or will be able to read instructions on medication, etc.
- Peer mentoring: providing training for Travellers and Gypsies to attend at appointments or liaising with medical staff on behalf of other Travellers, ensuring that culturally appropriate and accessible information is available to Travellers who are willing to act as mentors and to share their knowledge among their community.
- Community Mothers scheme (predominantly based in Ireland): the programme[75] is based upon a recognition that some parents seek social support from other parents, rather than professionals. Community mothers are experienced local mothers living in disadvantaged areas. They have unique and informal access to parents during the first year of parenthood, through monthly home visits and parent-led support groups. Although some projects exist in the UK, it is uncertain how greatly Gypsy and Traveller mothers have been targeted, or to what extent the service would be required amongst the Travelling communities. In Ireland, a number of projects work extensively with Traveller women.[76]
- Primary Health Care for Travellers Project (Ireland): although we are unaware of such a scheme in mainland UK, we would commend these projects based upon an original model developed by Pavee Point[77] that have now spread to all areas of Ireland. The basis of the concept is training Travellers as community health workers who can then disseminate information in a culturally appropriate manner to members of their community. We look forward to seeing similar developments in Britain.
- Provision of audio and CD/DVD information on common health problems and how Travellers can access services.
- Outreach medical and dental care (for example, the Herefordshire mobile dental unit and GP bus that attend at sites).
- The NAHWT, a special-interest group comprising members of the Community Practitioners' and Health Visitors' Association: information sharing, involvement in research and good practice

Gypsy and Traveller
women making the
Health Banner
(courtesy of Friends,
Families and
Travellers Women's
Health Project)

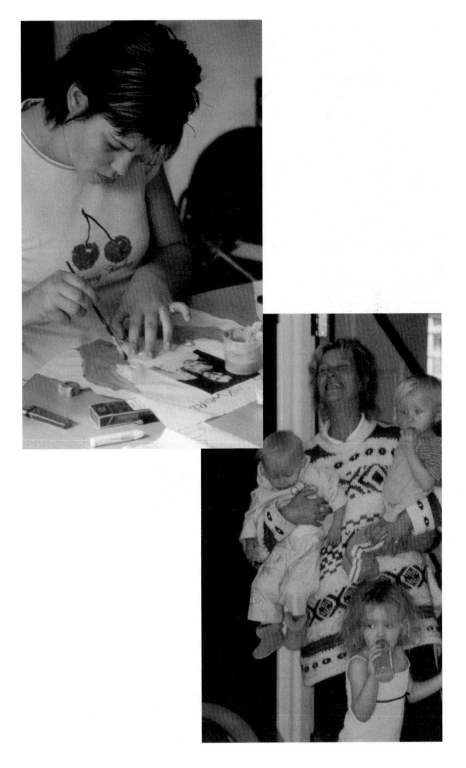

The finished Health Banner (courtesy of Friends, Families and Travellers'
Women's Health Project)

advice for health- and social-care staff working with Gypsies and
Travellers <http://www.msfcphva.org/sigs/sigtravellers.html>.

We welcome further suggestions from readers for inclusion into 'good
practice' updates.

Further research

At present a number of exciting large-scale health studies are being
undertaken in partnership with Gypsy and Traveller communities

aimed at exploring the extent of unmet health needs and the specialist services or outreach work that is required to enable Travellers to utilise their right to access health care. Although some of the studies will not be completed or published for some months or years, in conclusion to this chapter, we summarise the key research initiatives of which we are aware.

ScHARR: the health status of Gypsies and Travellers in England

Since the time this chapter was initially written (summer 2004), the first national study of Gypsy and Traveller health (carried out between 2002 and 2004) has been published.[78] The research, carried out by a team of leading health professionals and academics, was funded by the Department of Health under their 'Inequalities' programme and comprised a large-scale survey as well as qualitative interviews with Gypsies and Travellers from a range of ethnicities to explore major health difficulties experienced by the communities (e.g. stroke, heart disease, smoking, etc.), access to services, attitudes to the use of health services, availability of culturally appropriate information and (particularly importantly) how Travellers' health problems and needs compared to other non-Traveller communities. In a determined attempt to assess the extent of the inequalities experienced by Travellers (whether living on authorised or unauthorised sites or in housing) the team 'matched' every Traveller interviewee (by age and sex) with a comparative sample. The non-Traveller sample was drawn from White British *gorje* (both rural and urban and of low as well as average socio-economic status), Pakistani, and Black Caribbean British communities.

A series of follow-up qualitative (in-depth, one-to-one) interviews was also undertaken, giving Gypsies and Travellers an opportunity to discuss their own health needs and attitudes and experiences of accessing medical services. While key findings from this study were perhaps largely unsurprising given the results of localised projects and anecdotal knowledge of the inequalities experienced by Traveller communities, for the first time, major, rigorously undertaken research, funded by a government department, has confirmed the suspicions of all those who work closely with Travellers: that 'Gypsy Travellers have significantly poorer health status and significantly more self-reported symptoms of ill-health than other UK-resident, English speaking ethnic minorities and economically disadvantaged white UK residents' (ScHARR [2004] Executive Summary, p. 6).

Other key findings from the study include:

- Gypsy Travellers have poorer health than their age- and sex-matched comparators.
- Chest pain, respiratory problems and arthritis are more common amongst Travellers.
- Living in a house is associated for Gypsy Travellers with long-term illness, poorer health status and anxiety.
- Gypsy Travellers are between two and five times more likely to have health problems than the general UK population.
- Gypsy Travellers were likely to experience an excessively high rate of miscarriage, stillbirth and premature death of children.
- Accommodation (including access to good quality sites and a healthy environment) was mentioned by every respondent as the key to meeting their health needs.
- Barriers were identified in communication between health staff and Gypsy Travellers.
- Fear of a negative diagnosis may lead to a delay in seeking screening and ultimately treatment for certain conditions, for example, cancer.
- Rates of smoking and depression were high amongst Gypsy Travellers.

Maternity Alliance research

As a follow-up to their 1990 publication *Traveller Mothers and Babies: Who Cares for Their Health?*, in 2003 the Maternity Alliance commenced a new three-year study into the care offered to pregnant and recently delivered Traveller women, with the intention of highlighting need and raising awareness of good practice amongst health- and social-care professionals. Although no results have yet been published, the researchers are working closely with the NAHWT, and have accessed funding from both privately charitable foundations and the Department of Health. The first stage of the project has involved consulting with Gypsy and Traveller women on their experiences and concerns about the service they received while pregnant, talking to Travellers living on unauthorised and authorised

A BETTER ROAD

AN INFORMATION BOOKLET
FOR HEALTH CARE
&
OTHER PROFESSIONALS

This booklet has been produced by Derbyshire Gypsy Liaison Group in
collaboration with the Derbyshire Traveller Issues Working Group

Derbyshire Gypsy Liaison Group and Derbyshire Traveller Issues Working
Group information booklet (courtesy of Margaret Greenfields)

sites and in housing about attitudes to pregnancy, childbirth and
parenthood, and speaking to health professionals about their
perceptions of current maternity services provision and what could be
improved to best meet the needs of Gypsy and Traveller families. The
project will end in 2006.

Sheffield Adult Mental Health Collaborative Research Group

A certain degree of overlap exists between the team working on this study of Gypsy and Traveller mental health support needs and the staff who carried out the inequalities survey referred to above. The research into 'meeting the mental health needs of Gypsies and Travellers and facilitating access to appropriate support' (undated briefing note/information leaflet on research, T. Hagan et al.) has been developed as a result of the findings that depression is fairly common amongst Travellers, particularly those who are living in houses or unable to travel regularly.

The research has been developed to explore the prevalence of depression and other mental health issues amongst the Gypsy Traveller communities in Sheffield, and to examine the experiences of Travellers in accessing services. Based upon these experiences of Travellers who have been through mental health difficulties and who have agreed to take part in in-depth interviews and focus groups, the team will develop a package to assist health workers in overcoming barriers when working with Traveller communities and developing appropriate support mechanisms and information for Gypsy and Traveller people. To date only one publication has been produced,[79] which outlines the findings from focus groups with socially excluded Gypsy and Traveller women. Concepts of powerlessness, unemployment and lack of adequate space or privacy proved important to the analysis and it would appear that existing psychological services are little used amongst this community. The authors concluded that:

> it is clear to them that it is the practical difficulties in their life that are the origin of their unhappiness and discussing these with a mental health worker is not going to change this. The participants in this study adopted strategies to maximise the resources they have ... [however] it is clear that any significant improvement in their lives will need to address of distal powers over which they have no control which results in deprivation and thus distress.   Appleton et al. (2003: 45)

Although we have only been able to list certain good practice initiatives and forthcoming research projects within this chapter, we welcome receiving information from readers and health professionals about projects of which we may not be aware.

CHAPTER EIGHT

Education
Colin Clark

Travellers from Star Hill present tutor with bouquet on successful completion of IT course (courtesy of Sam Wilson)

Introduction

This chapter shows that many Gypsies and Travellers across Britain are being denied access to relevant education and mainstream schooling in a number of different ways. This denial, although certainly not formalised in the policy language of 'equal opportunities', is manifested in practice at many levels of the education system across Britain. This is not a recent development as many official reports from England, Wales and Scotland have identified, to varying degrees, Gypsy and Traveller education as an area of concern and a site for appropriate government intervention. The Office for Standards in Education (OFSTED), the HM Inspectorate of schools and local education authorities (LEAs) in England and Wales in whose 1999 report, for example, identified 'Gypsy and Traveller pupils as the group most at risk in the education system today.'[1] Likewise, the influential Parekh Report on *The Future of Multi-Ethnic Britain* (2000) noted the 'generally low [educational] attainment' of Gypsy and Traveller children and suggested that this was 'a matter of serious concern.'[2] Such 'concerns', however, have long been highlighted in the literature and in government circles. In 1967, for example, the famous Plowden Report stated that Gypsies and Travellers are 'probably the most deprived group in the country'.[3] What has changed since this time? For one thing, devolution has had a profound impact on social and public policies across Britain. Certainly, since the passing of the Scotland Act in 1998, and the convening of the Scottish Parliament and Executive a year later, it has been apparent that devolution has allowed for some substance to be given to once abstract notions of social justice and social inclusion. A good example of this in the 'race' equality field has been the efforts put into the 'One Scotland, Many Cultures' initiative since 2002. Similar moves have happened in Wales at the behest of the Assembly. However, it is also clear that this argument regarding the supposed 'liberating' aspects of devolution vis-à-vis progressive policy reforms can sometimes be overstated. It is noted that although there are important institutional and implementation differences in social policies between London, Cardiff and Edinburgh, there are still many more similarities and, crucially, the social relations that lie at the heart of all this do not seem to differ much across supposed national borders.[4]

History and contexts

Tracing the history of Gypsy and Traveller education in Britain is a lengthy and problematic affair, and it is difficult to fully explore and analyse this history across the three countries under discussion, in the space restrictions of this chapter. While some distinguished commentators, such as Mary Waterson, have attempted to chart such a history, even this detailed and lengthy study was concerned only with England.[5] Likewise, Sandra Clay has investigated Traveller education in one part of Wales and, as part of that micro-study, has commented more broadly on the development of Traveller education in that particular country.[6] In Scotland, the influential work of the Scottish Traveller Education Project (STEP), based at the University of Edinburgh, stands out in this regard and it has produced a wealth of valuable data on the Scottish Gypsy/Traveller pupil experience of public education in this country.[7]

In England, individual LEAs, supported by central government, began setting up Traveller Education Services (TESs) in the 1970s. In Wales, there is only one main TES that is based in Cardiff, although other less well-funded services operate out of Swansea, Wrexham and Flintshire (so, in effect, four services operate). Scotland operates quite different services with regard to Gypsy and Traveller education and these will be discussed in due course.

As no 'area pool' money was centrally provided, not all local authorities in England and Wales have TESs. At the time of writing, there are specialist teams of teachers for Gypsies and Travellers in over 100 LEAs in England and Wales.[8] Typically, a Traveller education team consists of various specialist support staff, such as peripatetic and school-based staff who can work on-site or in school. Although TESs have a direct input into the teaching of Gypsy and Traveller students, they are principally there as an additional resource which schools can call upon to help them carry out their responsibilities. For example, TESs help to find school places for Gypsy and Traveller children, and they work with each other to provide an 'alerting service', giving advance notice to each other of likely Gypsy and Traveller arrivals. They may supervise the use of distance-learning materials and can also provide general back-up support. TESs also support schools who accept Gypsy and Traveller students, seeking to provide a degree of continuity of education by liaising with other TESs in areas where the children have been previously.[9] The policy emphasis in England and Wales has shifted from separate provision to mainstream access. This is also, largely, the case in Scotland although across all three countries there are still some parents who feel that on-site education may be of more benefit to their sons and daughters. Although outside the remit of this chapter, it is worth pointing out the fact that in Belfast, Northern Ireland, there is a separate school for Traveller children, St Mary's (formerly St Paul's) School for Travelling Children. There are no examples of such segregated schooling provision in England, Wales or Scotland. For TESs, however, the aim is to work in *partnership* with the mainstream staff to enable them to meet the needs of Gypsy and Traveller pupils as and when it is required.

Some TES teams also have a youth and community development worker and classroom assistants. In addition there are education welfare officers and home/school liaison officers whose job is to ensure the education system serves the needs of Traveller children as effectively as possible. This is done through visits and contacts between home and school and by supporting the work of the education welfare service and other departments such as in the local authority. Home visits aim to encourage the family to send their children to school, giving advice and help with forms for free school meals and uniform grants, attendance issues, problems with bullying, exclusions and transport difficulties amongst many others. School visits are often linked to the above but also include: taking Traveller children to be registered and enrolled, gathering attendance figures, improving attainment, teaching support and the provision of in-service training.

Site stability is often seen as a relevant factor in parents deciding whether or not to send children to mainstream school. Some families make use of services provided by non-statutory organisations such as the Travellers' School Charity (TSC) for advice and support in educating their children. It is evident that TESs in England appear to have mixed experiences of working with New Traveller families. Some TESs have substantial experience of supporting New Traveller children and see it as an important aspect of their work, particularly true in the south-east and west of England. Others, however, have not worked with New Travellers, giving the reason that there are few families residing in their area, this being especially true in the north of England. A few TESs have noted that New Travellers tend to opt for 'home education', thus falling outside of their remit, as the Auckland (2000)[10] study has reported.

Section 210 of the Education Reform Act 1988 was replaced by Section 488 of the Education Act (1996). The Section 488 Specific Grant for Traveller Education offered a specific grant to local authorities from central government, which principally funded the TES network across England and Wales. The primary aim of this grant was to promote unhindered access to, and full integration into, mainstream education. This grant was merged in April 2000 with the

TSC teachers' workshop. Arthur Ivatts (HMI) and the reporter from *TES* talking with those running the TSC programme in 1997 (photograph by Alan Dearling)

grant for other minority ethnic achievement, namely, the Ethnic Minority Achievement Grant (EMAG). It then became the Ethnic Minority and Traveller Achievement Grant (EMTAG), falling within the then DfEE (Department for Education and Employment) Standards Fund. In 1999/2000 the grant supported a total expenditure of £13.7 million for England.[11] This was allocated within a framework of a competitive bidding process with local projects being planned for three-year periods at a time. The EMTAG was targeted specifically at raising the achievement of ethnic minority and Gypsy and Traveller pupils, including pupils for whom English is not their first language. Some saw the formation of the new EMTAG grant as having negative implications for Gypsies and Travellers. Friends, Families and Travellers (FFT), for example, argued that the grant meant less money was specifically available for Gypsy and Traveller education. Second, by being subsumed into a broader funding category, it reinforced the view that Gypsy and Traveller education was a 'non-priority'.[12] Funding has changed again, more recently, and this is discussed below in the form of the Vulnerable Children Grant (VCG).

According to the then Schools Minister, Jacqui Smith, LEAs received £162.5 million for 2000–1. However, this was to help raise the educational achievement of ethnic minority pupils, more generally, as well as Gypsy and Traveller children. From April 2001, the EMTAG was separated back into two separate grants creating a new Traveller Achievement Grant (TAG) (still within the then DfEE Standards Fund). From April 2002, this grant moved away from competitive bidding to a formula-based grant, although this will not entail more funds.

It is apparent that the then DfEE contributions to TES funding were steadily being reduced during the late 1990s and individual TES projects felt the pinch. From April 2000 they have been 58 per cent (originally they used to be 75 per cent), matched by a contribution of 42 per cent by the LEAs. In addition to this grant, there is also a development fund, set up in 1998, which aimed to meet with innovative approaches towards Traveller education needs. Local authorities were invited to bid competitively for grants from this fund. The areas prioritised in this fund were: transfer to and retention at secondary level, early years' provision and access to new educational opportunities. The DfEE defined the latter as the provision of 'work-related' (i.e. vocational) learning for all Traveller children who desire it at Key Stage 4. The National Association of Teachers of Travellers (NATT) was critical of this competitive element to funding, however, seeing it as undermining continued and sustained funding for the education of Gypsy and Traveller children.[13]

The collection and analysis of data of ethnic minority pupil performance is another area of policy development that has implications for Gypsy and Traveller education. Such 'ethnic monitoring' analysis is becoming recognised as a key management tool by an increasing number of schools as they look to improve their 'league table' performance. The 1999 OFSTED Report noted that *all* the primary schools surveyed with Gypsy Traveller pupils had supplied their LEA with national-curriculum attainment information, as required by Section 488 funding.[14] This information was necessary as part of the annual report which each LEA was required to supply to the then DfEE at the end of each grant year. For no explained reason, annual reports were not requested for 1999/2000 or for 2000/1.

As of 2004, the TES service was placed within the school improvement team of LEAs. The funding is centrally managed through the VCG that was introduced in April 2003 to ensure that school-aged Gypsy and Traveller children receive their full entitlement to education.[15] The funding extends to include from infancy to the age of nineteen, which is seen to encourage further and higher education take-up. Schools in England and Wales receive funding for Gypsy and Traveller children in the same way as for other pupils on their roll. In addition, where LEAs and schools are faced with significant financial burdens in responding to the particular educational needs of Gypsy or Traveller children, they may benefit from additional funding, the TAG part of the Standards Fund. From April 2003, the TAG merged with a number of other small grants to form the VCG, also part of the Standards Fund. The VCG is worth £84 million, which represents a substantial increase on the grants it replaced, which totalled £31 million in 2002. The VCG, it is argued, not only allows more services to be provided but also gives the opportunity for LEAs to allocate funding based on local needs and practices and to provide coherent support across the different groups of vulnerable children.[16] Practical examples of how the VCG has supported the inclusive education of Gypsy and Traveller children have been highlighted by the Department for Education and Skills (DfES) in a working paper from April 2003 and include factors such as: a welcoming ethos at the school, support with homework, a 'safe area' for pupils to go when they are troubled within the school and a positive intercultural curriculum.[17]

A recent government initiative in the area of Information and Communication Technology (ICT) and multimedia resources for pupils has had an impact on Gypsy and Traveller education and this is worth noting. Sections of DfES funding (via Standards Fund Grant 31c) now go via LEAs to individual schools for Electronic Learning Credits (ELCs). These need to be spent on multimedia resources, either at a school level or by individual staff. LEAs have allocated £100 million of ELCs to schools this academic year (2004/5). This is in addition to the Standards Fund ICT in Schools grant and TESs can apply so that Gypsy and Traveller children can benefit from the use of ICT.

It is widely accepted that schools themselves can have a vital role to play in promoting access and raising achievement for Gypsy and Traveller pupils. Effective and monitored 'race' equality and equal opportunities policies are generally seen as important and should specifically mention Gypsy and Traveller children and their educational needs, in order to establish an inclusive ethos in the school (a point raised by Smith [1997] as well[18]). Crucially, the DfEE (2000) report argues that where the commitment of senior managers and school governors to an inclusive ethos and equal opportunities is *matched* by high teacher expectations and the inclusion of Traveller issues in the curriculum, Gypsy and Traveller children can share in the Government's drive to raise standards for all. The most important finding, according to the authors, is that the way schools handle the initial induction process can greatly impact on future attendance and achievement of Gypsy and Traveller children in the school classroom. This is a factor that seems to be endorsed by many Gypsy and Traveller parents across Britain.

The 'Sure Start' programmes introduced initially in England, Wales and Scotland and then later Northern Ireland aim at improving the health and education status of newborns to three-year-olds by activities targeted at children and families.[19] Sure Start has implications for Gypsy and Traveller education in that it does not exclude them per se – indeed there are a few local programmes in all three countries that at least have Gypsy and Traveller elements to them. In Hackney, for example, the Dalston and Queenbridge Sure Start project supports Gypsy and Traveller projects, including a childminding network.[20]

It should be noted at this point that the Race Relations Act (RRA) (1976, amended 2000) has helped increase the focus on monitoring discrimination in service provision with respect to Gypsy and Traveller education. For example, OFSTED, with support from the Home Office, has been undertaking the systematic collection and analysis of minority performance data. Likewise, the setting up of the Advisory Group on Raising Ethnic Minority Pupil Achievement (AGREMPA) by the former Conservative Government has also helped to bring issues of performance, achievement and barriers to a successful education into the spotlight. AGREMPA covered England, Wales and Scotland. At that time there was a Gypsy and Traveller representative on the group but no one person specifically from a professional Traveller education background.

In terms of the general policy framework in Scotland, it should be noted that the Caravan Sites Act of 1968, which led to the creation of local authority sites, only ever applied to England and Wales. This is due to Scotland having a quite separate legal system and to the fact that, in many areas, separate legislation applies to the country, especially following devolution in the late 1990s. Regarding Scotland, in place of the clearer statutory framework that existed under the 1968 Act, the Scottish Office, in 1971, established an Advisory Committee on Scotland's Travelling people (as discussed earlier) which was renewed at intervals for three-year periods. The membership of the committee included some limited representation of Gypsy-Travellers. The ninth of its regular reports, covering the period 1998–9, was completed and published in 2000 and the Scottish Executive, as mentioned earlier in this book, felt that the work of the advisory committee was complete it looked to mainstream equality measures.[21]

In Scotland, prior to the last decade, there was only ever very limited governmental guidance or publications on Gypsies and Travellers. The most significant was a guidance letter issued by the Scottish Education Department in April 1989. This offered guidelines on how to support Gypsies and Travellers in respect of education. It was largely based on the English model and experience and outlined topics such as the integration of schooling, teaching support, teacher liaison, secondary education and community education. Regarding education, there is no special grant for Gypsy and Traveller education in Scotland as exists in England and Wales. Funding is instead allocated within the overall framework of funding provided for local authorities. As a consequence, there are fewer than ten whole-time equivalent staff employed in education departments in five of the twenty-nine authorities who work directly with Gypsies and Travellers.[22] Other recent developments in Scotland do show some signs for optimism and a potential for access to the decision-making process. Many Gypsies and Travellers had high expectations of the 2001 Equal Opportunities Committee (EOC) inquiry, hoping that it would provide a mechanism through which the discrimination faced by Gypsies and Travellers could be recognised and discussed. Members of the EOC visited a number of sites throughout Scotland and spoke directly with residents. The Social Inclusion Unit in Scotland also potentially offers a route to discuss Gypsy and Traveller education needs with the Scottish Parliament and Executive.[23]

As discussed above, like in England, TESs have developed in Wales although much more slowly and in much smaller numbers. There are four TESs overall, Cardiff (by far the most established and effective due to size and funding), Wrexham, Swansea and Flintshire. However, there are at least a dozen 'projects' operating at the moment (as of 2004). The transfer of powers to the National Assembly for Wales impacts directly on the development of education policy, which now falls within the remit of the Assembly.[24] In Wales there is no unit dedicated to social exclusion as such. There is, however, a national assembly minister responsible for social inclusion, who (at the time of writing) is Edwina Hart, Minister for Finance and Communities. Like Scotland, Wales has chosen to focus on social inclusion rather than exclusion, and again like Scotland, the Minister may be able to have some say in new directions in Gypsy and Traveller education, if lobbied successfully by the various bodies interested in Welsh Gypsy and Traveller education.

Access and attendance

During the past three decades there have undoubtedly been, with varying degrees of success in different parts of Britain, improved rates of attendance at schools for Gypsy and Traveller children. This is due to a range of factors that will be outlined below. Most LEAs in England and Wales collect data on the number of Gypsy and Traveller children and their attendance at school. Most of this data is collected and reported to the DfES on an annual basis. OFSTED, in 2003, estimated there were at least 70,000–80,000 school-age Gypsy and Traveller children in England and Wales but commented that participation rates were relatively low – 84 per cent at Key Stage 2 and 47 per cent at Key Stage 4.[25] The DfES has undertaken research recently (2003–4) to look at Key Stages 3 and 4 and examine why drop-out rates rose during this period.[26] Official evidence collated by the then DfEE (during 1997–8) records 28,000 school-aged Traveller children identified by TESs.[27] The same report suggests a further 8,500 additional children in the newborn to five-year-old age range. Since 1990, with the introduction of the New Specific Grant (Section 488) and the requirement to complete an annual report for the then DfEE by all LEAs in receipt of a grant, the number of identified Gypsy and Traveller children has maintained a year-on-year increase. Between 1996/7 and 1997/8, the increase reported by the then DfEE was 7 per cent. The factors behind this annual increase are unclear. Two possible influences are thought to relate to the normal demographic increase predicted of communities with an above average percentage of persons below the age of fifteen years, and the 'willingness of disclosure' effect in which Gypsy and Traveller families may be more willing to disclose their 'presence' because of the growing level of trust between the community and the local TESs.[28]

However, an earlier report from 1996 gave a different picture to this one.[29] The OFSTED report estimated that the total size of the nomadic communities in England at that time was in the region of 90,000 (with some 50,000 school-aged children). Gypsy and Traveller numbers were thought to account for 70,000 of this total. Estelle Morris, while a minister at the then DfEE, estimated the total number to be nearer to 150,000.[30] Some progress has also been made in improving attendance and achievement among Gypsy and Traveller children of secondary age although it is still estimated that around 12,000 secondary age children are not registered at any school in England.[31] A recent study by Derrington and Kendall (2004) found that whether a Gypsy or Traveller child lives in a house or on the roadside, their engagement in secondary education can be equally precarious. Whilst this study has shown that positive developments are being made in terms of increasing numbers of Traveller students transferring to secondary school and being retained in Key Stage 3, a worrying number are still not being retained. Furthermore, evidence from the study confirmed that Traveller students continue to under-achieve, are disproportionately excluded and are likely to encounter racism at school.[32]

Similarly, in Scotland, Save the Children estimated that approximately 20 per cent of those Gypsy and Traveller children of secondary-school age attended with any degree of regularity.[33] More recent research from Scotland has also highlighted the fact that Gypsy and Traveller children's exclusion from school may be even higher than these figures suggest in the more remote parts of that country.[34] This is likely to be the case in the remoter parts of England and Wales as well.

Whilst it is important to acknowledge the positive work carried out by statutory and voluntary organisations, including the NATT, the official response to Gypsy and Traveller education, as illustrated above, tends to focus on enrolment and attendance rates rather than the actual *quality* of education received while attending. This is illustrated, for example, in the targets set for England by the then DfEE back in March 1999:[35]

- 100 per cent of four-year-old Traveller children, whose parents want one, to have a nursery place;
- 25 per cent of eleven-year-old Travellers in school to reach national expectations at Level 4 in literacy by 2002 – up from 10 per cent;
- a 40 per cent increase in the number of Traveller children successfully enrolled in secondary schools;
- all Key Stage 4 Travellers who want access to a work-related curriculum, to do so (this is recognition of the different priorities required for Gypsies and Travellers);
- a 30 per cent increase in the number of Travellers participating in further education.

One attempt at incorporating the different needs of Gypsy and Traveller communities was the special provision of dual registration introduced for Gypsies and Travellers in England in January 1998. Parents are able to inform the main school that their child would be away for a certain period, but that they intended to return. Regulation 9(1)(b) (registration at another school) and (g) (absence in excess of four weeks) no longer require the pupil to be removed from the base school's register. Also legislation (passed in September 2001) aimed at limiting infant class sizes to no more than thirty pupils will not always have to apply if a child wishes to register with a class already at its limit outside of normal admission times.

As is the case for all parents across Britain, Gypsy and Traveller parents whose children do not attend school are at risk of enforcement actions and legal prosecution. It is normally seen as a last resort when all other forms of support have been tried. Although many see this 'last resort' as a highly negative approach for encouraging attendance, it has been observed by some organisations as effective in some instances. Save the Children in Wales and the School of Education, University of Wales, for example, in their joint 1998 report *Traveller Children and Educational Need*, noted that prosecutions in Cardiff for non-registration and non-attendance did lead to improvements in attendance rates without unduly affecting the healthy rapport between Gypsies and Travellers and the TES.[36] But what reasons do Gypsy and Traveller parents have for not sending their children to school? To answer this question we need to look at what goes on inside schools: what is taught and broader issues regarding the culture of schooling.

Curriculum issues

For many Gypsy and Traveller children and adults it appears to be the case that the present school system is not meeting their needs, especially at the secondary-level stage. Many parents, when questioned, are largely happy with primary schools and the curriculum and culture they adopt. At the secondary level, however, it can be quite a different story and many parents have real concerns about bullying, in particular, as well as social and moral issues (such as boys and girls mixing freely with one another, sex-education classes, the potential availability of illegal drugs, etc.).[37] However, regarding the curriculum, it is still the case that a school-based education is often perceived as being largely irrelevant, at least above a certain age, and is regarded as not telling children anything that they either need to know or would want to know. At this juncture it is important then to examine the processes behind the development of the curriculum and what inputs are being made into this by Gypsies and Travellers of all ages. It seems, to date, that little effective input is being made for a variety of reasons. It should be noted that not all these reasons are to do with so-called 'cultural' factors of Gypsies and Travellers themselves. It can be much more to do with rigid and inflexible structures of the education system itself – especially via the national curriculum in England and Wales – and the organisation of the consultation process.

Attempts have been made in recent years to ensure curriculum development in the general area of 'minority' education. For example, the general statement on inclusion for the national curriculum in England states that teachers should take specific action to respond to pupils' diverse needs by 'using materials which reflect social and cultural diversity and provide positive images of race'.[38] The Report of the Stephen Lawrence Inquiry (recommendation 67) more specifically stresses that: 'consideration be given to the amendment of the National Curriculum aimed at valuing cultural diversity and preventing racism, in order better to reflect the needs of a diverse society'.[39]

Other general education initiatives in England, however, do not usually take into consideration the needs of Gypsies and Travellers, such as the Education Development Plan. This in spite of attempts by some branch officials to ask LEAs to include Gypsies and Travellers. Other initiatives that on the whole do not deal with Gypsies and

Travellers include Early Years Development Plan, Lifelong Learning
Plan, Literacy Strategy, Numeracy Strategy, Equal Opportunities
Strategy and the Care and Education Plan. There are of course some
exceptions, but these remain few and far between. Ultimately, these
initiatives are all examples of what Rachel Morris has termed the
'invisibility' of Gypsies and Travellers in official discourses and policy
discussion.[40]

It is helpful when explicit statements from the government
reinforce the message that each child has the right to a school place
and that local authorities must provide for all children. This is not
exactly revolutionary, of course, but Gypsies and Travellers may
benefit from provisions that require local authorities to make special
arrangements for the pupil to receive education elsewhere than at an
educational establishment. This could mean, for example, on-site
provision or supported distance-learning.

In August 2000 the Committee on the Elimination of Racial
Discrimination (CERD) published a report entitled *Concluding
Observations Report* on the UK. The Committee noted some positive
developments in terms of formal education, such as recent legislative
measures in the areas of 'race' and human rights and the use of ethnic
monitoring to ascertain numbers according to ethnic group in various
settings. The committee, however, also expressed a number of
concerns regarding admission and access to schools for Gypsies
and Travellers, continued racist bullying in schools and the
disproportionate number of ethnic minorities that continue to be
excluded from schools.[41]

For many Gypsy and Traveller parents, the idea of sending their
children to mainstream schooling is not an attractive one, despite
many valuing education. On the other hand, problems can start
immediately when attempting to get children into schools: they may
simply refuse to take Gypsy and Traveller children on. Instead of
'mainstream' schooling, alternative learning systems have developed
that place the family and Gypsy and Traveller culture at the centre.
There is much evidence of resistance on the part of Gypsies and
Travellers to attend school for a myriad of reasons, such as the
perceived loss of culture and the fear of persecution. However, there
are many Gypsies and Travellers who do want their children to be
educated in school, or at least to have a meaningful choice between
different types of home and school learning.[42]

The National Association of Gypsy Women (NAGW) argues that education for Gypsies and Travellers is more essential than ever, in light of advances made in ICT. They believe that if this generation of Gypsies and Travellers miss out on learning in this area, it will further widen the educational gap between themselves and the majority settled society.

For New Travellers the situation is different in that parents are usually more numerate and literate and may have had a higher level of education (for example, attending university). However, some New Traveller parents tend to view state education as inappropriate to the needs of their children whom they see as 'growing up in a world of crisis'.[43] Many younger New Travellers therefore are home educated, making use of the 'education otherwise' option.[44] However, children of secondary age are more likely than their Gypsy and Traveller counterparts to attend schools, often because the importance of 'paper qualifications' is recognised by parents. This is a complex issue with many different perspectives.

Accommodation and education

When discussing issues of access, attendance and the curriculum, we again have to look at the connection between accommodation and education. It is often assumed that the commercial nomadism of Gypsy and Traveller families can undermine regular school attendance and educational progress. In essence, this translates as cultural difference being regarded as one of the main barriers towards Gypsies and Travellers accessing a school education. It is also argued by some researchers and policy-makers that nomadism can also be 'used' as an 'excuse' to allow Gypsies and Travellers to 'self-exclude' themselves from attending school.[45] Thus, when you place nomadism alongside other aspects of Gypsy and Traveller culture this can lead to supposed inevitable barriers between Gypsy and Traveller children obtaining a school education.[46] However, this is not always the case, as we see below.

Certainly, with *unplanned moves* due to constant evictions, families without a secure pitch on a local authority or private site will have difficulty in accessing regular schooling for their children. Faced with such circumstances, school attendance can be a low priority: lack of school provision near to stopping places, transport difficulties and strict uniform requirements can add to the reasons that deter some parents from sending their children to school. Indeed, the voluntary organisation FFT have recorded numerous enquiries which involve the inability to secure school places due to a lack of adequate site provision.

Common to all those Gypsies and Travellers who do live on stable and secure sites is the question of *where* schooling should take place: on-site provision or attending mainstream schooling or, indeed, 'education otherwise'. This is one aspect of a wider debate about what legitimate choices and options can give children a meaningful education and necessary skills for later life. This part of the debate is linked to issues of 'education otherwise' and has centred on whether provision should be separate, that is, on-site, or integrated in mainstream schools. The current philosophy is that the placing of Gypsies and Travellers in mainstream classes is the most appropriate method. On-site provision is therefore considered a short-term option to enable the child to gain skills, which she or he will need later on in school. It has been described as a 'stepping stone' into school where trust and a respectful relationship can be built up between the local school and Gypsy and Traveller children and parents.[47] This debate is ongoing.

Forms of exclusion

Exclusion from school can take many different forms. Formal exclusion is administered by the school and can be either for a short fixed term or permanent. There is also informal exclusion, which can take the form of self-exclusion, parental exclusion or long-term non-attendance. As noted earlier, the 1996 OFSTED Report notes that there are a disproportionate number of Gypsy and Traveller pupils, particularly at the secondary phase, who are formally excluded from school. This is despite the general assessment by OFSTED that the behaviour of Gypsy and Traveller pupils is 'good'.[48] The report therefore recommends that the whole staff, teaching and non-teaching, should participate in appropriate awareness raising in-service training before Gypsy and Traveller pupils arrive, to enable the school to respond positively and appropriately to their needs. However, it must also be acknowledged that racist bullying is a major factor in exclusion from school. It is not, of course, the only reason but it is a major reason given by Gypsy and Traveller parents and children for withdrawing or not attending school. Other forms of independent home tuition, such as that offered by non-governmental organisations (NGOs) and community projects, are attractive to some parents because of their flexibility and being able to adapt to the specific needs and circumstances of their children. The actual successes and failures of such alternative options vary greatly across the country.

Parents and older brothers and sisters can, and do, have a strong influence in transmitting the 'worth' of a school education. As mentioned earlier, if negative experiences (bullying, for example) or non-attendance (due to social and moral concerns) is the norm within the family and extended family then it will be more likely that younger children will be 'protected' and not attend or attend infrequently. So, there are families who, with regard to education, see a *positive element* in withdrawing from non-Gypsy school-based educational provision. It is an act of resistance, in a symbolic way, and an act of good business sense from an economic perspective. However, as 'times change', as noted above, it seems likely that more mainstream education is being accessed by Gypsy and Traveller children. The issue comes to a head when a school education is seen by Gypsies and Travellers as a route to an independent life whilst at the same time there should be respect for cultural difference within the school setting. This is the square that needs to be circled regarding access. Segregation can take place formally and informally in a number of different ways. Children can be segregated within a classroom, for example, children can be made to sit in a different part of the room away from their classmates. More formally, arrangements can be made to instruct children in separate classrooms, but within the same school, such as, for example, so-called 'special classes'. Finally, entire schools can be established, designed to cater for one particular group, that remain segregated from mainstream schools, such as one school in Belfast (briefly discussed above).

In Scotland there have been reports of segregation both within and outside the classroom at school. For example, it was reported to the Equal Opportunities Committee hearings in May 2000 that a school in Larkhall, which had four Travellers attending, put the Gypsy and Traveller children in a room on their own and gave them a separate part of the playground at breaktimes and lunchtimes.[49] This type of experience does nothing to enhance the attraction of school to Gypsy and Traveller parents. In Wales, research findings into the educational needs of Gypsies and Travellers have also noted that some of the Gypsy and Traveller children included in the study were often seen as 'disrupting' normal classroom life by being 'too loud' and were segregated from other pupils. Many children reported being given a book or some other work and told 'to get on with it' in the corner whilst the rest of the pupils were taught separately.[50] This is a common sentiment and is echoed throughout various parts of Britain.

The limited uptake of places by Gypsy and Traveller young people at the secondary level of schooling is an issue that concerns many educationalists with an interest in the matter. The low figures are at least some reflection of how schools are perceived as being inappropriate to their needs and interests as an ethnic minority group. There are numerous reasons for the low take-up of secondary education. The failure of schools to be adaptable and flexible in this way represents an important issue and is one that not only relates to Gypsy and Traveller pupils, but to many pupils. Although there are examples of TESs in England and Wales working on differentiated education, such initiatives rarely penetrate mainstream schools. There is a tendency in some schools to see the TES as responsible for Gypsy and Traveller pupils and as the 'go-between' with the parents which often means that schools fail to confront the issue directly on their own terms. This is a critical factor in poor communication between parents and the school. Reluctance on the part of schools to accept full responsibility for Gypsy and Traveller children has been noted by DfEE/OFSTED as militating against the development of coordinated action with TESs and other bodies in improving attendance and raising levels of attainment.[51]

Although many schools throughout Britain have written policies for combating racial harassment and promoting good 'race relations', far fewer appear to actively monitor their implementation or effectiveness.[52] The racist element to bullying can often be dismissed as 'peer teasing' or 'name-calling'. The failure to investigate racist incidents is widespread but has particular ramifications for Gypsies and Travellers. Ultimately, the way racist incidents are treated within the school directly affects the willingness of victims to come forward and this certainly seems to be the case with Gypsy and Traveller pupils. The number of racist incidents reported by Gypsies and Travellers would appear to be considerably less than those reported by other groups although exact data on this is hard to trace. In one London borough, which commissioned a study into the needs of the Traveller community, it was found that Gypsy and Traveller parents were experiencing difficulty in registering children once it became known they were from Gypsy and Traveller families. Research carried out for Save the Children in Wales confirms this reluctance to admit Traveller children: 'Those on unauthorised sites report difficulties with obtaining education provision for their children since many local authorities refuse to acknowledge their presence.'[53]

The DfEE/OFSTED 1999 Report noted that teacher expectations of Gypsy and Traveller children when in school are generally unreasonably low.[54] The report stated that although many of the schools 'recognise and celebrate' ethnic diversity, there is considerable hesitancy with regard to Gypsies and Travellers. Racist name-calling and bullying is a problem often experienced by Gypsy and Traveller children once in school, which often goes unchallenged. What also happens, of course, when schools do not perhaps respond as encouragingly as they should to the needs of Gypsy or Traveller pupils (when they are bullied, for example) is that Traveller parents feel justified in withdrawing them. To be clear, so-called 'self-exclusion' can be another factor when examining Gypsy and Traveller non-attendance at both primary and secondary level schooling.[55] Concern has been expressed at both the ground level and at policy level on this issue of Gypsy and Traveller families being denied access to schooling for their children and the outcomes of self-exclusion when negative experiences are felt.

From various testimonies there is a general theme of young Gypsy and Traveller pupils being ignored, not being believed and subjected to harassment and abuse on account of their 'difference': that is, of being Gypsies and Travellers. Likewise, there is a deficiency or 'gap' in the structures and mechanisms which should be encouraging children to challenge or report the racism they are facing at school. This is all the more worrying in light of the supposed 'tightening up' of the systems following the critical findings of the Macpherson Report on institutional racism. Indeed, Save the Children in Scotland have felt it necessary to say that: '[our] experience indicates a lack of perceived awareness or commitment on the part of some schools to take racist issues and prejudices seriously.'[56]

Giving a talk at Leeds University, working for the Traveller Education Service
(from *Gypsies & Travellers in their own words*, courtesy of the Leeds Traveller
Education Service)

Further and higher education

'I've never heard of a Gypsy girl going to college ... no Gypsy goes to
school after the age of thirteen or fourteen. Perhaps one in ten might.'[57]

Unfortunately there is no empirical research to date which has looked
exclusively at how Gypsy and Traveller children experience further
and higher education in Britain.[58] Such a project is long overdue and
is urgently needed. In place of such evidence, we instead have scraps
of anecdotal evidence and personal testimony across the country
obtained from families whose children have either tried to get a place
at college or university or those who have gone on to study at this
level. What also exists is some research at the secondary level of
schooling, and the literature and research on secondary schooling and
Gypsies may provide some clues.[59] For example, one survey from
2001 stated that in the Republic of Ireland there were just thirty-eight
sixth-year Gypsy and Traveller pupils in secondary schools across

the country and just one Traveller enrolled in further education.[60] However, anecdotally, the situation does seem to be improving. Some examples from around the country can be cited – local colleges, when approached directly or via third parties (e.g. Gypsy civil-rights groups or voluntary agencies that work with Travellers), are providing specific courses to meet the needs of the community in their local areas. This has been evident in the central belt of Scotland, the north-east of England and in Cambridgeshire. These courses tend to be vocational in nature (such as welding, building and construction work, car mechanics, nursery nursing, landscape gardening and child care, etc.) or in the arts and humanities field (with a view to access to university). Young Gypsies and Travellers are breaking through into certain professional areas such as the law, journalism, academia, the voluntary sector and town planning. With regard to legal and public administration training, the respected European Roma Rights Centre (ERRC) offers scholarships to students from a Roma/Gypsy or Traveller background study degree courses in such subjects in their own countries at local universities and a few British students have taken up these scholarships.[61]

There is a certain degree of high visibility and attention for those who enter such occupations, but some individuals, for very understandable reasons, do not want to be 'public' and identified as someone from a Gypsy or Traveller background. Prejudice and discrimination can operate in even the most liberal of institutions. Beyond undergraduate studies at university, there are an increasing number of postgraduates who are doing critical work on their own culture and on different topics – again, there is anecdotal evidence of this taking place at Greenwich, Leicester and Durham Universities. There is an important issue here of 'ethnic invisibility'. Unlike many other ethnic minority groups in Britain some Gypsies and Travellers will have an option as to whether they choose to disclose their ethnicity or not. An identifier or clue may well be an address, if living on a caravan site, or a surname and style of appearance, for example, but in terms of physiology and skin colour then there is room for manoeuvre and negotiation. Witness what one female Traveller has said regarding her identity and how it is both presented and received by others within a higher-education setting:[62]

> There are only a few teachers at college who know I'm a Traveller ... it's a hard thing to come out with. If I were to tell other students, some

Childrens' entertainment field at the Big Green Gathering
(photograph by Alan Dearling)

wouldn't speak to me again and some would say 'So?' You just can't tell what their reaction will be, even though, being a Traveller, you come to be a good judge of character.[63]

Institutionally, we would suggest that there is room for improvement in the admissions process and looking closely at the basis of how decisions are made (coincidentally at a time when the Government is also interested in how this is conducted across the higher-education sector). Further, funding mechanisms need to be examined and how the Government-backed partners/widening participation programmes are working or not working with regard to the Gypsy and Traveller populations. Are such valued initiatives stretching to Traveller sites and those sixth-form colleges that may have Traveller students? There is also a role, we would argue, for solid and more proactive careers advice at the secondary-school level that respects the opinions and wishes of both Gypsy and Traveller pupils and parents, whilst also pushing the boundaries of what may be considered a feasible career. Stereotyped ideas of Gypsies and Travellers 'looking after their own' (as is the case for other ethnic minority groups) is not a reason to deny good advice that may make the difference in students at least thinking of applying for a course in further or higher education.

Conclusion

This chapter has drawn on a range of experiences and practices across the three countries of England, Scotland and Wales. It draws out important similarities and differences within Britain. Distinct legal and policy frameworks exist in the three countries and this is especially true when comparing England and Wales with Scotland. However, what this chapter continually demonstrates is that, in spite of different legal and policy frameworks, the actual *disadvantaged experiences* of school and education systems by Gypsy and Traveller children and young people is actually very similar. We have outlined the ways in which public education policies are experienced in Britain by Gypsy and Traveller pupils. Much discussion has focused on the political and cultural context of these policies and illustrated the general policy framework that exists regarding Gypsy and Traveller education, especially in England. It was noted that the education systems across Britain, as with other European countries, are highly politicised and the curriculums are subject to an intense amount of lobbying which sees the 'swinging pendulum' rock back and forth across the shades of the political spectrum. We also briefly examined the situation of Gypsies and Travellers in further- and higher-education sectors and found that much is still to be done in this area when compared to the relative progress that has been made at primary level and, increasingly, at the secondary level as well.

CHAPTER NINE

Nomads and newspapers

Rachel Morris

Introduction

'Journalists often seem to think only in terms of stereotypes: innocent victims, great leaders, evil killers, vicious dictators, tragic children, vengeful wives, love rats. Under this kind of treatment the complexity of life, which is its truth, evaporates almost instantly.'1

I apologise if I have left anyone who hasn't seen a mobile squatter close-up thinking the majority are poverty-stricken and deserving sympathy. For the majority, that image is as far from true as romantic notions of old ladies roasting hedgehogs over open fires while hand-crafting wooden clothes pegs ... They have all the material possessions of Milton Keynes' better heeled residents – except legitimate incomes, VAT numbers, Schedule D numbers, demands for council tax and water rates. Cash in hand is their ONLY style.'2

On 2 July 2005, the 'In Brief' section of the *Guardian* newspaper reported that postal deliveries to a Travellers' site in Essex had been suspended due to a dog attack on a postal worker. No actual injuries were reported. I remembered delivering mail in Brighton, years before, and the countless times I was snarled at, leapt at, and generally terrified, by pet dogs (often after the owner had said, 'Don't mind him, he's harmless'). Why, I thought, should news of a dog attack make the pages of a national newspaper, not least when it seemed insufficiently severe to merit a detailed account? 'Dog bites man' is, famously, not news.

That piece pales in comparison to a campaign mounted on 9 March 2005 by a newspaper from the other end of the press spectrum, *The Sun*. Following an announcement by Deputy Prime Minister John Prescott that local authorities must include Travelling people's needs in housing and planning policies and schemes, *The Sun* urged readers to 'Stamp On the Camps'. It ran a series of front-page articles: the headline on 9 March ran 'Sun War On Gipsy Free-For-All', accusing the Government of sparking 'invasion' by people it represented as being law-breaking, dishonest and parasitic. The newspaper unreservedly quoted an Essex man who described Travelling people as 'animals', and it described a school as being 'swamped' by Traveller children. A 'Comment' piece on page 8 that day stated: 'These people are far removed from the traditional Romany people with their admirable moral code' (thereby distancing the paper from possible accusations of racism).

The National Union of Journalists (NUJ) has over 25,000 UK members, who agree to abide by a Code of Conduct, Clause 10 of which states: 'A journalist shall mention a person's age, sex, race, colour, creed, illegitimacy, disability, marital status, or sexual orientation only if this information is strictly relevant. A journalist shall neither originate nor process material which encourages discrimination, ridicule, prejudice or hatred on any of the above-mentioned grounds'.

The Press Complaints Commission (PCC) – a regulatory body established and operated by representatives of the press itself – also has a code, which counsels against discrimination and suggests the avoidance of prejudicial or pejorative remarks about race and other personal traits and social groupings.

Yet the print media, as I will argue, suggests to readers as a matter of course, through select representations of Travelling people, that as a group they routinely display 'typical' negative characteristics, that is, they are all portrayed through prejudicial stereotypes regardless of individual traits. The relationship of reality to representation is that which exists for any group of people, be they politicians or plumbers. Some Travelling people break the criminal law, some break the civil law, some don't clean up after themselves, some simply annoy. The salient difference being that while some settled people have those characteristics, all other settled people are not assumed also to possess them, but this is generally what is suggested about Travelling people collectively.

Additionally, the press reports on Travelling people where there exists a negative angle – such as the dog attack – but in most other circumstances simply overlooks them and any inequities they may suffer. Thus my argument is twofold: that Travelling people are invisible to the press and settled society until some few are seen as a problem, at which point *all* Travelling people are made highly visible by the press, and in a derisory way.

> 'A journalist is a grumbler, a censurer, a giver of advice, a regent of sovereigns, a tutor of nations. Four hostile newspapers are more to be feared than a thousand bayonets'.[3]

There has been considerable academic debate as to whether there are 'media effects'. One view is that media powers of mass persuasion cannot be proven, and to suggest their existence insults the intelligence of media consumers. '[F]ew social scientists today think that the mass media have the power to sway huge audiences to the extent once believed likely.'[4] But there seems little question that not only do the news media 'largely determine our awareness of the world at large, supplying the major elements for our pictures of the world, they also influence the prominence of those elements in the picture.'[5] The media may not tell us what to believe, but they provide much of the raw material by which our beliefs are created and developed.

Factors influencing the appearance of Travelling people in this raw material include: psychology, the degree to which journalists are informed about actual Travelling people and laws affecting them, the pressure of editorial and public opinion (i.e., whether a simple, complex, balanced or biased viewpoint is deemed acceptable or desirable), the level of input from Travelling people or their allies, and the nature of any influence applied by media regulators and the state. The impact of these on content, and of the resulting press coverage on the lives of Travelling people, are explored below.

> The worst is what the papers say about us. People panic automatically when we first arrive and too much is written in the papers to frighten people against us.[6]

Stereotyping and 'typical' Travelling people

Stereotyping is the product of a standard mental process carried out by all humans and many animals: categorisation. We need to categorise from an early age: which foods do I like or not like? To which people should I respond or not? By dividing people or things into groups based on perceived characteristics and then creating a hierarchy of

Travellers turn rec into toilet

Feelings are running high in Sutton Scotney, near Winchester, as travellers have been accused of turning a recreation ground into a health hazard.

Fourteen caravans are camped illegally on the Gratton recreation ground. Since their arrival nine days ago, the play area has been padlocked shut for "hygienic reasons", after human excrement was found in and around the playbus.

Dirty nappies, faeces and toilet paper have also been left on a riverside footpath and in surrounding woods.

Mother-of-two, Emma van Leest, of Gratton Close, said: "I can't take my kids to the playground any more or walk my dog. I wouldn't mind if the travellers just stayed for two or three days and cleaned up after themselves. But this really is horrible."

Dave Gibbon, also of Gratton Close, said: "People are getting really cross. The playbus is going to have to be disinfected and I don't know how they're going to get rid of the stuff in the grass."

Eagle Star, which owns the recreation ground, served the travellers with a court order evicting them on Tuesday (June 25th.)

Giles Wordsworth, managing agent for the Sutton Scotney estate, said: "I witnessed a child walking into the playbus and defecating. They are using it as a public lavatory."

Mr Wordsworth had hoped to persuade the travellers to leave voluntarily. He said: "The problem with injunctions is that there is a 28-day period before we can call in the bailiffs in to remove them.

"Quite often if they are given 28 days, they will take 28 days."

He said a joint clean-up operation would be mounted with Winchester City Council and the Gratton Trust, which runs the recreation ground.

Meanwhile, a notice has been posted in the children's playground warning youngsters not to play on the bus.

Although the gate to the play area is padlocked, the traveller children, some just toddlers, still play in it, usually unattended by grown-ups.

David Small, chairman of the Gratton Trust, said a cricket match last Saturday had been disrupted.

He is worried about forthcoming events on the recreation ground over the next month, including a church fete at nearby Mill House and the village carnival.

Mr Small said: "We have no protection as ordinary citizens from the law in this country. But the law protects them. It's crazy because if any one of us was caught using the kids' playground as a toilet, we would be prosecuted. It really is as simple as that."

One of the travellers, a young mother, admitted that the group had no toilet facilities, but said her family used the toilet in a nearby garage.

Inspector Mark Wise, of Alresford Police, said the travellers set up camp at Sutton Scotney service station last summer. This site has now been rendered inaccessible with trenches and earth mounds.

"This time, they've got into the heart of the community. I have great concerns about the effects."

But he said there had been relatively few complaints from the public and most of those had been about fouling in the play area.

www.thisishampshire.net

Some of the 14 'vans illegally parked in Sutton Scotney's Gratton Rec F723A *Photographs: Frank Riddle*

No-go area...The children's playbus has been declared out of bounds after excrement was found inside F723C

A negative newspaper article
(courtesy of Sam Wilson)

preferences to which we adapt our behaviour, we find our way around a complex and occasionally dangerous world.

All people belong to groups that can be stereotyped in some way, to positive or negative effect: 'the student', 'the feminist', 'the academic'. Stereotyping, while useful as a means of simplifying complex people or things, can be problematic when used by people to deal with that of which they are afraid and do not understand. As has been stated, a side effect of this process for Travelling people is that some features of their lives are rendered invisible.

> Like fictions, they are created to serve as substitutions, standing in for what is real ... Stereotypes abound when there is a distance. They are an invention, pretence that one knows when the steps that would make real knowing possible cannot be taken or are not allowed.[7]

Adults are experienced enough to know that behind every stereotype is a complex reality, but some find it simpler to leave it unexplored. If everything they read about the object of their fears – from childhood books to newspapers – confirms reductive assumptions, they are encouraged to continue in simplistic and sometimes prejudicial thinking. Prejudice can lead to discrimination, which is more adverse than simple differentiation as it may involve some element of assumption, capriciousness, and denial of rights and services (as can be seen in *The Sun* piece outlined above).

> The mental age of an average adult gypsy is thought to be about that of a child of ten. Gypsies have never accomplished anything of great significance in writing, painting, musical composition, science or social organization. Quarrelsome, quick to anger or laughter, they are unthinkingly but not deliberately cruel. Loving bright colours they are ostentatious and boastful but lack bravery ... They betray little shame, curiosity, surprise or grief and show no solidarity.[8]

Stereotypes stem not just from categorisation but also an evaluation of those being stereotyped. Even if there is some reality in a stereotype, it may apply to one person or a few members in a group but may disproportionately and dramatically disadvantage the whole. Yet stereotypes are difficult to dismantle, as they are deeply rooted in socialisation and thought processes, and their very strength relies on the fact that the features of the stereotyped are assumed to be fixed by nature.

Some stereotypes tie a group to *opposed* images: 'They seem to be represented through sharply opposed, polarized, binary extremes – good/bad, civilized/primitive, ugly/excessively attractive, repelling-because-different/compelling-because-strange-and-exotic. And they are often required to be *both things at the same time!*'[9]

Gypsies are in an unusual position in this respect. A complaint often levelled at them is that they do *not* fit the stereotype carved out for them, that of the 'true' Gypsy. This is then employed to justify denial of their rights and access to goods and services. Again, this process makes the false face chosen for Travelling people by settled people[10] more apparent, while rendering the real and more complex visages imperceptible, and places them in an excluded position where they are less able and likely to prevent the process.[11]

> There is a myth about those people we call travellers. The image we treasure, conditioned by Enid Blyton children's books, is of a gaily-painted, horse-drawn caravan, meandering its way down country lanes.
>
> We tolerate the fact that Mrs Gippo sells heather and clothes pegs door-to-door while Mr Gippo does the odd spot of scrap metal dealing. They add colour, after all, to our sad, grey suburban lives.
>
> The reality of the situation is that these people are nothing but scum ... They content themselves with resurfacing pensioners'

driveways at £1,000 a throw while Cousin Joey slaps a bit of mortar on the chimney pot for another five hundred notes.
      And they steal babies.[12]

The 'true Gypsy' stereotype is the 'positive' branch, whereby they are seen as mysterious, darkly beautiful and sultry, close to nature, bestowing good luck or ill as the mood takes them, wearing plenty of gold jewellery and brightly coloured clothes and scarves, leading a carefree and romantic life which is tantalising for but unattainable by settled people. (In 2005, 'Gypsy' fashions such as sequined slippers and long, wafting skirts were highly in vogue in the UK.)

> The settled population is generally intolerant of contacts and relations with nomads ... The further away the nomad is the better. When the gypsies [sic] are so far away that they verge on myth, they suddenly become alluring: handsome, artistic, living untrammelled lives, symbols of freedom.[13]

As I have come to realise from my interactions with Travelling people, these representations bear no more (and no less) of a relationship with actual Gypsies and Travellers than with settled people. Some are spiritual, some are sultry, few could be described as carefree. But settled people draw on a 'memory' of Gypsies derived from childhood books, operas, nursery rhymes and local anecdote – and some Travelling people know and play on this to obtain respect and advantage – to establish who does and does not constitute a 'real', and therefore marginally more acceptable, Gypsy. It is as if Travelling people are only 'genuine', and therefore 'well-behaved', if they travel by horse and wagon and get warm by a campfire. If they use modern conveniences such as the internal combustion engine they do not match settled people's 'memories', that is, they are no longer 'real' and therefore are 'bad'.

> If Gypsies have expressed ... aspirations, they are charged with having been contaminated by the outside world, and with no longer being 'proper' Gypsies ... When non-Gypsies go from wagon to automobile, it is called progress, when Gypsies do the same thing, it is disappointment.[14]

Many 'memories' of Travelling people, then, consist of another, more 'negative' stereotype. The 'bad' Gypsy survives on wits rather than skill and so necessarily lives outside the mores and laws of settled society, is dirty in person and habits, provides a low standard of goods and services to settled people and then uses nomadism to 'slip the net' of the law, is scrounging and parasitic, living off the scraps and through the loopholes of settled society and taking it for what he or she can get, leaves trails of human and industrial waste behind, is potentially violent, and creates expense and fear by his or her very nature. This belief about the so-called Gypsy character is so firmly held by settled people that 'to gyp' has come to mean 'to be cheated'. (The construct appears to apply to all Travelling people who do not look like the 'good Gypsy' construct, whether or not they are actually Gypsies.)

While binary oppositions may 'have the great value of capturing the diversity of the world within their either/or extremes, they are also a rather crude and reductionist way of establishing meaning'.[15] Put another way, to bluntly divide Gypsies into two 'types' and then punish them for being one and not the other may have developed as a device to combat feelings of fear and ignorance, but it can only lead to an increase in those fears among settled people and between the settled and Travelling communities generally. Arguably, Travelling people have become a socially excluded societal sub-class because they have been placed in that position by another culture that does not fully see and therefore fears them.

> It is recommended that the County adopts a proactive strategy towards all local newspapers … many such newspapers appear obsessed with negative aspects of the gypsy presence. New site proposals are therefore rarely presented in a positive or even a neutral light.[16]

By creating categories into which they expect the world to fit neatly, people create a false and tidy world out of which some things and some other people might step and transgress contrived boundaries. Those things and people must then be stigmatised and discouraged if society is to feel safe and orderly, because they do not fit neatly into society as many would like to see it. These 'others' become both despised and intriguing, humans being drawn to that which is threatening or taboo. This makes them easy subjects for frequent and colourful newspaper coverage.

The role of Travelling people

Travelling people experience exclusion from the process of reportage, in that they are rarely involved as interviewees and next to never as journalists. They are partially visible within media images of them but invisible within and through the process, and therefore a complete picture is usually missing from the outcome. 'Groups that are heavily stereotyped (as "problems") are likely to have less access to influential positions in the media, or to other kinds of power. This can ... mean there may be few images or stories that centre on them sympathetically.'[17]

Prevailing attitudes to Travelling people can put them into positions tallying with the common views, lending a patina of 'truth' and 'objectivity' to press representations. It is easy to sell the 'dirty Gypsy' image when societal dislike of Gypsies forces them to live on the margins of society, under motorways, next to sewage plants and railways, where no one else must live. Problems of access to health, education and stability, over-policing and lack of access to land experienced by some Travelling people are rarely depicted, not least because they are not themselves a part of the reporting process. Their physical and social placement can exclude them from participation in the creation of news stories.

Regarding an audit of local press coverage Liz Fawcett noted that, even in positive pieces, non-Traveller spokespeople were quoted rather than Travelling people themselves. 'I would argue that this pattern of coverage helps to render members of ethnic minorities *invisible* [her italics] to the white community and to give the impression that such individuals are incapable of speaking out for themselves'.[18] So stereotypes are reproduced in a continuous loop.

Groups with little power may experience layers of discrimination in their lives: as they are less likely to become members of the group carrying out stereotyping or labelling, it is difficult for them to counter such representations with other, more complex realities. While it is generally unhelpful to create hierarchies of disadvantage, it is asserted that Travelling people have less power to influence their image in the UK press than other minority ethnic groups, especially as illiteracy is a major issue for their communities.[19] In addition, often Travelling people have moved on or been moved on by the time the local press has printed a story involving their group. Therefore many Travelling people will not see or cannot read the things that are written about them. Not only are they being reduced to simple, negative images, it may be done behind their backs by people who have for the most part never met them.

There are many factors making it unlikely that Travelling people will pursue participation or a profession in the media, perhaps including their fear that a business which so often represents them negatively would make neither a good source of employment nor an appropriate forum or ally for their interests and concerns.[20] This might also explain why newspapers that have previously presented Travelling people unfairly or incompletely, subsequently complain that they refused to be interviewed.[21]

It is a cultural feature of Travelling people that they are reluctant to be seen to speak for more than their immediate group, which could lead to difficulties in encouraging them to assert their viewpoints. Some may therefore only be prepared to comment on other groups, for example, a Gypsy person giving his views on Irish Travellers, which can lead to a deepening of settled society's belief that there are legitimate, 'real' Travelling people, and then there are impostors who are not entitled to any sympathy, understanding or assistance.

The role of news providers

> This paper, and the hundreds of thousands of words it contains, has been produced in about fifteen hours by a group of fallible human beings, working out of cramped offices while trying to find out about what happened in the world, from people who are sometimes reluctant to tell us and, at others, positively obstructive. Its content has been determined by a series of subjective judgements made by reporters and executives, subject to what they know to be the editors' and owners' prejudices. Some stories appear here without essential context as this would make them less dramatic or coherent and some of the language employed has been deliberately chosen for its emotional impact, rather than accuracy.[22]

> A bullet in the head is what they need ... If I were dying of cancer I'd buy a shotgun and take out six of them.'[23]

The press, both tabloids and broadsheets, local and national alike, routinely represents Travelling people in a manner that actively increases dislike of them and their way of life. The local press, in particular, more often than not covers Travelling-related issues in a tone and from a viewpoint which seem deliberately designed to inflame local tensions and damage relations between settled and Travelling communities. I reached this conclusion after monitoring the national press, and as much of the local press as possible, over a two-year period (1999–2001). The press office of the CRE in London operates its own clippings service, and its media-office staff concurred with my findings in private conversations during that time. My research also showed that press regulators do little to redress the situation, and simply cannot be approached by most of the readers who might wish to apply pressure regarding standards of fairness and balance.

> KEEP THIS SCUM OUT (And it IS time to hound 'em, Chief Constable). They call themselves tinkers. Itinerants. New age travellers. We call them parasites. The scum of the earth who live off the backs of others. They contribute nothing but trouble ... They set up filthy, disease-ridden camps on roadsides and in parks and offend every decent citizen.[24]

If this assertion as to regular and inflammatory coverage appears to contradict my hypothesis that Travelling people are made invisible, I must reiterate that it is *selected* elements of them and their lives that such coverage does not portray or promote. Only the more controversial aspects of the lives of some Travelling people are encompassed – and sometimes amplified – by such reportage, breeding fears and prejudice in the process. Indeed, other research has found 'that the announcement of a large number of small sites had been used by some local newspapers to produce the image of a major gypsy [*sic*] "invasion", even though the gypsies [*sic*] concerned were already regularly resident in the area.'[25]

> The use of racist language, prejudicial images and stereotyped coverage of Travellers endorses the principle of prejudice and so gives to those members of the public who it may influence the suggestion that racist attitudes to others are an acceptable and rational approach ... You do not have to read the papers for very long to see the consequences: writing which has no other purpose than to play upon – and so reinforce – prejudices.[26]

A review between January 1998 and July 1999 of coverage of minority ethnic groups by five regional newspapers in Northern Ireland found such groups were the subject of marginalisation, by a media culture which was reactive and overly narrow in its definition of what constituted 'news'. 'At times, coverage in the Northern Ireland press reinforced stereotypes of minority-ethnic groups as criminal or deviant. This was particularly true with regard to Travellers who were often depicted as "outsiders" whom the settled community was being forced to accommodate.'[27] The report noted:

Without any doubt, the minority ethnic group which is accorded the most media prominence in Northern Ireland is the Traveller community ... they tend to be reported when they are the subject of controversy. As many local weekly newspapers simply report council debates without additional interviews or information, the media provides a platform for those councillors who take a dim view of Travellers.[28]

The report devotes five of fifteen pages to press coverage of Travellers, and describes instances in which Travellers were represented in ways that demonised them and reinforced common stereotypes. The author gives as possible reasons: first, that a paper 'would see such views as having popular support among readers, just as Enoch Powell's racist views once won popular support in Britain; secondly, it is clear from news reports of council debates that some councillors in Northern Ireland view Travellers as 'second-class citizens'. The report also expressed shock at the stark manner in which one editorial had compared Travellers to animals.[29]

Residents quiz council – who's moving into empty homes?
'We don't want gipsies [sic] next door'[30]

Citizenship and the unseen

It is not difficult to see why the media plays a role in promulgating false but recurring images, thus reinforcing the position of Travelling people as perhaps the most maligned of minorities in Britain and in Europe.[31] The 'difference' element makes stories that stand out from the ordinary, that always sell and stir up emotions. The plethora of stereotypes around Travelling people provides writers with rich imagery and 'hooks' upon which they can hang a story, public sympathies upon which they know they can draw. Such vibrant simplifications are easier to write about and easier to read.

The similarities in tone, language and imagery between local coverage of Travelling people and national coverage of asylum seekers, especially Roma (Gypsies), are striking. This indicates that in neither case are the people portrayed considered to 'belong', to be 'local', to be citizens, and are therefore neither welcomed nor deemed deserving of the benefits that might flow from belonging.

Negative attitudes frequently manifest themselves in the refusal to admit Travelling children or in delay or the imposition of difficult or discriminatory conditions. In some cases, threats and acts of physical violence by members of the settled community have been sufficient to deter Gypsy parents from placing their children in school.[32]

'Over-reporting' frequently occurs both when Travelling people arrive in a locality and with arrivals of asylum seekers, including Roma, from other countries to the UK. This style of reporting is so common that 'the media and their audiences have lost even a tenuous hold on the meaning of the words they use. How is a town "beaten up"or "besieged"? How many shop windows have to be broken for an "orgy of destruction" to have taken place?'[33]

> Every time the press attacks asylum seekers ... it doesn't help on the ground. As soon as it appears in the press, feelings begin to rise, you can feel it.[34]

In 1998, reporting on Roma asylum seekers in Kent was so avid and biased that Kent police threatened to charge newspaper editors with incitement to racial hatred under the Public Order Act 1986. A police spokesman described some reports as 'inflammatory' and 'unacceptable', and blamed them for attracting extreme right-wing groups to the area. A newspaper spokesman replied: 'I'm merely reflecting my mailbag. I don't think we are making the news, we are merely reflecting it.'[35]

> 'I'm not saying that all these gypsies [sic] are the same ... there may be genuine cases. But it is the ones who are just hoping to get a free ride on the gravy train that we are talking about.'[36]

> 'We were told your country really is the land of milk and honey': the Sun joins spongers on refugee express.

> Cheeky Bulgar: Immigrant blows £67 dole on lotto.[37]

> Gypsies invade Dover, hoping for a handout.[38]

Some of the reportage during that time had no apparent purpose other than the broad desire to play upon and reinforce existing prejudices and fears. Other issues that might be important, even central, to the arrivals of these people were downplayed, derided or ignored, made invisible by neglect. Again, it is clear that some perceived elements of the (negative) 'natural Gypsy character' were put forward, and other individual attributes made unobservable by oversight.[39] Seven months later a journalist wrote, in an article entitled 'Plight of the gypsies [sic] Britain branded as scroungers', that a number of the Roma had been granted asylum, as they would face racist persecution if returned to countries which had statutorily removed their citizenship (and rendered them stateless) in 1993.[40] This was the only example of follow-up on the story I could find.

> When hostility occurs in a large proportion of a population ... it implies that frustrations and inadequacies might be built into the social structure. The resulting public anxiety can then focus on a 'scapegoat group' which is seen as symbolic of all manner of social ills. It is this we suggest which constitutes the functional inter-changeability of travellers and immigrants.[41]

The negative imagery and language characteristic of most reporting around Roma arrivals by the national press, including emphasis on lack of citizenship and deservingness for welfare assistance, is commonly found in local-press treatment of arrivals of *British* Travelling people. As noted, while the local press is more difficult to monitor, many clippings were sent to me and to organisations such as the CRE between 1999 and 2002. The positive/neutral pieces in our collections are outweighed by negative by a ratio of around ten to one.[42] Other extant research would suggest that this is to be expected, and is a longstanding issue.

In 1977 UNESCO analysed media reporting of race in the UK, Canada and Ireland. UK analysis focused on the West Midlands, in particular on Black and Asian issues, but UNESCO's attention was drawn to the high rate of press coverage of Travelling people in the years 1968–70. UNESCO noted, 'it seemed that certain constraints operating on the coverage of race did not apply in the case of travelling people.'[43] UNESCO stated that it used the overtly hostile and racist reportage to allow them to pick up on issues that might usually be subtler, as newspapers were more sensitive to criticism where other minorities were concerned.

The main analysis was of the *Walsall Observer*, which they determined was 'a blanket of white hostility, unruffled by any contrary opinions or organizations. Comment on legislation was also mostly hostile. The framework of reference most frequently employed was one which portrayed travellers as dirty, criminal, alien, etc., giving rise to communal tension.'[44] The use of common themes created:

> a composite negative image of travellers as causing conflict, creating health hazards, committing criminal acts and as having special legislative rights and immunity from immigration control. News with any positive reference to any travellers activity is minimal throughout

the period ... The status of travellers as a foreign-born, culturally different, minority is used to raise questions of nationality, cultural conformity and majority interests.[45]

UNESCO concluded that:

> The need to provide scapegoats who symbolize the potential undermining of traditional values may have particular salience for the self-conception of a local community and the newspaper which serves it. An alien group such as immigrants or tinkers may be used to overcome ambiguities and contradictions present within the community itself ... used as a negative symbol for all that was good and decent in local life.[46]

This may well be a reason why Travelling people never seem to belong, or be accepted as belonging to – as being citizens of – the place where they are. It would also explain why hateful representations of them are less common in the national than in the local press, which UNESCO accuses of operating a form of 'institutionalized intolerance'.[47] (In addition to which, 'unauthorised encampments', the issue most commonly reported on with respect to Travelling people, are a national issue but generally perceived as a local matter.) The available research, and my own, suggests a strong relationship between citizenship and sympathetic – or at the very least thorough and even-handed – newspaper coverage, and the benefits of participation and respect which might flow from it.[48] Travelling people are often presented as a social burden, deepening and worsening images of them as deviants worthy of social hatred.

> Fury as travellers set up illegal camp ... Families 'in fear of raids on homes'[49]

> Delight as Gypsy plan is dropped[50]

> Cycling route 'threatened by gipsy [sic] site'[51]

In December 2004, The European Commission against Racism and Intolerance (ECRI, a CoE body) adopted its third report on the United Kingdom, in which it notes, at paragraph 129:

> Roma/Gypsies and Travellers are reported to be the ethnic minority group which faces the highest level of societal prejudice. By reporting in an often sensational way and using stereotypes and racist language, the media, both print and electronic, have contributed to making prejudice and sometimes outright hostility towards Roma/Gypsies and Travellers, commonplace.

The problem is notable from outside the UK, and has been for decades. As the ECRI report highlights, the dissemination of misleading reporting is even more of a widespread problem now that newspapers simultaneously publish on the Internet.

At a 1998 meeting at the CRE in London on the press and Travelling people, a staffer from the *Bristol Evening Post* (home of 'Barry Beelzebub') said his paper could not ignore a 10,000-signature petition by local residents against the building of a Gypsy site. This is fair comment, yet the same paper ignored, and therefore effected the invisibility of, the legislative and historical background giving rise to the need for a site. In choosing to lend credence to one 'side', the paper conferred the benefits of citizenship upon one group at the expense of another.

> It is a tragedy that our society continues to tolerate and even subsidise these ragbag vagabonds who sponge off the state and steal it blind ... Set up a Gypsy site next to Sellafield where they can pinch as much radiation as they like.[52]

Travelling people are so *very* 'other'. While there are many cultural and other differences between black, white and Asian communities, between religious and secular groups, between the poor and privileged, what they all have in common (aside from the homeless) is that they live in perceptibly permanent dwellings. (Although, in fact, some 'settled' people change residence fairly often, for reasons including employment opportunities, social mobility, and family growth. The wide and varied network of available 'static' accommodation in the UK facilitates their version of 'nomadism'.) Nomadic people, even those now settled on sites or in housing, may bewilder and therefore both beguile and panic settled people. A local paper could as easily campaign for the building of a site for Travelling people as it could call for their eviction, but antipathy against Travelling people is so widespread that readership could suffer greatly as a result. There are economic reasons to take one viewpoint over another. In addition, the very definition of 'news' constrains more in-depth coverage of such issues:

> The media's inherent bias towards novelty (encapsulated in the journalistic maxim that while Man Bites Dog is a news story, Dog Bites Man is not) means that many things whose importance almost everyone would acknowledge very rarely receive coverage simply because they happen all the time ... Structural inequalities in society, which by definition have their effects every day, are thus not news.[53]

Power and responsibility

The media can hardly be expected to single-handedly undo centuries of prejudice, fear and ignorance, but nor should it continue to breed them. The broadcasting media has shown a marked improvement in its representations of ethnicity in recent years; the press has improved but only with regard to some minorities. Asylum seekers and Travelling people still come in for rough and racist treatment with very little public outcry. Those who watch the press therefore, whether regulators or commentators, are clearly also worthy of examination.

The NUJ guidelines on race reporting (at <http://www.nuj.org.uk>) counsel that someone's race or nationality should only be mentioned if strictly relevant, that the temptation to sensationalise issues which could harm race relations should be resisted, and that journalists should not forget 'travellers and gypsies [*sic*]. Cover their lives and concerns. Seek the views of their representatives.'

It has been shown that these ideal principles are not always followed, indicating a role for press regulators. However:

> Not one of the 600 or so complaints made to the Press Complaints Commission (PCC) since 1991 about alleged racism in the Press has been upheld. In fact, the vast majority of them are not even allowable complaints under PCC rules. Article 13 of the Code of Practice only recognises racist reporting made against a specifically named Person, and even then there is no violation unless the named victim complains.[54]

Therefore an Irish Traveller finding press remarks to be offensive, inaccurate or personally harmful cannot lodge a complaint because they are not directed at that particular Traveller personally. Yet in October 1997, the PCC upheld a complaint about a *Time Out* magazine article in which a 'humour' column expressed denigrating opinions. Some of the remarks related to 'a dozen varieties of sweating ethnic minorities', to which the Association of Greater London Older Women (AGLOW) objected. The objection was not upheld, but the PCC did uphold its complaint about harsh remarks in the same piece concerning elderly people and the mentally ill.

This provides an example of a third-party complaint about general offence being discretionarily administered and upheld by the PCC in relation to the 'spirit', not the letter, of their code. This is something it has not done regarding coverage of Travelling people, but has opted to do in relation to royal privacy and other matters.[55]

In July 1996 Vernon Coleman made remarks in the *Glasgow Evening Times* regarding Maltese people, about which the PCC received thirty to forty complaints. Coleman wrote: 'Malta is a noisy, squalid, smelly, Godforsaken, grubby little corner of Hell populated by petty crooks, racists and barbarians'. A consequent complaint was from the High Commissioner for Malta; others were made by MPs. All complaints were 'third party' in nature, but the PCC nonetheless issued a statement that Mr Coleman was writing 'in a manner clearly designed to shock'.[56] According to a statement by the PCC, the Editor of the newspaper contended that 'such extreme use of hyperbole to make a point was a legitimate journalistic tactic. He noted that it was so extreme in this particular instance that no reasonable person reading the column would take it literally.'

The PCC stated that the complaints fell within the realm of issues such as taste and decency, which are not covered by the commission's code and so could not be adjudicated upon. However, members of the commission expressed 'their own abhorrence at the offensiveness of the language which, they believed, was a rare example of that worst type of journalism which all too easily can bring the whole of the press into disrepute.' The commission examined whether any aspects of the Coleman piece breached Clause 3 of its code.[57] It found that, throughout the articles, the writer's opinions were presented not as conjecture but as fact.

However, it considered that reasonable people were unlikely to be misled into believing that the articles were intended to be accurate in view of the hyperbolic language employed. It therefore declined to adjudicate under this clause. This would suggest a state of affairs whereby, the more outrageously racist and offensive the language used, the more likely that the writer will not be taken seriously, at least by the PCC. The commission is seemingly of the view that all readers are 'reasonable' and that such language can never be taken seriously by any reader. (It is difficult to accept that a writer would not wish to be taken seriously, unless he or she – unlike Mr Coleman – were a renowned satirist.)

The PCC was created for the purpose of allowing redress for individuals adversely affected by press coverage, not to determine and police a set of standards for the press. However, as no other organisation or individual is charged with the setting of standards, there is a vacuum filled only by the press itself. Additionally, the system of redress administered by the PCC is arguably piecemeal, discretionary and inadequate.

While breaches of the law or even of public expectations on the part of Travelling people are dealt with by rigid enforcement of the law and other standards, breaches of NUJ guidelines and other standards expected of the press with regard to other minorities are ungoverned when Travelling people are the subject. It could be said that the regulators are toothless but in fact the regulators are themselves the regulated. Therefore if they are toothless it is because they choose to be. The PCC has been described by a well-known writer and journalist as 'a rather ludicrous body set up by the industry out of the fear that if it didn't regulate itself the government would come in and do the job less indulgently.'[58] My experience with complaints to the PCC has inclined me to concur.

In 1999 the CRE issued guidelines to every newspaper editor in Britain, outlining a fair and practical approach to reporting on Gypsy and Traveller issues.[59] While these were useful and welcome, it is hard to believe that journalists pay any more attention to the CRE than to the PCC or NUJ. Given the current state of standards in relation to reporting on Travelling people, it is apparent that codes are not enough. Without willingness or incentive on the part of people employing and employed in the media, and those who consume its output, to pursue truth and fairness, codes of conduct are meaningless.

In March and April 2000 parts of the national press conducted a crusade against 'bogus' asylum seekers, egged on by some politicians including the then leader of the opposition, William Hague. Many stories complained about Romanian Roma women 'aggressively' begging in the streets of London while carrying babies in their arms. The most arguably racist and offensive of these articles appeared on the cover of *The Sun* newspaper on 9 March 2000. The article appeared the day after a Treasury report had identified that £15 billion in lost taxes were incurred in the UK each year because of the 'black economy'. Next to the headline 'FLEECED' and the sub-head 'Scandal of Britain's scroungers and dole cheats who rake in £80 billion a year' was a photograph of a Romanian Roma woman, who in previous days had been reported as being in court for begging aggressively. The highlighted word to the right of the sub-head said, simply, 'GIPSIES'.

The response was different than that to the anti-Roma campaign of October 1997; this time a large number of complaints were sent to newspapers and the PCC. The Campaign Against Racism and Fascism and the National Coalition of Anti-Deportation Campaigns organised an electronic protest against *Daily Mail* and *London Evening Standard* coverage of asylum seeker issues, and over 1,000 emails were sent. The *Guardian* 'Diary' for 20 April 2000 reported that the *Mail* seemed 'to be in retreat from its usual splenetic frenzy on right-wing causes … Management at the paper have been rattled by the hostile response from readers over its asylum rantings, and staff are unhappy to find themselves targeted by protests'.

The Hackney Refugee and Migrant Support Group held a protest in April 2000 outside the offices of the *Daily Mail* and the *Evening Standard* to show opposition to consistent inflammatory attacks on asylum seekers. Supporters included the National Coalition of Anti-Deportation Campaigns, Campaign Against Racism and Fascism and the National Assembly Against Racism. Over 100 people attended, chanting 'Daily Mail, hate mail, Evening Standard, racist standards'.

The PCC asked *The Sun* for its comment on complaints received about the aforementioned front page. Editor David Yelland insisted in correspondence to the PCC on 10 April 2000 that *The Sun* was:

> not a racist newspaper: in line with the PCC Code we never discriminate against anyone on grounds of either race or colour … it is clear that our stories were not about genuine asylum seekers rightly seeking refuge in this country – but about illegal immigrants who defraud the state and the taxpayer … We believe it is wrong for these women to use their children for begging. It is a matter of opinion – and it is not one that is discriminatory. Let me finish by underlining again that this newspaper would never do anything that is intended to promote discrimination or stir up racial hatred.

The PCC examined carefully the complaints against the newspaper but its resultant June 2000 adjudication was arguably one-dimensional. The commission appeared simply to have accepted the Editor's defence of stating that his was 'not a racist newspaper', and that it was simply exposing cheating and tax avoidance as a matter of public interest. The PCC side-stepped the issue of placement of words and images on the cover implying that Gypsies – and immigrant Gypsies at that – are solely responsible for all the tax evasion, black-marketeering and benefit fraud in Britain.

However, the PCC did take the opportunity, in announcing that they would not uphold these complaints, to remind newspapers of their duty under the PCC code to avoid discriminatory reporting and the incitement of racial hatred. The adjudication stated that 'Discrimination has no place in a modern society and the Commission would censure most heavily any newspaper found guilty of racist reporting'. It is unclear, at 2005, whether the PCC were walking a safe line or issuing a warning for the future.

The RRA 1976 was amended and strengthened by the RRA 2000. The Act now applies to all public bodies, the definition of such bodies being as broad in scope as in the Human Rights Act 1998, i.e. all bodies performing a public function. The PCC arguably fall within this definition and, indeed, have been involved in a case under the Human Rights Act 1998 in which it was taken for granted that it is such a body.[60]

In that case, the court concluded that the commission's membership and expertise make it better equipped than the courts to balance the conflicting rights of a claimant to privacy and of the newspapers to publish. It remains to be seen whether the judiciary will take an equally deferential line if a case concerning both race-relations law and press regulation comes before them. It does not appear that the Government will take a less reverent approach to media regulation in the near future, although arguably it *must* intervene in order to meet its own duties under race-relations laws.

> ECRI encourages the authorities of the UK to impress on the media, without encroaching on their editorial independence, the need to ensure that reporting does not contribute to creating an atmosphere of hostility and rejection towards asylum seekers, refugees and immigrants or members of any minority group, including Roma/Gypsies, Travellers and Muslims, and the need to play a proactive role in countering such an atmosphere.[61]

Conclusion

The media has a powerful societal position in deciding what is seen of people and what is not. It acts as a filter, a prism through which only some images of some Travelling people, and some aspects of their lives, are made publicly available. Those people and aspects that are filtered out are not then visible to the public eye. Ideas and assumptions about Travelling people are subsequently, and selectively, (in)formed as a result. They are reduced to a set of simple, broad, externally defined snapshots.

In creating reflexively negative, flat images of Travelling people, the press may argue that they are merely reflecting standard public opinion, and they may be correct.[62] But in reflecting it, if indeed this is their proper role, they condone, encourage and confirm generalising or racist assumptions, whereas, some might argue, it is part of their role to counter bigoted simplifications. It is a strange system that will retroactively condemn one racist comment in the press if and only if there is an active and valid complainant, but which allows Gypsies in general to be referred to as 'scum', 'gyppos' and 'parasites' and so on with impunity. It is neither fair nor logical to assert that freedom of speech should give columnists the right to present racist remarks as fair opinion, when they are in a more powerful position than most to disseminate such opinions.

With power comes responsibility. All freedoms come with limitations; individuals can only live in society together if their individual freedoms are balanced against each other in some way, and under the rule of law the press should not and must not be exempted from this principle. Reporting can be done in a provocative and profitable way without denigrating entire groups. '[T]here is a large amount of evidence today to suggest that people use the mass media selectively in such a way as to reinforce existing attitudes that they hold'.[63]

The press alone cannot combat prejudice, especially as readers may read selectively and look for material that will confirm rather than challenge their beliefs. The 'media have their greatest influence when they reinforce rather than attempt to change the opinions of those in their audience.'[64] However, it can be argued that journalists should work towards the raising rather than lowering of standards. NUJ guidelines on race reporting state that 'its members cannot avoid a measure of responsibility in fighting the evil of racism as expressed through the mass media.'

Journalists who send responsible, thorough, thoughtful messages can promote informed and fair debate in society with some success. There is no doubt that press coverage in general has improved enormously over the past ten to fifteen years. The type of media statements that could have been made about Black and Asian people

Positive media images of Gypsies and Travellers: Richard O'Neill, Founder of
National Men's Health Week, with Steve Davis, the international snooker
champion, at NMHW 2002 (courtesy of Richard O'Neill)

in the late 1970s, for example, could not be made today. But it is
evident that this is not yet the case for nomadic peoples.

There are at least some hopeful developments. A union
representative for *Daily Express* journalists advised recently that staff
there had twice reported their own newspaper to the PCC for its
reporting on Gypsies (and on asylum seekers): 'In the case of the
stories on the Roma people we felt it was a cynical campaign to boost
circulation. They saw the effect headlines had, and exploited it by
having as many scare stories about Gypsies "overrunning" the country
as possible.' Reporters at the paper tried, unsuccessfully, to convince
the PCC to adopt a 'conscience clause' so that journalists could refuse
to contribute to news stories they felt were unethical.[65]

The UK's G&TLRC and individual Travelling people have been
increasingly active in lodging (so far ineffective) complaints, to the
PCC and to the police, against racist reporting, and in some cases have
even successfully demanded that newsagents remove offending papers
from their shelves. And, to my personal joy, police have censured

'Barry Beelzebub', who recently wrote, attacking police recruitment of Travelling people: 'Putting gippos in uniform is like asking Louise Woodward to babysit. Does this mean that the next time you're burgled the CID will pop round and offer to tarmac your drive?'[66]

Racist invective by the press infects society in a way that racist remarks by one individual to another cannot. It confirms existing prejudices and creates new ones, much as parents do in transferring unexamined aversions to children. There are few other sources of information for settled people, so every word published about Travelling people is a pebble dropped into a very still pool.

> We don't realise the amount of prejudice against us when we're on the road. If we get trouble, we just hook the trailer on and move. So we don't see what the local papers say about us. We don't buy them. What's the use, if you can't read them? So we've never complained of what's said of us. And so those paper people think it's okay, what they do. But it's time we spoke up.[67]

CHAPTER TEN

Europe
Colin Clark

OPRE ROMA!
Gelem gelem lungone dromençar
Maladilem baxtale romençar.
A Roma len!, katar tumen aven
E caxrençar, bokhale chavençar?
A-a Roma len!, a-a chava len!

GYPSIES ARISE!
I have travelled, travelled long roads
Everywhere meeting happy Gypsies
Oh, Gypsies, where are you coming from
With your tents and hungry children?
Oh, Gypsies! Oh, my Gypsy lads![1]

Introduction

This chapter broadens the questions and issues out by taking into consideration the European context and situation of Roma, Gypsies and Travellers. Increasingly, what happens at a European level has a direct bearing on how the various parts of Britain tackle various social, economic and political problems. When it comes to issues that affect Gypsies and Travellers this is also very much the case. In light of this, it should be noted that the main purpose of this chapter is not to be comparative, in any strict sense, but to be contextual – to illustrate how certain issues impacting on Gypsies and Travellers in Britain are being directed and influenced by European movements and policies. As well as reviewing the wider social and legal context of Europe and the European Union (EU) and how this impacts on Britain, the chapter will relate this to the broader position of ethnic minority groups in

Travellers in Strasbourg flying the European flag, 1968 (from *Gypsies & Travellers in their own words*, courtesy of the Leeds Traveller Education Service)

Europe. In particular, the chapter looks at the specific institutions in Europe and their stance on Gypsies and 'nomad populations'. Can the Gypsies and Travellers of Britain look to Europe for answers to their situation?

Civil rights and European action

> People with an awareness of possibilities and of their rights are in a better position to negotiate with their environment and to see that their rights are respected: familiarity with existing guidelines and decisions taken by democratic bodies, and with the progress of ideas of respect for individuals and cultures, makes it possible to participate in ongoing debates and to support others active in the field ... In the current period, as international institutions develop more and more activities aimed at Gypsy communities, it is well to take stock of the internal dynamics of these institutions.[2]

As this chapter is essentially contextual, it is important to first review the general social and legal context of Europe and the EU. It is true to say that when Britain became a member of the European Economic Community (now EU) in 1973 this had a major impact on British social policy. One example of this is the fact that as a member state, Britain is now under certain legal obligations to introduce particular social law that emerges and takes shape on the European stage.[3] At the time of writing, there are twenty-five member states of the EU and it seems very likely that others will join in the near future, especially from the central and eastern parts of Europe (such as Bulgaria, Croatia and Romania). Indeed, for member states from this area who have only recently joined, such as the Czech Republic, Slovakia and Slovenia, one of the conditions of joining serves to illustrate the importance of the Romani people as a transnational policy issue: the integration, equal treatment and respect of the human rights of their Romani, and other, ethnic minorities.[4] Having said this, as Bill Jordan (1998) has noted, for entry to the EU the final test for applicants is less to do with abstract ideas of 'political democracy' and 'human rights' than with the creation of viable 'market economies': 'From the perspective of existing member states, the main advantage of an enlargement of potentially 100 million EU citizens is in their opportunities as markets, and sites for profitable industrial expansion'.[5]

One of the first things worthy of comment in opening this chapter is the fact that on the European stage, social policy looks very different in its definition and scope to that traditionally seen in Britain. The key areas of British social policy, such as housing and health, have, until the passing of the 1993 Maastricht Treaty, been largely neglected. What we find at the European level is, historically, only a minor level of interest in redistributive issues such as social security. Nonetheless, as the years have passed, it has become increasingly apparent that some decisions taken at the EU level, especially in matters relating to social intervention (such as the environment, for example), can have a big impact on politics and policies of the states who are part of the EU network.[6] However, this seems to be the exception rather than the rule: for although critics of the European 'social dimension' continually assert how damaging the type of social intervention that is taking place is and how binding the legislation can be, in practice this is not the case.

Indeed, in practice, there is no coherent model of EU social policy, despite various Green and White secondary legislation papers on the matter.[7] Rather, as Cram, Dinon and Nugent (1999) have suggested, EU social policy efforts have developed in a 'stop-go' fashion.[8] A telling example of this is the fact that few proposals have made it to the statute books intact: those that have made it usually go through a process which leaves them watered down and only shadows of their original versions. As Leibfried (1993: 143) has argued, EU legislation, in most areas, 'is mainly procedural and not substantive'.[9] That is, it can have only incremental and modest impact on member states' legislative systems and can very rarely make major changes quickly. Although changes have been incremental and modest, it is still the case that EU social policy concerns have had some impact on Britain. As Kassim and Hine (1998: 212-13) have argued, 'the impact of EU action on national policy is ... complex and highly differentiated'.[10] In practice – in the British experience – we can observe that this impact has been both direct and indirect, directly through a few limited legislative interventions in specific policy fields and indirectly through EU interest in social fields.[11]

The actual power of the EU in traditional social policy affairs is still limited, largely through the problematic principle of subsidiarity (that is, EU institutions only getting involved in a policy area where member states are unable to deal with tasks themselves). Indeed, as Spicker (1991: 3) has noted, a more realistic definition of subsidiarity would see it as 'a synonym for national sovereignty'.[12] Roberts and Bolderson (1999) highlight a relevant example of such a problem area.[13] They assessed the settlement rules and disentitlements of non-EU migrants in relation to social security benefits in the EU and examined how widespread this exclusion is, what forms they take and how significant a problem this is. In general terms, their study found little consistency within member states and the differences tended to reveal how 'open' or 'closed' a country was to outsiders (in terms of immigration, employment and asylum procedures). One implication of this is examining the discriminatory aspects of different legislative provisions across different member states in relation to settlement rules and social security entitlement and the case for a more focused EU-led approach to resolving the tensions.

It is perhaps because of issues like subsidiarity that EU interest in social policy is, broadly speaking, about setting minimum standards and proposing regulatory policies and rule making only. Again, in practice, what this means is more activity around non-binding or so-called 'soft law' declarations on social policy matters.[14] In other words, there are a plethora of statements or recommendations made to member states in a variety of policy areas that have little legal obligation attached to them in terms of implementation. Examples of this abound, such as agreements on parental leave and part-time work. In essence, a lot of 'social dialogue' does take place at the EU level but very rarely does it lead to legislation.

However, there is some limited 'binding' legislation at the EU level which must not be overlooked in this brief overview. This legislation is largely about developing institutional frameworks that will help establish decision rules (such as the European Social Fund), setting up and monitoring advisory and standing committees and, on occasion, even creating permanent organisations (such as the Foundation for the Implementation of Living and Working Conditions).[15] Also, in terms of provisions that have a direct and 'real' impact on European citizens (and citizenship), we can see that certain equality measures (in relation to gender and pay especially), health and safety guidelines and worker protection methods are good examples of positive EU intervention. It should also be noted that in some social areas, the EU funds programmes – such as HELIOS – which work with people with disabilities. Indeed, the operation of the European Social Fund has been a major success for the EU in many member state countries.

So, despite some positive and meaningful interventions, the overall picture is one that suggests it is the 'soft law' non-binding provisions that dominate social policy areas within the EU and this means, in effect, that although there are many statements and declarations made their impact is slight and weak. In part, this is explained by the very history of the EU: it was, after all, primarily established for economic progress and monetary goals, not social ones. The many statements made at the EU level on the 'social dimension' tend to be overlooked when economic matters are pressing and also on the agenda, as Bonoli, George and Taylor-Gooby (2000: 156-7) have suggested: 'The long-term vision of the founders of the EU was the creation of a Europe that was united in the economic, political and social field. So far, however, progress has been made only in the economic field'.[16]

In summary, we can see that although EU social legislation is limited in its reach, it is nonetheless important for British social policy. We can also see that the attention given to 'social dialogue' within the EU has increased in recent years and this shows some signs of continuing in the twenty-first century. For Britain specifically, 1997 was a year of great change, we saw the election of a more 'Europe-friendly' New Labour government and its acceptance of the social-led Amsterdam Treaty, passed in the same year. It seems likely that Britain will be more willing to listen and contribute to ideas for inclusive European-led social justice initiatives – even those that feature Roma, Gypsies and Travellers perhaps. At the same time, however, on a wider platform, it is unlikely that the controversy surrounding the 'social dimension' will just disappear. For example, it is still the case that member states are refusing to extend qualified majority voting on social issues in the EU, this illustrating the unwillingness of some member states to cede power in this sensitive and political area.

For the purposes of this chapter, it should be noted that amongst the mixed outcomes on social matters the EU has often led the way on matters of 'race' and other social divisions, especially gender and disability. Indeed, the inclusion of issues which affect marginalised groups in the EU may lead to more encouragement being given to such groups – including Romanies, Gypsies and Travellers – to participate at the EU level in pushing for equality and social inclusion/justice. Clearly, however, this is a long-term project and needs to be sustained and monitored to ensure real progress. We now move on to examine the racial dimension of the 'New Europe' and EU influence in this area.

The racial dimension of the 'New Europe'

This brief section aims to provide an overview of the way Europe and the EU have framed policy questions about 'race' and racial/ethnic (in)equality. In doing this, it will lead us onto examining the position of the International/European Romani movement and how Europe and the EU has engaged, and not engaged, with groups of Romanies, Gypsies and Travellers in the area. Bearing in mind the context of this book, we will do all this with reference to Britain and with particular reference to important ideas about 'citizenship'.

One of the starting points in examining 'race' in the European policy setting is to see how the EU has had an impact on the concept on citizenship, both formally and substantively. Citizenship, within the social science literature, has a long established history with the work of T. H. Marshall being especially important.[17] According to Marshall (1950), citizenship was essentially a question of full and active membership within the national political structures. Thus, when Britain joined the EEC (now EU) in 1973, an interesting and wider dimension was brought to the nature and scope of this definition. It is interesting that the rights which accompanied citizenship, as Marshall saw it, were ones of 'gradual incorporation'. That is, the extension of citizenship rights in Britain occurred over time and was a way of accommodating the mass demands of the population and drawing in previously excluded classes into the 'body politic'.[18] In this way, Marshall was essentially arguing that citizenship rights were a type of 'alternative outcome' for the class struggle – not dramatic working-class revolution but instead the gradual incorporation and accommodation of all social classes within 'the system' (bourgeois capitalist parliamentary Western liberal democracy in the case of Britain). These rights that Marshall discussed were of three types: civil (equality before the law), political (extension of the franchise) and social (state support for material and social well-being).[19]

On this basis, we can say that in the early twenty-first century in Britain most sections of the community are able to identify themselves, and be identified by others, as 'citizens' with the rights (and responsibilities) this status brings. However, it also means that for those who cannot associate themselves with some or all of these rights then the status of 'outsider' might be more applicable: that is, they are seen as 'not belonging' and are excluded or marginal to mainstream society.[20] It should be noted that this can happen at both an individual and group level, depending on circumstances and context.

When examining the British experience, we can see that exclusion from citizenship rights occurs most obviously for those who are legally defined as being 'non-citizens', that is, there is a direct connection here with immigration and British nationality legislation. Nonetheless, this is not to say it is just legal 'non-citizens' who are excluded from citizenship rights – even though Marshall's early account might suggest this to be the case. Today, Marshall's original account of citizenship is recognised as being limited. It is now considered, by some commentators, as being too bound up in the British experience and concerned only with class, thus presenting a rather static and one-dimensional evolutionary model of citizenship which ignores, for example, dynamics of gender, sexuality and 'race'.[21]

An important distinction must be made at this point. As touched on previously, there is a crucial difference between formal and substantive citizenship rights. Whilst one may possess the formal rights of citizenship on paper, this is not always matched by the practice of being able to exercise those rights: for example, a Gypsy family who cannot access social security benefits due to their classification as being of No Fixed Abode (NFA). This distinction becomes quite important in the next section where we look at the European dimension on citizenship much closer. With regard to Europe, it might seem that this is a stage on which citizenship rights of British people – including Gypsies and Travellers – might be enhanced. However, there is another side which warns us that 'counter-forces' may be of threat to the substantive citizenship rights of British people from minority ethnic backgrounds.[22] Indeed, despite my earlier comment about the EU often leading the way on challenging social divisions, the 'race' dimension to this challenge has certainly not kept pace with the many gender initiatives aimed at tackling inequalities. We can see, in fact, when comparing Britain with other EU member states on the issue of 'race-relations' legislation, that the island nation shows itself to be quite developed and progressive in areas of anti-discrimination law.[23]

Still, there is much concern in Britain and Europe today about immigration and asylum, not least about Romani immigration and asylum.[24] Against this background, and for quite some time now, there has been talk of EU proposals to tighten controls on entry procedures and give rise to what was termed in the early 1990s as 'fortress Europe'.[25] What with large populations in some EU states of non-citizens, it has been apparent that ethnic minority 'difference' and skin colour are sometimes taken as evidence of, and equated with, illegal entry and 'bogus' citizenship status. This trend, often buttressed by sections of the press, has serious implications for the EU principle of 'freedom of movement' and the human rights of such individuals falling into this widely cast net. This fact is often overlooked in commentaries on the matter, as is the impact such questioning of status and denial of substantive citizenship rights has on sections of the ethnic minority population.

Another aspect to this is the migrations of the 1990s, which to a large degree were kick-started by the break-up of the former USSR, the demise of Communism in central and eastern Europe and the reunification of Germany. Such migration trends did generate social strains on a number of western EU states and it was not helpful that this happened to coincide with a period of economic slowdown and rising unemployment across Europe.[26] During the 1990s and 2000s, perhaps as a consequence of such unstable political and economic environments, we have seen a rise in the popularity of right-wing groups who play on themes of xenophobia, racism, extreme nationalism and support policies of forced repatriation. Increased neo-fascist activity has seen outbreaks of racial violence across Europe, and in turn, this has raised real fears about pan-European forms of organisation which might emerge among such racist organisations and the potential impact on the safety and future of Britain's ethnic minority population.[27] In Britain itself, of course, it is worth noting that there has been a long history of racist violence and encouragement from Europe has rarely been needed to see it take root and develop.[28]

However, as Jordan (1998: 205) has noted, such neo-fascist movements have 'loomed and faded in the past decade, just as its progenitors did in the 1920s'.[29] In other words, the pervasiveness of racism in a 'New Europe' dominated by neo-fascist tendencies and racist political activity can be seen as a 'doomsday'-like scenario for some commentators. Robert Miles (1994) has suggested that rather than seeing a qualitative increase in levels of racism in Europe during the 1980s and 1990s we have seen instead a continuing thread of ethnocentrism and racism in European politics more generally.[30] Likewise, it has been noted by some people that for every racist group in Europe there is at least one, if not more, trying to counter its messages via anti-racist networks and alliances.[31] Miles also makes this point and usefully reminds us that human beings are not wholly powerless and do have *agency*. Indeed, if we fail to appreciate this fact then we could very easily absolve the racists from responsibility for their actions and treat the marginalised and oppressed as little more than 'victims', incapable of independent thought and action. On this note – and set within this context – we should move on to focus on what impact European matters have had on the Gypsy and Traveller population in Britain. Using a historical approach, we can trace the emergence of the European Romani movement and also examine when and how Europe became interested in the Romani minority within its borders and the impact of this, in particular, in Britain. Before doing this, it is important to say a little more regarding the migration and immigration patterns of Roma in Europe.

Immigration and migration

> Gypsy migrations came about both as the outcome of dynamic change
> in order to adapt to new circumstances and as a response to historical
> opportunities.[32]

At the start of the twentieth century, western Europe witnessed many
population movements both between and within its many countries
and nation states. The reasons for such movements were many and
complex. Suffice to say, groups of Romanies were amongst those on
the move in countries such as France, Germany, Italy and Switzerland
and the newspapers commented on the Gypsies and their migratory
ways. As Matras (1996: 5) has noted, 'Migration forms a repetitive
pattern throughout Romani history. It is part of the collective
recollection and cultural and historical legacy of the Roma as a
nation'.[33]

It is widely acknowledged, and documented, that the Roma were
subject to persecution, harassment and expulsion from around the late
fifteenth and early sixteenth centuries causing them to leave their
areas of residence.[34] Earlier episodes are deemed to have been very
likely, with scholars such as Ian Hancock (2000) suggesting a
connection between the Romani migration into Europe and the Islamic
victories in northern India during the tenth century.[35] Likewise,
connections are frequently made between the fall of the Byzantine
Empire and Ottoman conquests and Romani migrations from the
Balkans to north and west Europe in the fourteenth and fifteenth
centuries. The exodus of groups of *Vlach* Roma (including *Kalderash*,
Lovari and others) from Romania toward the end of the nineteenth and
early twentieth centuries was in part connected to the abolition of
Romani slavery and the resulting freedom of movement.[36] The
descendants of those migrants are now located in most parts of Europe
and the Americas. Romani refugees from central and eastern Europe
were displaced during the Second World War and many have opted to
stay in the West. In some parts of the East, the migration of Roma was
enforced by post-war industrialisation policies, such as the shift of
Roma from Slovakia to Bohemia in the late 1940s and 1950s.[37]

More recently, Romani migration patterns have changed and these
need to be examined. Matras (1996), in a report for the CoE, has
usefully summarised these patterns as falling into three phases.[38]

Photograph of Roma (from Alan Dearling's private collection)

- **Phase 1, pre-mid-1970s**: this phase allowed for recent migrants not only to find employment and take up residence permits but also, in some cases, to be granted formal and substantive citizenship rights.
- **Phase 2, late 1970s to early 1990s**: during this phase migration was only possible by entering and staying illegally or by applying for political asylum.
- **Phase 3, post 1992–3**: this phase started with the introduction of regulations which concerned 'safe countries' of origin and transit and provisions for the speedy refusal of asylum applications and readmission to the countries of origin or transit. For eastern European Romani migrants in this phase, this has involved either entering the West on tourist visas and 'overstaying' or entering illegally.

It is evident from examining the history and phases of Romani migration patterns that these patterns differ from general European migration trends and routes. This is due to a number of reasons. Mainly, it is because Romani migration is often triggered by external developments which specifically affect the community. These external developments can take a number of forms but include events such as social conflict and ethnic tensions, violence or change in socio-political status (such as the citizenship law changes in the former Czechoslovakia during the earlier part of the 1990s).[39] In addition to these external factors, there are also other 'push' factors, such as Romani non-confidence or non-identification with the state institutions of the current 'host' society.[40] Taken together, the high risks of emigration seem minor compared with the dangers and threats of staying in a country which rejects them at all levels and has historically marginalised and segregated them, as has the former Czechoslovakia.[41]

Prior to the events of 1997, which saw Roma from the former Czechoslovakia emigrate to Canada then Britain, other Romani migrations were taking place. The main countries of origin of Romani migrants who travelled to various countries in western Europe since about 1990 have been Romania, Macedonia and Bosnia-Herzegovina. It is estimated that the total number of Romani individuals from these three countries who have applied at least once for political asylum in western Europe is anywhere between 50,000 and 150,000. Small numbers of Romani refugees, from a group known as the *Serbaya Kalderash* from Bosnia and Serbia, have arrived in the UK since 1990.[42] What is also apparent is that similar numbers, if not more, have been prevented from crossing the borders into western Europe since the collapse of 'actually existing socialism' at the beginning of the 1990s. Other countries whose Romani populations have headed west in recent times include Bulgaria, Croatia and Poland, although figures have been much lower than for the main three countries.[43]

The favoured Western locations for Romani migrants have been Italy, Germany, France and Austria, with some movement into Sweden, Spain and the Netherlands. In June and July 1999 small groups of Romanies from Slovakia arrived in Finland claiming political asylum, although the first group of 150 that arrived had their applications for asylum almost instantly rejected.[44] Of course many, if not most, of these Romani migrants have since returned to their countries of origin, usually as a result of their asylum applications being rejected.

The International Romani movement

In 1959 Ionel Rotaru, a member of the *Ursari* clan and a writer, adopting the old chieftain's title Vaida Voevod, emerged in Paris as would-be leader of the world's Gypsies. He founded an international organisation: Communauté Mondiale Gitane (CMG). This was banned by the French Government in 1965 but Vanko Rouda and other ex-members of the CMG then formed a new movement, the Comité International Tzigane (CIT). As they never officially registered it, the French Government was not able to dissolve it. Grattan Puxon and the Dublin-based Itinerant Action Group were in contact with both the CMG and the CIT, and Vanko Rouda spoke at the foundation meeting of the Gypsy Council in Kent, 1966.

From the beginning, members of the British Gypsy Council were to have a significant impact on the emerging European scene. For example, the Gypsy Council hosted the First World Romani Congress in 1971 which was held in the premises of a boarding school near London.[45] The CIT, now called the Comité International Rom, was active in mustering support for this meeting which was attended by delegates and observers from sixteen, mainly European, countries. At the congress there emerged a flag (blue and green with a red wheel[46]), an anthem ('Opre Roma!', reproduced at the beginning of this chapter) and five commissions that were to meet between congresses.[47]

The Second Congress was held in Geneva in 1978 with 120 delegates and observers from twenty-six countries. The link with India was the dominant theme of this congress which opened with the presentation by W. R. Rishi from Chandigarh of a symbolic package of earth from the historical 'mother country' of the Romanies.[48] New statutes were elaborated and a fresh organisation emerged, the International Romani Union (IRU), which was to operate between congresses and which, in the following year, gained recognition from the United Nations Educational, Scientific and Cultural Organisation (UNESCO).[49]

The Third Congress was held in Göttingen, Germany, in 1981, with even larger numbers: some 300 delegates and observers mainly from eastern Europe. Prominence was given to recalling the Nazi period and invited Jewish speakers included Simon Wiesenthal and Richard Hauser. A new demand was made for global reparations from the German Government. This has not yet been met, but Berlin does now support the national German Sinti (Gypsy) Union based in Heidelberg. An international Presidium or committee was elected with Peter Mercer MBE as the British member.[50]

As the frontiers of eastern Europe began to open up, the Fourth Congress in 1990 was held near Warsaw in Poland. Over 300 persons from twenty countries attended, including delegations from Bulgaria, Czechoslovakia, Romania and the Soviet Union. It was decided to set up commissions to produce a standard Romani literary language and an encyclopaedia for Romanies by Romanies. These tasks are still being undertaken by working parties attached to the Centre de Recherches Tsiganes in Paris, largely funded by the European Commission in Brussels.[51] The congress reaffirmed the Indian origin of the Romanies while recognising that they would remain citizens of the countries where they now live. Ideas about a new homeland called 'Romanestan' were not on the agenda at this meeting. The British and Irish delegations stressed the need for a good network of caravan sites, access to relevant education and the right to a nomadic way of life.

Following the Fourth Congress, the International Romani Union took part in setting up a new overall international body on which all Gypsy organisations can be represented – the Standing Conference for Co-operation and Co-ordination of Romani Associations in Europe (SCCCRAE). This was founded on 30 July 1994, in Strasbourg and there have been meetings at various locations where issues such as the rise of anti-Gypsyism in Europe have been discussed.[52]

In July 2000 the Fifth Congress was held in Prague and delegates from thirty-nine different countries attended the five-day event, for the first time in ten years. Emil Scuka, a Slovak-born Romani lawyer, was elected President of the IRU and the majority of the cabinet were from central and eastern European countries. Peter Mercer MBE was elected as a Member of Parliament representing England and Martin Collins was elected to represent Ireland.[53]

Progress was made in the meetings: a new statute calling for the recognition of a Roma nation was drawn up, there was a fresh call for Germany to issue an apology for the Roma Holocaust, and the election of the new president took place. Speaking to a reporter from the *Independent on Sunday* about the 'Gypsy nation' issue, Scuka said:

> The world does not behave towards the Gypsy nation at all. The world only behaves towards Gypsy minorities. We have all the attributes of a nation: our own language, our own culture and traditions. We had to

declare ourselves a nation because we are convinced no one else will do it for us.[54]

The Sixth Congress was held in Lanciano, Italy, during October 2004.[55] A new President was elected, Stanislaw Stankiewicz from Bialystok in Poland, but the congress was not without its controversy. There was widespread criticism of the congress organisers who had sent out invitations only a month before it was due to take place. As a result, many who had planned to attend were unable to obtain visas for entry into Italy in the required time. To avoid a repeat of this unsatisfactory situation, the congress adopted a constitutional amendment proposed by Veerendra Rishi, of the Trans-European Roma Federation (TERF), stating that notice of future sessions must be posted at least six months before the event to allow for proper consultation, preparation and dialogue. Other positions filled via election were First Vice-President (Nadezda Demeter from the Russian Federation) and Viktor Famulson of Sweden and Normundus Rudevics of Lithuania as Vice-Presidents. The new General-Secretary of the IRU is Zoran Dimov, from Macedonia, Head of the TV BTR Nacional (television station) and Dragan Jevremovic, of *Romano Centro*, has been re-elected Chairman of the IRU Parliament. From a UK perspective, and despite the timing issue, a large delegation travelled to Italy. Peter Mercer remains IRU representative in the UK. Cliff Codona, Vice-Chair of TERF and Head of the National Travellers Action Group, Valdemar Kalinin (elected to the Language Commission), Veerendra Rishi, Editor of *Roma* (elected Indian representative), Sylvia Dunn, Rachel Francis and Janie Codona, Members of the National Association of Gypsy Women, and Florina Zoltan, of the London-based Romani Resource Centre, all attended.

Although the venue and date of the next congress is undecided it seems likely it may be held in Mexico City. An offer to host the next meeting in Mexico by SKOKRA, the coalition of North and South American Romani groups, was met with enthusiasm at the Sixth Congress as it would help build links between Roma and Gypsies in the Americas and Europe.

European organisations: the Council of Europe

Although the CoE covers over thirty countries, it has no powers over its members and has until now had a relatively low profile in countries such as Britain. Nevertheless, it has played a part in at least raising consciousness of the Gypsy issue at international level.[56] As early as 1969 the Consultative Assembly made a recommendation that member states should try and improve the conditions of life of their Gypsy citizens (Recommendation 563, 1969 'On the situation of Gypsies and Nomads in Europe').[57]

In 1975, the Committee of Ministers of the Council, noting that little had been done by member states as a result of this recommendation, passed a strongly worded resolution. This Resolution (75–13), on the 'Carrying Recommendations on the Social Situation of Nomadic Populations of Europe', invited 'the governments of the Member States to inform the Secretary General of the CoE in due course of measures taken to implement the recommendations contained in this resolution'.[58]

Resolution 75–13 called for an end to discrimination, the safeguarding of the culture of nomadic populations, the building of caravan sites and the encouragement of the education and training of children and adults. It also established a sizeable fund for promoting Romani educational work.

The Parliamentary Assembly of the CoE of 1993 proposed a number of measures in its Resolution 1203 which declared that Gypsies were 'a true European minority'.[59] These measures covered a range of issues from culture to civil rights. Unfortunately, the council has no power to enforce these proposals. The council also financed and published a useful educational survey on Gypsies in all the member states, *Roma, Gypsies and Travellers*, of which a second edition came out in 1994.[60] Meetings for teachers and others involved in education have been held in Donaueschingen and elsewhere and reports of the discussions and conclusions have been widely circulated.[61] The CoE initiated a project for the history of minorities, including Gypsies, for inclusion in history textbooks and teaching programmes of member states (what is now known as the 'Interface Project'). This has been very successful and has led to numerous publications in a range of languages.[62]

In 1995, the council established a new advisory body – the Specialist Group on Roma/Gypsies (MG-S-Rom). The seven original members of this group came from Finland, Spain, the Netherlands, Romania, Bulgaria, Italy and Poland. The latter was represented by the Romani activist Andrzej Mirga. This group drew up a number of policy documents in various fields during the 1990s and in 1999 the pivotal role of the group was demonstrated when the EU adopted its document Guiding Principles for Improving the Situation of the Roma.[63]

The European Convention on Human Rights

The European Convention on Human Rights is a good example of where European policy has been of benefit to a number of Gypsy families in Britain. In particular, it has given some hope to those families who have been refused planning permission on appeal to Inspectors from the Planning Agency and then taken their cases to the European Court of Human Rights. They claimed that their 'right to a home' was denied contrary to Article 8 (the right to respect for private and family life) of the European Convention on Human Rights (ECHR), which states:

> Everyone has the right to respect for his private and family life, his home and his correspondence. There shall be no interference by a public authority with the exercise of this right except such as is in accordance with the law and is necessary in a democratic society in the interests of national security, public safety or the economic well-being of the country, for the prevention of disorder or crime, for the protection of health or morals, or for the protection of the rights and freedoms of others.[64]

One of the first cases of this kind was that of Mrs June Buckley who took the UK Government to court in 1996. In *Buckley* v. *UK* (App.23/1995/529/616 [1996] JPL 10018), Mrs Buckley of Cambridgeshire alleged that the planning system effectively made it impossible for her to pursue her way of life as a Romani Gypsy, as her only other available option was to move onto an unsuitable pitch on a public site. In January 1995 the European Commission on Human Rights concluded by five votes to four that her Article 8 rights had been breached. This was to be a hollow and short-lived victory, however, as in September 1996 the European Court of Human Rights took the opposite view.[65] Central to the court's reasoning was that the state had not employed 'disproportionate means' to enforce planning control (as Mrs Buckley was subject only to 'small fines' – these small fines still amounting to several thousand pounds, however). Nonetheless, Gypsy organisations in Britain took some hope from the fact that other cases, where eviction and harassment are employed or where non-planning options and personal circumstances are more problematic, might succeed.

It is important to note that Mrs Buckley's legal case began before the abolition of the 1968 Caravan Sites Act in November 1994 and other cases are now working their way through the long and complicated legal procedures. For example, on 4 March 1998 the European Commission on Human Rights considered a number of cases regarding British Gypsies who owned their land. The commission declared as admissible the applications of Mr and Mrs Coster of Maidstone, Mr and Mrs Beard and three others (Chapman, Lee and Smith). In each case there was a lack of alternative sites in the area they lived. The results of these appeals to the court were announced on 18 January 2001 (unfortunately, Mr and Mrs Coster had already been driven off their site by enforcement proceedings and accepted housing in November 2000). In this case, the European Court of Human Rights held, by ten votes to seven, that there had been no violation of Article 8 of the European Convention on Human Rights, in all five cases. Further, the court held unanimously that there had been no violation of Article 14 (prohibition of discrimination), in all cases and that, again unanimously, there had been no violation of Article 1 of Protocol No.1 (right to peaceful enjoyment of possessions), in the cases of Chapman, Coster, Jane Smith and Lee. The court also ruled unanimously that there had been no violation of Article 6 (access to court) (Chapman and Jane Smith) and that there had been no violation of Article 2 of Protocol No. 1 (right to education) (Coster, Lee and Jane Smith).[66]

This was a disappointing outcome for the five families involved. It was noted by one observer, Hector McNeil, that of the seven judges from the EU, four dissented the decision, i.e. a majority of EU judges did not agree with the final decision. However, the weight of their opinion was countered by the other non-EU judges in the court.[67]

From October 2000, major legal changes made the process much smoother and less costly for Gypsy families in Britain taking the UK Government to court. The implementation of the Human Rights Act 1998 on 2 October 2000 has incorporated the ECHR into British law, and people no longer have to undertake the long pilgrimage to Strasbourg to find a remedy for breaches of their rights. The Act enables anyone involved in criminal or civil proceedings, at any level from the magistrate's court to the House of Lords (including social security and other tribunals), to invoke their rights where relevant. The Act makes it unlawful for any public authority to act in a way which is, and for any other law to be, incompatible with the convention.[68]

Recent cuts in legal aid mean that some people who need protection for their rights will be unable to afford to enforce them, and it has been mooted by some legal commentators that the Act will never represent a revolution until the judiciary are more 'rights minded' and less fearful of being too powerful in relation to the Government.[69] Nonetheless, a more immediate and domestic remedy for the breach of rights is to be welcomed, and local authorities and the police will have to conduct a review of all of their working practices and procedures to ensure that they are fair, balanced, and 'necessary in a democratic society'. If they do not undertake a review they face the prospect of losing in court. It does seem that the days of police raids on Gypsy sites involving 100 officers, fifty Gypsies, and one resulting arrest, for example, may well be at an end.

The European Union

As early as 1981, members of the International Romani Union first approached the European Community (as it then was) to press the case for aiding Gypsies. There was a delay until 1984 when the European Parliament decided to study school provision.[70] Information was collected from all member countries and published in 1989 (set out in Resolution 89/C153/02). At the end of the study there were forty-three recommendations. They are far-sighted and include:

- that teaching material incorporating elements of Gypsy and Traveller culture, language and history be developed;
- that Travellers be employed as paid assistants in connection with the schooling of their children.

Needs other than education were not forgotten entirely: 'Nomadism must be officially recognised and provision made for nomads'.[71] The study was accepted by the Education Committee and has been published in many of the EU languages. Since then, a number of meetings of teachers and educationalists, as well as representatives of various Gypsy groups, have been held, and the study has been enlarged to cover Spain and Portugal. A new edition was published in

A truck parked up near a stream, Provence (photograph provided by Julie
Harvey for the book *No Boundaries, new Travellers on the road (outside of
England)* compiled by Alan Dearling)

1998.[72] Gypsies await further positive action in the form of pressure
on governments to provide a framework within which their children
can receive education, as well as finance for adult training
programmes. This may come about as a result of resolutions on the
general situation of the Romanies passed by the Council of Ministers
in 1989 and reaffirmed by the Parliament in 1994.

The Decade of Roma Inclusion

A recent development, with much potential promise, is the 'Decade of
Roma Inclusion' project. This is a bold and far-reaching programme
that has been adopted by eight countries in the central and south-
eastern parts of Europe: Bulgaria, Croatia, the Czech Republic,
Hungary, Macedonia, Romania, Serbia and Montenegro and Slovakia.
The inclusion plan, endorsed by the wider European and international
community, is attempting to push ahead some clear 'joined-up' policy
thinking on how best to change the lives of socially and economically
excluded Roma families in Europe. An action framework for those
states in the central and eastern parts of Europe with large Roma
minorities, simply known as 'the Decade', runs from 2005 to 2015, and

will ensure that cooperative efforts in accelerating social inclusion and improving the economic and social status of Roma across the region are actually happening. The monitoring of such efforts is a crucial and important element to 'the Decade' project.

'The Decade' grew out of a major conference entitled 'Roma in an Expanding Europe: Challenges for the Future' that was held in Hungary in June 2003.[73] The conference was organised by the Open Society Institute, the World Bank, and the European Commission, with support from the United Nations Development Program (UNDP), the CoE Development Bank, and the governments of Finland and Sweden.[74] At the conference, prime ministers and other high-level government officials from the eight countries made a political and economic commitment to close the gap in welfare and living conditions between the Roma and the non-Roma and to break the cycle of poverty and exclusion. The backing of the World Bank is particularly important here and is yet another signal of their revealing interest in Roma issues.[75] The backing of such senior officials and organisations has indicated the potential for a dramatic change in Roma policy and the political will necessary for urgent reform. It remains to be seen what 'the Decade' will produce but the early signs are that governments appreciate the need for changes – if the economics of Roma inclusion can be funded.

Conclusion

In this chapter we have reviewed the wider social and legal context of Europe and the EU and how this impacts on Britain. This review has also considered some issues that emerge when relating this context to the position of 'race' and ethnic minority groups in Europe. In particular, we have examined the specific institutions in Europe and the EU and their stance on Roma, Gypsies and 'nomad populations'. It is apparent that European and EU interest in the Gypsy and Traveller population has, over time, increased and certain institutions – such as the CoE and the EU – have particular 'Gypsy issues' on their agendas. We also noted in this chapter that the role of the European Court of Human Rights has been quite significant for British Gypsy families taking the Government to court for breaches of their human rights, in particular regarding planning decisions. Although no cases have been successful, and from October 2000 Gypsy families have been able to

Taking the cherries to be weighed near Nyons, France (photograph provided
by Julie Harvey for the book *No Boundaries, new Travellers on the road
(outside of England)* compiled by Alan Dearling)

use the Human Rights Act 1998 to pursue cases in British courts, the
ECHR has at least demonstrated the *possibility* to families that they can
access justice and question the legality of what, to them, seems a very
unfair system of planning. The chapter closed with some positive
developments coming to light under the 'Decade of Roma Inclusion'
project and it will be interesting to see what has changed by 2015.

Conclusion

Colin Clark

What do you see, when you look at me?
Your idea of my identity
Am I the Gypsy you've read books about?
Am I the Traveller you heard talk about?
Will you see the folki [people] not in the books?
Will you judge my cousins just by their looks?
Will you know the Gypsy who lives in your street?[1]

There are many themes that have run throughout this book, but the ones that perhaps stand out best are the same ones that have stood out in similar books that have Gypsies and Travellers as the subjects of their attention: family solidarity, economic independence and opposition to territorial state authorities and their boundaries.[2] As we have seen, times have changed quickly since legislation, such as the Caravan Sites Act 1968, was passed, and even more since the passing of the Criminal Justice and Public Order Act 1994, which effectively destroyed the work of the earlier Act. New battles are being faced by Gypsy and Traveller families today, for example, those concerning planning issues, political representation and human rights. In writing this book we have explored issues that touch on broader themes: 'race', family, community and nomadism. We have suggested that in Britain we need to take more seriously the issue of nomadism as well as questions regarding ethnicity and 'race'. For too long now the bogus 'race' schism has created false divisions between different Gypsy and Traveller groups in Britain – groups that should be forming strategic political alliances to dismantle anti-nomadic legislation and practices, rather than arguing over who is the 'genuine' Romani and who is the 'pretend' Traveller. The creation, therefore, of the G&TLRC in

Gypsy and Traveller children enjoying the activity area at Stow Horse Fair, 2004 (photograph by Margaret Greenfields)

September 2002 was a significant and important event, bringing together as it has many different Gypsy and Traveller groups under one collective, political, united and colourful banner.[3]

We have also, hopefully, provided an insight into the lives and experiences of various groups of Gypsies and Travellers who live in Britain and what they encounter on a day-to-day basis. We have sought to argue throughout the book that they constitute, in some ways, 'invisible' people. As a conceptual and theoretical argument, this may have seemed an odd route to travel. We may have given some readers the impression that hardly a day seems to pass by without some local newspaper complaining about a 'visible' roadside encampment that has just arrived in the area and the accompanying 'rubbish' and extra burden this poses to council-tax payers in the borough. But, upon further scrutiny, is it really such an odd argument? We have suggested in the previous chapters that the British vision or idea of who Gypsies and Travellers are – such as Jack Straw's in 1999 – is essentially misguided and divided into two.[4] This dichotomy includes, on one hand, the 'proper' or 'deserving' Gypsy who is fortunate to live in a nicely painted *vardo* (bow-topped wagon), tell fortunes, attend fairs, entertain us with music, sit by a campfire and, above all else, who appears to symbolise the freedom, mystery and romanticism of an earlier age where the winding lanes led you to the heart of a rural and idyllic Britain. The other dominant image – the 'pretend' or 'undeserving' Traveller – is instead to be feared, blamed and pushed from pillar to post, for they are dirty, dishonest and might steal 'our' children as well as our money. It is clear that the deep-rooted history of such dualistic stereotypes have not disappeared from the public, or political, consciousness.

These romanticised and demonised images do not actually reflect the contemporary reality of British Gypsy and Traveller life, of course, it is much more complicated than this. Like their settled neighbours, most Gypsies and Travellers will use a car, go on holiday and attempt to enjoy the benefits of modern technology. As their trailers have satellite dishes and central heating and the men engage in self-employed modern trades, they are regarded as being somehow 'not real' Gypsies or Travellers. Such 'pretend' groups do not meet or square with the images that are so heavily present within the nursery rhymes and fairy tales, operas and novels that popular culture has provided us with for so long.[5] The 'bogus' or 'pretend' Gypsies and Travellers do not have problems themselves, for they *appear* to live a charmed, simple and easy life without a mortgage or work deadlines to meet. In fact, if anything, they *deserve* such problems for engaging in such a masquerade – 'freedom' comes with a price and a potential sting in the tail.

To be clear, and it is worth repeating in this conclusion, that English Gypsies, since 1988, and Irish Travellers, since 2000, have been regarded as ethnic minority groups in the eyes of the Commission for Racial Equality and the Race Relations Act of 1976 (as amended 2000). The ethnic-status door is open for Scottish Gypsy/Travellers to walk through when a solid test case is forthcoming. The problem has been that *in general terms*, amongst the *majority* of the settled population and those people working for local authorities and other agencies who deal with Gypsies and Travellers, this legal status has largely not been recognised or the implications fully appreciated. Likewise, their right to live a nomadic way of life has been threatened and effectively criminalised by draconian legislation: the power of the state has been felt by many nomadic families in recent years. It is in this context that Gypsies are rendered as 'invisible people' and, further, considered as not even being 'real' people or having needs and rights. As we have shown in this book, this is not only the case in the public-policy context, but also in the academic context – with only a few exceptions, they are an 'invisible' group in the eyes of the ethnic and racial studies community.[6]

Politics, and the broader social-policy context, touches the ordinary and anxious lives of Gypsies and Travellers in Britain as it does everybody else. As we have examined throughout the book, the policies followed by the Blair 'New' Labour Government have been something of a disappointment for Gypsy and Traveller organisations and their supporters. Most worrying has been the moral panic whipped up by the Government and the tabloid press about Roma asylum seekers from central and eastern Europe as well as the recent furore over sites and planning matters. On a policy level, although lots of research has been commissioned, papers have been produced, select committees have met, there has been little felt at the ground level to ensure that many Gypsy and Traveller families have more secure places to station their caravans (thus allowing them to engage with and take up services such as education and health). It is important to note that despite New Labour rhetoric in the 1990s and 2000s on the importance of social justice, social cohesion and tackling social exclusion, there has been no move from the Government to repeal the anti-Gypsy sections (61–80) of the 1994 CJPOA. When this fact is put beside the stringent planning measures that continue to prevent families from parking their caravans on land they own, it is little wonder that the situation of accommodation is one of the most fundamental, and now politicised, issues that concerns Gypsies and Travellers in Britain.[7] Recent guidance and measures that have come via the Office of the Deputy Prime Minister (ODPM) continue a rich tradition in government advice and legislation in viewing Gypsies and Travellers as 'the problem' and we are still far away from a situation where the Government accepts that a statutory duty to provide sites is required.[8] The emphasis of such documentation clearly still has one, if not both, eyes firmly on helping local authorities to move roadside encampments on quicker, and with less legal complications, rather than actually preventing pointless evictions and the disruption and costs they bring with them. We would ask: when will this square be circled?

If one message comes across clearly within this book, it is hopefully that which suggests that guidance, advice and recommendations are not a replacement for, or to be preferred to, formal and substantive legal and human rights. It is against this background of rights (and responsibilities) that there has been a widespread movement, spearheaded by major charities and by lawyers dealing with Gypsy causes, to bring forward a Gypsy and Traveller Law Reform Bill.[9] Similarly, the implementation of the 1998 Human Rights Act in October 2000 has also, eventually, proved useful with many Gypsies and Travellers being able to lobby and challenge the discriminatory planning system for private sites. It is in the policy areas concerning land, law and planning that much work is still to be done, as well as tackling the anti-Gypsy prejudice, often promoted by the press as we have seen, and discrimination that infects and pollutes the policy process. These are the crucial issues that have featured heavily in much of the Gypsy and Traveller meetings and conferences that we have attended for many years. The question that many people are asking now is: What happens next?

Although what happens next is not clear in Britain, it is evident that the institutions of Europe and the EU, as well as European Romani NGO forums such as the European Roma Rights Centre, offer some hope for British Gypsy and Traveller groups. The 'Decade of Roma Inclusion' project (2005–15) offers much potential, even though there is some scepticism about what it will actually deliver to poor Roma communities across Europe. However, this is not to ignore the domestic base: on one hand, as discussed above, there have been some efforts at instigating a new culture of Romani lobbying and civil-rights work in Britain, not least those activities being undertaken by the G&TLRC. However, the European stage is increasingly seeing activity regarding British Gypsy and Traveller issues. Although we discussed in some detail the limitations of the European 'social dimension', we also noted that some impact is being made in certain social-policy areas across member state interests (such as the environment). Arguably, since the June Buckley human-rights case of the mid-1990s, many British Gypsy and Traveller families and their legal representatives regarded Europe as a friendly place to visit, particularly in relation to private-site development and challenging discrimination in other areas of social policy. In this regard, the European Convention on Human Rights has been very significant as has the Council of Europe and its specialist agencies on Gypsy and Traveller matters in Europe.[10] Clearly, the European arena remains a force for progressive change in some areas which may impact on Gypsy and Traveller interests in Britain.

A tack stall at Stow Horse Fair, 2004 (photograph by Margaret Greenfields)

We are keen to remember and highlight the case of those Gypsy and Traveller families who, through no fault of their own, are facing a difficult and legally precarious situation as they go about their daily lives. To be sure, in the year 2006, in democratic, tolerant Britain, some 3,500 to 4,000 Gypsy and Traveller families continue to live in a caravan, 'illegally', on the roadside.[11] This roadside might be on the edge of a busy motorway, next to a sewage farm, a quarry, electricity pylons or a refuse dump. Other families might be encamped on a local authority sports field or in the car park of an Ikea store.[12] They will probably have no water supply or rubbish collection, and the children are probably not attending school. They will be evicted, sooner rather than later, and moved on to another area where the camp/evict/camp cycle will begin again. This is hardly a good state of affairs, whether viewed from a social, political or economic perspective.

As we have seen, throughout the 1990s and 2000s, Gypsies and Travellers have been largely 'invisible' from the wider debates about social justice and inclusion. As a group, they are often overlooked as being not a 'real' ethnic group and are regarded instead as being an 'eyesore' or a 'nuisance' to be moved on to the next town or county.

Scene at Stow Horse Fair, October 2004 (photograph by Margaret Greenfields)

The 1968 Caravan Sites Act, in England and Wales, provided the means by which these 'homeless' families could be given pitches where they could legally stop while still preserving their independent culture, economy and way of life. In Scotland, it was supposed to be the 'Toleration Policy' that provided Travellers with a sense of security, even if they couldn't find a pitch on a local authority site. In practice, as we have seen, there was little security offered to families either by Acts or Toleration Policies. Good accommodation and sites, as we hope this book has shown, are the first important steps to justice and equality. For one thing, they allow people to register to vote. Also, being able to live legally in a caravan, on a well-planned and resourced site, can enable better access to services such as health and education. Further, a formal education is just one of the means by which some Gypsies and Travellers are better placed to stand up for themselves against officialdom, bureaucracy and institutionalised racism and discrimination. However, in tracing this rather simplistic and linear path, we must remember that schools and education systems, as we have shown, are not without their problems for Gypsy and Traveller children.

Horsetrading at Stow Horse Fair, October 2004 (photograph by Margaret Greenfields)

With the 1968 Caravan Sites Act gone, voluntary and private-site provision has never been able to catch up with the demand for good sites and pitches. This is continuing to be the case and will stay this way until local councillors and politicians risk losing votes and permit sites in their area, and the residents, that is, the general public, become more knowledgeable and able to distinguish the reality about Gypsies and Travellers from the many myths and stereotypes that this book has accounted for and explained in some depth.[13] The various 'race-relations' and public-order Acts should offer some form of legal protection against anti-Gypsy prejudice, but, as we have seen, they often do not.

Other options and roads ahead do exist. Common misunderstandings about the Gypsies and Travellers of Britain can be dispelled if some time, energy and commitment is put into improving community relations between Gypsies and non-Gypsies. In promoting a more tolerant climate in Britain, where Gypsies and Travellers may 'integrate' without being assimilated, we are seeking a new kind of multicultural future. This is a future that is rarely spoken of: not one that simply respects ethnic diversity but one that respects the rights of nomadic people to travel, live in caravans, seek employment and raise their children in a way that previous generations of Gypsies and Travellers have. This should not be at the discretion of individual local authorities and police forces; there should be a national policy on nomadic living and a proper network of sites to accommodate such families. However, whether nomadic, static or somewhere in between, Gypsy and Traveller families are indeed 'here to stay' in Britain and that fact has to be welcomed and celebrated, not just accepted or tolerated.

Notes

Introduction

1 Michael Howard's full speech from 21 March 2005 can be read here: <http://www.conservatives.com/tile.do?def=news.story.page&obj_id=1208 17>.

2 In fact, many high-profile individuals and organisations have stated full and public support for Gypsy and Traveller led organisations and the civil-rights issues they address, including the Commission for Racial Equality, the Institute for Public Policy Research, Liberty, Lord Avebury and, until recently, Kevin McNamara MP (who didn't stand for re-election at the General Election in 2005).

3 The G&TLRC website at <http://www.travellerslaw.org.uk>.

4 The full statement by the G&TLRC can be read at the website of the 'Stamp Out the Prejudice' campaign, hosted by the National Assembly Against Racism (NAAR), <http://www.naar.org.uk/newspages/050406b.asp>.

5 For a discussion of this idea, see Morris, R. (2000) 'The Invisibility of Gypsies and Other Travellers', *Journal of Social Welfare and Family Law*, 21(4): 397–404.

6 BBC News, 'Seven Arrests over Burnt Gypsy Effigy', 12 November 2003, <http://news.bbc.co.uk/1/hi/england/southern_counties/3259887.stm>.

7 BBC News, 'Bonfire Sparks Complaints of Racism', 30 October 2003, <http://news.bbc.co.uk/1/hi/england/southern_counties/3228833.stm>.

8 BBC News, 'Gypsy Effigies Burnt on Bonfire', 28 October 2003, <http://news.bbc.co.uk/1/hi/england/southern_counties/3222321.stm>.

9 BBC News, 'Seven Arrests over Burnt Gypsy Effigy', 12 November 2003, <http://news.bbc.co.uk/1/hi/england/southern_counties/3259887.stm>.

10 BBC News, 'Gypsy Effigies Burnt on Bonfire', 28 October 2003, <http://news.bbc.co.uk/1/hi/england/southern_counties/3222321.stm>.

11 The CPS decision on Firle bonfire case, 7 July 2004, <http://www.cps.gov.uk/news/pressreleases/archive/132_04.html>.

12 CRE response to CPS decision on Firle bonfire case, 7 July 2004, <http://www.cre.gov.uk/Default.aspx.LocID-0hgnew04c.RefLocID-0hg00900c002.Lang-EN.htm>.

13 Firle Bonfire Society, Legal Fees Fighting Fund,

<http://www.firlebonfire.com/legal-fees.html>.

14 BBC News, 'Boys Guilty of Killing Gypsy', 28 December 2003,
    <http://news.bbc.co.uk/1/hi/england/merseyside/3246518.stm>.

15 The *Kirkby Times* – 'Justice for Johnny Delaney', 2003,
    <http://www.kirkbytimes.co.uk/news_items/2003_news/justice_for_
    johnny_delaney.html>.

16 The Monitoring Group News Service, 'Boys Guilty of Killing "Gypsy"',
    28 December 2003, <http://www.monitoring-
    group.co.uk/News%20and%20Campaigns/news-
    stories/2003/regions/north%20west/boys_guilty_of_killing_gypsy.htm>.

17 The *Kirkby Times* – 'Justice for Johnny Delaney', 2003,
    <http://www.kirkbytimes.co.uk/news_items/2003_news/justice_for_
    johnny_delaney.html>

18 Travellers in Leeds: The Death of Johnny Delaney,
    <http://www.travellersinleeds.co.uk/_information/delaney.html>.

19 CRE response to Johnny Delaney verdict, 2 December 2003,
    <http://www.cre.gov.uk/Default.aspx.LocID-0hgnew04x.RefLocID-
    0hg00900c002.Lang-EN.htm>.

20 Okely, J. (1983) *The Traveller-Gypsies*, Cambridge: Cambridge University
    Press, p. 28.

21 This is not to suggest that it is always played out this way. Amongst the
    hostility and largely negative comments there are some politicians and
    newspapers that do speak out and write in a more balanced, sympathetic
    and engaged way about issues impacting on the lives of Gypsy and
    Traveller families. The *Guardian* newspaper, via its regular columnist
    George Monbiot, and Lord Avebury in the House of Lords stand out as
    being supportive of Gypsy and Traveller rights. It does have to be said that
    these people and publications are, however, very much in the minority.

22 A recent debate in May 2005 on the activities of so-called 'anti-social
    Travellers' in Nottingham serves as a case in point. A full account is
    available at <http://www.parliament.the-
    stationeryoffice.co.uk/pa/cm200506/cmhansrd/cm050519/debtext/50519-
    30.htm>. Recent examples of anti-Gypsy newspaper headlines include
    'Gipsies' £30 Million Handout' from *The Sun* and 'Prison Threat to
    Travellers' from the *Daily Mail*, both from 21 March 2005. *The Sun* also
    launched a 'Stamp on the Camps' campaign that month to stop what it
    regarded as a 'gipsy [*sic*] free-for-all' in terms of the development of 'illegal
    sites'. The 'Gypsy Invasion' theme has been used many times in
    newspaper campaigns, see <http://www.dzeno.cz/?c_id=3554> for
    examples.

23 Turner, R. (2002) 'Gypsies and British Parliamentary Language', *Romani
    Studies*, 12(1): 26.

24 The Government introduced new powers to deal with unauthorised
    camping in the Anti-Social Behaviour Act 2003. The use of ASBOs against
    Gypsies and Travellers is also occurring in Northern Ireland, as shown in

the *Belfast Telegraph*, 13 June 2005,
<http://www.belfasttelegraph.co.uk/news/story.jsp?story=646562>.

25 As quoted in the CRE strategy on Gypsies and Travellers for 2004–7. The
full strategy can be read at <http://www.uk-romani.org/cregytra.pdf>.

26 Monbiot, G. (2003) 'Acceptable Hatred', *Guardian*, 4 November 2003, also
available at <http://www.monbiot.com/archives/2003/11/04/acceptable-
hatred>.

1 Who are the Gypsies and Travellers of Britain?

1   Kohn, M. (1996) *The Race Gallery: The Return of Racial Science*, London:
Vintage, pp. 212–13.

2   An exhaustive and recent account of this issue can be found in the early
chapters of Mayall, D. (2004) *Gypsy Identities 1500–2000: From Egipcyans
and Moon-men to the Ethnic Romany*, London: Routledge.

3   Liégeois, J.-P. and Gheorghe, N. (1995) *Roma/Gypsies: A European
Minority*, London: Minority Rights Group, p. 6.

4   Anderson, B. (1991) *Imagined Communities: Reflections on the Origins
and Spread of Nationalism*, rev. edn, London: Verso.

5   Although now out of date, the following essay is still a very useful source
to appreciate the complexities of 'who' and 'what' a Gypsy is in different
policy and legal contexts: Kenrick, D. (1999) 'What is a Gypsy?', in R.
Morris and L. Clements (eds) *Gaining Ground: Law Reform for Gypsies
and Travellers*, Hatfield: University of Hertfordshire Press.

6   At the moment, we would direct interested readers to the following
resources on Fairground Travellers and Circus Travellers: The National
Fairground Archives are located at Sheffield University,
<http://www.shef.ac.uk/nfa/index.php> and, for a more historical tour,
The Galloper is an excellent website, <http://www.thegalloper.com>.
Useful books would include: Dallas, D. (1971) *The Travelling People*,
London: Macmillan; Toulmin, V. (2003) *Pleasurelands*, Sheffield: National
Fairground Archive in association with Projection Box; Green, E. (2004)
My Travelling Family: The Story of the Mitchell Family, Tweedale: New
Era.

7   See Acton, T. A. and Gallant, D. (1997) *Romanichal Gypsies*, London:
Wayland Press (Threatened Cultures Series).

8   See Jarman, A. and Jarman, E. (1991) *The Welsh Gypsies: Children of
Abram Wood*, Cardiff: University of Wales Press and also
<http://sca.lib.liv.ac.uk/collections/gypsy/woods.htm> on the Woods
family in Wales. Another famous and valuable source to consult on
language issues is Sampson, J. (1926) *The Dialect of the Gypsies of Wales*,
Oxford: Clarendon Press (although do note this work has been open to
much interpretation and, indeed, sharp criticism).

9   For a full account of the figures on Irish Travellers see Vol. VIII of Census
2002. This can be read online at <http://www.cso.ie/census/Vol8.htm>.

10 See Gmelch, G. and Gmelch, S. B. (1985) 'The Cross-Channel Migration of Irish Travellers', *Economic and Social Review*, 16(4): 287–96. For a full account of Irish Travellers in America see McDonagh, M. and McVeigh, R. (1996) *Minceir Neeja in the Thome Munkra (Irish Travellers in the United States)*, Belfast: Belfast Travellers Education and Development Group.

11 The best recent collection of work on Irish Travellers is McCann, M., Ó Síocháin, S. and Ruane, J. (eds) (1994) *Irish Travellers: Culture and Ethnicity*, Belfast: The Institute of Irish Studies, The Queen's University of Belfast and The Anthropological Association of Ireland.

12 See the website of the Scottish Traveller Education Project, where many resources are available: <http://www.scottishtravellered.net/resources/articles.html>. The Scottish Gypsies website is useful for a short review of the history of Travellers in Scotland: <http://www.scottishgypsies.co.uk>. A very good recent book on Scottish Gypsy/Travellers, focusing on their traditions of storytelling, is Braid, D. (2002) *Scottish Traveller Tales: Lives Shaped through Stories*, Jackson, Miss.: University of Mississippi Press.

13 For a comprehensive overview of New Traveller history, culture and lifestyle, see the website run by 'Tash', aka Alan Lodge, <http://tash.gn.apc.org>.

14 See Earle, F. et al. (1994) *A Time to Travel: An Introduction to Britain's Newer Travellers*, Lyme Regis: Enabler Publications; Hetherington, K. (2000) *New Age Travellers: Vanloads of Uproarious Humanity*, London: Cassell; Martin, G. (1998) 'Generational Differences amongst New Age Travellers', *Sociological Review*, 46(4): 734–56; and the recently published Worthington, A. (ed.) et al. (2005) *The Battle of the Beanfield*, Teignmouth: Enabler Publications.

15 See Kenrick, D. (1997) 'Foreign Gypsies and British Immigration Law after 1945', in T. Acton (ed.) *Gypsy Politics and Traveller Identity*, Hatfield: University of Hertfordshire Press.

16 Birkett, D. (1996) 'The Show on the Road', the *Guardian Weekend Magazine*, 14 December, pp. 12–20.

17 Gillian, L. (2000) 'Trailer Flash', *The Observer*, 16 April.

18 Quoted in Toulmin, V. (1997) *World's Fair*, Sheffield: National Fairground Archives (Sheffield University), available at <http://www.shef.ac.uk/uni/projects/nfa/newspap/wf/vtarticles/vtart2.html>.

19 The Yorkshire section of the guild has its own website, <http://www.showmensguild.com/p_01.htm>.

20 McVeigh, R. (1997) 'Theorising Sedentarism: The Roots of Anti-Nomadism', in T. Acton (ed.) *Gypsy Politics and Traveller Identity*, Hatfield: University of Hertfordshire Press.

21 We would also note here that certain reports and sources that might be expected to at least mention Gypsies and Travellers have largely failed to do so, such as the influential Policy Studies Institute's (PSI) research on Britain's ethnic minority populations. In this report they do not feature in

any of the chapters nor even in the footnotes or index. See Modood, T., Berthoud, R., Lakey, J., Nazroo, J. and Smith, P. et al. (1997) *Ethnic Minorities in Britain: Diversity and Disadvantage*, London: Policy Studies Institute. We would hope that this inexcusable oversight is not repeated if another PSI survey is conducted in the near future.

22 See <http://www.cre.gov.uk/gdpract/g_and_t_facts.html>#three>.

23 See <http://www.travellerslaw.org.uk> and <http://www.thegypsycouncil.org> for further details.

24 At the time of writing, a consultation exercise is taking place on the 2011 Census. <http://www.statistics.gov.uk/about/consultations/2011Census.asp>.

25 For further details of the Gypsy Sites Policy at the ODPM, see <http://www.odpm.gov.uk/stellent/groups/odpm_control/documents/ contentservertemplate/odpm_index.hcst?n=1190&1 =3>.

26 ODPM (2004) *Count of Gypsy Caravans, July 2004 (England)*, London: ODPM. Donald Kenrick, in his initial analysis of these figures, believes them still to be too low, even though they indicate an increase of about 700 caravans from the previous year. For the numbers of caravans on council sites, he suggests that there is the need for careful analysis here, as much of the increase from last year will be due to families acquiring a second caravan rather than an increase in the number of families per se. Finally, in terms of the numbers of caravans on private sites, he notes that the decrease indicates fewer planning permissions being issued. Donald Kenrick (2004) *Count of Gypsy Caravans, July 2004 (England)*, some comments and personal communication by email, 18 November 2004.

27 Gentleman, H. and Swift, S. (1971) *Scotland's Travelling People: Problems and Solutions*, Edinburgh: HMSO and Scottish Development Department; Gentleman, H. (1993) *Counting Travellers in Scotland: The 1992 Picture*, Edinburgh: Scottish Office Central Research Unit.

28 See the following website for further information on the July 2004 count: <http://www.scotland.gov.uk/library5/development/gttyc-01.asp>. At the time of writing, the figures for the January 2005 count are not available.

29 Welsh Office (1997) *Gypsy Count Survey*, Cardiff: Welsh Office.

30 School of Education, Cardiff University and Save the Children Wales (1998) *Traveller Children and Educational Need*, October.

31 For a fuller discussion of this important issue, see Druker, J. (1997) 'Present but Unaccounted for', *Transitions*, 4(4): 22–3 and also Clark, C. (1998) 'Counting Backwards: The Roma "Numbers Game" in Central and Eastern Europe', *Radical Statistics*, 69: 35–46, available at <http://www.radstats.org.uk/n0069/article4.htm>.

32 Hancock, I. (1993) 'Anti-Gypsyism in the New Europe', *Roma: The Journal of the Indian Institute of Romani Studies*, 38(1/2): 5–29, p. 6.

33 The Gypsy Lore Society, <http://www.gypsyloresociety.org>. See also, for details of the special collection at Liverpool University, <http://sca.lib.liv.ac.uk/collections/gypsy/intro.htm>.

34 See Hancock, I. (2000) 'The Emergence of Romani as a Köiné Outside of India', in Acton, T. (ed.) *Scholarship and the Gypsy Struggle: Commitment in Romani Studies*, Hatfield: University of Hertfordshire Press; Lucassen, L., Willems, W. and Cottaar, A. (1998) *Gypsies and Other Itinerant Groups: A Socio-Historical Approach,* London: Macmillan; Matras, Y. (2004) 'The Role of Language in Mystifying and Demystifying Gypsy Identity', in Saul, N. and Tebbutt, S. (eds) (2004) *The Role of the Romanies: Images and Counter-Images of Gypsies / Romanies in European Cultures*, Liverpool: Liverpool University Press; Okely, J. (1983) *The Traveller-Gypsies*, Cambridge: Cambridge University Press.

35 Hübschmannová, M. (1972) 'What Can Sociology Suggest about the Origin of Roms?', *Archiv Orientalni*, 40(1): 51–64.

36 Hancock, I. (1987) *The Pariah Syndrome: An Account of Gypsy Slavery and Persecution*, Ann Arbor, Mich.: Karoma Publishers Inc.

37 Fraser, A. (1995) *The Gypsies*, 2nd edn, Oxford: Blackwell.

38 Fraser, A. (2000) 'The Present and Future of the Gypsy Past', *Cambridge Review of International Affairs*, 13(2): 17–31.

39 Barth, F. (1986) *Nomads of South Persia: The Basseri Tribe of the Khamseh Confederacy*, Prospect Heights, Ill.: Waveland Press.

40 MacRitchie, D. (1894) *Scottish Gypsies under the Stewarts*, Edinburgh: D. Douglas.

41 Fraser, A. (1995) *The Gypsies*, 2nd edn, Oxford: Blackwell, p. 112.

42 The Patrin Web Journal (April 1999): 'A Brief History of the Roma', <http://www.geocities.com/Paris/5121/history.htm>.

43 Okely, J. (1983) *The Traveller-Gypsies*, Cambridge: Cambridge University Press; Willems, W. (1997) *In Search of the True Gypsy: From Enlightenment to Final Solution,* London: Frank Cass.

44 Liégeois, J.-P. and Gheorghe, N. (1995) *Roma/Gypsies: A European Minority*, London: Minority Rights Group.

45 Liégeois and Gheorghe (1995) op. cit., p. 8.

46 See Mayall, D. (1988) *Gypsy-Travellers in Nineteenth Century Society*, Cambridge: Cambridge University Press.

47 See Burleigh, M. and Wippermann, W. (1991) *The Racial State: Germany 1933–1945*, Cambridge: Cambridge University Press, pp. 112–35; Huttenbach, H. R. (1991) 'The Romani Porajmos: The Nazi Genocide of Gypsies in Germany and Eastern Europe', in Crowe, D. and Kolsti, J. (eds) *The Gypsies of Eastern Europe*, New York: M. E. Sharpe Inc.

48 Kenrick, D. and Puxon, G. (1972) *The Destiny of Europe's Gypsies*, London: Heinemann.

49 Kenrick, D. (ed.) (1999) *In the Shadow of the Swastika: The Gypsies during the Second World War*, Hatfield: University of Hertfordshire Press.

50 For example, Michael Stewart, in his 1997 book *The Time of the Gypsies* (Oxford: Westview Press) accounts very well how this manifested itself in central and eastern Europe, especially in Hungary. Under the former Socialist regimes, the process of reintegration or assimilation of Gypsies

was what Stewart terms 'proletarianization'. The 'rigorous discipline of socialist labour' was to be the saviour of the Hungarian Gypsies and free them from the shackles of 'peasantdom and social parasitism'.

51 Liégeois, J.-P. (1998) *School Provision for Ethnic Minorities: The Gypsy Paradigm*, The Interface Collection, Vol. XI, Hatfield: University of Hertfordshire Press.

52 Clark, C. (1997) 'New Age Travellers: Identity, Sedentarism and Social Security', in Acton, T. (ed.) *Gypsy Politics and Traveller Identity*, Hatfield: University of Hertfordshire Press.

53 Simmel, G. (1950) 'The Stranger', in Wolff, K. (ed.) The Sociology of Georg Simmel, New York: Free Press.

54 This fact has been pointed out by various social scientists including Sway, M. B. (1981) 'Simmel's Concept of the Stranger and the Gypsies', *The Social Science Journal*, 18(1): 41–50.

55 Opotow, S. (1990) 'Moral Exclusion and Injustice: An Introduction', *Journal of Social Issues*, 46(1): 1–20.

2 Family, community and identity

1 See Van Dijk, A. (1998) *Ideology: A Multidisciplinary Approach*, London: Sage.

2 'Ethnicity', while an imprecise term, is used within this text in the sense of 'a collective identity, including cultural, religious, national and sub-cultural forms' (*Collins Dictionary of Sociology*, 1995, 2nd edn, Glasgow: HarperCollins). Definitions of 'ethnicity' may also include 'a shared history of which the group is conscious and where the ethnic group is characterised by involuntary membership mechanisms for boundary maintenance such as through marriage and other cultural practices' (O'Connell, J. (1994), 'Ethnicity and Irish Travellers' in McCann, M. et al. (eds) *Irish Travellers: Culture and Ethnicity*, Belfast: Institute of Irish Studies. Thus, for example, a person defining themselves as 'Sikh' or 'Jewish' lays claim to a combination of religious, cultural and genetic heritage which are collectively recognised as constituting their 'ethnicity'. Similarly, English Romanichal, Irish Travellers, Scottish Traveller/Gypsies and Roma are members of separate 'ethnic' groups, despite often being collectively identified as 'Gypsies' or 'Travellers' by people who may not recognise the cultural variations between Travelling communities. Finally, members of any or all of the above distinct Travelling groups might at times decide for political purposes to demonstrate a *collective* identity as 'Travellers' (see, for example, the G&TLRC in the Conclusion to this book and at Appendix 1) to identify themselves as distinct from the sedentary population, and with a communality of interest which overcomes differences and variations in cultural practice between the various communities.

3 Cultural change (not necessarily viewed by individuals as positive) that

occurs in response to extended close contact between two or more previously separate groups, for example, *gorje* and Romanichal or co-residence on the same site between members of different Travelling groups such as Irish Travellers and Scottish Gypsy/Travellers.

4   Deculturation is the process of loss of an individual's own cultural heritage either through assimilation into mainstream culture, or resulting from acceptance of a dominant group's cultural preferences over those of one's own community. See Berry, J. W. (1987) 'Finding Identity: Separation, Integration, Assimilation or Marginality?', in Driedger, L. (ed.), *Ethnic Canada: Identities and Inequalities*, Toronto: Copp, Clark Pitman.

5   See Acton, T., Caffrey, S. and Mundy, G. (1997) 'The Theory of Gypsy Law', in Acton, T. (ed.) *Gypsy Politics and Traveller Identity*, Hatfield: University of Hertfordshire Press.

6   Avoidance techniques are practised across a wide range of traditional cultures and are internally mediated mechanisms for restoring the status quo by identifying and acknowledging behaviour which is shameful or contrary to social and cultural norms. In general, following a period of avoidance or ostracisation deemed appropriate to the offence, attempts will be made to reintegrate the 'offenders' into the community through bringing about a reconciliation between the parties most affected by the infringement of rights. See further, Wardak, A. (2000) *Social Control and Deviance in a South Asian Community in Scotland*, Aldershot: Ashgate; Stewart, T. (1996) 'Family Group Conference with Young Offenders in New Zealand', in Hudson, J. (ed.) *Family Group Conferencing: Perspectives on Policy and Practice*, Annandale, NSW: Federation Press.

7   In cultural anthropology, sociolinguistics and a number of related fields, it is commonly agreed that 'culture' is about 'performing' actions and behaviours that constitute cultural markers which identify us as members of a particular community or ethnic group. As culture includes aspects such as clothing, music, cooking, etc., someone can 'perform culture' by cooking foods that are traditional to their community. Similarly, someone can 'perform' an identity if they are consciously behaving, dressing or acting in ways that project their identity as, for example, parent, spouse, trader or Traveller. The performance of identity can vary according to the role played – a spouse will behave towards their partner in a different manner from the way in which they will relate to their cousin or mother, and language will be used in different ways in different contexts. See Rajendran, C. (2002) 'Performing Identity: A Stage for Multi-Lingual English and Multi-Cultural Englishness', British Council website, <http://elt.britishcouncil.org.pl/intper.htm> and Carlson, M. (1996) *Performance*, London: Routledge.

8   See, for example, Carter, B. and McGoldrick, M. (1999) *Expanded Family Life Cycle: The Individual, Family, and Social Perspectives*, Boston, Mass. and London: Allyn & Bacon. Specific texts that refer to culture-specific identities across the life cycle of Gypsies and Travellers include: Okely, J.

(1983) *The Traveller-Gypsies*, Cambridge: Cambridge University Press, and Refugee Women's Resource Project: Asylum Aid (2002) 'A Fourth World, or Experience of Multiple Discrimination (Romani Women from Central and Eastern Europe)', available at <http://www.asylumaid.org.uk/Publications/ Roma%20reports/RWRP%20A%20Fourth%20World.pdf>.

9 For a discussion of the ways in which individuals and families negotiate to whom they owe allegiance, reciprocal duties of responsibility and care, and how these arrangements vary in different contexts, see the key texts by Finch, J. (1989) *Family Obligations and Social Change*, London: Polity Press, and Finch, J. and Mason, J. (1993) *Negotiating Family Responsibilities*, London: Tavistock. These texts discuss not only cultural and gendered attitudes towards care (which is mainly negotiated and carried out by women) but also the ways in which levels of responsibility can alter across time according to the carer's other responsibilities, sense of family duty and personal liking for the recipient party. Sal Buckler has explored this issue further in her 2003 research 'Fire in the dark: telling Gypsy-ness in North East England' (unpublished Ph.D. thesis, University of Durham) which will be published as a book late in 2006.

10 Trevor Phillips, Chair of the CRE, cited by Nicholas Hellen, in '"Ethnic" Whites Replace Blacks on Race Board' *Sunday Times*, 5 October 2003.

11 'Profiles of Prejudice: The Nature of Prejudice in England: In-Depth Analysis of Findings', carried out by MORI in May 2003 on behalf of Stonewall's Citizenship 21 project in May 2003, report summary available at <http://www.c21project.org.uk/docs/finalpop.pdf>.

12 See Greenfields, M. (2002) 'New Traveller Families and Post-Separation Parenting Arrangements' unpublished Ph.D. thesis, University of Bath; Earle, F., Dearling, A., Whittle, H., Glass, R. and Gubby (1994) *A Time to Travel: An Introduction to Britain's Newer Travellers*, Lyme Regis: Enabler Publications.

13 Greenfields, M. (1999) 'Travelling Light: The Impact on Family Relationships of "Going on the Road"' unpublished M.Sc. thesis, University of Bath.

14 Greenfields, M. (2002) op.cit.

15 Greenfields, M. (2002) op.cit.

16 For a discussion on changing patterns of family formation see Silva, E. and Smart, C. (eds) (1999) *The 'New' Family?*, London: Sage.

17 'Handfasting': to make a contract of marriage between (parties) by joining of hands (*Oxford English Dictionary*). In past centuries, a public avowal of betrothal between a couple, made in the presence of witnesses, was counted as a binding form of marriage, and was widely practised in Britain by poorer couples who could not afford to marry. This form of marriage ceased to be legally recognised in England following Lord Harwicke's Marriage Act of 1753, although in Scotland (particularly Gretna Green) similar ceremonies were practised until a considerably later date and were held to be valid. Among many 'alternative' communities in the UK today

(most particularly those who adhere to pagan religions) 'handfasting' is recognised as conferring either the status of a permanently married couple or may be an agreement to a contract of marriage lasting for 'a year and a day' which can be renewed by the participants at the end of that period if they so choose.

18 Greenfields, M. (2002) op. cit.; Webster, L. 'A Positive Form of Homelessness' (1999) unpublished Ph.D. thesis, University of Bath.

19 The discussion on community earlier in this chapter takes as given that identity attained through membership of a group involves recognition of a set of beliefs and ideologies which are common to that community, in essence creating a 'moral contract' to which members will adhere. Typical examples of core values which are central to the ideologies of Travelling communities include: respect for the family unit; offering support to relatives; participating in shared responsibility for children and care of elders, etc. A person will obtain a 'moral' reputation through demonstrating their willingness to adhere to core tenets of community life and, conversely, will obtain a bad reputation if they breach the 'moral contract' that defines 'Traveller-appropriate' behaviour. See Gmelch, G. (1977) *The Irish Tinkers*, Menlo Park, Calif.: Cummings Publishing Company; and Bredemier, H. and Stephenson, R. (1962) *The Analysis of Social Systems*, New York: Holt, Rinehart & Winston.

20 A person who has grown up understanding the social rules that define their society (for example, how a Traveller should behave) and has acquired skills which are of value within their particular culture (for example, 'trading' for males, domestic and caring skills for females) possesses 'cultural capital' (Bourdieu, P. [1989], 'What Makes Social Power? On the Theoretical and Practical Existence of Groups', *Berkeley Journal of Sociology*, Vol. 32, 1–18). However, the value placed upon cultural capital will vary according to different contexts, as the skills and knowledge which are highly valued by Travellers are often not appreciated or respected by people from *gorje* cultures.

A person who has a high degree of cultural capital will, over time and through adhering to the set of values of their community (Traveller-appropriate behaviours), also acquire access to 'social capital', which can best be defined as access to inter- and intra-group resources through their set of relationships and connections with other members of the Travelling community. Where a person fails to adhere to the moral contract that binds members of their particular community, whether we are talking about Travellers, *gorje*, members of a motor-cycle gang or a group of Spanish teenagers, their access to social capital will become diminished as their networks contract or as people are reluctant to involve them in opportunities or assist them beyond a basic level, until they once again conform to the values and appropriate behaviours for their society (see Bowles, S. 'Social Capital and Community Governance', 1999, Department of Economics seminar paper, University of Massachusetts,

<http://www.Unix.oit.umass.edu/~bow>.

21 Greenfields, M. (2002) op. cit.

22 Webster, L. and Millar, J (2001) *Making a Living: Social Security, Social Exclusion and New Travellers*, Bristol: Policy Press.

23 See Davis, J. and Hoult, H. (2000) 'Travelling Families Health Needs', in Rowbotham, A. and Sheldrake, D. (eds) *Health Visiting: Specialist and Higher Level Practice*, Edinburgh: Churchill Livingstone; and West Yorkshire Travellers Project (1992) *Bringing Up Children in a Traveller Community: The Final Report of the West Yorkshire Travellers Project*, Leeds: West Yorkshire Travellers Project.

24 See Okely, J. (1983) *The Traveller-Gypsies*, Cambridge: Cambridge University Press; Sutherland, A. (1987) *Gypsies: The Hidden Americans*, London: Tavistock, for anthropological descriptions of the 'meaning' of *marime* and *mochadi* taboos. Within some Traveller cultures (most particularly east European Roma) the strength of adherence to certain customs (for example, long dresses and hair covered by scarves for women) and ritual taboos (on mixing laundry by age or gender, etc.) may be more strongly enforced than amongst some British Travellers, but many customs of cleanliness are still critical to all Travellers and are practised as rigorously as ever. For example, the strict use of separate bowls for preparation of food, laundry and personal washing are both ritually important and exemplary practical health and hygiene regulations, as are the taboos on placing food containers on the floor, shoes on the table, etc. Essentially, the rules that govern the divisions between *mochadi* (polluted) and *wuzho* (clean) are as much a code of life for traditional Travellers as are the ethical, practical and dietary laws enshrined in the Torah and followed by Jewish families. In a manner similar to Jews, some Traveller families may be stricter in their interpretation of the code than others, but certain behaviours and concepts are so fundamental that it can be said that an individual's identity as a Traveller is bound up with their practice of these daily customs. It is important to note that examples of *mochadi* include the fact that Travellers will often consider *gorje* homes 'dirty' as a result of having an inside lavatory (polluting so near to living and food-preparation spaces), litter bins in each room and only one sink in the kitchen where hand-washing, food preparation, etc., all take place.

25 On boys' transitions to employment and the role of male relatives in teaching skills/arranging for apprenticeships, see, for example, Ryrie, A. and Weir, A. (1978) *Getting a Trade*, London: Hodder and Stoughton; Willis, P. (1977) *Learning to Labour*, Farnborough: Saxon House; and Carter, M. (1962) *Home School and Work*, London: Pergamon Press.

   For oral-history narratives of working-class children working alongside their female relatives and spending time out of school to participate in field or domestic work, see particularly: Leane, M. and Kiely, L. (2004) 'Women Domestic and Farm Workers in Munster, 1936–1960: Insights from Personal Testimonies', conference paper,

Economic History Society, Annual Conference; and O'Neill, G. (1990) *Pull No More Bines: Hop-picking, Memories of a Vanished Way of Life*, London: The Women's Press (East End Londoners' hop-picking memoirs).

26 See Chapter 8 on education and, for specific government responses, DfES (2003) *Aiming High: Raising the Achievement of Gypsy Traveller Pupils*, Annesley: DfES; Bhopal, K., Gundara, J., Jones, C. and Owen, C. (2000) *Working towards Inclusive Education: Aspects of Good Practice for Gypsy Traveller Pupils*, Nottingham: DfEE; OFSTED (1996) *The Education of Travelling Children. A Survey of Educational Provision for Travelling Children*, London: OFSTED; OFSTED (1999) *Raising the Attainment of Minority Ethnic Pupils: School and LEA Responses*, London: OFSTED.

27 'Family practices' is a term coined by a leading sociologist of the family (Morgan, D. (1996), *Family Connections*, Cambridge: Polity Press) to describe how new family behaviours are fluid and change organically, enabling a group of kin to adapt their methods of ascribing roles and responding to particular circumstances, in a manner that meets both the norms of their particular society and the needs of their household. In this way the concept of 'family practices' recognises that ways of 'doing family' may include kinship and friendship networks and moral responsibilities which go beyond the conventional 'Westernised' ideas of 'the family'. 'Family practices' therefore permits an explanation of the centrality of 'community' to Travellers across a wide range of interactions.

28 Crawley, H. (2004) *Moving Forward: The Provision of Accommodation for Travellers and Gypsies*, London: IPPR, p. 38.

3 Stopping places

1   In this context (unlike the definition within planning law, see Chapter 4) 'Gypsies' equates to people of Romani origin – recognised as an ethnic minority in the case of *CRE* v. *Dutton [1989] 1 All ER 306,* with other Travellers (Irish, Welsh, Scottish and 'New') considered as a separate category.

2   See Chapter 5 for further information on 'Travellers in houses'.

3   Shoard, M. (1987) *This Land Is Ours: The Struggle for Britain's Countryside*, London: Paladin.

4   See Acton, T. (1999) 'Authenticity, Expertise, Scholarship and Politics: Conflicting Goals in Romani Studies', inaugural professorial lecture, available at <http://www.groundswelluk.net/~fft/pdfs/acton_article.pdf>.

5   Beier, A. (1985) *Masterless Men: The Vagrancy Problem in England 1560–1640*, London: Methuen; Slack, P. (1987) *Vagrants and Vagrancy in England 1598–1664*, London: Hutchinson.

6   Mayall, D. (1995) *English Gypsies and State Policies*, Hatfield: University of Hertfordshire Press.

7   Chapters 4 and 10 expand on the impacts of human rights legislation and EC law on British Travellers.

8   Hawes, D. and Perez, B. (1995) *The Gypsy and the State: The Ethnic Cleansing of British Society*, Bristol: SAUS.

9   Okely, J. (1983) *The Traveller-Gypsies* (Cambridge: Cambridge University Press) quotes from a number of parish and newspaper reports from the nineteenth and twentieth centuries which recite claims of increased 'criminality' in localities, supposedly perpetrated by 'worthless' and 'idle' Gypsies who were passing through or stopping in the area (see further Chapters 6 and 9).

10 See Acton, T. (1974) *Gypsy Politics and Social Change*, London: Routledge & Kegan Paul, and Okely, J. (1983), op. cit., for a discussion on nineteenth-century philanthropic and religious missions to Travellers.

11 It has been estimated that as many as 90 per cent of traditional stopping places, such as green lanes, have been blocked off or otherwise made inaccessible between the early 1980s and the present time (see Traveller Law Research Unit, 2002, 'Factsheet on Travelling people in the UK', Cardiff: Cardiff University.

12 See, for example, Smith, L. (2004) *Romany Nevi-Wesh: An Informal History of the New Forest Gypsies*, Minstead: Nova Foresta Publishing.

13 Pateman, J. (2002) *Seven Steps to Glory: Private Pateman goes to War*, [Great Britain]: Romany & Traveller Family History Society; Berlin, S. (1970) *Dromengro,* London: Collins; Boswell. S, (1973) 'Gypsy Boy on the Western Front', *Journal Gypsy Lore Society, 3rd Series*, 52(2/Jan.–Apr.); Hearn, J. (2001) *John's Story*, [Great Britain]: Romany & Traveller Family History Society.

14 Acton (1974) notes (p. 130) that during the Second World War military authorities, in recognition of the role of Gypsies and Travellers in the services, provided sites specifically for the families of forces personnel.

15 Kenrick, D. and Clark, C. (1999) *Moving On: The Gypsies and Travellers of Britain*, Hatfield: University of Hertfordshire Press, p. 26.

16 Friend, A. (1980) 'The Post-War Squatters', in Anning, N. et al. *Squatting: The Real Story*, London: Bay Leaf. Extracts available at <http//www.squat.freeserve.co.uk/story/index.htm>; Mass Observation Archives, Topics Collection, 'Squatting' (1946–48)', Sussex University, UK.

17 Kenrick and Clark (1999) op. cit., p. 26.

18 Okely (1983) op. cit., p. 36.

19 Personal communications (2003/4).

20 Hawes and Perez (1995) op. cit.; Acton (1974) op. cit.; Kenrick and Clark (1999) op. cit.

21 See Sibley, D. (1981) *Outsiders in Urban Society*, Oxford: Basil Blackwell; Samuel, M. (1973) 'Comers and Goers', in Dyos, H. and Wolff, M. (eds) *The Victorian City: Images and Reality*, London: Routledge & Kegan Paul.

22 Kenrick and Clark (1999) op. cit.

23 See Smith (2004) op. cit. for a detailed description of the regulatory schemes that ended the free movement of Gypsies within the New Forest by requiring that they live within 'compounds' or newly provided

housing. Much of the political debate on the viability of 'compound life' focused on the 'necessity' of bringing Romanies to accept twentieth-century ways of life and improving their 'stone-age' conditions. With the subsequent abolition of 'compounds' in the 1950s and the enforced eviction of those families who refused to leave voluntarily, a 500-year-old tradition of Travellers' freedom to camp in the forest finally came to an end.

24 Dodds, N. (1966) *Gypsies, Didikois and Other Travellers*, London: Johnson Publications; Evans, S. (2004) *Stopping Places: A Gypsy History of South London and Kent*, Hatfield: University of Hertfordshire Press; Stanley, B. (1998), in Keet-Black, J. (ed.) *Memories of the Marsh: A Traveller Life in Kent*, South Chailey: Romany & Traveller Family History Society.

25 Indeed, in their subtitle of their 1995 book, Hawes and Perez (op. cit.) refer to the post-war policies of assimilation of Travellers and the restriction on movement and encampment as 'the ethnic cleansing of British Society'; see also Dodds (1966) op. cit.

26 Dodds (1966) op. cit., throughout his text, cites this phrase as recurring in communications from local authorities and in parliamentary debates on Traveller accommodation needs.

27 Cited in Dodds (1966) op. cit., pp. 61–2.

28 See Evans (2004) op. cit.; Stanley (1998) op. cit.; Dodds (1966) op. cit. and <http://www.ideal-homes.org.uk/bexley/belvedere/gypsy-encampment.htm>.

29 See Kenrick and Clark (1999) op. cit.; Acton (1974) op. cit.; Dodds (1966) op. cit.; and Evans (2004) op. cit.

30 Dodds (1966) op. cit. quotes (p. 61) an outraged editorial from *The Times* condemning the actions of the Church Commissioners (who had initially owned the woodland) and Dartford Rural District Council (who purchased the land with the intent of ousting the long-term residents) as 'marshalling a bureaucratic machine against victims whose helplessness merits sympathy'. See Chapters 4 and 9 generally for instances of national press comments.

31 Conservative Prime Minister, 1957–63.

32 Minister for Local Government, 1964–6, a cultured social democrat by leaning, who expressed considerable concern over the poor quality of accommodation available to wide sections of the British public.

33 See Dodds (1966) op. cit. Dodds formed a committee in 1947, consisting of Gypsies and committed *gorje* who drew up a charter with nine objectives (all equally valid today) that were aimed at alleviating the plight of Travellers and ensuring equality of access to education and accommodation. In addition, he asked the first ever parliamentary questions on Gypsy site provision in November 1950, and in 1951 arranged for Hugh Dalton (then Minister for Local Government and Planning) to meet a deputation of Gypsies who were facing eviction from large sites in Kent. It was the first time that Gypsies had ever entered the

House of Commons. Sadly, Dodds was to die suddenly in 1965, three years before the Caravan Sites Act 1968 (see below) was piloted through Parliament by the equally determined Liberal MP Eric Lubbock (now Lord Avebury), who is still politically active in Gypsy and Traveller matters.

34 Academic and author of *Gypsies of Britain*, 2nd edn (1973) Newton Abbot: David and Charles Holdings, first published 1944.

35 The NCCL, a lobbying and monitoring organisation (renamed 'Liberty' in the 1990s), was still concerned with Traveller issues some forty years later, producing a report on the notorious 'Battle of the Beanfield' where a group of New Travellers (including small children and pregnant women) were forced off the road into a beanfield and their vehicles burnt and damaged by a large number of police from several forces, acting to keep them away from a festival site to which they were travelling in convoy. Many severe injuries were sustained by the Travellers during this action (for which damages were in some cases awarded) and widespread public condemnation greeted the police action which had been captured on film by television crews following the group on their travels. Similar although not so brutal actions were repeated in the following year when New Travellers once again attempted to attend their longstanding festival at Stonehenge in Wiltshire. See NCCL (1986) *Stonehenge: A Report into the Civil Liberties Implications of the Events Relating to the Convoys of Summer 1985 and 1986,* London: NCCL.

36 See Kenrick and Clark (1999) op. cit., p. 85, for a description of the way in which local authorities used local Acts of Parliament dating from the 1930s to enable them to create 'exclusion zones', banning Travellers from pulling up with a trailer. This technique was subsequently revived during the 1980s by local authorities anxious to ensure that Travellers could not return to a site from where they had just been evicted, or that others would not join them, or move onto the land once they had left. Dodds (1966) op. cit. provides graphic evidence of the cycle of evictions, removal of Travellers across district and parish boundaries and re-eviction which drove many Gypsies into houses and in some cases led to the death of family members through lack of adequate medical care or ability to stop long enough to tend injuries or to enable safe childbirth. See also Chapter 7, which deals with evidence of poor outcomes for maternal and child health resulting from lack of site provision.

37 See Hawes and Perez (1995) op. cit., p. 20; Dodds (1966) op. cit.

38 See Hawes and Perez (1995) op. cit.; Dodds (1966) op. cit.

39 See Kenrick and Clark (1999) op. cit., p. 87.

40 Okely, J. (1983) op. cit., p. 106.

41 Miss Wilmot-Ware, a Gloucestershire tenant farmer who had allowed Travellers to stop on her farm land since the Second World War was repeatedly prosecuted for not possessing a site licence. Over a number of years she fought repeated legal battles, mobilised clergy and political support and did her utmost to bring attention to the situation of unsited

Travellers. Ultimately, Miss Wilmot-Ware lost her farm as a result of the actions of the local authority who proceeded against her relentlessly. Many other well-disposed farmers, aware of the outcome of her battles and unwilling to risk their own livelihood, reluctantly informed Travellers that unless they were actually *working* on the farm, they could only stay for the twenty-eight-day period stipulated in the Act and must then move on elsewhere. See Acton (1974) op. cit.

42 See Dodds (1966) op. cit.

43 Published in 1967 as *Gypsies and Other Travellers*, London: HMSO.

44 See Acton (1974) op. cit. for the definitive analysis of the Gypsy Council campaign and government responses.

45 See Kenrick and Clark (1999) op. cit., p. 91.

46 See, for example, Drakakis-Smith, A. and Mason, K. (2001) 'Out for the Count: A Critical Examination of the DETR Biannual Count of Gypsies and Travellers in England with Special Reference to Staffordshire', available at <http://www.radstats.org.uk/n0078/drakakis-smithandmason.htm>; and the ODPM-commissioned review of the census: Niner, P. (2004) *Counting Gypsies and Travellers: A Review of the Gypsy Caravan Count System*, London: ODPM, which, whilst supporting the concept of a Gypsy 'census', identified significant weaknesses in the counting methods used.

47 Cripps, J. (1976) *Accommodation for Gypsies: A Report on the Working of the Caravan Sites Act 1968*, London: HMSO.

48 See Morris, R. and Clements, L. (2002) *At What Cost? The Economics of Gypsy and Traveller Encampments*, Bristol: Policy Press.

49 The dreadful concept of 'toleration', despite carrying racist overtones and a grudging sense of acceptance of members of our oldest minority ethnic community, is the phrase used in various government guidance – for example, *Managing Unauthorised Camping: A Good Practice Guide* (1998) London: Department of the Environment, Transport and the Regions; Circular 18/94, DoE – to refer to situations where delays in eviction are permitted while welfare enquiries are carried out, a date is agreed when Travellers will move on, or a lengthy compliance period is granted prior to enforcement of eviction proceedings.

50 In 2002, Dr Donald Kenrick estimated that, based on numbers of nomadic Travellers in the UK at that time, not allowing for population growth, and the number of sites in existence at that date, it would take twenty-seven years to find accommodation for all of the unsited families who were counted in the January 2002 biannual census (personal communication, spring 2002). Crawley, H. (2004) *Moving Forward: The Provision of Accommodation for Travellers and Gypsies*, London: IPPR, notes (at p. 16) that research undertaken for the ODPM found that between 5,000–7,000 additional pitches will be required by 2009 to meet the needs of the growing community.

51 See Niner, P. (2002) *The Provision and Condition of Local Authority Gypsy and Traveller Sites in England*, London: ODPM.

52 It is only recently that Gypsies and Travellers have achieved some measure of security of tenure on local authority sites following the leading case of Connors where a challenge was brought in the European courts against the power of local authorities to evict an entire family at very short notice following the alleged anti-social behaviour of adult relatives who did not reside on their plot. Under earlier legislation a local authority did not need to prove anti-social behaviour prior to terminating residents' site licences. <http://www.travellersinleeds.co.uk/_information/RaceConnors.html>.

53 Niner, P. (2003) *Local Authority Gypsy Traveller Sites in England*, London: ODPM; Kenrick and Clark (1999) op. cit.

54 Morris and Clements (2002) op. cit.

55 Crawley (2004) op. cit.

56 Statistics prepared by the DoE, April 1994, cited in Hawes and Perez (1995) op. cit., p. 40.

57 See Niner (2003) p. 6 and notes to p. 41.

58 Sir George Young, Housing and Planning Minister, cited in the *Independent*, 19 August 1992.

59 See also Chapter 9 and Hetherington, K. (2000) *New Age Travellers: Vanloads of Uproarious Humanity*, London: Cassell; Martin, G. (2002) 'New Age Travellers: Uproarious or Uprooted?', *Sociology*, 36(3): 723–35; and Kenrick and Clark (1999) op. cit.

60 See Campbell, S. (1995) 'Gypsies: The Criminalisation of a Way of Life?', *Criminal Law Review* (1995), pp.28-37.

61 DoE analysis of responses to the consultation paper, 25 November 1992 (unpublished), cited in Morris and Clements (2002) op. cit., p. 14.

62 See Advisory Council for the Education of Romanies and other Travellers analysis of responses from local authorities to the consultation paper, which demonstrates that the great majority of such respondents considered that the proposals 'do not provide workable solutions' (93 per cent); that it was necessary to retain the 100 per cent grant for provision of sites (73 per cent); and that the statutory requirement to provide sites should be retained (56 per cent). Cited in Morris and Clements (2002) op. cit., p. 15.

63 Liberty (2003) 'Your Rights: The Rights of Travellers: The Right to Stop', <http://www.yourrights.org.uk/your-rights/chapters/rights-of-gypsies-and-travellers/index.shtml>

64 Niner (2002) op. cit., p. 39.

65 See Kenrick and Clark (1999) op. cit., p. 109.

66 Emphasis in the original. Letter from Anne Bagehot to Hazel Blears MP, 26 November 2003, cited in Crawley (2004) op. cit., p. 26.

67 See Chapter 4 for a discussion on private-site provision, planning permission and the impact of Circular 1/94. Although authorised private sites have increased in number over the years since the CJPOA came into force, rising from 3,271 (1/94) to 4,760 (1/03), Niner (2003), op. cit., demonstrates that the increased private provision has signally failed to

fulfil the accommodation needs of Travellers to the extent that in the region of 4,500 extra pitches would be required by 2010 to enable the current population access to sites. (Note that these estimated figures fail to take account of the Travellers and Gypsies – numbers of whom cannot be calculated given the present level of administrative statistics – who would prefer to dwell on a site, but who are living in housing.)

68   Although dealing *only* with New Travellers, patterns of movement and aspirations for accommodation, see Greenfields, M. (1999) 'Travelling Light: The Impact on Family Relationships of Going on the Road', unpublished M.Sc. thesis, University of Bath; and Dearling, A. (1998) *No Boundaries: New Travellers on the Road in Europe*, Lyme Regis: Enabler Publications. In addition, we are aware of anecdotal evidence that a number of Gypsies and Travellers reported moving to Ireland, or travelling more frequently into Europe in the mid-1990s as a strategy to avoid the restrictions imposed by the CJPOA. It is important to note that recent legislation passed in Ireland (The Housing [Miscellaneous Provisions] Act 2002 commonly known as the 'Anti-Trespass' Act) has imposed very similar restrictions to the UK CJPOA. It has been anecdotally suggested that the implementation of this piece of legislation in Ireland has led to an increased rate of movement of Travellers from the Republic of Ireland to the UK in the past few years.

69   Webster, L. (1995) 'A Report for the Children's Society on the Impact of the Criminal Justice and Public Order Act on the Lives of Travellers and their Children', Children's Society; FFT (1996) *Confined, Constrained and Condemned: Civil Rights and Travellers*; Davis, J. (1997) 'New Age Travellers in the Countryside: Incomers with Attitude', in Milbourne, P. (ed.) *Revealing Rural 'Others'*, London and Washington: Pinter.

70   Press release from the Chartered Institute of Environmental Health (CIEH), 1 July 1998, cited in Morris and Clements (2002), p. 27.

71   Liberty (1995) *'Criminalising Diversity, Criminalising Dissent'* NCCL.

72   Cowan, D. and Lomax, D. (2003) 'Policing Unauthorised Encampments', *Journal of Law and Society*, 30(2), June 2003, pp. 283-308(26); Webster, L. (1999) 'A Positive Form of Homelessness', unpublished Ph.D. thesis, University of Bath.

73   The Office of the Deputy Prime Minister (ODPM) retains overall responsibility for Gypsy and Traveller policy and collates statistics on numbers of caravans present on authorised and unauthorised sites within local authority districts. In addition, final appeals on planning applications for Gypsy sites are decided by the Deputy Prime Minister.

4 The planning system and the accommodation needs of Gypsies

1   Niner, P. (2003) *Local Authority Gypsy Traveller Sites in England*, London: ODPM; Drakakis-Smith, A. and Mason, K. (2001) 'Out for the Count: A Critical Examination of the DETR Biannual Count of Gypsies and

Travellers in England with Special Reference to Staffordshire', available at
<http://www.radstats.org.uk/n0078/drakakis-smithandmason.htm>.

2 Morris, R. and Clements, L. (2002) *At What Cost? The Economics of Gypsy and Traveller Encampments*, Bristol: Policy Press.

3 Home Office (2003) *Draft Framework Guide on Managing Unauthorised Gypsy and Traveller Encampments*, London: HMSO.

4 Crawley, H. (2004) *Moving Forward: The Provision of Accommodation for Travellers and Gypsies*, London: IPPR.

5 The name by which the Gypsy and Traveller Law Coalition was formerly known.

6 House of Commons (2004) 'Gypsy and Traveller Sites', Housing, Planning, Local Government and the Regions Committee, 13th Report of Session, 2003–4.

7 Niner, op. cit.

8 Including high turnover, non-payment of rent, vandalism of facilities, anti-social behaviour, complaints from neighbouring land users, conflict between different occupiers and difficulty in enforcing maximum length of stay.

9 Brand, C. M. (1986) *Mobile Homes and the Law*, London: Sweet & Maxwell.

10 Hawes, D. and Perez, B. (1996) *The Gypsy and the State: The Ethnic Cleansing of British Society*, 2nd edn, Bristol: Policy Press, p. 18.

11 Quoted in Hawes and Perez, op .cit., p. 4.

12 Ministry of Housing and Local Government (1969) *Caravan Sites Development Control Policy Note 8*, paras 11–14.

13 Booth, P. (1999) 'From Regulation to Discretion: The Evolution of Development Control in the British Planning System 1909–1947', *Planning Perspectives,* 14: 277–89.

14 Home, R. K. (1982) 'Planning Problems of Self-Help Gypsy Sites', *Journal of Planning Law,* 217–4; and Home, R. K. (2002) 'Negotiating Security of Tenure for Peri-Urban Settlement: Traveller-Gypsies and the Planning System in the United Kingdom', *Habitat International,* 26(3): 335–46.

15 Circular 1/94, 'Gypsy Sites and Planning', DoE.

16 Wilson, M. A. (1997) *Directory of Planning Policies for Gypsy Site Provision in England*, Bristol: Policy Press.

17 Resolution 249 (1993), Standing Conference of Local and Regional Authorities of Europe.

18 *R v. Kerrier DC ex p Uzell* [1996] 71 P&CR 566 at 571.

19 *Buckley v. United Kingdom* [1996] 23 EHRR 101.

20 *Chapman v. United Kingdom* [2001] 33 EHRR 399.

21 For detail of case law, see Johnson, C. and Willers, M. (eds) (2004) *Gypsy and Traveller Law,* London: Legal Action Group.

22 In this context the term 'gypsy' is not capitalised in line with planning legislation terminology which does not refer to ethnic status but nomadism to confer 'gypsy status'.

23 Morris and Clements, op. cit., p. 11.

24 Planning Policy Guidance 3, *Housing* (2000).

25 See *Clarke* v. *Secretary of State for the Environment, Transport and the Regions and Tunbridge Wells BC* [2001] EWHC 800 Admin; upheld by the Court of Appeal JPL 552; July 2002 Legal Action 27.

26 *R* v. *Brent LBC ex parte Awua* [1996] AC 55; [1995] 3 All ER 493; (1995) 27 HLR 453, HL.

27 Williams, T. (1999) *Private Gypsy Site Provision*, report for ACERT, Harlow.

28 Williams, op. cit.

5 Bricks and mortar accommodation: Travellers in houses

1   There are large settled Traveller populations in Southampton, Kent, Leicestershire, Worcestershire, Somerset, Herefordshire and Devon (see local authority websites and community and race-equality statements issued within these regions). In the south-west of England in particular, Romani Gypsies are widely noted as being the largest single minority ethnic community (see Dorset County Council website). In addition, there are fairly substantial housed Traveller populations in the cities of Cardiff, Manchester (see Irish Community Care Traveller Family Project), Birmingham and Liverpool, as well as a housed population of unknown size in London (for example, in Greenwich and Ealing) and surrounding conurbations such as Bromley.

2   Hopkinson, G., Ingram, M. and Wishart, B. (2001) *Where's the Real Choice? What are the Accommodation Needs of Travellers in Wychavon?*, Evesham & Pershore HA Ltd./The Housing Corporation/UCE discusses the accommodation preferences of Travellers in houses and on sites, and refers to the large housed population in Worcestershire who have to some extent successfully recreated community structures within housing estates containing a high percentage of Romani Gypsy occupants. Irish studies on 'group housing' and other accommodation options touch upon the experiences of Travellers in conventional housing. See McKeown, K. and McGrath, B. (1996) *Accommodating Travelling People*, Dublin: Crosscare. O'Dwyer, M. (1997) *Irish Travellers Health Access Project Draft Report*, London: Brent Irish Advisory Service. Irish Travellers Project refers to the social isolation experienced by Travellers who are placed in housing, away from their immediate family and support structures. Oral history provides us with rather more information on personal experiences of Travellers in housing, for example, Evans, S. (2004) *Stopping Places: A Gypsy History of South London and Kent*, Hatfield: University of Hertfordshire Press, which refers extensively to the move into 'bricks and mortar' for Travellers displaced from traditional sites in the 1950s and 1960s; and Stanley, B. (2002) *Memories of the Marsh: A Traveller Life in Kent*, South Chailey: Romany & Traveller Family History Society, which deals with the same period of 'resettlement'. The classic anthropological-

biographical text *Nan: The Life of an Irish Travelling Woman* (1986), edited by S. Gmelch, London: Wayland Press, presents considerable information on the eponymous heroine's movement in and out of housing over the course of her long life.

3   See Niner (2003) *Local Authority Gypsy Traveller Sites in England*, London: ODPM, for reference to budgeting problems experienced by newly housed Travellers.

4   Interviews conducted by Margaret Greenfields (MG) in 2000 with Travellers who had experienced living in houses and subsequently returned to unauthorised sites as a result of 'an inability to settle' or financial problems.

5   Booth, C. (1902) *Life and Labour of the People in London*, Vol. III, pp. 151–2. From Booth manuscripts, seventeen volumes, London School of Economics.

6   The Westway local authority Traveller site is renowned for its dreadful location beneath one of the busiest motorways (free-ways) in London. Despite the terrible health risks faced by residents (e.g. constantly breathing in petrol and diesel fumes and enhanced levels of lead in children's blood-streams, risks of vehicles crashing and spilling loads onto the site below, vermin, etc.) they retain an exceptionally strong community spirit and one of the founder members of the Gypsy and Traveller Law Reform Coalition (Mr Tom Sweeney) is a leading light of the Westway site, having successfully campaigned for the provision of a computer suite, Sure Start childrens' services and homework clubs for children who reside on the small plots surrounded by unsanitary recycling provisions and frequent fly-tippers. See further <http://www.mynottinghill.co.uk/nottinghilltv/revealed4.htm>; Kyriacou, S. (1989) *The Forgotten Lives: Gypsies and Travellers on the Westway Site,* London: Ethnic Communities Oral History Project <http://unseen.nlb-online.co.uk/webpages/theforgottenlives.html> and Strehow, C. (1980) *The Westway Gypsy Caravan Site* (unpublished report on behalf of Westminster and St Mary's Hospital Medical Schools which found dangerous levels of lead in air and soil).

7   See Booth (op. cit.) and references in Whetlor, S. (undated) *The Story of Notting Dale: From Potteries and Piggeries to Present Times*, London: Kensington & Chelsea Community History Group; and Gladstone, F. and Barker, A. (1924) *Notting Hill in Bygone Days*, Anne Bingley (1969 reprint).

8   Borrow, G. (1923) *Romano Lavo-lil: Word Book of the Romany or English Gypsy Language*, London: Dent, pp. 207–40. First published 1874.

9   See Samuel, R. (1973) 'Comers and Goers', in Dyos, H. and Wolff, M. (eds) *The Victorian City: Images and Realities*, London: Routledge & Kegan Paul.

10 The first British census was carried out in 1801 and thereafter at ten-yearly intervals apart from 1941. From 1851 greater information on the occupation and relationship between household members was required

than in earlier years, enabling historians to map demographic data and patterns of ethnicity fairly accurately. Census data is released into the public domain after 100 years, so that the most recent available census statistics date from 1901. The 1881 and 1891 census returns are widely available on the Internet and microfiche for public use. Some extremely useful analyses of Gypsy and Traveller families' presence in the 1881 and 1891 census have been carried out by Jackie Blackman, <http://www.passing-through.co.uk>, and by Pauline Gashinski, <http://www.nwon.com/pauline/Travellers.html>, who have also undertaken some work on parish registers and the 1901 census returns.

11 See, for example (1881 Census), the Lee family and a Gumble 'brother-in-law' occupy a house at Bertram Street, St Pancras, Middlesex, while in 'Gipsey Tents', also in St Pancras, a large number of Gumbles are found, along with a Lee and his wife (surnamed Gumble Lee), and a family of Smiths.

12 White, J. (2003) *Campbell Bunk: The Worst Street in North London between the Wars*, London: Pimlico, p. 55. First published 1986.

13 Rudge, T. (2003) *Brumroamin: Birmingham and Midland Gypsy and Traveller Culture*, Birmingham: Birmingham Library & Information Service.

14 See comments by Rundell, J. (unreported decision dated 9 January 2002) who, on being asked to grant an injunction against an unauthorised private Gypsy site by Nuneaton and Bedworth Borough Council on the grounds that some residents of the new site had left the council facility, refused certain aspects of the application, finding that the Griff local authority site was 'a disgrace', riddled with vermin, surrounded by a high concrete wall where passers-by fly-tipped and had left burnt-out cars and with insufficient sanitary or safety features.

15 See Chapter 3 and also, Kenrick and Clark (op. cit.); Niner (2003) op. cit.

16 Cited in Arden, A. and Hunter, C. (2002) *Homelessness and Allocations*, London: Legal Action Group.

17 *Clarke* v. *Secretary of State for the Environment, Transport and the Regions and Tunbridge Wells Borough Council* (2002) EWCA civ 819(2002); and *R (Margaret Price)* v. *Carmarthenshire County Council* (2003) EWHC 42 (Admin).

18 Avebury, E. (2003) 'Travellers and the Homelessness Act', available at <http://www.travellerslaw.org>.

19 (Update since the time of writing.) Note that the requirements implemented under the Housing Act 2004 (subject to Draft Guidance from the ODPM as of June 2005) now mean that all local authorities shall carry out an accommodation needs assessment which explicitly includes the needs of Gypsies and Travellers. Although no date has been given by which local authorities shall have provided additional sites as identified through these means, needs assessment must be completed by 2007.

20 The Homelessness Act 2002 (and the Housing Act 1996 Parts VI and VII

amended by the 2002 legislation) has essentially revived the old Poor Law concept of an applicant needing to show a connection to a local area prior to receiving assistance with accommodation. In common with the Poor Law legislation the requirement of 'local connection' means that authorities can attempt to remove homeless people from their area and return them to their place of origin on the grounds that they are the financial responsibility of another authority.

21 Much of the information pertaining to ethnicity in these areas is anecdotal due to a lack of census and administrative statistics. However, many families are very aware that they are the descendants of Gypsies and Travellers who moved into housing when large sites were cleared in the localities and who then subsequently married local people who they met in school, employment or daily life. The extent to which Gypsies and Travellers retain an awareness and pride in their ethnicity can be demonstrated by the fact that both the Traveller Project in Yately (Hampshire) and Bromley Gypsy Project (Kent) work closely with families who settled into 'bricks and mortar' accommodation fairly recently as well as second- or third-generation housed Gypsies. Similar projects (often in receipt of some funding from local authorities who recognise the size of the Traveller population in their areas) function in Leeds, Manchester, London and other locations.

22 See publications by the Romany & Traveller Family History Society, <http://website.lineone.net/~rtfhs/index2.html>

23 See Evans, S. (2004) *Stopping Places: A Gypsy History of South London and Kent*, Hatfield: University of Hertfordshire Press; Rudge, T. (2003) op. cit.; Stanley, B. (2002) *Memories of the Marsh: A Traveller Life in Kent*, South Chailey: Romany & Traveller Family History Society.

24 Smith, L. (2004) *Romany Nevi-Wesh: An informal history of the New Forest Gypsies*, Minstead: Nova Foresta Publishing.

25 See Forestry Commission Memo, August 1962, which, using language that would not be out of place in Stalinist or Nazi documents of some decades earlier, notes that policy would advocate that 'the first purge will be to rehouse those families who are capable of recreating the species. When they have been dealt with, the older people will follow', cited in Smith (2004) op. cit., p. 115.

26 Probably the most acceptable form of 'conventional' accommodation for Travellers as the fact that they are single-storey removes the difficulty of becoming used to stairs, lessens the noise issues associated with housing, precludes that someone may be residing above the living accommodation and importantly, by the nature of such accommodation, often means that the structure is detached with some small plot of land attached.

27 See, for example, Hopkinson, G., Ingram, M. and Wishart, B. (2001) 'Where's the Real Choice? What Are the Accommodation Needs of Travellers in Wychavon?' Birmingham: Evesham & Pershore HA Ltd./The Housing Corporation/University of Central England, Birmingham.

Travellers in this particular study perceived themselves as only being offered houses on certain estates that contained 'hard to let' properties, and housing officials referred to 'clustering' in the neighbourhood (pp. 29–31). Thomas, P. and Campbell, S. (1992) *Housing Gypsies*, Cardiff: Cardiff Law School (p. 11) (available in PDF at <http://www.law.cf.ac.uk/tlru/publications.html>) cite a former senior housing officer on the 'many complaints from neighbours [where families are housed in isolation, leading to] a real possibility of Gypsy ghettos in areas of housing'.

28 A study undertaken for the DoE (Davies, E. (1987) *Gypsies and Housing*, London: HMSO) found that in the years 1981–5, approximately 20 per cent of Traveller families who sought housed accommodation had been unable to settle and returned to roadside life within a short period of time. The 'Wibberley Report', DoE (1986) *A Report on the Analysis of Responses to Consultation on the Operation of the Caravan Sites Act 1968*, London: DoE, however, considered that the failure of placements into housing was in the region of 50 per cent. Whilst Niner (2003) did not seek to make a quantitative assessment of numbers of Gypsies and Travellers moving in and out of conventional accommodation, she noted (at p. 56) 'only slightly more than half of postal survey respondents were able to estimate what proportion of Gypsy and Traveller tenancies end within a year. Of those who made an estimate, 60 per cent think it is a minority, 16 per cent about half and 24 per cent the majority'.

29 See, particularly, McKeown, K. and McGrath, B. (1996) *Accommodating Travelling People*, Dublin: Crosscare.

30 Local authority or housing association provided accommodation available to families on housing waiting lists, or who are counted as being in priority need as a result of having nowhere legally to park their caravan or who have children, are in ill health, disabled, etc. (see above).

31 Personal communication from Traveller support group staff.

32 Examples of Traveller adaptation of accommodation cited by housing officers in Thomas, P. and Campbell S. (1992) op. cit.

33 *Profiles of Prejudice: The Nature of Prejudice in England: In-Depth Analysis of Findings*, carried out by MORI in May 2003 on behalf of Stonewall's Citizenship 21 project. Report summary available at <http://www.c21project.org.uk/docs/finalpop.pdf>.

34 Duncan. T. (1996) 'Neighbours' Views of Official Sites for Travelling People', Glasgow: The Planning Exchange, Joseph Rowntree Foundation, 'Findings' available at: <http://www.jrf.org.uk/knowledge/findings/housing/H201.asp>.

35 See further findings on mental health and depression from the 2004 Sheffield University study of Gypsy and Traveller health at <http://www.shef.ac.uk/scharr/about/publications/travellers.html>.

36 Thomas and Campbell (1992) op. cit. and Drakakis-Smith, A. (2002) 'Moving On? An Examination and Analysis of the Representation of

Gypsies and Travellers and How this Informs and Perpetuates their Socio-Economic Exclusion via Policy, Practice and Service Delivery in the County of Staffordshire', unpublished Ph.D. thesis, University of Bristol. See specifically Drakakis-Smith on 'how space is controlled and manipulated and how far Gypsy and Traveller movement and settlement is organised and controlled within it revealing nomadism to be a "moving myth"'.

37 Lomax, D., Lancaster, L. and Gray, P. (1999) 'Moving On: A Survey of Travellers' Views', Scottish Executive/Scottish Homes; Niner (2003) op. cit.

38 Cooper, C. and Stott, S. (2003) 'Meeting the Mental Health Needs of Gypsies and Travellers: Facilitating Access to Appropriate Support', Sheffield Adult Mental Health Collaborative Research Group (ongoing project, background information on study); O'Dwyer, M. (1997) 'Irish Travellers' Health Access Project Draft Report', Brent Irish Advisory Service, Irish Travellers' Project; Hennick, M., Cooper, P. and Diamond, R. (1993) 'Primary Healthcare Needs of Travelling People in Wessex', University of Southampton; and see quotations from housed or formerly housed Travellers in Thomas and Campbell (1992) op. cit.; Niner (2003) op. cit.

39 Personal communication and requests for information on cultural support patterns made to the authors by probation staff, social workers and court welfare officers; see also Cemlyn, S. (1998) *Policy and Provision by Social Services for Traveller Children and Families*, Bristol: (university of) SPSS/Nuffield Foundation.

40 See also Power, C. (2004) *Room to Roam: England's Irish Travellers*, London: Action Group for Irish Youth.

41 Calculated by the CRE (2004) *Gypsies and Travellers: A Strategy 2004–2007* (available at <http://www.cre.gov.uk/policy/gypsies_and_travellers.html> and based in part upon CoE statistics from CoE (1995) 'The Situation of Gypsies (Roma and Sinti) in Europe', European Committee on Migration, CDMG (95) 11, 5 May. See also Morris, R. and Clements, L. (2002) *At What Cost? The Economics of Gypsy and Traveller Encampments*, Bristol: Policy Press, p. 8. The figure of 300,000 equates to a population similar to the British Jewish and Sikh communities. (See comments made by Trevor Phillips, Chair of the CRE, at the National Association for Teachers of Travellers Conference, March 2004.)

42 <http://england.shelter.org.uk/home/index.cfm>.

6 Gypsies, Travellers and legal matters

1 'Institutional racism': those forces, social arrangements, institutions, structures, policies, precedents and systems of social relations that operate to deprive certain racially identified categories equality, from

<http://www.socialpolicy.ca>.

2   For example, the presumption that specific requirements imposed by
    professions or legal regimes will not cause hardship over and above that
    experienced by a non-Traveller. See below for a discussion on the Children
    Act 1989 and Gypsies and Travellers involved in criminal proceedings.
    See further Greenfields, M. (2002) 'The Court Experience of New
    Travellers Engaged in s8 Children Act Proceedings', unpublished
    conference paper, Socio-Legal Studies Association Annual Conference,
    April 2002.

3   Greenfields, M. and Home, R. (forthcoming: 2005) 'The Gypsy "Problem"
    or the Paradox of the Settled Nomad', in Bottomley, A. and Lim, H. (eds)
    Feminist Perspectives on Land Law, London: Glasshouse Press.

4   McVeigh, R. (1997) 'Theorising Sedentarism: The Roots of Anti-
    Nomadism, in Acton, T. (ed.) *Gypsy Politics and Traveller Identity*,
    Hatfield: University of Hertfordshire Press.

5   Beier, A. L. (1985) *Masterless Men: The Vagrancy Problem in England,
    1560–1640*, London: Methuen.

6   'The people over the hill' has been used as anthropological shorthand to
    refer to the virtually universal sense of mistrust and fear associated with
    the strange and/or appalling behaviour of communities, tribal groupings or
    other strangers who break taboos, have a disorganised or perverse sense of
    community and are essentially less than human (or 'not like us'). The
    point of the term 'the people over the hill' is that nobody has ever met
    anyone from these particular communities who behaves in such an
    obscene manner; it is always someone further away who has met these
    people and who has passed back the stories about their lifestyles.
    However, everyone has heard about these other communities and their
    actions, and a mythological or warped version of community practices is
    developed. In this way, the terminology 'the people over the hill'
    represents a socio-cultural map, with people who are closer morally and
    socially to the speaker being represented as nearer physically (the next
    village, etc.). People who are further away geographically are represented
    as more distant in terms of culture and behaviour, enabling the speaker to
    demonise them. With the advent of mass media and the growth of
    understanding about a variety of cultures, it is harder for all but the most
    determinedly biased person to adhere to the most extreme beliefs about
    'the people over the hill' and to avoid considering the ways in which
    Gypsies, asylum seekers, the mentally ill, residents of 'rough' housing
    estates, homeless people, lone parents, etc. are often presented as
    perverted and dangerous whilst sharing many characteristics with the
    viewer/reader who is not part of their community. In general, the more
    obviously 'different' a person or community is and the less contact that is
    had with the 'others', the easier it is to construct an idea of their life that
    often bears no resemblance to reality. See Boeree (1999)
    <http://www.ship.edu/~cgboeree/prejudice.html> for further discussion.

The reverse of this demonisation of 'others' is the romanticism associated with certain groups, for example, when Gypsies and Travellers are presented as singing, dancing, exotically dressed mysterious strangers. See various texts by Borrow (1851, 1857); early 'lorists'; romantic novels that feature beautiful Gypsy women and tall, dark and handsome travelling men and the popularity of books such as Davies, J. (1997) *Tales of the Old Gypsies*, Newton Abbot: David and Charles; and websites dedicated to the 'freedom' of life on the road/mysticism. See <http://www.welcomehome.org/rainbow/clans/gypsy.html> and other examples, too numerous to mention, which utilise romanticised images of dubious historical accuracy as part of a marketing ploy (for example, the 'definition' of 'Gypsy' on the following website: <http://www.gypsytea.com>). The construction of an overtly romantic image of Gypsy life reached its apogee in the nineteenth century and should be considered as mirroring the 'Orientalism' common in Britain and France at that time, which reified the (generic) 'East', presenting it as a lush, overblown and corrupt cultural location, more mythologised than based in reality; a discourse that permitted colonialists to present it as 'Othered' and thus inferior to the 'civilised', Christian 'West'. See Edward Said (2003) *Orientalism*, London: Penguin, for a thought-provoking account of the essentialism within such modes of thought, and <http://www.personal.psu.edu/staff/k/x/kxs334/academic/theory/said_orientalism.html>.

7   Hancock, I. (1987) *The Pariah Syndrome: An Account of Gypsy Slavery and Persecution*, Ann Arbor, Mich.: Karoma, extract available at <http://www.geocities.com/Paris/5121/pariah-contents.htm>.

8   <http://www.derbyshire.police.uk/news/354.html>.

9   See <http://www.dglg.org> for further information on the wide-ranging activities of the Derbyshire Gypsy Liaison Group (DGLG).

10 This unduly simplistic explanation of an extremely complex area is further expanded and explained in the excellent legal handbook *Gypsy and Traveller Law* (2004) edited by Chris Johnson and Marc Willers and published by the Legal Action Group. At the time of writing, the text detailed above is the definitive guide to planning and human rights law pertaining to members of the community.

11 See section within the body of the FFT website <http://www.gypsy-traveller.org/noticeboard.htm> under 'Woodside', where an eyewitness account of the aborted eviction is given; see also <http://news.bbc.co.uk/1/hi/uk/2395679.stm>.

12 A large family site, which was home to approximately 150 adults and children. The majority of the fifty children were attending local schools, and a relatively high proportion of the residents (both children and adults) were receiving often long-overdue medical treatment for a variety of conditions. After a lengthy planning case and series of appeals, enforcement notices were issued that required the residents to move off

their own land without receiving provision for removal to alternative accommodation on a caravan site. Education and health treatment were inevitably disrupted and (at the time of writing), some eighteen months after the subsequent brutal eviction, a number of families are still living on roadside sites in the area after failing to achieve access to authorised sites.

13 'Land-swaps' are an innovative concept proposed by the G&TLRC <http://www.travellerslaw.org.uk/pdfs/land_swap.pdf> and subsequently endorsed by a range of religious, social and other organisations, for example, the Cottenham Residents Association, a campaigning group who were initially bitterly opposed to the existence of an unauthorised development within their locality but who, over time and as a result of the negotiations with residents and the G&TLRC, realised that calls for simple eviction failed to deal with the lack of authorised Gypsy sites.

   'Land-swap' schemes involve the exchange of land occupied by Travellers, which is deemed to be on an inappropriate location and where planning permission has not been granted, for land that is considered suitable for site development. Essentially, the local authority provides pitches of equal or higher quality than those vacated, with the local authority taking ownership of the returned pitches. Generally, the concept is underpinned by the understanding that there should be a cut-off date for such a process, and that the original land was bought in 'good faith' for a site, without residents being aware of outstanding planning refusals or the need to apply for permissions. See also <http://www.middleenglandinrevolt.co.uk/jointsta.html>.

14 See <http://www.advocacynet.org/resource_view/link_397.html> for a first-hand account of the brutal eviction carried out at that site.

15 Brearley, M. (1996) 'The Roma/Gypsies of Europe: A Persecuted People', Research Report No. 3, December, London: Institute for Jewish Policy Research.

16 The International Centre on Housing Rights and Evictions publishes an 'evictions monitor' detailing state actions against insecurely accommodated and socially excluded communities around the world. Each edition provides a round-up of recent events. The overall picture of marginalised and poverty-stricken communities experiencing the erosion of their civil rights as their accommodation options are diminished presents a depressing and alarming picture of worldwide loss of land rights. In a number of international reports, similar (although more extreme) tactics to those used in bailiff-led evictions in the UK are detailed, leading in some cases to the deaths of those evicted from formerly commonly held or tolerated land, <http://www.cohre.org/downloads/Evictions-Monitor-N02-V011-Dec2004.pdf>.

17 See Cemlyn, S. (2000) 'Assimilation, Control, Mediation or Advocacy? Social Work Dilemmas in Providing Anti-Oppressive Services for Traveller Children and Families', *Child and Family Social Work*, Vol. 5: 4: 327–41; and <http://www.greenleaf.demon.co.uk/h850601.htm> for an account of

children being removed into care when New Travellers were attacked and arrested at Stonehenge in 1985.

18 See <http://www.schnews.org.uk/archive/news25.htm>; and also discussion on animals being destroyed and attempts to remove children from Travellers facing eviction by use of Emergency Protection Orders at Stoney Cross in 1986 in Earle et al. (1994) *A Time to Travel? An Introduction to Britain's Newer Travellers*, Lyme Regis: Enabler Publications.

19 Kenrick and Clark (1999) op. cit.; Morris, R. and Clements, L. (2001) *Disability, Social Care, Health and Travelling People*, Cardiff: TLRU, p. 62.

20 Scottish Equal Opportunities Committee/SCF (2001) 'Having Our Say: A Peer Research Project with Young Gypsy/Travellers in Scotland', <http://www.scottish.parliament.uk/business/committees/historic/equal/reports-01/eor01–01-v0102–05.htm>, evidence from Clementine MacDonald, para 9.

21 Kundnani, A., Independent Race and Refugee News Network, <http://www.irr.org.uk/2004/june/ak000012.html>, 24 June 2004.

22 A land charge means that the local authority registers a debt to a particular value against the deeds of the land. On the sale of the land, the local authority is able to reclaim the cost of the action, or even force a sale to meet the debt.

23 <http://www.statewatch.org/news/2005/jun/coe-uk-report.pdf>.

24 European Roma Rights Centre (2005) 'Greece Systematically Frustrates Fundamental Rights of Roma to Adequate Housing', <http://www.errc.org/cikk.php?cikk=2265>, 8 June 2005.

25 For further information on basic child-protection proceedings in the UK and duties of local authorities towards children and families, please see <http://www.frg.org.uk> (advice sheet downloads); <http://www.dh.gov.uk/assetRoot/04/06/13/03/04061303.pdf>; <http://www.ntas.org.uk/childrenact.htm> and <http://www.cafcass.gov.uk>.

26 See Cemlyn, S. (2000) 'From Neglect to Partnership? Challenges for Social Services in Promoting the Welfare of Traveller Children', *Child Abuse Review*, Vol. 9: 5: 349–63, for a discussion on attitudes towards and concerns about children's removal into care.

27 See, for example, the Patrin Timeline of Romani History <http://www.geocities.com/Paris/5121/timeline.htm>; Jourdan, L. (2000) on the Yenish children in Switzerland <http://lists.errc.org/rr_nr4_2000/past_abuses.shtml>; and Petterson, K.-S. (2005) 'Norwegian Tatere Children and State Intervention/Removal from their Parents (Assimilation Policies)' <http://www.nova.no/index.gan?objid=8047&subid=0&language=1>.

28 See Chapter 8 where cultural and social attitudes to education are considered and evidence on bullying and racism within educational environments is presented.

29 Cemlyn, S. (1998) *Policy and Provision by Social Services for Traveller*

Children and Families, Bristol: University of Bristol/Nuffield Foundation.

30 Aspects of family law that impact on children's place of residence after divorce or parental separation; contact with parents and other relatives with whom they do not live, etc.

31 The sections of the Children Act that govern social services involvement with children, for example, fostering, adoption, child protection and 'preventative services' that can be put in place to help families who are under stress.

32 A form of agreement is commonly made where parents are coerced into assenting that a child is cared for by social services without the need for the department to go to court for a care order. In some cases, local authorities are unsure whether they would be able to provide enough evidence of child-protection issues to obtain a court order and use 'accommodation' as an alternative option on the grounds that the parents retain greater say in what happens to their child if a care order is not in existence, and that technically a parent can remove the child from 'accommodation'. In practice, if a parent seeks to remove a child from accommodation the local authority will usually apply for a care order on the grounds that the child may be or is in danger. See further fact sheets on 'accommodation' at <http://www.frg.org.uk>.

33 Greenfields, M. (2002) 'New Travellers and Post-Separation Parenting', unpublished Ph.D. thesis, University of Bath; see also Greenfields, M. (2002) 'Equal in the Eyes of the Law? New Travellers and S8 Children Act Applications', conference paper given to the Socio-Legal Studies Association Annual Conference.

34 A court order made under Section 8 of the Children Act, which specifies particular aspects of a child's upbringing, for example, which school they should attend; if they should be allowed to go to certain places or meet specific people, etc.

35 Power, C. (2004) *Room to Roam: England's Irish Travellers*, London: Action Group for Irish Youth.

36 Stewart, R. and Kilfeather, J. (1999) 'Working with Travellers in Northern Ireland', in Henderson, P. and Kaur, R. (eds) *Rural Racism in the UK*, London: Community Development Publications.

37 Pemberton, D. (2001) 'Fostering in a Minority Community: Travellers in Ireland', in Greeff, R. (ed.) *Fostering Kinship: An International Perspective on Kinship Foster Care*, London: Ashgate.

38 See data on Black children in mainland Britain for a comparative discussion on how and why some communities may come into contact with the care system, and their experiences of racism and cultural isolation. Useful background documents on this subject include: Barn, A. (1993) *Black Children in the Public Care System*, London: Batsford; Candappa, M. (2004) *Improving Services to Black and Ethnic Minority Children and their Families*, London: Understanding Children's Social Care 6 DH/TCRU (Institute of Education); Selwyn, J., Frazer, L. and

Fitzgerald, A. (2005) *Finding Adoptive Families for Black, Asian and Black Mixed-Parentage Children: Executive Summary and Best Practice Guide*, London: National Children's Homes <http://www.bristol.ac.uk/sps/downloads/FPCW/recruiting2.pdf>.

39 A small charity formed by a group of Travellers, lawyers and civil-liberties campaigners in the mid-1980s to administer small grants and to offer a range of specialist advice and support services to Gypsies and Travellers, including assisting with the set-up of community projects. Travellers Aid Trust is a recipient of a percentage of the royalties received from the sale of this book <http://www.travellersaidtrust.org>.

40 One of the authors of this text has direct experience of local authorities who have (for example) refused to provide statutory services for disabled Travellers and then indicated that without access to disabled adaptations in trailers it would not be possible to return someone from hospital or permit them to remain living on a site.

41 <http://www.cre.gov.uk/policy/gtstrat/opportunities.html>.

42 Romani Gypsies have been recognised in law as a racial group since 1988 (*CRE* v. *Dutton*). Irish Travellers, who have been travelling in England as a distinct social group since the 1800s, received legal recognition as a racial group in England and Wales in 2000 (*O'Leary* v. *Allied Domecq*).

43 See Chapter 8 of the LAG Handbook on *Gypsy and Traveller Law* (2004), Johnson, C. and Willers, M. (eds) London: Legal Action Group.

44 *Smith and Smith* v. *Cheltenham Borough Council*, 7 June 1999 (Bristol County Court unreported); see also <http://www.yourrights.org.uk/your-rights/chapters/rights-of-gypsies-and-travellers/racim-and-discrimination/racism-and-discrimination.shtml>.

45 op. cit. (and see Bibliography).

46 <http://www.cre.gov.uk/policy/gtstrat/role.html>.

47 Morris and Clements (2002) op. cit., p. 90.

48 James, Z. (2005) 'Policing Space: Managing New Travellers in England', *British Journal of Criminology*. Advance Access Published 15 August 2005, 10; Barton, A. and James, Z. (2003) '"Run to the Sun": Policing Contested Perceptions of Risk. Policing and Society', 13 (3): 259–270. 1093/bjc/azi077; Cowan, D. and Lomax, D. (2003) 'Policing Unauthorised Camping', *Journal of Law and Society* 30(2): 283–308.

49 For one of the few academic papers on policing of Travellers, see Cowan, D. and Lomax, D. (2003) 'Policing Unauthorised Camping', *Journal of Law and Society*, 30 (June): 283–308.

50 <http://www.monitoring-group.co.uk/News%20and%20Campaigns/news-stories/2003/Asylum%20seekers%20and%20refugees/death_of_asylum_seekers_rise.htm>.

51 <http://news.bbc.co.uk/1/hi/special_report/1999/02/99/stephen_lawrence/285357.stm>.

52 <http://observer.guardian.co.uk/race/story/0,11255,1086301,00.html>.

53 <http://news.bbc.co.uk/1/hi/england/southern_counties/3237841.stm>

and <http://news.bbc.co.uk/1/hi/england/southern_counties/
3272309.stm>.

54 <http://www.cps.gov.uk/news/pressreleases/archive/132_04.html>.

55 See discussion on the CD *Del Gavvers Pukker-Cheerus: Advice from
    Gypsies and Travellers on Sorting Out Racists*, Gypsy Media
    Company/Home Office. As a footnote to the Firle incident, it is pleasant to
    recount that a Gypsy Bonfire Society was formed that held its own highly
    successful 'alternative' firework celebration in 2004 as a way of laying to
    rest the previous year's events:
    <http://news.bbc.co.uk/1/hi/england/southern_counties/3969201.stm>.

56 Home, R., Greenfields, M. and the Cambridge Gypsy and Traveller
    Advisory Group (2006) *The Cambridge Sub-Region Traveller Needs
    Assessment*, Cambridge: Anglia Ruskin University/Buckinghamshire
    Chilterns University College ('The Cambridge Project'). This study, which
    was undertaken to fulfil a regional accommodation needs assessment as
    required under the Housing Act 2004, was unique in being carried out by
    members of English Gypsy, Irish Traveller and Showmen communities
    working in full partnership with the academic team. Although the
    research axis concentrated on accommodation need and aspiration, key
    elements of the study included 'new public health' agendas including
    community safety, physical and mental health, education, employment,
    access to services and indices of social inclusion. Gypsy and Traveller
    community members were trained in interviewing and research methods
    and the study was undertaken using the Modified Andalusian
    Snowballing technique, a mixed methodology consisting of triangulating
    data gleaned from primary surveys, documentary analysis, depth
    interviews, focus groups and community validation events. At the time of
    writing this is the largest study of Gypsy and Traveller needs undertaken
    in the UK. The methodology is currently being successfully replicated in a
    number of local regions, assisting in local capacity building for Gypsy and
    Traveller communities.

    Further similar evidence may be heard by listening to *Del Gavvers
    Pukker-Cheerus* (op. cit.).

57 See website <http://www.pridenotprejudice.org.uk>.

58 <http://news.bbc.co.uk/1/hi/uk/2370883.stm>.

59 <http://www.met.police.uk/job/job952/live_files/8.htm>.

60 Judicial Studies Board 'Equal Treatment Bench Book' at 1.5.7 and 1.5.8,
    <http://www.jsboard.co.uk/etac/etbb/benchbook/et_01/et_mf08.htm>.

61 <http://www.homeoffice.gov.uk/crime/antisocialbehaviour/orders>.

62 See the following links for articles that detail when and how some ASBOs
    have been granted: <http://icbirmingham.icnetwork.co.uk/
    birminghampost/news/tm_objectid=15556828&method=full&siteid=5000
    2&headline=teenagers-given-asbos-for-car-minding-racket-outside-villa-
    park-name_page.html>;
    <http://www.cleansafeworldwide.org/doc.asp?doc=1982&cat=159>;

<http://news.bbc.co.uk/2/hi/uk_news/magazine/3900369.stm>;
<http://news.bbc.co.uk/1/hi/uk/3948821.stm>.

63 Home Office statistics, 1999–2004
<http://www.crimereduction.gov.uk/asbos2.xls>.

64 <http://observer.guardian.co.uk/uk_news/story/0,6903,1504906,00.html>;
<http://www.redpepper.org.uk/civ/x-apr2005-asbos.htm>.

65 Indeed the ethnicity or other characteristics of people issued with ASBOs
are not collected centrally. See Hazel Blears's written answer to
parliamentary question, Hansard, 7 June 2005, Column 501W,
<http://www.publications.parliament.uk/pa/cm200506/cmhansrd/cm050
607/text/50607w15.htm>.

66 <http://news.bbc.co.uk/1/hi/uk_politics/4263113.stm>.

67 <http://society.guardian.co.uk/localgovt/story/0,7890,1497375,00.html>
and see further James (2005) and Barton and James (2003) op. cit.

68 <http://www.yorkshiretoday.co.uk/
ViewArticle2.aspx?SectionID=55&ArticleID=1054132>.

69 <http://www.guardian.co.uk/racism/Story/0,2763,202987,00.html>;
<http://news.bbc.co.uk/1/hi/uk_politics/4365287.stm>.

70 Temporary stop notice guidance (ODPM) March 2005,
<http://www.odpm.gov.uk/stellent/groups/odpm_planning/documents/
page/odpm_plan_035784.pdf>.

71 See chapter on planning and private sites and statutory definition of a
'gypsy' for planning purposes.

72 <http://news.bbc.co.uk/1/hi/business/3417401.stm>; see also
<http://money.guardian.co.uk/personal/story/0,13970,1451928,00.html>.

73 For examples of newspaper headlines referring to this problem see
<http://icberkshire.icnetwork.co.uk/0100news/slough/tm_objectid=15643
286&method=full&siteid=50102&headline=cleaning-up-travellers-mess-
costs-thousands-name_page.html>;
<http://www.accringtonobserver.co.uk/news/s/49/49222_fury_over_travel
lers.html>;
<http://www.metronews.co.uk/news/article/0/638_travellers_leave_thous
ands_of_pounds_worth_of_damage_behind.html>.

74 See 'Stamp Out the Prejudice' campaign seven-point charter
<http://www.naar.org.uk/newspages/050406b.asp>; and minutes of the
ODPM Select Committee report (Anti-Social Behaviour) at para 193,
<http://www.parliament.the-stationery-
office.co.uk/pa/cm200304/cmselect/cmodpm/633/63318.htm>.

75 Crawley, H. (2004) op. cit., p. 37.

76 See <http://www.parliament.the-stationery-
office.co.uk/pa/cm200304/cmselect/cmodpm/633/63318.htm>,
particularly paras 201 and 207; see also 'Stamp Out the Prejudice'
campaign seven-point charter
<http://www.naar.org.uk/newspages/050406b.asp>.

77 Kent and Medway Council, *Statistical and Behaviour Analysis of*

Unauthorised Encampments in 2004, p. 2. (internally circulated reports, Kent and Medway Councils) and <http://www.redcar-cleveland.gov.uk/YrCounc1.nsf/7C69A56600302C3880256F2000381057/$File/GTS05.pdf>, para 3.3.

78 Although see the Joseph Rowntree Foundation findings (1996) on 'Understanding and Preventing Youth Crime' for a discussion on children's risk factors pertaining to crime and social exclusion <http://www.jrf.org.uk/knowledge/findings/socialpolicy/SP.93.asp>.

79 Pizani-Williams, L. (1998) 'Gypsies and Travellers in the Criminal Justice System: The Forgotten Minority?', Institute of Criminology Occasional Paper No. 23, Cambridge: University of Cambridge.

80 Given the age of the Pizani-Williams data (research carried out in 1993/4), it is possible that the profile of young people's economic activities and contacts with the police has altered post-publication. Certainly, more recent anecdotal evidence indicates the increasing criminalisation of youth, aided perhaps by the rapid rise in the use of ASBOs (see above); higher rates of substance abuse amongst socially excluded young people, particularly those resident on 'sink' housing estates; the enhanced pressures to enforce educational attendance; and powers such as prosecution for parents who condone 'truanting'. The conflation of these changing legislative and social pressures would go some way to accounting for the apparent trend in earlier criminalisation of young people from Gypsy and Traveller communities reported by community workers and family members.

81 The 'Moving Forward' project aims to develop materials and best practice to help combat stereotyping, prejudice and discrimination against Gypsies and Travellers. Best-practice training and materials are specifically designed for use by decision-makers and trainers in public services whose staff come into contact with Travelling communities. The project is the brainchild of Derbyshire Gypsy Liaison Group working with John Coxhead, Gypsy and Traveller Liaison Officer with Derbyshire Constabulary, Professor Marie Parker-Jenkins of the University of Derby and a network of community activists. The project is being supported by the community-cohesion team at the Centre for Policing Excellence and the Home Office: <http://www.dglg.org>.

82 The Macpherson Report into the circumstances surrounding the tragic murder of Stephen Lawrence, a young Black man, highlighted the failures in policing and 'institutional racism' inherent in many police practices. As a result of the lengthy recommendations made in the report, <http://www.archive.official-documents.co.uk/document/cm42/4262/sli-47.htm>, the subsequent political and policy debate and the police service's sober rethink of their handling of racist incidents, the past few years have brought about significant changes in responses to BME communities and the development of enhanced community-liaison strategies and good-practice models. Whilst it will inevitably take some

time for many 'rank and file' police officers to come to terms with the expectation that 'a racist incident is any one incident which is perceived to be racist by the victim or any other person' and that such incidents, however minor they may appear, *must and will be investigated*, the report has proved a benchmark for good practice. Despite the overhaul of policing that the report has brought about and the implementation of the Race Relations (Amendment) Act 2000, perhaps unsurprisingly in the light of earlier discussions, statistical reports, articles and studies of policing and prison populations from BME communities signally fail to refer to Gypsies and Travellers (see, for example, <http://www.bmecrackingcrime.org.uk/docs/library/154.doc>). Similarly, the Youth Justice Board, when carrying out their excellent review of minority ethnic young people in the youth justice system, 'Differences or Discrimination' <http://www.youth-justice-board.gov.uk/Publications/Scripts/prodList.asp?idCategory=17&menu=ite m&eP=YJB> also managed to exclude members of Travelling communities from consideration.

83 See Every Child Matters, a Government website which details policy changes and targets that identify children 'at risk' of abuse and social exclusion at an early stage of their lives, enabling support and monitoring to be put in place to assist in social integration and achievement for all children in the UK: <http://www.everychildmatters.gov.uk/aims>. The policy initiative arose following an interdepartmental review which explored the barriers to achievement for children and outlined a fundamental change in young people's services and public responsibility for youth well-being and protection: <http://archive.treasury.gov.uk/docs/2001/ccr_children_tor.html>. Whilst the proposed monitoring and identification arrangements that will seek to 'flag up' concerns about children and young people 'at risk' have been the subject of considerable criticisms (not least on civil liberties and 'labelling' grounds) (see <http://society.guardian.co.uk/children/comment/0,1074,1186315,00.htm l>), at the time of writing, a range of projects are under development across the UK. Particular cornerstones of the core aims include minimising risks of youth offending, steering children 'at risk' in positive directions and addressing potential offending behaviours. <http://www.crimereduction.gov.uk/youth56.htm>.

84 Stanton, A. (1994) 'An Impressionist Account of the Discrimination Suffered by White Ethnic Minorities in Newark', unpublished paper cited in Fletcher, H., Hutton, S., McCarthy, J. and Mitchell, H. (1997) *The Irish Community: Discrimination and the Criminal Justice System*, London: National Association of Probation Officers/Federation of Irish Societies/Action Group for Irish Youth/Irish Commission for Prisoners Overseas and The Bourne Trust, available at: <http://www.irish.org.uk/pdfs/discrimi.pdf>.

85 Power, C. (2003) 'Irish Travellers: Ethnicity, Racism and Pre-Sentence Reports', *Probation Journal*, 50(3): 252–66.

86 Devereaux, D. (1999) 'Enforced Invisibility: The Irish Experience of the Criminal Justice System', unpublished M.A. thesis, School of Law, Manchester Metropolitan University, quoted in Power (2003) op. cit.

87 Heavens, J. (2003) *Review of Deaths in Custody at HM Prison Brixton*, London: HM Prison Service.

7 Travellers' health

1   See, for example, 'GP Shortage Threatened by Pay Differential', *The Scotsman*, 28 May 2003; and 'Postcode Lottery in GP Services', BBC News/Health <http://www.bbc.co.uk>, 9 July 2002.

2   Although the General Medical Council Ethical Guidance specifies in the 'Contractual Arrangements in Health Care: Professional Responsibilities in Relation to the Clinical Needs of Patients' guidance of May 1992 that a GP should not simply refuse to accept or alternatively remove a patient from their books because of the expense/impact on targets of provision of treatment, this is an ethical rather than legal or contractual matter and, in practice, GPs make their own decisions. The same set of guidelines also specify that GPs should not refuse to accept or treat patients because of their ethnicity, religion, the GP's personal beliefs, etc.

3   <http://www.msfcphva.org/sigs/sigtravellers.html>.

4   <http://society.guardian.co.uk/primarycare/story/0,8150,900034,00.html> and <http://society.guardian.co.uk/primarycare/story/0,8150,981036,00.html>.

5   <http://www.tin.nhs.uk/events-calendar/success-2005/category-definitions/working-partnerships/gypsy-travellers-newark>.

6   <http://www.dh.gov.uk/assetRoot/04/07/80/39/04078039.pdf>.

7   See Race Equality Scheme: PCT and in particular para 5.2 of the report at <http://www.herefordshire.nhs.uk/Portals/0/race%20equality%20scheme%20internet.pdf>.

8   See the Sheffield Health Study (2004) <http://www.shef.ac.uk/scharr/about/publications/travellers.html>.

9   Van Cleemput, P. and Parry, G. (2001) 'Health Status of Gypsy Travellers', *Journal of Public Health Medicine*, 23(2): 129–34.

10 The risk of ill health and increased morbidity experienced by Travellers is exacerbated by the percentage of Travellers living on roadside sites who have no or limited access to clean water, which was found to be between 14 per cent and 30 per cent of Travellers depending on location in the UK: Feder, G. S. (1989) 'Traveller Gypsies and Primary Care', *Journal Royal College of General Practitioners*, 39 (October): 425–9. The figure was 16 per cent in Ireland: Clarke, B. (1998) 'The Irish Travelling Community: Outcasts of the Celtic Tiger? Dilemmas for Social Work', *Social Work in Europe* 5(1): 28–34. Similarly, the percentage of Travellers with no access

to water or chemical lavatories on site has been found to vary between 33 per cent and 58 per cent of those resident in the UK (Feder, op. cit.) and 36 per cent in Ireland (Clarke, op. cit.).

11 Chartered Institute of Environmental Health (CIEH) (1995) *Travellers and Gypsies: An Alternative Strategy*, CIEH; Pahl, J. and Vaile, M. (1988) 'Health and Health Care Among Travellers', *Journal of Social Policy*, 17: 195–213.

12 Nelligan, D. (1993) *Report of the Specialist Health Visitor for Travelling Families 5/90–11/92*, Bristol: internally published report from the United Bristol Healthcare Trust not in general public domain.

13 Strehow, C. (1980) 'The Westway Gypsy Caravan Site', unpublished survey for the Westminster and St Mary's Hospital Medical Schools of environmental factors affecting residents of the above-named London site.

14 The Children's Society (1998) *My Dream Site*, Bath: The Children's Society.

15 Beach, H. (1999) 'Injury Rates in Gypsy-Traveller Children', unpublished M.Sc. dissertation, University of Wales College of Medicine.

16 NHS Action Plan (2001), London: Department of Health, see especially Chapters 9, 13 and 16.

17 See below and Power, C. (2004) *Room to Roam: England's Irish Travellers*, London: Action Group for Irish Youth.

18 See, for example, Black Country Inter-Authority Health Group (BCIAHG) (1992) *Gypsy and Traveller Families in the West Midlands*, (internally published report): Black Country Inter-Authority Health Group; Cornwell, J. (1984) *Improving Health Care for Travellers*, London: King's Fund.

19 Feder, G. (1989) op. cit.

20 Bancroft, A., Lloyd, M. and Morran, R. *The Right to Roam: Travellers in Scotland 1995/96*, Dunfermline: Save the Children Fund (Traveller Section).

21 Cardiff Gypsy Sites Group (1991) *The First Decade: Cardiff Gypsy Sites Group 1981–1991*, Cardiff: CGSG.

22 See 'Gypsy Mistrust of Jabs Hits GP Targets' the *Guardian*, 2 August 1990; BCIAHG (1992) op. cit.; and Bell, E., Riding, M. and Collier, P. (1983) 'Susceptibility of Itinerants (Travelling people) in Scotland to Poliomyelitis', *Bulletin of the World Health Organisation*, 61: 839–43, which found that over 50 per cent of Travellers aged between five and sixty-one had no recollection of receiving vaccinations against polio or other infectious diseases.

23 FFT (1998) 'Report of the Pilot Health Promotion Project with Travellers in Dorset 1997–1998', FFT on behalf of Dorset Health Authority; Davis, J. and Hoult, H. (2000) 'Travelling Families Health Needs', in Rowbotham, A. and Sheldrake, D. (eds) *Health Visiting Specialist and Higher Level Practice*, London: Churchill Livingstone, Chapter 17; and see MacAuley, D. (1991) 'Care of the Travelling Community', *Journal of the Irish College of GPs*, 8: 58–60, citing the exceptionally low percentage of women aged

twenty-five to sixty-five who had received cervical smear testing, although ironically this appeared to correlate to their degree of mobility and hence access to services rather than refusal to participate in the scheme.

24 See Chapter 2 of this text; Hennick, M., Cooper, P. and Diamond, R. (1993) *Primary Healthcare Needs of Travelling People in Wessex*, Southampton: University of Southampton/Department of Social Statistics (Working Paper 95–01); see also, for references to pregnancy and family size, Durward, L. (1990) *Traveller Mothers and Babies: Who Cares for their Health?* London: Maternity Alliance; Hawes, D. (1997) *Gypsies, Travellers and the Health Service: A Study in Inequality*, Bristol: Policy Press.

25 Maternity Alliance (1992) *Safe Childbirth for Travellers Information Pack*, London: Maternity Alliance; Pahl and Vaile (1988) op. cit., and Linthwaite, P. (1983) *The Health of Traveller Mothers and Children in East Anglia*, London: Save the Children Fund.

26 Pahl, J. and Vaile, M. (1986) *Health and Health Care among Travellers*, Canterbury: University of Kent.

27 Davis and Hoult (2000) op. cit.

28 See Power (2004) op. cit.; Nelligan (1993) op. cit.; Van Cleemput, P. (2000) 'Health Care Needs of Travellers', *Archives of Disease in Childhood*, 82(1): 32–7.

29 Sutherland, A. (1992) 'Cross-Cultural Medicine: A Decade Later', *Western Journal of Medicine* 157: 276–80; Lehti A. and Mattson, B. (2001) 'Health, Attitude to Care and Pattern of Attendance among Gypsy Women: A General Practice Perspective', *Family Practice*, 18(4): 445–8.

30 Power (2004) op. cit., p. 44.

31 <http://www.nhs.uk/england/noAppointmentNeeded/ walkinCentres/default.aspx>.

32 Davis and Hoult (2000) op. cit., p. 387; Van Cleemput, P. (2000) 'Health Care Needs of Travellers', *Archives of Disease in Childhood*, 82(1): 35.

33 See Lehti and Mattson (2001) op. cit.

34 Davis and Hoult (2000) op. cit., p. 391.

35 Durward (1990) op. cit.; Hawes, D. and Perez, B. (1996) *The Gypsy and the State: The Ethnic Cleansing of British Society*, Bristol: Policy Press; Heller, T. and Peck, B. (1983) 'Health Policy for Gypsies', unpublished paper, University of Sheffield; Linthwaite, P. (1983) op. cit.

36 Pahl and Vaile (1986) op. cit.

37 Crout, L. (1987) *Traveller Health Care Project: Facilitating Access to the NHS*, Walsall Health Authority; Pahl and Vaile (1988) op. cit.

38 Barry, J. and Kirke, P. (1997) 'Congenital Abnormalities in the Irish Traveller Community', *Irish Medical Journal*, 90: 223–4; Barry, J., Herity, B. and Solan, J. (1987) *The Travellers' Health Status Study: Vital Statistics of Travelling People*, Dublin: Dublin Health Research Board; Hennink et al. (1993) op. cit. Although the first two studies are specifically concerned with Irish Traveller populations in the Republic of Ireland, there is limited evidence (often anecdotal and identified by health workers and planning

consultants working with Travelling families) which indicates that clusters of specific (and often unusual) metabolic diseases, genetic abnormalities or other conditions (for example, congenital deafness) are found amongst some Romani Gypsy and Irish Traveller families in Britain. Formal research evidence is sparse, yet Hennick et al. in their literature review suggest that this may be related to the relatively high degree of consanguinity found within the population. See also, the executive report from Health ASERT (Wales) 'A Research Programme to Enhance the Evidence Base on Health Promotion Issues amongst Ethnic Minorities, Refugees and Travellers in Wales', which cites a trend towards a greater prevalence of congenital abnormalities amongst Traveller children where parents are married to their first cousins. <http://www.mdx.ac.uk/www/rctsh/asert/executive_summary_gypsy_travellers.htm#5>.

39 Linthwaite (1983) op. cit.; Pahl and Vaile (1988) op. cit.; Hennick et al. (1993) op. cit.

40 Linthwaite (1983) op. cit. found extreme variations from the national average when exploring perinatal death rates amongst Travellers in East Anglia, but the methodology of her study has been questioned. Pahl and Vaile (1988) op. cit. found an increase of 1.48 for stillbirths for women on private and unauthorised sites when compared to those on local authority facilities, and 1.38 for highly mobile Traveller women. Both studies found considerably increased rates of perinatal death amongst insecurely sited women when compared with the general population.

41 Office for National Statistics (2003) Series DH3 Mortality Statistics: Childhood, Infant and Perinatal. Review of the Registrar General on Deaths in England and Wales, 2001, London: The Stationery Office.

42 Fitzpatrick, J. and Cooper, N. (2001) 'Patterns and Trends in Stillbirths and Infant Mortality', in Griffiths, C. and Fitzpatrick, J. (eds) Geographic Variations in Health, London: The Stationery Office, pp. 162–81.

43 Kramer, M., Seguin, L., Lydon, J. et al. (2000) 'Socio-Economic Disparities in Pregnancy Outcome: Why Do the Poor Fare So Poorly?', Paediatric Perinatal Epidemiol, 14: 194–210.

44 McAuley, D. (1991) 'Care of the Travelling Community', Journal of the Irish College of GPs, 8: 58–60, an Irish study that found that less than 15 per cent of women whose records were surveyed showed evidence of having had cervical smear tests, and of those women who had been screened, the majority were resident on 'settled' sites. McAuley's findings bear a marked resemblance to qualitative research reports within the UK. See Power (2004) op. cit., Chapter 3; Durward (1990), op. cit. and anecdotal evidence gathered from health visitors and medical staff, as well as one of the authors of this text who routinely interviews female Travellers involved in planning applications on their health needs and status.

45 National Institute for Clinical Excellence/Scottish Executive/Department of Health, Social Services and Public Safety: Northern Ireland (2001) 'Why

Mothers Die 1997–1999', London: Confidential Enquiries into Maternal Deaths/Royal College of Obstetricians and Gynaecologists available at <http://www.cemach.org.uk/publications/CEMDreports/cemdrpt.pdf>.

46 Within the body of the report, 'Direct' causes are those directly related to pregnancy; 'Indirect' are those in which an underlying medical condition was aggravated by pregnancy and 'Coincidental' refers to unrelated causes of death. 'Late' deaths are those that occur later than six weeks postpartum but within a year of delivery and *may* potentially relate to illnesses or events that would, had mortality occurred at an earlier date, have been included under 'Direct' or 'Indirect' categories.

47 Hennick et al. (1993) op. cit.

48 Barry, J. et al. (1987) op. cit.

49 <http://www.travellersinleeds.co.uk/travellers/downloads/ BaselineCensus.pdf>.

50 O'Dwyer, M. (1997) *Irish Travellers Health Access Project Draft Report*, London: BIAS Irish Travellers Project/NHS Ethnic Health Unit.

51 Pavee Point (2004) 'Factsheet: Irish Travellers'. Data taken from the 2002 Irish Census <http://www.paveepoint.ie>.

52 Crout (1987) op. cit.; Crout, E. (1988) 'Have Healthcare, Will Travel', *The Health Service Journal*, 14 January: 47–8. Thomas, J., Doucette, M. and Thomas, D. C. (1987) 'Disease, Lifestyle and Consanguinity amongst 58 American Gypsies', *The Lancet* 2: 377–9; Wilson, G. (1988) 'On the Road', *Nursing Times*, 84(3): 26–7; Hawes, D. (1997) *Gypsies, Travellers and the Health Service*, Bristol: Policy Press; O'Dwyer, M. (1997) *Irish Travellers Health Access Project: Draft Report*, Brent Irish Advisory Service; *Bromley Gypsy Traveller Community Project Annual Report 1995–6* (1996), Bromley: BGTCP, which expressed concern at 'the number of Travellers dying of heart disease at a young age'. See also medical reports seen by the authors of this text when undertaking planning enquiries, numerous interview data gathered from Travellers seeking access to secure sites who report that they have received treatment for 'bad hearts' and information obtained from health workers with Travelling communities. The booklet entitled *On the Road to Better Health for Travelling Men* (2003) published by The Men's Health Forum in conjunction with NAHWT explicitly refers to Travellers as being at risk from cardiovascular conditions.

53 Although the authors have been advised by many Travellers that they are prone to urinary tract and renal conditions, the only study that refers to this tendency within the communities is the American research carried out by Thomas et al. (1987) op. cit., which found 20 per cent of the (small) sample suffered from chronic renal problems.

54 Although cancer is a relatively common cause of death among Travellers (and in common with most communities perhaps the most feared diagnosis a patient can be given), in the absence of clear data or research, it is unclear whether a hereditary tendency towards the disease exists in the population and, if so, which cancers are most prevalent, or whether the

relatively high number of Travellers who smoke cigarettes and late diagnosis of the condition associated with poor access to health care create a misleading impression of the prevalence of the disease amongst Travelling people.

55 A number of localised UK research studies record the extremely high incidence of asthma amongst Travellers. See, for example, Crout, E. (1987) 'Trailer Bound Community Outlook', *Nursing Times*, May; Crout (1988) op. cit.; Hennink et al. (1993) op. cit.; Anderson, E. (1997) 'Health Concerns and Needs of Travellers', *Health Visitor* 70 (April): 148–50; Kearney, P. M. and Kearney, P. J. (1999) 'The Prevalence of Asthma in Schoolboys of Travellers' Families', *Irish Medical Journal* 91: 203–6. The findings bear out the experience of health and community workers and planning consultants who routinely discuss the state of health of client groups with whom they have contact. Whilst once again this condition may be linked to both 'lifestyle', for example, active and passive smoking, environmental conditions on poor quality sites and genetic inheritance, it would appear uncontroversial to note that quality of life is severely diminished for many Travellers as a result of the need to either use inhalers, or, in severe cases, nebulisers to control this condition. See, for example, Konstantinos, I., Gourgoulianis, I., Tsoutsou, P., Fotiadou, N., Samrasa, K., Dakis, D. and Molyvdas, P. (2000) 'Lung Function in Gypsies in Greece', *Archives of Environmental Health*, 55(6): 453–4.

56 Again, limited published research means that we are largely dependent upon anecdotal reports, but see the Men's Health Forum (2003) op. cit.; Hennink et al. (1993) op. cit.; Hawes (1997) op. cit.; Davis and Hoult (2000) op. cit.

57 Arthritic symptoms may be exacerbated by living in poorly heated or damp conditions or by previous muscular-skeletal injury (see above), although it is also an inheritable condition. See Hennick et al. (1995) op. cit.; Hawes (1997) op. cit.

58 Written by Vincenzo Mesce (who also designed the booklet), Richard O'Neill, Sarah Rhodes and Patrice Van Cleemput.

59 Men's Health Forum (2003) op. cit.; Hennick et al. (1993) op. cit.; Crout, E. (1987) op. cit.

60 See Lothian Anti-Poverty Alliance website for a review of literature pertaining to the expense of 'healthy eating', and the nutritional defects of much convenience food that 'fills' without providing a balanced diet. The National Children's Homes report *Going Hungry* (2004), London: NCH, further highlights the additional premium on food costs and limited choices experienced by poorer families or those who do not have the space or equipment to purchase in bulk, store food adequately, or who live some distance from shops.
    <http://www.nch.org.uk/news/news3.asp?ReleaseID=261>.

61 See Hennik (1993) op. cit.; Crout (1987) op. cit.; Hawes (1997) op. cit.; Konstantinos et al. (2000) op. cit.; Health ASERT Wales (2003) *Executive*

Summary: Gypsy-Travellers, ASERT/University of Middlesex
<http://www.mdx.ac.uk/www/rctsh/asert/executive_summary_gypsy_
travellers.htm#4>.

62 See in particular the Economic and Social Research Council (ESRC)
    funded study by Power, C., Graham, H. and Manor, O. (2003) 'Socio-
    Economic Life Circumstances at Different Stages and Adult Smoking',
    ESRC Regard database <http://www.regard.ac.uk/research_findings/
    R000239579/summary.pdf> which found that 'men and women in the
    most disadvantaged circumstances ... were most likely to be smokers.
    Those from manual backgrounds tended to start smoking earlier than in
    non-manual groups and to keep smoking through adulthood'. Jackson, N.,
    Prebble, A. and Smith Rose, C. (2002) 'Perceptions of Smoking Cessation
    Products and Services amongst Low Income Smokers', NHS Health
    Development Agency <http://www.hda-online.org.uk/documents/
    perceptions_smoking_cessation.pdf> note that individuals living under
    stress, particularly in insecure circumstances (for example, social,
    financial or in terms of accommodation), whilst aware of the health
    benefits of ceasing smoking, tend to feel that the 'disadvantages' of
    stopping smoking (such as social exclusion if most friends and relatives
    smoke, cravings, weight gain, loss of a 'luxury' with no immediate reward)
    outweighed the positive aspects.

63 Most information pertaining to excess or problem drinking is anecdotal by
    nature, for example, see Dorset County Council Gypsy and Traveller policy
    statement which refers to 'Gypsy and Traveller Liaison Services
    identifying growing problems associated with drug and alcohol addiction
    ... problems can be compounded by difficulties in accessing health and
    other services'
    <http://www.dorsetcc.gov.uk/media/pdf/Gypsy%20&%20Traveller%20Po
    licy%202003.pdf>. Although we are unaware of any reliable UK study of
    alcohol use amongst Travellers, some limited research has been carried out
    in Ireland. See Butler, S. (1996) 'Drinking Problems amongst Irish
    Travellers', *Irish Social Worker*, 14 (summer): 8–9.

64 See, for example, National Aboriginal Community Controlled Health
    Organisation publications and, in particular, the Chair's address to the
    Fifteenth International Conference on the Reduction of Drug Related
    Harm, April 2004 <http://www.naccho.org.au/body.cfm?paraID=146>; and
    statistics on drug use in Australia (2002) wherein '1 in 5 Aboriginal and
    Torres Strait Islander people reported patterns of alcohol drinking which
    substantially increased the risk of harm in the long term',
    <http://www.aihw.gov.au/publications/phe/sdua02/sdua02.pdf>. While
    excessive alcohol use has been regarded as less common and problematic
    amongst the Maori populations of New Zealand than the Australian
    Aboriginal communities, there is evidence that indicates increased use of
    the drug when individuals felt cut off from their heritage or socially
    excluded. See Hutt, M. (2003) *Maori and Alcohol: A History*, Health

Service Research Centre, New Zealand. Alcohol consumption over and above healthy limits appears to have declined with the rise of Maori involvement in policy and legal institutions and statutory recognition of the rights of the Maori communities to self-determination, indicating the impact of discrimination and social exclusion on substance use patterns <http://www.alac.org.nz/InpowerFiles/Publications/CategorisedDocument. Document1.1488.0005d36e-e207–4a86-a32b-e77e22027e50.pdf>.

The difficulties experienced by Native American communities with regard to alcohol consumption and excessive drinking are well documented and are clearly associated with issues of poverty, social exclusion, limited life opportunities and confinement to reservations. See also Lobb, M. (1989) *Native American Youth and Alcohol: An Annotated Bibliography*, New York: Greenwood Press; The Harvard Project on American Indian Economic Strengthening (2004); *The Context and Meaning of Family Strengthening in Indian America* (2004), Harvard: The Annie E Casey Foundation <http://www.ksg.harvard.edu/hpaied/rp_family.htm>; and the report 'Banning Booze at Blackfeet' (April 2004) on *Native America Calling*, a radio station/website by and for Native American and indigenous Canadian populations <http://www.nativeamericacalling.com/nac_past20032.shtm>.

65 See Crout, E. (1987b) op. cit.; O'Dwyer, M. (1997) op. cit.; Hawes, D. (1997) op. cit.; Daly, M. (1990) *Anywhere But Here: Travellers in Camden*, London: London Race and Housing Research Unit; Hyman, M. (1989) *Sites for Travellers*, London: London Race and Housing Research Unit.

66 McKeown, K. and McGrath, B. (1996) *Accommodating Travelling People*, Dublin: Crosscare.

67 See Kirsch, M. (2002) 'Hard Habit to Break', *The Observer*, 3 February; Ashton, H. (1997) 'Benzodiazepine Dependency', in Baum, A., Newman, S., Weinman, J., West, R. and McManus, C. *Cambridge Handbook of Psychology and Medicine*, Cambridge: Cambridge University Press, pp. 376–80.

68 Bowers, J. and Taylor, B. *Ladged No Longer: Advice from Gypsies and Travellers about Drugs*, Gypsy Media Company, funded by the Home Office National Drugs Strategy.

69 Consumer Which? (2001) 'Serious Shortage of NHS Dentists', press release, 28 September <http://www.which.net/media/pr/sep01/general/dentists.html>.

70 O'Dwyer (1997) op. cit.

71 Edwards, D. M. and Watts, R. G. (1997) 'Oral Health Care in the Lives of Gypsy Travellers in East Hertfordshire', *British Dental Journal*, 183: 252–7.

72 Bromley Gypsy and Traveller Project Annual Report (1995–6) op. cit.

73 See Hennink et al. (1993) op. cit.

74 A government-funded initiative that targets monies at areas of high social deprivation to assist in delivering high-quality child care; supporting

projects that improve the health and emotional development of young children and assisting parents in attaining employment or educational aspirations. Health visitors and a range of health and other social-care staff are critical partnership workers in Sure Start areas as they (health visitors in particular) are a universal point of contact with all parents of under-fours.

75 <http://www.oneplusone.org.uk/projects/CommunityMothers.asp>.

76 Fitzpatrick, P., Molloy, B. and Johnson, Z. (1997) 'Community Mothers' Programme: Extension to the Travelling Community in Ireland', *Journal of Epidemiology and Community Health*, 51: 299–303.

77 <http://www.paveepoint.ie/progs_health.html>.

78 Parry, G.,Van Cleemput, P., Peters, J., Moore, J., Walters, S., Thomas, K. and Cooper, C. (2004) *The Health Status of Gypsies and Travellers in England*, University of Sheffield (ScHARR) op. cit.
<http://www.shef.ac.uk/scharr/about/publications/travellers.html>.

79 Appleton, L, Hagan, T., Goward, P., Repper, J. and Wilson, R. (2003) 'Snail's Contribution to Understanding the Needs of the Socially Excluded: The Case of Gypsy and Traveller Women', *Clinical Psychology* 24(April): 40–5.

8 Education

1 DfEE/OFSTED (1999) *Raising the Attainment of Minority Ethnic Pupils*, London: HMSO, para 8.

2 Parekh, B. et al. (2000) *The Future of Multi-Ethnic Britain: The Report of the Commission on the Future of Multi-Ethnic Britain*, London: Profile Books, p. 146.

3 Department of Education and Science (1967) *Children and their Primary Schools*, The Plowden Report, London: HMSO.

4 Mooney, G. and Poole, L. (2004) ' "A Land of Milk and Honey"? Social Policy in Scotland after Devolution', *Critical Social Policy*, 24(4): 458–83.

5 Waterson, M. (1997) 'I Want More than Green Leaves for my Children: Some Developments in Gypsy and Traveller Education, 1970–1996', in Acton, T. A. and Mundy, G. (eds) *Romani Culture and Gypsy Identity*, Hatfield: University of Hertfordshire Press.

6 Clay, S. (1999) 'Traveller Children's Schooling', unpublished Ph.D. thesis, Cardiff University of Wales.

7 For details of the range of work that the Scottish Traveller Education Project has been involved with, see <http://www.scottishtravellered.net>. A good example of this work includes this report: STEP/LTS (2003) *Inclusive Educational Approaches for Gypsies and Travellers within the Context of Interrupted Learning: Guidance for Local Authorities and Schools*, Edinburgh: STEP, available at <http://www.scottishtravellered.net/research/enrolment/STEP_enrolment report.pdf >.

8   For example, see Norfolk,
    <http://www.norfolkesinet.org.uk/pages/viewpage.asp?uniqid=1298>.
9   See <http://www.becta.org.uk/inclusion/sen/resources/
    travellers/directory.html> (provided by Brian Foster, Cross-Boroughs Co-
    ordinator for Traveller Education, Camden Language and Support
    Service).
10 Auckland, R. (2000) 'The Educational Needs of New Traveller Children',
    Travellers' School Charity,
    <http://www.travellersschool.plus.com/rr01.html#research>.
11 The Standards Fund does not operate in Wales. Existing projects
    continued to be funded via Section 488 (still at 75 per cent) until March
    2001.
12 Comment from Susan Alexander from FFT. Likewise, the National
    Association of Teachers of Travellers (NATT) pointed out that not all
    travelling/mobile communities are necessarily 'ethnic': some are
    occupational (fairground/circus communities). NATT argued that bringing
    lots of different groups under the one 'ethnic' funding umbrella served to
    add to the confusion and complexity of the situation rather than easing it.
    NATT (2000) *Travellers Times*, Cardiff: TLRU, Cardiff Law School, January
    2000, p. 4.
13 NATT *Social and School Exclusion and Truancy*, quoted in Morris, R. and
    Clements, L. (eds) (1999) *Gaining Ground: Law Reform for Gypsies and
    Travellers*, Hatfield: University of Hertfordshire Press, p. 72.
14 OFSTED (1999) *Raising the Attainment of Minority Ethnic Pupils*, London:
    OFSTED, para 50, p. 14.
15 The Vulnerable Children Grant is used to secure improved access to
    education; to provide high-quality education for those unable to attend
    school or whose circumstances make it difficult for them to do so; to
    support attendance, integration and reintegration into school and to
    provide additional educational support to enable vulnerable children to
    achieve their full potential. Clearly Gypsy and Traveller children fall into
    many of these categories.
16 For further information see <http://www.teachernet.gov.uk/management/
    atoz/g/Gypsy_and_traveller_children>.
17 See the DfES document here for further details of this case study (April
    2003): <http://www.dfes.gov.uk/standardsfund/gtc#gtc>.
18 Smith, T. (1997) 'Recognising Difference: The Romani "Gypsy" Child
    Socialisation and Education Process', *British Journal of the Sociology of
    Education*, 18(2): 243–56.
19 See the 'Sure Start' web page for further details:
    <http://www.surestart.gov.uk/home.cfm>. Its mission statement reads as
    follows: 'The aim of Sure Start is to work with parents and children to
    promote the physical, intellectual and social development of pre-school
    children – particularly those who are disadvantaged – to ensure that they
    are ready to flourish when they get to school'.

20 For further details on the work conducted under the Hackney Sure Start programme: <http://www.surestart.gov.uk/surestartservices/ surestartlocalprogrammes/localprogrammes/index.cfm?prog=74>.

21 The Scottish Executive (2000) *The Ninth Term Report 1998–99*, Edinburgh: The Scottish Office/HMSO.

22 Save the Children Fund (Scotland) (2000) *Moving Targets*, Edinburgh: Save the Children, Scotland.

23 The web page for the Social Inclusion Unit in Scotland can be found at <http://www.scotland.gov.uk/socialjustice>. See also the work of the Scottish Centre for research on Social Justice at <http://www.scrsj.ac.uk/Information/PovertyScotland.html>.

24 This is 'badged' as 'Learning Wales': <http://www.learning.wales.gov.uk/index.asp>.

25 OFSTED (2003) *Provision and Support for Traveller Pupils* (HMI 455), London: HMSO, <http://www.ofsted.gov.uk/publications/ index.cfm?fuseaction=pubs.displayfile&id=3440&type=pdf>.

26 The DfES ran a Gypsy-Traveller project focusing on Key Stages 3 and 4 to raise the attendance and achievement of all Gypsy and Traveller pupils, ensuring their educational and social inclusion. The project involved six LEAs and ran from November 2003 until August 2004. Further details of the project outline are here: <http://www.standards.dfes.gov.uk/ ethnicminorities/resources/Traveller_Project_Aims_May04>.

27 DfEE (1999) *Traveller Education: Annual Report 1997–1998*, London: DfEE.

28 Bhopal, K. et al. (2000) *Working towards Inclusive Education: Aspects of Good Practice for Gypsy Traveller Children*, London: DfEE/HMSO. Research Report No. 238.

29 OFSTED (1996) *The Education of Travelling Children*, HMR/12/96/NS.

30 *The Times Higher Educational Supplement*, 26 September 1997.

31 OFSTED (2003) *Provision and Support for Traveller Pupils* (HMI 455), London: HMSO, <http://www.ofsted.gov.uk/publications/ index.cfm?fuseaction=pubs.displayfile&id=3440&type=pdf>.

32 See Derrington, C. and Kendall, S. (2004) *Gypsy Traveller Students in Secondary Schools: Culture, Identity and Achievement*, Stoke on Trent: Trentham Books.

33 Bancroft, A., Lloyd, M. and Morran, R. *The Right to Roam: Travellers in Scotland 1995/96*, Edinburgh: Save the Children Fund (Traveller Section), p. 17.

34 McKinney, R. (2001) *Different Lessons: Scottish Gypsy/Travellers and the Future of Education*, Edinburgh: Scottish Traveller Consortium.

35 DfEE/OFSTED (1999) *Raising the Attainment of Minority Ethnic Pupils*, London: HMSO.

36 School of Education, Cardiff University and Save the Children Wales (1998) *Traveller Children and Educational Need*, October, p. 30.

37 Kenny, M. (1997) *The Routes of Resistance: Travellers and Second-Level*

Schooling, Aldershot: Ashgate.

38 See <http://www.dfes.gov.uk/curriculumonline> for further details.

39 See <http://www.official-documents.co.uk/document/cm42/ 4262/4262.htm> for further details.

40 Morris, R. (1999) 'The Invisibility of Gypsies and other Travellers', *Journal of Social Welfare and Family Law,* 21(4): 397–404.

41 CERD (2000) *Concluding Observations of the Committee on the Elimination of Racial Discrimination: United Kingdom of Great Britain and Northern Ireland,* CERD/C/CRP.3/Add.9, 18 August.

42 Jordan, E. (2001) 'From Interdependence, to Dependence and Independence: Home and School Learning for Traveller Children', *Childhood,* 8(1): 57–74.

43 Dearling, A. (1997) '*Almost ... Everything You Wanted to Know about Travellers' School Charity,* Lyme Regis: Enabler Publications/TSC, p. 8.

44 'Education Otherwise'. See <http://www.education-otherwise.org> for more details.

45 See, for example, Jordan, B. (2001) 'Exclusion of Travellers from State Schools', *Educational Research,* 43(1): 117–32.

46 This issue is discussed in some depth in the following recent report from Scotland: McKinney, R. (2001) *Different Lessons: Scottish Gypsy/Travellers and the Future of Education,* Edinburgh: Scottish Traveller Consortium, p. 11.

47 As in the case of the local authority site at Collin, near Dumfries. Discussed in McKinney (2001) op. cit., p. 22.

48 OFSTED (1996) *The Education of Travelling Children,* HMR/12/96/NS, London: HMSO, p. 8.

49 CMc (2000) Testimony at the Equal Opportunities Committee of the Scottish Parliament, May.

50 School of Education, Cardiff University and Save the Children Wales (1998) *Traveller Children and Educational Need,* October, p. 10.

51 DfEE/OFSTED (1999) *Raising the Attainment of Minority Ethnic Pupils,* London: HMSO, para 760.

52 Morris, R. and Clements, L. (eds) (1999) *Gaining Ground: Law Reform for Gypsies and Travellers,* Hatfield: University of Hertfordshire Press, p. 17.

53 School of Education, Cardiff University and Save the Children Wales (1998) *Traveller Children and Educational Need,* October, p. 10.

54 DfEE/OFSTED (1999) *Raising the Attainment of Minority Ethnic Pupils,* London: HMSO, para 63.

55 Jordan, E. (2000) 'The Exclusionary Comprehensive School System: The Experience of Showground Families in Scotland', *International Journal of Educational Research,* 33: 253–63.

56 Lloyd, M. and Morran, R. (1999) *Response to the Stephen Lawrence Enquiry: An Action Plan for Scotland,* Edinburgh: Save the Children Fund, p. 9.

57 Anonymous Gypsy, Heath Common Site, Wakefield, as quoted in Daley, I.

and Henderson, J. (eds) (1998) *Static: Life on Site*, Yorkshire Art Circus, p. 70.

58 For a fuller discussion of Gypsies and Travellers in further and higher education, see Clark, C. (2004) 'It is Possible to Have an Education and Be a Traveller: Education, Higher Education and Gypsy-Travellers in Britain', in Law, I., Phillips, D. and Turney, L. (eds) *Institutional Racism in Higher Education*, Stoke-on-Trent: Trentham Books.

59 See, for example, Kenny, M. (1997) *The Routes of Resistance: Travellers and Second-Level Schooling*, Aldershot: Ashgate; Derrington, C. and Kendall, S. (2004) *Gypsy Traveller Students in Secondary Schools: Culture, Identity and Achievement*, Stoke on Trent: Trentham Books.

60 Birkett, D. (2002) 'School for Scandal', *Guardian*, 15 January.

61 See <http://errc.org/capacitation/index.shtml>.

62 Interestingly, the majority of students going on to further and higher education appear to be female, challenging non-Gypsy held stereotypes that assume Gypsy society is overtly patriarchal. Gypsy men, as with many of their working-class peers in the wider settled society, are still concerned to have 'real jobs' and carry on family businesses working with uncles, brothers and cousins. The family name, whether associated with being a general dealer, landscape gardener or scrapping, is important to pass on, although there is room to adapt to new business opportunities as and when they arise.

63 Hester Hedges, Traveller, female student, as quoted in Klein, R. (1997) 'Upwardly Mobile', *Times Educational Supplement (2)*, 23 May: 4–5.

9 Nomads and newspapers

1 Simpson, J. (2001) *A Mad World, My Masters*, London: Pan Books, p. 323.

2 Johnson, T. (1997) *Milton Keynes on Sunday*, 6 July.

3 Napoleon Bonaparte, quoted in Randall, D. (1996) *The Universal Journalist*, London: Pluto Press, p. 4.

4 Petty, R. E. and Priester, J. R. (1994) 'Mass Media Attitude Change: Implications of the Elaboration Likelihood Model of Persuasion', in Bryant, J. and Zillmann, D. (eds) *MediaEffects: Advances in Theory and Research*, Hove: Lawrence Erlbaum Associates, p. 91.

5 McCombs, M. (1994) 'News Influence on our Pictures of the World', in Bryant, J. and Zillmann, D. (eds) op. cit., p. 4.

6 A Traveller, in Smith, D., Gmelch, G. and Gmelch, S. (1982) *The Accommodation Needs of Long-Distance and Regional Travellers*, London: DoE, p. 9.

7 Hooks, B. (1992) *Black Looks: Race and Representation*, Boston, Mass.: South End, p. 170.

8 *Encyclopaedia Britannica* (1956), Vol. XI, pp. 43–4.

9 Hall, S. (ed.) (1997) *Representation: Cultural Representations and Signifying Practices*, Milton Keynes: The Open University, p. 229.

10 It is a given that a person constructing a representation is more likely to

faithfully portray a person or experience with which or whom they have had direct experience.

11 Gandy, O. (1998) *Communication and Race: A Structural Perspective*, London: Arnold, p. 97.

12 *Bristol Evening Post* 'columnist' 'Barry Beelzebub' (a nom de plume), 28 March 1998.

13 Liégeois, J.-P. (1986) *Gypsies: An Illustrated History*, London: Al-Saqi.

14 Hancock, I. (1991) 'The East European Roots of Romani Nationalism', in Crowe, D. and Kolsti, J. (eds) *The Gypsies of Eastern Europe*, Armonk, NY and London: M. E. Sharpe, Inc., p. 138.

15 Hall, S. (ed.) (1997) *Representation: Cultural Representations and Signifying Practices*, Milton Keynes: The Open University, pp. 235.

16 Todd, D. and Clark, G. (1991) *Gypsy Site Provision and Policy: Research Report*, London: HMSO, p. 21.

17 Branston, J. and Stafford, R. (1996) *The Media Student's Book*, London: Routledge, p. 83.

18 Fawcett, L. (1998) 'Ethnic Minorities and the Media', in Hainsworth, P. (ed.) *Divided Society: Ethnic Minorities and Racism in Northern Ireland*, London: Pluto Press, p. 112.

19 Seventy per cent of adult Travelling people may have limited literacy. UK Gypsy and Traveller adult literacy rates, by percentage, compiled by Thomas Acton and Donald Kenrick, in Liégeois, J.-P. (1998) *School Provision for Ethnic Minorities: The Gypsy Paradigm*, Hatfield and Paris: Centre de Recherches Tsiganes and University of Hertfordshire Press, pp. 74–5.

20 There are of course exceptions to every rule, one such being Jake Bowers, a Romani journalist who has written for the *Guardian* and other publications.

21 This is anecdotal: I witnessed such complaints at meetings with local reporters, 1998–2002.

22 Suggested disclaimer for most newspapers, Randall, D. (1996) *The Universal Journalist*, London: Pluto Press, p. 15.

23 A 'settled' man quoted, uncritically, in the *Independent*, 16 June 1993.

24 The *Birmingham Evening Mail*, 29 June 1993, front page.

25 Todd, D. and Clark, G. (1991) *Gypsy Site Provision and Policy: Research Report*, London: HMSO, p. 21.

26 From a speech by Hugh Harris, then Deputy Chair of the CRE, at a meeting to discuss press standards and Travelling people held at the Commission in London in June 1998.

27 Fawcett, L. Equality Commission for Northern Ireland (1999) *Racial Equality Bulletin No. 2: Press Reporting on Minority Ethnic Issues and Racism*, Belfast: Equity Commission for Northern Ireland, December, p. 1.

28 Fawcett (1999), op. cit., p. 5.

29 Fawcett (1999), op. cit., p. 7.

30 The *Biggleswade Chronicle*, 16 May 1997.

31 I assert that press items about Travelling people that are considered acceptable would be subject to national outcry if they concerned other minority groups. Imagine that the pieces included here concerned Jewish, Pakistani or Irish people.

32 OFSTED (1996) 'The Education of Travelling Children', ref. HMR/12/96/NS, p. 10, <http://www.osted.gov.uk/public>.

33 Cohen, S. (1873) *Folk Devils and Moral Panics*, St Albans: Paladin, p. 229. 'The Coming Hordes', a February 2004 article by the Roma Press Agency reprinted on the Domino Forum (<http://www.dofo.sk>), complains that Western journalists are determined to report 'hordes' of Roma moving to the UK, even in the face of evidence to the contrary.

34 A Dover police officer, from a *Guardian* newspaper article quoted in Amnesty International (UK) magazine *Amnesty*, May/June 2000, p. 5.

35 Jason Bennett, the *Independent*, 17 December 1998.

36 The *Daily Telegraph*, 25 October 1997. Quote from one of 3,000 signatories to a petition demanding that Roma asylum seekers be denied any access to social assistance.

37 This quote and that above it are from the *Sun*, 23 October 1997.

38 The *Independent*, 20 October 1997, front page, published the day after the Roma in question arrived, before any hearing had taken place as to their motives for seeking entry. The accompanying photograph of a boy with hands reaching towards the camera could be seen as 'cute' but, in the context of the headline, he looks grasping.

39 Clark, C. and Campbell, E. (2000) ' "Gypsy Invasion": A Critical Analysis of Newspaper Reaction to Czech and Slovak Asylum-Seekers in Britain, 1997', *Romani Studies*, 10(1): 23–47.

40 Ian Burrell, the *Independent*, 21 May 1997. On 8 July 2004, the Independent Race and Refugee News Network (<http://www.irr.org.uk>) reported: 'Earlier this year, the *Daily Express* dedicated numerous front pages to the threat of "1.6 million Gipsies" who were "ready to flood in" to Britain on 1 May, when the EU was expanded. Today, an article on page eight of the paper admits that only 10,000 have come.'

41 The United Nations Educational, Scientific and Cultural Organization (UNESCO) (1977) *Ethnicity and the Media*, Paris: UNESCO, p. 160. I refer to such dated research partly because I believe the issues raised by it are largely unchanged and because there is otherwise such a paucity of research specifically relating to Travelling people and the press.

42 Alert to the possibility that people are more likely to send in clippings they are angry about rather than approving of, I checked newspaper databases available through the Cardiff University computer network over the same period for all pieces concerning Travelling people. This search confirmed that the majority – as much as 94 per cent – of such coverage was racist, or objectionable on other standards-based grounds.

43 UNESCO (1977) *Ethnicity and the Media*, Paris: UNESCO, p. 138.

44 UNESCO (1977), op. cit., p. 145.

45 UNESCO (1977), op. cit., p. 160.

46 UNESCO (1977), op. cit., p. 164.

47 UNESCO (1977), op. cit., p. 166.

48 Kymlicka, W. and Norman, W. (eds) (2000) *Citizenship in Diverse Societies*, Oxford: Oxford University Press; Campbell, S. (1999) *Gypsies and Travellers in England and Wales: Political and Civic Participation*, M.Phil. thesis, University of Wales, Cardiff.

49 *Weston-super-Mare Daily Post*, 11 June 1998, front page.

50 *Clacton and Harwich Evening Gazette*, 11 November 1997, front page, about the failure of the local council to build a site in the face of local opposition. Delight for whom?

51 The *Western Daily Press*, South Gloucestershire edition, 25 March 1997, page 14.

52 *High Wycombe Midweek*, 6 July 1993.

53 Fintan O'Toole (2001) 'Equality and the Media', *Equality News* (the newsletter of the Equality Authority, Dublin), (spring), p. 4.

54 Publisher and former journalist Bob Borzello (1998) *Telling It Like It Is ... Report of the Ethnic Minorities and the Media Forum 1997*, Bristol: PressWise.

55 During the Euro '96 football championship, the PCC received many hundreds of third-party complaints of anti-German language and took action outside its code.

56 PCC Report No. 36, Oct.–Dec. 1996, pp. 13–14.

57 Clause 3 relates to the right for privacy, similar in wording to that under Article 8.1 of the European Convention on Human Rights.

58 Barnes, J. (1995) *Letters from London 1990–1995*, London: Picador, p. 150. 'The quiescent approach of governments is partly attributable to the political parties' reliance on the press, but was also the result of changes to the structure of the Press Complaints Commission giving majority weight to members from outside the industry' (Feldman, D., 2002, *Civil Liberties and Human Rights in England and Wales*, 2nd edn, London: Oxford University Press, p. 815). Just over half of the seventeen members of the PCC are non-press.

59 <http://www.cre.gov.uk/media/guidetj.html>.

60 *R* v. *Press Complaints Commission, ex parte Anna Ford* [2001] EWHC Admin 683.

61 European Commission against Racism and Intolerance (ECRI) (2005) *Third Report on the United Kingdom* (CRI(2005)27), CoE, Strasbourg, 14 June, para 79.

62 Connolly, P. and Keenan, M. (2000) *Racial Attitudes and Prejudice in Northern Ireland*, Belfast: Northern Ireland Statistics and Research Agency.

63 Roshier, B. 'The Selection of Crime News by the Press', in Cohen, S. and Young, J. (eds) (1973) *The Manufacture of News*, London: Constable, p. 36.

64 Wilson II, C. and Gutiérrez, F. (1995) *Race, Multiculturalism, and the*

Media: From Mass to Class Communication, 2nd edn, London: Sage, p. 44.
65 <http://news.bbc.co.uk/1/hi/uk/3992575.stm>, 11 March 2005.
66 Reported at <http://www.MediaWise.org.uk>, 6 December 2004.
67 Sylvia Dunn, President, National Association of Gypsy Women, speaking
    to me on the telephone in December 1999, shortly after she was made a
    Woman of the Year in the UK (although this was not a widely reported
    fact).

10 Europe

1   Excerpt from the 'Romano Kongreso' anthem, composed for the first World
    Romani Congress held in London in 1971 by Zarko Jovanovic Jagdino,
    from Liégeois, J.-P. (1994) *Roma, Gypsies, Travellers*, Brussels: CoE, p. 17.
2   Danbakli, M. (1994) *On Gypsies: Texts Issued by International Institutions*,
    Toulouse: CRDP, pp. 7–8.
3   Burrows, N. and Mair, J. (1996) *European Social Law*, Chichester: J. Wiley
    & Sons.
4   Castle-Kanerová, M. (2001) 'Romani Refugees: The EU Dimension', in Guy,
    W. (ed.) *Between Past and Future: The Roma of Central and Eastern
    Europe*, Hatfield: University of Hertfordshire Press.
5   Jordan, B. (1998) *The New Politics of Welfare*, London: Sage.
6   Wurzel, R. (2001) *Environmental Policy-Making in Britain, Germany and
    the European Union*, Manchester: Manchester University Press.
7   For example, EU (1993) *Green Paper on European Social Policy: Options
    for the Union*, (COM(94) 333, 27 July); EU (1994) *White Paper on
    European Social Policy: A Way Forward for the Union*, (COM(94) 333, 27
    July); EU (1994) *Community of Learning: Intercultural Education in
    Europe*, Brussels: OPEC.
8   Cram, L., Dinon, D. and Nugent, N. (eds) (1999) *Developments in the
    European Union*, London: Palgrave.
9   Leibfried, S. (1993) 'Towards a European welfare state?', in Jones, C. (ed.)
    New Perspectives on the Welfare State in Europe, London: Routledge,
    p. 143.
10 Kassim, H. and Hine, D. (1998) 'Conclusion: The European Union,
    Member States and Social Policy', in Hine, D. and Kassim, H. (eds) *Beyond
    the Market: The EU and National Social Policy*, London: Routledge,
    pp. 212–13.
11 Roberts, I. and Springer, B. (2000) *Social Policy in the European Union:
    Between Harmonisation and National Autonomy*, London: Lynne Rienner
    Publishers.
12 Spicker, P. (1991) 'The Principle of Subsidiarity and the Social Policy of
    the European Community', *Journal of European Social Policy*, 1(1): 3–14,
    p. 3.
13 Roberts, S. and Bolderson, H. (1999) 'Inside Out: Migrants' Disentitlement
    to Social Security Benefits in the EU', in Clasen, J. (ed.) *Comparative*

Social Policy: Concepts, Theories and Methods, Oxford: Blackwell.

14 Geyer, R. (2000) *Exploring European Social Policy*, Cambridge: Polity Press.

15 Hantrais, L. (2000) *Social Policy in the European Union*, 2nd edn, London: Palgrave.

16 Bonoli, G., George, V. and Taylor-Gooby, P. (2000) *European Welfare Futures: Towards a Theory of Retrenchment*, Cambridge: Polity Press, pp. 156–7.

17 Marshall, T. H. (1950) *Citizenship and Social Class and Other Essays*, Cambridge: Cambridge University Press.

18 Mason, D. (2000) *Race and Ethnicity in Modern Britain*, 2nd edn, Oxford: Oxford University Press, p. 122.

19 Craig, G. (2001) ' "Race" and Welfare: Social Justice and Britain's Ethnic Minority Groups', inaugural lecture, 19 March, University of Hull, p. 2.

20 Dean, H. and Melrose, M. (1999) *Poverty, Riches and Social Citizenship*, Routledge: London.

21 See, for example, Lister, R. (1997) *Citizenship: Feminist Perspectives*, Basingstoke: Macmillan; Williams, F. (1989) *Social Policy: A Critical Introduction*, Oxford: Blackwell.

22 Castles, S. (2000) *Ethnicity and Globalisation*, London: Sage.

23 MacEwen, M. (1995) *Tackling Racism in Europe: An Examination of Anti-Discrimination Law in Practice*, Oxford: Berg.

24 For a critical review of newspaper coverage in Britain, see Clark, C. and Campbell, E. (2000) '"Gypsy Invasion": A Critical Analysis of Newspaper Reaction to Czech and Slovak Romani Asylum-Seekers in Britain, 1997', *Romani Studies* (continuing *Journal of the Gypsy Lore Society*), 10(1): 23–47.

25 Kohli, J. (1998) ' "Race": An Emergent Policy Issue in the European Union', in Sykes, R. and Alcock, P. (eds) *Developments in European Social Policy: Convergence and Diversity*, Bristol: Policy Press.

26 Mitchell, M. and Russell, D. (1998) 'Immigration, Citizenship and Social Exclusion in the New Europe', in Sykes, R. and Alcock, P. (eds) *Developments in European Social Policy: Convergence and Diversity*, Bristol: Policy Press.

27 Favell, A. (ed.) (1998) 'The European Union: Immigration, Asylum and Citizenship', *Journal of Ethnic and Migration Studies* (special issue), 24(4).

28 Virdee, S. (1997) 'Racial Harassment', in Modood, T. et al. *Ethnic Minorities in Britain: Diversity and Disadvantage*, London: Policy Studies Institute.

29 Jordan, B. (1998) *The New Politics of Welfare*, London: Sage, p. 205.

30 Miles, R. (1994) 'A Rise of Racism and Fascism in Contemporary Europe? Some Sceptical Reflections on its Nature and Extent', *New Community*, 20(4): 547–62.

31 Sivanandan, A. (1988) 'The New Racism', *New Statesman and Society*, 1 (24): 8–9.

32 Reyniers, A. (1995) *Gypsy Populations and their Movements within Central and Eastern Europe and towards Some OECD Countries*, Paris: International Migration and Labour Market Policies Occasional Papers, 1, p. 8.

33 Matras, Y. (1996) *Problems Arising in Connection with the International Mobility of the Roma in Europe* (CDMG (98) 14, pp. 1–25), Strasburg: European Committee on Migration/CoE, p. 5.

34 Liégeois, J.-P. and Gheorghe, N. (1995) *Roma/Gypsies: A European Minority*, London: Minority Rights Group, pp. 7–10.

35 Hancock, I. (2000) 'The Emergence of Romani as a Köine Outside of India', in Acton, T. (ed.) *Scholarship and the Gypsy Struggle: Commitment in Romani Studies*, Hatfield: University of Hertfordshire Press.

36 Hancock, I. (1987) *The Pariah Syndrome: An Account of Gypsy Slavery and Persecution*, Ann Arbor, Mich.: Karoma.

37 Powell, C. (1994) 'Time for Another Immoral Panic? The Case of the Czechoslovak Gypsies', *International Journal of the Sociology of Law*, 22: 105–21.

38 Matras, Y. (1996) op. cit.

39 See Bancroft. A. (1999) 'Gypsies to the Camps!: Exclusion and Marginalisation of Roma in the Czech Republic', *Sociological Research Online* 4 (3), <http://www.socresonline.org.uk/4/3/bancroft.html>; O'Nions, H. (1999) 'Bonafide or Bogus?: Roma Asylum Seekers from the Czech Republic', *Web Journal of Current Legal Issues*, 5 (3), <http://webjcli.ncl.ac.uk/1999/issue3/onions3.html>; Young, M. (1999) *Unwanted Journey: Why Central European Roma are Fleeing to the UK*, London: Refugee Council.

40 Matras, Y. (1998) *The Recent Emigration of Roma from the Czech and Slovak Republics* (MG-S-ROM (98) 9. pp. 1–11), Strasbourg: CoE Population and Migration Division.

41 For examples of such treatment, see Kalvoda, J. (1991) 'The Gypsies of Czechoslovakia', *Nationalities Papers*, 19(3): 269–96; Kostelancik, D. (1989) 'The Gypsies of Czechoslovakia: Political and Ideological Implications in the Development of Policy', *Studies in Comparative Communism*, 22(4): 307–2; Ulc, O. (1991) 'Integration of the Gypsies in Czechoslovakia', *Ethnic Groups*, 9: 107–17.

42 Acton, T. (1996) 'Romani Refugees from Bosnia and Serbia in the UK', unpublished paper, University of Greenwich, pp. 1–5.

43 Kenrick, D. (1997) 'Foreign Gypsies and British Immigration Law After 1945', in Acton, T. (ed.) *Gypsy Politics and Traveller Identity*, Hatfield: University of Hertfordshire Press.

44 Radio Free Europe (1999a) 'Slovak Authorities Suspect "Plot" Behind Romani Exodus to Finland', (Jolyon Naegele), 14 July. Posted to Romnet on 14 July 1999 by Erika Schlager; Radio Free Europe (1999b) 'Finland Rejects First 150 Slovak Roma', 14 July. Posted to Romnet on 14 July 1999 by Wally Keeler.

45 Kenrick, D. (1971) 'The World Romany Congress, April 1971', *Journal of the Gypsy Lore Society*, 10(3–4): 101–8.

46 The Patrin Web Journal:
<http://www.geocities.com/Paris/5121/rromflag.gif>

47 For a detailed review, see Puxon, G. (2000) 'The Romani Movement: Rebirth and the First World Romani Congress in Retrospect', in Acton, T. (ed.) *Scholarship and the Gypsy Struggle: Commitment in Romani Studies*, Hatfield: University of Hertfordshire Press.

48 Fraser, A. (1995) *The Gypsies*, 2nd edn, Oxford: Blackwell, p. 318.

49 Puxon, G. (2000) op. cit.

50 Hawes, D. and Perez, B. (1996) *The Gypsy and the State: The Ethnic Cleansing of British Society*, 2nd edn, Bristol: Policy Press.

51 For further details, see <http://www.isn.ethz.ch/osce/networking/ research&programmes/research_other/doc_related/gypsy_center_F.htm>.

52 Liégeois, J.-P. (1994) *Roma, Gypsies, Travellers*, Brussels: CoE.

53 For a full and detailed review of the Fifth Meeting, see Acton, T. and Klímová, I. (2001) 'The International Romani Union: An East European Answer to West European Questions?', in Guy, W. (ed.) *Between Past and Future: The Roma of Central and Eastern Europe*, Hatfield: University of Hertfordshire Press.

54 The *Independent on Sunday* (2000) 'Gypsy Leader Demands EU Help', 30 July.

55 This section on the Sixth Congress is based on a field report from Grattan Puxon posted to IMC-UK-Reports on 10 October 2004, <http://lists.indymedia.org/mailman/listinfo/imc-uk-reports>.

56 Liégeois (1994) op. cit., pp. 278–84.

57 Danbakli, M. (2001) *Roma/Gypsies: Texts Issued by International Institutions*, Interface Collection Vol. 5 (new edition), Hatfield: University of Hertfordshire Press.

58 Liégeois (1994) op. cit., pp. 279.

59 Verspaget, G. (1993) *On Gypsies in Europe*, CoE Parliamentary Assembly, ADOC6733, 1403–7/1/93–4-E, Strasbourg: CoE, 7 January.

60 Liégeois (1994) op. cit.

61 Fraser, A. (1995) *The Gypsies*, 2nd edn, Oxford: Blackwell, p. 288.

62 For full details of European Interface publications, see <http://www.herts.ac.uk/UHPress/interface.html>.

63 Van der Stoele, M. (2000) *Report on the Situation of Roma and Sinti in the OSCE Area*, Organisation for Security and Co-operation in Europe (OSCE), Office of the High Commissioner on National Minorities, The Hague: OSCE.

64 CoE (1950) *Convention for the Protection of Human Rights and Fundamental Freedoms (ETS No. 5)*, Rome, 4 November. (Ratified 1953), Brussels: CoE.

65 O'Nions, H. (1996) 'The Right to Respect for Home and Family Life: The First in a Series of "Gypsy Cases" to Challenge UK Legislation', *Web*

Journal of Current Legal Issues, 5,
<http://webjcli.ncl.ac.uk/1996/issue5/o'nions5.html>.

66 European Court of Human Rights (2001) *Press Release Issued by the Registrar: Results of Recent Cases*, Strasbourg: ECHR.

67 McNeil, H. (2001) Email contribution to the electronic discussion list *Patrin*. Posted 18 January.

68 Drabble, R. (2000) *Local Authorities and the Human Rights Act 1998*, London: Blackstone Press.

69 Morris, R. and Clements, L. (eds) (1999) *Gaining Ground: Law Reform for Gypsies and Travellers*, Hatfield: University of Hertfordshire Press.

70 Noble, A. (1996) *From Rome to Maastricht: The Essential Guide to the European Union*, London: Warner Books.

71 Danbakli, M. (1994) *On Gypsies: Texts Issued by International Institutions*, Toulouse: CRDP, p. 59.

72 Liégeois, J.-P. (1998) *School Provision for Ethnic Minorities: The Gypsy Paradigm*, The Interface Collection, Vol. 11, Hatfield: University of Hertfordshire Press.

73 For a news report on the conference, see <http://www.soros.org/initiatives/roma/news/decade_20030708>.

74 For further details, see <http://www.romadecade.org>. This website can be read in either English or Romani.

75 For full details on the interest the World Bank has in issues impacting on Roma in Europe, see <http://web.worldbank.org/wbsite/external/countries/ecaext/extroma/0,,menupk: 615993~pagepk: 64168427~pipk: 64168435~d: y~thesitepk: 615987,00.html>.

Conclusion

1 Extract from a poem, 'Identity', by the late Charles Smith in Smith, C. (1995) *Not All Wagons and Lanes*, Essex: Essex County Council/Traveller Education Services, p. 28.

2 See, for example, the discussion in Chapter 1 of Acton, T. (1974) *Gypsy Politics and Social Change*, London: Routledge & Kegan Paul.

3 The banner of the G&TLRC consists of the Romani flag colours to the left half and the Irish tricolour to the right half. Upon this is an intertwined emblem of the Romani Chakra and a symbolic shamrock, with a superimposed dove of peace, holding a multi-coloured peace ribbon in its beak. The banner symbolises 'unity without dominance' of all the main Gypsy and Traveller groups. Designed and drawn by Len Smith.

4 According to Jack Straw, then Home Secretary, Gypsies are people who 'think that it's perfectly OK for them to cause mayhem in an area, to go burgling, thieving, breaking into vehicles, causing all kinds of other trouble including defecating in the doorways of firms and so on' (Jack Straw, 22 July 1999, interview with Annie Oathen, Radio West Midlands).

5 One only needs to think here of the D. H. Lawrence classic 'The Virgin and

the Gypsy', Bizet's 'Carmen' or the often-recorded folk song 'The Raggle-Taggle Gypsy'.

6   It is useful to note that amongst these exceptions is a new generation of critical social scientists who are directly engaging with Gypsy and Traveller/Roma-related matters. This would include the likes of Angus Bancroft, Peter Vermeersch, Helen O'Nions and Robert Vanderbeck who develop and extend the work of more established scholars such as Judith Okely, Thomas Acton and David Mayall.

7   ODPM (7 March 2005) 'Supplement to the Guidance on Managing Unauthorised Encampments'. This is the latest publication from the ODPM that attempts to advise interested parties (landowners, the police, etc.) on how 'best' to 'manage' Gypsy and Traveller sites that appear in 'unauthorised' locations. It adds further measures to those set out in the 2004 document 'Managing Unauthorised Encampments', which can also be downloaded from the ODPM website,
    <http://www.odpm.gov.uk/stellent/groups/odpm_housing/documents/page/odpm_house_035805.hcsp>.

8   See the following article from the <http://www.politics.co.uk> website entitled 'ODPM: Duty is not Necessarily the Appropriate Solution' (8 November 2004) <http://www.politics.co.uk/issueoftheday/odpm-duty-not-necessarily-appropriate-solution-$7010370.htm>.

9   See <http://www.law.cf.ac.uk/bill.html> and <http://www.travellerslaw.org.uk/>.

10 One of the important organisations worth mentioning here is the OSCE's Office for Democratic Institutions and Human Rights whose Roma adviser is the sociologist Dr Nicolae Gheorghe.

11 The ODPM counted 3,558 unauthorised encampments across England in January 2005.
    <http://www.odpm.gov.uk/stellent/groups/odpm_housing/documents/page/odpm_house_028940.xls>.

12 This has regularly been the case at the Ikea store in Gateshead, part of Sir John Hall's 'MetroCentre' development in the north-east of England.

13 A good example of the general public becoming better informed and changing their minds is illustrated in the following study on sites: Duncan, T. (1996) *Neighbours' Views of Official Sites for Travelling People*, Glasgow: Joseph Rowntree Foundation and Planning Exchange. This report is interesting as it examines what settled residents felt both before and after the construction of Gypsy and Traveller sites in their areas. In all cases settled people had real concerns about the construction of sites in their areas (traffic, crime, noise, etc.), but these fears were proved to be unfounded once the sites were up and running.
    <http://www.jrf.org.uk/knowledge/findings/housing/H201.asp>.

Useful resources and contacts
Margaret Greenfields

Please note that this resources and contacts list is up to date as of August 2005. However, individuals may move post, or organisations change address or cease operating, rendering details inaccurate. If this does occur, given the close-knit world of Gypsy and Traveller organisations, even if a website or person cannot be contacted, it is often worth getting in touch with one of the larger organisations who may be able to help with your enquiry.

Gypsy and Traveller organisations

Bromley Gypsy and Traveller Project
Contact: Sue Balaam
Address: 13–15 High Street, St Mary Cray, Orpington, Kent BR5 3NL
Tel: 01689 839052
Email: sue@bgtcp.fs.net.co.uk

Canterbury Gypsy and Traveller Support Group
Contact: Joe and Bridie Jones
Tel: 0845 644 8879 / 01227 453441

Cardiff Gypsy Sites Group
Address: 114 Clifton Street, Roath, Cardiff CF24 1LW
Tel: 029 2021 4411
Web: <http://www.switch-cymru.org.uk/html/CGSG/page1.htm>

Derbyshire Gypsy Liaison Group (DGLG)
Address: Ernest Bailey Community Centre, Office 3, New Street, Matlock
    DE4 3FE
Tel: 01629 583300
Web: <http://www.dglg.org>

East Anglian Gypsy Council
Contact: Peter Mercer MBE

Address: 3 Oxney Road Caravan Park, Peterborough PE1 5NX
Tel: 01733 347112
Email: peter@eagc.org.uk
Web: <http://www.eagc.org.uk>

Friends, Families and Travellers
Contact: Emma Nuttall/Anna Hinton
Address: Community Base, 113 Queens Road, Brighton BN1 3XG
Tel: 01273 234777
Fax: 01273 234778
Email: fft@communitybase.org
Web: <http://www.gypsy-traveller.org>

The Gypsy Council
Contact: Hughie Smith
Address: Spring Lanes Caravan Park, Bickerton, Near Wetherby, North
    Yorkshire LS22 5ND
Tel: 01937 842782

The Gypsy Council for Education, Culture, Welfare and Civil Rights
Contact: Charlie Smith/Anne Bagehot
Address: (European and UK office), 8 Hall Road, Aveley, Essex RM15 4HD
Tel/Fax: 01708 868986
Web: <http://www.thegypsycouncil.org>

Gypsy and Traveller Community Development Project
Address: Community Central Halls, 304 Maryhill Road, Glasgow G20 7YE
Tel: 0141 576 5333

The Gypsy and Traveller Law Reform Coalition
Contact: Andrew Ryder (Policy Development Worker)
Email: romanistan@yahoo.com
Web: <http://www.travellerslaw.org.uk>

Gypsy Traveller Education and Information Project (North East)
Address: c/o Aberdeen Foyer, Marywell Centre, Marywell Street, Aberdeen
    AB11 5RN
Tel: 01224 596156

Irish Travellers Movement in Britain
Address: c/o Brent Irish Advisory Service, 156–62 Kilburn High Road, London
    NW6 4JD
Tel: 020 7625 2255
Email: info@irishtraveller.org.uk

Leeds Gypsy and Traveller Exchange
Contact: Helen Jones
Address: 7 Shafton Lane, Holbeck, Leeds LS11 9LY
Tel: 0113 2346556 / 07974 574889

Leeds Justice for Travellers
Contact: Tommy Collins
Address: 9 Mowbrary Court, Seacroft, Leeds LS14 6UN
Tel: 0113 264 8658 / 07980 031616

London Gypsy Traveller Unit (LGTU)
Contact: Frieda Shiecker
Address: 6 Westgate Street, London E8 3RN
Tel: 020 8533 2002

The National Association of Gypsy Women
Contact: Catherine Beard/Rachel Francis
Address: CVS Building, Church Row, Darlington DL1 5QD
Tel: 01268 782792 (South office) / 01325 240033 (North office) / 07748 670200
Email: rachelfrancisingham@yahoo.co.uk

National Gypsy and Traveller Affairs
Contact: Sylvie Dunn
Address: Meadowview, Goldsmith Drive, Lower Holbridge Road, Rayleigh,
    Essex SS6 9QX

**National Romani Gypsy and Traveller Alliance/Gypsy and Traveller Drugs
    Helpline**
Contact: Barrie Taylor
Email: drugshelpline@uk49.fsnet.co.uk / nrgta@uk49.fsnet.co.uk

National Romany Rights
Contact: Basil Burton
Address: 10 Dugdell Close, Ferndown, Dorest BH22 8BH
Tel: 01202 893228

National Travellers Action Group
Contact: Cliff and Janie Codona (currently on the roadside following local
    authority eviction from their Woodside site)
Address: (formerly) 7 Woodside Park, Hatch Road, Sandy, Bedfordshire
    SG19 1PT
Tel: 01767 689736 / 07890 596718
Email: codona@aol.com

New Futures Association (NFA)
Address: c/o 42 Wade Meadow Court, Lings, Northampton NN3 8ND
Tel: 07880 758713
Email: calnfa@hotmail.com / mail@newfutures.fsnet.co.uk

Ormiston Trust: Cambridgeshire Travellers' Advocacy Service
Contact: Sherry Peck
Address: Cambridgeshire Travellers Initiative, Travellers' Advocacy Service,
      7e High Street, Fenstantion, Cambs PE28 9LQ
Tel: 01480 496577
Email: advocacy@ormiston.org

Pavee, Advice, Assist and Direction: Representing Irish Travellers in the UK
Contact: Phien
Address: PO Box 429, Margate, Kent CT9 9A
Tel: 0779 1327842 (for donations or membership details)
Email: phien@beeb.net

Scottish Gypsy/Traveller Association
Contact: Mark Kennedy
Address: 37 Guthrie Street, Edinburgh EH1 1JG
Tel: 0131 650 6314

The Showmen's Guild (National)
Contact: Denise Ablett (Secretary)
Address: 151a King Street, Drighlington, Bradford BD11 1EJ
Tel: 0113 285 3341
Web: <http://www.showmensguild.com>

Showmen's Guild Offices (Scotland)
Address: 8 Fitzroy Place, Glasgow G37 RH
Tel: 0141 221 7297

Society for the Promotion and Advancement of Romany Culture (SPARC)
Address: c/o 27 Yarm Road, Stockton on Tees TS18 3NJ
Web: <http://www.sparcnortheast.org.uk>

Travellers Aid Trust
Small grants for Travellers and occasional targeted funding.
Contact: Susan Alexander
Address: PO Box 16, Llangyndeyrn, Kidwelly SA17 5YT
Email: travellersaidtrust@yahoo.co.uk
Web: <http://www.travellersaidtrust.org/>

The Travellers Project
Address: Castlebrae Community Education, Greendykes Road, Edinburgh
    EH16 4DP
Tel: 0131 661 4754

Legal advice and representation

British Committee on Romani Emancipation (BCRE)
British section of the European Committee on Romani Emancipation.
Address: 128 Copnor Road, Portsmouth PO3 5AN
Email: info@uk-romani.org
Web: <http://www.eu-romani.org/legal.htm>, which is dedicated to the
    elimination of the enforced exclusion, dependency and poverty of the
    Roma. BCRE provides a single non-exclusive representation on behalf of
    British citizens wishing to promote common rights of equity of treatment,
    protection and improvement in the conditions of the Roma.

Commission for Racial Equality
Address: St Dunstan's House, 201–211 Borough High Street, London SE1 1GZ
Tel: 020 7939 0000
Fax: 020 7939 0001
Email: info@cre.gov.uk
Web: <http://www.cre.gov.uk/gdpract/g_and_t_facts.html>

European Roma Rights Centre
International Human Rights Law and policy updates
Web: <http://errc.org>

Guide to the Legal Rights of Gypsies and Travellers
Web: <http://www.yourrights.org.uk/your-rights/chapters/rights-of-gypsies-
    and-travellers/index.shtml>

Liberty
Formerly National Council for Civil Liberties.
Address: 21 Tabard Street, London SE1 4LA
Tel: 020 7403 3888

Traveller Advice Team (Community Law Partnership)
Address: Ruskin Chambers, 191 Corporation Street, Birmingham B4 6RP
Tel: 0845 120 2980 (Monday–Friday 10 a.m.–1 p.m. and 2 p.m.–5 p.m.) /
    07768 316755 (emergencies)

The Traveller Law Research Unit
Now closed but many documents still available free to download.
Web: <http://www.cf.ac.uk/claws/tlru>

Education contacts and resources

Advisory Council for the Education of Romanies and Other Travellers (ACERT)
Address: Moot House, The Stow, Harlow, Essex CM20 3AG

The Children's Society
Educational and social-care advocacy and support for Gypsy and Traveller children.
Contact: Debbie Harvey
Address: 92b High Street, Midsomer Norton, Somerset BA3 2DE
Tel: 01761 411771

Educational Advice for Travellers
Contact: Fiona Earle
Address: PO Box 36, Grantham, Lincolnshire NG31 6EW

European Federation for the Education of Travelling Communities
Promoting educational resources and methods adapted to the particular needs of Occupational Travellers.
Web: <http://www.efecot.net>

National Association of Teachers of Travellers (NATT)
The official association for teachers working with Travelling families. Educational resources and links to local TES services.
Web: <http://www.natt.org.uk>

The National Playbus Association
Address: Brunswick Court, Brunswick Place, Bristol BS2 8PE
Tel: 0117 916 6580
Email: playbus@playbus.org.uk
Web: <http://playbus.mysite.wanadoo-members.co.uk>

Scottish Traveller Education Programme
Information about Traveller education in Scotland supported by access to academic research findings.
Web: <http://www.scottishtravellered.net>

Travellers in Leeds
Leeds TES-hosted website for Gypsies and Travellers. Education and health resources, journal articles and children's area.
Web: <http://www.travellersinleeds.co.uk>

The Travellers' School Charity (TSC)
Address: PO Box 2, Goodwick SA64 0ZQ
Tel: 07717 055378
Email: stigstrunk@aol.com
Web: <http://www.travellersschool.plus.com>

Health contacts and resources

Gypsy and Traveller Drugs Helpline
Contact: Barrie Taylor
Email: drugshelpline@uk49.fsnet.co.uk

The Health Status of Gypsies and Travellers in England
A Sheffield University report to the Department of Health, 2004. The leading
    study on the health situation of Travelling people in the UK.
Summary of report: <http://www.shef.ac.uk/content/1/c6/02/55/71/
    GT%20report%20summary.pdf>
Qualitative findings: <http://www.shef.ac.uk/content/1/c6/02/55/71/
    GT%20qualitative%20report.pdf>
Final report: <http://www.shef.ac.uk/content/1/c6/02/55/71/
    GT%20final%20report.pdf>

Maternity Alliance Gypsy and Traveller Women's Project
Running between 2003 and 2006, this project aims to raise awareness
    amongst, and demonstrate good practice to, health and social care
    professionals on the care given to Gypsy and Traveller women during
    pregnancy and childbirth.
Web: <http://www.maternityalliance.org.uk/prof_health.htm#2>

National Association of Health Workers with Travellers
Address: c/o Balsall Heath Centre, 43 Edward Road, Birmingham B12 9LB
Tel: 0117 922 7570 / 0121 446 2300
Web: <http://www.msfcphva.org/sigs/sigtravellers.html>

Central and local government contacts and information

National Association of Gypsy and Traveller Officers
Contact: George Summers (Secretary)
Address: c/o Hampshire County Council, The Castle, Winchester S023 9DS
Email: george.summers@hants.gov.uk
Web: <http://www.nagto.co.uk>

Office of the Deputy Prime Minister (ODPM) Gypsy and Travellers Branch
Address: Eland House, Bressenden Place, London SW1E 5DU
Tel: 020 7944 4400
Web: <http://www.odpm.gov.uk/stellent/groups/odpm_about/
documents/sectionhomepage/odpm_about_page.hcsp> (Search under
'Gypsies and Travellers' for data on sites, counting caravans, statistics and
relevant policy documents.)

The Social Exclusion Unit (Frequent Movers project)
Government website (part of the ODPM) aiming at maximising social
inclusion and minimising the disadvantages of marginalised UK citizens
and residents including Gypsies and Travellers with no stable sites.
Web: <http://www.socialexclusionunit.gov.uk/page.asp?id=588>

Other organisations and useful resources

Connexions
A Governmental service available to all young people aged 13–19 offering a
range of information and support services including careers and education
advice or access to specialist services such as help with drugs,
relationships or alcohol issues.
Web: <http://www.connexions.gov.uk/partnerships/index.cfm?CategoryID=3>

Gypsy Expressions
The first UK Gypsy Traveller site hosting writing and creative skills.
Contact: Richard O'Neill
Email: gypsyexpressions@aol.com
Web: <http://www.gypsyexpressions.org.uk>

The Liverpool Gypsy Collection
Hosted by the University of Liverpool, an unparalleled collection of early
Gypsy Lore Society resources and photographs.
Web: <http://sca.lib.liv.ac.uk/collections/gypsy/intro.htm>

National Association of Boat Owners
Resource for Boaters and Water Gypsies, focused on mooring rights and access
to services.
Tel: 01749 677195

National Fairground Archive
Academic resources, circus and fairground information, articles and
photographs.
Web: <http://www.shef.ac.uk/nfa>

Patrin Web Journal
Romani culture and history resources.
Web: <http://www.patrin.com>

Pride Not Prejudice
Romani Gypsies and Irish Travellers working in partnership with the police to
develop an annual conference on community policing, to provide cultural-
awareness training for police forces and to enhance community relations
and cooperation. An annual conference is held to celebrate the
partnership, hosted by a rotating group of police forces and contributors to
the seminar. A Home Office-funded initiative, originally started by DGLG.
Web: <http://www.pridenotprejudice.com>

The Romany and Traveller Family History Society
An excellent organisation and website for those wishing to trace their Gypsy
and Traveller family history. Census data, journals and articles available
online and to purchase.
Web: <http://website.lineone.net/~rtfhs>

Travellers' Times / Travellers' Times magazine
Articles by and about Gypsies and Travellers. Free downloadable copies,
including previous editions, available.
Web: <http://www.travellerstimes.org.uk>

New Traveller and festival resources

Enabler Publications
Books on New Traveller culture, alternative living and DIY culture.
Contact: Alan Dearling
Email: adearling@aol.com
Web: <http://members.aol.com/adearling/enabler>

George Dice's Homepage
Stonehenge campaign, tribal voices, links and more.
Web: <http://www.phreak.co.uk/stonehenge/psb/george>

Tash's Homepage
Festivals, Travelling and environmental articles and photographs.
Web: <http://tash.gn.apc.org/INDEX.htm>

How to complain
Colin Clark

Below is some guidance on how to complain about anti-Gypsy or Traveller press coverage. If you want to complain about an item in the press that you think is discriminatory or biased against Gypsies and Travellers, then the best way to do this is by writing very quickly to the Editor of the publication, expressing your concerns. This can sometimes produce positive results and an apology or retraction. However, if the Editor of the publication does not agree with you and refuses to issue an apology then you can take things further and write a letter of complaint to the Press Complaints Commission <http://www.pcc.org.uk/index2.html> (the PCC helpline is 0845 600 2757). Do bear in mind that you must write within two months of the article being published.

As a general rule, you should send the PCC a cutting of the complete article, if at all possible, or the name of the publication and the date that the article was featured. It is also useful to note the name of the journalist who wrote the article, if it is a 'named' piece. In addition to this you should write a short summary of why you are complaining and why you think it breaches the PCC Code of Practice (for details of the full Code of Practice, see <http://www.pcc.org.uk>. The final thing you should do is include any relevant letters or any other documentation that will help the PCC assess the complaint. The address to send your complaint, and any other materials, to is: The Press Complaints Commission, 1 Salisbury Square, London EC4Y 8JB.

We would also recommend, for members of the media, the useful guidance put together by the Traveller Law Research Unit and the CRE. It is a short guide on how to best report issues that may involve Gypsies and Travellers: *Travellers, Gypsies and the Media: A Good*

Practice Guide from the CRE (in association with Cardiff Law School/Traveller Law Research Unit, 1999).

Coverage of race and ethnic issues across the media has significantly improved over the past twenty years. There has been a wider and more constructive exploration of many questions and a reduction in the use of language that is offensive to members of different ethnic groups. However, many problems remain. These recommendations are designed to help in dealing with one of them: the way parts of the media report on Traveller and/or Gypsy issues.

Poor quality reporting that exploits or panders to stereotypes can cause much hurt to those about whom the stories are written. By repeating false and negative stereotypes, the media can encourage bad practice on the part of those with whom Travellers and Gypsies deal and can validate the expression of language and attitudes that in any other circumstances would be seen as totally unacceptable.

The CRE has handled cases under the Race Relations Act for Travellers and Gypsies for over twenty years. The number of such cases continues to run at several dozen each year. The majority of these cases involve clear breaches of the Act.

These guidelines are not intended to make the media shy away from covering issues and stories to do with Travellers and Gypsies. Quite the contrary. The CRE and those organisations representing Travellers and Gypsies want to see more coverage in the media but are keen to help the media develop a coverage that is honest and fair, open and inclusive.

Steer clear of exploiting prejudice

The public wants a media that is campaigning, but those campaigns should be built on matters of genuine public concern, not simply prejudices against particular groups.

Check the facts

Go to the experts who can help to set the context. With these recommendations, we include a list of contacts of individuals and organisations that can help you with various aspects of your story. Make sure that wherever possible you check the details with a relevant source and don't just rely on expressions of local or popular prejudice.

Many allegations are made about Travellers, Gypsies and now Roma asylum seekers from eastern Europe, but can those making the allegations actually substantiate them?

Don't let your new agenda be driven by the way others are handling the issue

Certain story lines easily dominate media discussion of Travellers or Gypsies while issues of great importance to the communities involved are downplayed or ignored altogether. Don't write about Travellers and Gypsies only in the context of disputes over stopping places; look also at the problems Travellers face.

Look behind the story line

Don't assume there is only one point of view. Always seek the views of Traveller and Gypsy organisations to see whether or not there is an alternative interpretation or a different and more significant story line to be presented.

Listen to the people you are writing about

This is particularly important when it comes to the terms and language you use. Terms like 'tinker', 'itinerant' or 'gypo' are all highly offensive to those about whom they are used and should be avoided. The terms 'Traveller', 'Gypsy' or 'Irish Traveller' should be used with initial capital letters. Offensive stereotypes (for example, 'scroungers', 'dole dodgers', 'bogus asylum seekers') should only be used when they are accurate descriptions of particular individuals and should not be employed to negatively stereotype whole groups.

Don't label people if it is not relevant

Reference to the fact that an individual is a Traveller, Gypsy or Irish Traveller should only be made when it is relevant and appropriate.

APPENDIX 3

Glossary

Colin Clark

These are some of the key terms and references used in the book, and we detail here what we mean when we use these terms:

atchin tan: stopping place.

buffer: a term used by Irish Travellers for a house-dweller, someone who is not a Traveller.

caravan: the term 'caravan' (as defined by the 1960 Caravan Sites Act) includes a mobile home comprising a maximum of two units which is, in spite of the name, not mobile. It is brought onto a site in two parts on a lorry and put together on site. It cannot be towed by a lorry and, for practical purposes (as opposed to legal niceties), is the same as a chalet.

ethnicity: this concept is used in the book to refer to cultural awareness/identity within groups of people who share a common history/heritage. For Gypsies and Travellers, cultural/linguistic identification and family 'pedigrees' are also usually important (for example, at a first meeting the question will more likely be 'Who are you one of?' rather than 'Who are you?').

flattie: a term used by Scottish Gypsy/Travellers and Showpeople for a house-dweller, someone who is not a Traveller. Scottish Gypsy/Travellers might also use the term 'scaldie'.

gorje: an Anglo-Romani term meaning an 'outsider', someone who is not a Gypsy, Traveller or Romani. There are many different spellings of this term (e.g. *gorgio*).

green lanes: there is no legal definition of 'green lanes'. However, the term is generally accepted to indicate an unsurfaced, often hedged, track in the countryside, 'a routeway without a tarmac surface, bounded on either side by hedges which was once well used for a variety of practical purposes but is now often only used for leisure activities' <http://greenbooks.co.uk/glworksheet.php>.

Gypsy: an abbreviation of the word 'Egyptian', a name given to the Romani people in the Middle Ages as it was thought they came from Egypt. The word can be derogatory to some people we might think of as 'Gypsies' (such people may prefer the term 'Romani'). However, for this book we use it (and Traveller) throughout as a general term for anyone of nomadic habit of life (as British law currently suggests).

mobile home site: a site consisting entirely of mobile homes, popular with retired people or for holidays. Gypsies are rarely allowed on these sites.

poggerdi jib: a term that refers to the language of English Gypsies. The term translates as 'broken tongue/language'. Some examples can be found in Appendix 5. Please note that this term can be regarded as offensive as it implies ('broken') that Anglo-Romani is somehow not a 'proper' language. Many commentators argue that it very much is.

Romani: (noun) a member of a nomadic people said to originate in north India, the Romanies; (adjective) relating to the culture, customs and language of the Romanies. It is derived from the word 'Rom' (plural 'Roma').

Romanes: a more general term for the language of the Romanies.

Totting: slang for the trade of a 'Rag and Bone man' or person who bought up (or traded for) old rags, scrap metal, rabbit skins and anything else people would sell to him. Totting was a form of early recycling – and although often regarded as a trade with a dirty/sleazy reputation, one which provided a valuable service. Rag and Bone merchants or 'totters' had essentially disappeared from the streets of London by the late 1970s.

Traveller: (1) an Irish or Scottish nomad; (2) an overall term for nomads covering Romani Gypsies as well as Irish, New and Scottish Travellers.

unsited: without access to any authorised site (rather than simply travelling temporarily).

APPENDIX 4

Acronyms

Colin Clark and Margaret Greenfields

ACERT	Advisory Council for the Education of Romanies and other Travellers
ACSTP	Advisory Committee on Scotland's Travelling People
A&E	Accident and Emergency (Casualty) Departments at hospitals for treatment of injuries
AGLOW	Association of Greater London Older Women
AGREMPA	Advisory Group on Raising Ethnic Minority Pupil Achievement
ASBO	Anti-Social Behaviour Order
BBC	British Broadcasting Corporation
BCRE	British Committee on Romani Emancipation
BME	Black and Minority Ethnic
CERD	Committee on the Elimination of Racial Discrimination
CGSG	Cardiff Gypsy Sites Group
CIT	Comité International Tzigane
CJPOA	Criminal Justice and Public Order Act 1994
CMG	Communauté Mondiale Gitane
CoE	Council of Europe
CPS	Crown Prosecution Service
CRE	Commission for Racial Equality
CSA	Caravan Sites Act 1968
DfEE	Department for Education and Employment
DfES	Department for Education and Skills
DGLG	Derbyshire Gypsy Liaison Group
EEC	European Economic Community
EC	European Community
ECHR	European Convention on Human Rights and Fundamental Freedoms

ECRI	European Commission against Racism and Intolerance
EDP	Education Development Plan
EU	European Union
ECHR	European Court of Human Rights
ECRE	European Committee on Romani Emancipation
EFECOT	European Federation for the Education of Travelling Communities
ELC	Electronic Learning Credits
EMAG	Ethnic Minority Achievement Grant
EMTAG	Ethnic Minority and Traveller Achievement Grant
EOC	Equal Opportunities Committee
ERRC	European Roma Rights Centre
ESF	European Social Fund
FFT	Friends, Families and Travellers
GATE	Leeds Gypsy and Traveller Exchange
GCECWCR	The Gypsy Council for Education, Culture, Welfare and Civil Rights
GP	General Practitioner (Family Doctor)
G&TLRC	Gypsy and Traveller Law Reform Coalition
HA	Housing Act 2004 (inserts a requirement into existing legislation to assess the accommodation needs of Gypsies and Travellers as distinct from residents of 'bricks and mortar' accommodation)
HRA	Human Rights Act 1998
IAG	Itinerant Action Group
ICT	Information and Communication Technology
IRU	International Romani Union
ITM	Irish Traveller Movement in Britain
LEA	Local Education Authority
LGTU	London Gypsy Traveller Unit
MORI	Market and Opinion Research International
NAAR	National Assembly Against Racism
NACRO	National Association for the Care and Resettlement of Offenders
NAGTO	National Association of Gypsy and Traveller Officers
NAGW	National Association of Gypsy Women
NAHWT	National Association of Health Workers with Travellers

NATT	National Association of Teachers of Travellers
NAW	National Assembly for Wales
NCCL	National Council for Civil Liberties (now called Liberty)
NFA	No Fixed Abode
NGO	Non-Governmental Organisation
NHS	National Health Service
NTAG	National Travellers' Action Group
NUJ	National Union of Journalists
ODPM	Office of the Deputy Prime Minister
OFSTED	Office for Standards in Education
OSI	Open Society Institute
PCC	Press Complaints Commission
PCT	Primary Care Trust
PMS	Personal Medical Services (GP contract for provision of health care)
PSR	Pre-Sentence Reports
RRA	Race Relations Act 1976 (as amended 2000)
RTFHS	Romany and Traveller Family History Society
SC	Save the Children
SCCCRAE	Standing Conference for Co-operation and Co-ordination of Romani Associations in Europe
ScHARR	University of Sheffield School of Health and Related Research
SGTA	Scottish Gypsy/Traveller Association
SKOKRA	Federation of Romani Organisations in the Americas
SPARC	Society for the Promotion and Advancement of Romani Culture
STEP	Scottish Traveller Education Project
TAG	Traveller Achievement Grant
TAT	Travellers Aid Trust
TERF	Trans-European Roma Federation
TES	Traveller Education Service
TLRU	Traveller Law Research Unit
TSC	Travellers' School Charity
UNDP	United Nations Development Programme
UNESCO	United Nations Educational Scientific and Cultural Organisation
VCG	Vulnerable Children Grant

Gypsy and Traveller languages of Britain

Donald Kenrick

Please also see Acton, T. and Kenrick, D. (eds) (1984) *Romani Rokkeripen To-Divvus: The English Romani Dialect and its Contemporary, Social, Educational and Linguistic Standing*, London: Romanestan Publications, for some good examples of the languages used by the different groups of Gypsies and Travellers in Britain. The section below on languages is reproduced from Kenrick, D. and Clark, C. (1999) *Moving On: The Gypsies and Travellers of Britain*, Hatfield: University of Hertfordshire Press.

Each of the groups of traditional Gypsies or Travellers has its own language. The Romanies and some of the Kalé still speak the Romani (Romanes) language, using its traditional grammar.

Romani died out among the Romanichals early in the twentieth century and has been replaced by a variety of English (known as *poggerdi jib*) using many Romani words (some of the most common Romanichal words have made their way into the English language – such as *kushti* (good), *wonga* (money) and *chavvies* (children). If you have watched the television programmes *Only Fools and Horses* and *Minder*, you will probably know a few of these words below, for example, 'The *rakli jell*ed to the *gav* to *kin* some *pobbels*' [The girl went to the village to buy some apples].

The Irish Travellers used to speak a variety of Irish using many words from vocabularies known as Gammon or Shelta. They now speak a variety of English known as Cant, but incorporating the same words. Sometimes a whole sentence will be in Cant, for example, '*Bug muilsha gather skai*' [Give me a drink of water].

Most Scottish Travellers speak English but again with many words that are not used by the general population. Some of these words are of Romani origin, bearing out the theory that the Scottish Travellers have intermarried with Romanichals over the years. An example of

Lowland Scottish Travellers' Cant: '*Bing avree, gheddie,* and get some *peeve*' [Go out, lad, and get some beer].

The dialect of the Borders is closer to that of the English Romanichals, while some of the Highland and Islands Scottish Travellers who travel in the Highlands and to the Western Isles speak a Cant based on Scottish Gaelic. For example, '*S'deis sium a' meartsacha* air a *charan*' [We are going on the sea].

The Romani language

The following sketch of European Romani is intended to illustrate the connections with north Indian languages and to show that it is *not* just slang or a pidgin but has a grammar. Inflected (grammatical) Romani died out in England late in the nineteenth century and in Wales sometime in the middle of the twentieth century.

These examples of Romani words are taken from W. R. Rishi's *Multilingual Romani Dictionary*. Prakrit is a later form of Sanskrit. People who speak Hindi, Punjabi or Gujerati will recognise many common Romani words. Bengali or Sylheti speakers may know a few.

Romani	Sanskrit/Prakrit	English
byav	vivaha	wedding
kako	kakka	uncle
kalo	kala	black
nakh	nakka	nose
puch	pracch	ask
thuv	dhuma	smoke

kako, kalo, nakh and *puch* are used in English Romani, while *thuv* survives in the word *thuvalo*, 'cigarette'.

Romani has a case system not unlike Latin and Classical Greek and, of course, Sanskrit, to which it is related. To give one example, the word for 'boy' changes its endings where English would use a preposition.

raklesa	with a boy
rakleske	to a boy
raklengo	of boys

The verbs change their endings to show the person doing the action and also the time (past, present, future). The verb *dikh-* ('to see') takes thirty-two different endings. For example:

dikhav   I see
dikhlias   he (or she) saw

There were three genders (like Latin and German) when the speakers left India, but the neuter disappeared in the Middle East, probably under the influence of Persian. The definite article and adjectives have to change depending on whether they accompany a masculine or feminine noun.

O parno bakro   the white sheep [masc.]
I parni bakri   the white ewe [fem.]
E parne bakre   the white sheep [pl.]

It should also be noted that amongst some groups of New Travellers in Britain there is a form of 'slang' language/terminology used. See Earle, F. et al. (1994) *A Time to Travel: An Introduction to Britain's Newer Travellers*, Lyme Regis: Enabler Publications, pp. 41–2 for examples of this. Some appear below:

bender, a dome-shaped shelter made out of flexible poles and covered in tarpaulin
blim, small (as in a blim trailer/caravan)
blag, to gain something through articulate persuasion/argument
burner, wood-burning stove
decker, someone who lives in a double-decker bus (i.e. 'Decker John')
flat-bed, the flat-bed of a truck behind the cab (used for scrap work)
nylon nightmare, a tent
tarp, abbreviation for tarpaulin (used for making a bender tent)
tat, possessions
wood run, going to collect wood for the burner

Select bibliography
Colin Clark

Below are some of the key books that are useful to read when looking further into the situation and experiences of Roma, Gypsies and Travellers in Britain. We have also referred to some of the best books that look at the wider European situation.

You are likely to find some of these books from the following recommended booksellers:

University of Hertfordshire Press specialises in books that deal with Roma, Gypsy and Traveller issues. University of Hertfordshire, LRC, College Lane, Hatfield, Hertfordshire AL10 9AB, UK; Telephone: +44 (0)1707 284654; email: UHPress@herts.ac.uk; <http://www.herts.ac.uk/UHPress>.

Cottage Books: if you would like to receive the Cottage Books catalogue of new and second-hand books on Gypsies and Travellers please write to Cottage Books, Gelsmoor, Coleorton, Leicestershire LE67 8HR, UK (please note this is a postal service only).

Enabler Publications specialises in publications about New Travellers. To buy books from Enabler Publications please contact Alan Dearling at Enabler Publications, 16 Bitton Avenue, Teignmouth, Devon TQ14 8HD, UK; email: adearling@aol.com; <http://members.aol.com/adearling/enabler>.

Romanestan Publications: to receive the Romanestan Publications catalogue of new and second-hand books by email please contact t.a.acton@greenwich.ac.uk.

Key books

Acton, T. (1974) *Gypsy Politics and Social Change: The Development of Ethnic Ideology and Pressure Politics among British Gypsies from Victorian Reformism to Romani Nationalism*, London: Routledge & Kegan Paul.

Acton, T. (ed.) (1997) *Gypsy Politics and Traveller Identity*, Hatfield: University of Hertfordshire Press.

Acton, T. (ed.) (2000) *Scholarship and the Gypsy Struggle: Commitment in Romani Studies*, Hatfield: University of Hertfordshire Press.

Acton, T. and Gallant, D. (1997) *Romanichal Gypsies*, London: Wayland Press (Threatened Cultures Series).

Acton, T. and Mundy, G. (eds) (1997) *Romani Culture and Gypsy Identity*, Hatfield: University of Hertfordshire Press.

Adams, B. et al. (1975) *Gypsies and Government Policy in England*, London: Heinemann.

Alt, B. and Folts, S. (1996) *Weeping Violins: The Gypsy Tragedy in Europe*, Kirksville, Miss.: Thomas Jefferson University Press.

Banary, Z. (2002) *The East European Gypsies: Regime Change, Marginality and Ethnopolitics*, Cambridge: Cambridge University Press.

Bancroft, A. (2005) *Roma and Gypsy-Travellers in Europe*, Aldershot: Ashgate Press.

Braid, D. (2002) *Scottish Traveller Tales: Lives Shaped through Stories*, Jackson, Miss.: University of Mississippi Press.

Brearly, M. (1996) *The Roma/Gypsies of Europe: A Persecuted People, Policy Paper No. 3*, London: Institute for Jewish Policy Research.

Crowe, D. M. (1994) *A History of the Gypsies of Eastern Europe and Russia*, New York: St Martin's Griffin.

Crowe, D. and Kolsti, J. (eds) (1991) *The Gypsies of Eastern Europe*, New York: M. E. Sharpe Inc.

Dallas, D. (1971) *The Travelling People*, London: Macmillan.

Danbakli, M. (1994) *On Gypsies: Texts Issued by International Institutions*, Toulouse: CRDP.

Dearling, A. (ed.) (1998) *No Boundaries: New Travellers on the Road Outside of England*, Lyme Regis: Enabler Publications.

Dodds, N. (1966) *Gypsies, Didikois and Other Travellers*, London: Johnson Publications.

Earle, F. et al. (1994) *A Time to Travel: An Introduction to Britain's Newer Travellers*, Lyme Regis: Enabler Publications.

Evans, S. (2004) *Stopping Places: A Gypsy History of South London and Kent*, Hatfield: University of Hertfordshire Press.

Fonseca, I. (1995) *Bury Me Standing: The Gypsies and their Journey*, London: Chatto & Windus.

Fraser, A. (1995) *The Gypsies*, 2nd edn, Oxford: Blackwell.

Gay Y Blasco, P. (1999) *Gypsies in Madrid: Sex, Gender and the Performance of Identity*, Oxford: Berghahn.

Gmelch, G. (1985) *The Irish Tinkers: The Urbanization of an Itinerant People*, 2nd edn, Prospect Heights, Ill.: Waveland Press, Inc.

Grellmann, H. (1783) *Die Zigeuner (Dissertation on the Gypsies)*, trans. M. Raper, 1787 and also E. Wilson, 1807, Dessau and Leipzig/London.

Guy, W. (ed.) (2001) *Between Past and Future: The Roma of Central and Eastern Europe*, Hatfield: University of Hertfordshire Press.

Hancock, I. (1987) *The Pariah Syndrome: An Account of Gypsy Slavery and Persecution*, Ann Arbor, Mich.: Karoma Publishers Inc.

Hawes, D. (1997) *Gypsies, Travellers and the Health Service*, Bristol: Policy Press.

Hawes, D. and Perez, B. (1996) *The Gypsy and the State: The Ethnic Cleansing of British Society*, 2nd edn, Bristol: Policy Press.

Helleiner, J. (2000) *Irish Travellers: Racism and the Politics of Culture*, Toronto: University of Toronto Press.

Hetherington, K. (2000) *New Age Travellers: Vanloads of Uproarious Humanity*, London: Cassell.

Jarman, A. and Jarman, E. (1991) *The Welsh Gypsies: Children of Abram Wood*, Cardiff: University of Wales Press.

Johnson, C. and Willers, M. (eds) (2004) *Gypsy and Traveller Law*, London: Legal Action Group.

Kenny, M. (1997) *The Routes of Resistance: Travellers and Second-Level Schooling*, Aldershot: Ashgate.

Kenrick, D. (1993) *Gypsies: From India to the Mediterranean*, The Interface Collection, Toulouse: CRDP.

Kenrick, D. (1998) *Historical Dictionary of the Gypsies (Romanies)*, Lanham, Md.: Scarecrow Press.

Kenrick, D. (ed.) (1999) *In the Shadow of the Swastika: The Gypsies during the Second World War*, Hatfield: University of Hertfordshire Press.

Kenrick, D. and Clark, C. (1999) *Moving On: The Gypsies and Travellers of Britain*, Hatfield: University of Hertfordshire Press.

Kenrick, D. and Puxon, G. (1972) *The Destiny of Europe's Gypsies*, London: Heinemann.

Kirk, J. M. and Ó Baoill, D. P. (eds) (2002) *Travellers and their Language*, Belfast: Queen's University.

Klímová-Alexander, I. (2005) *The Roma Voice in World Politics: The United Nations and Non-State Actors*, Aldershot: Ashgate Press.

Lemon, A. (2000) *Between Two Fires: Gypsy Performance and Romani Memory*, Durham, Md. and London: Duke University Press.

Lewy, G. (2000) *The Nazi Persecution of the Gypsies*, Oxford: Oxford University Press.

Liégeois, J.-P. (1994) *Roma, Gypsies, Travellers*, Strasbourg: The Council of Europe.

Liégeois, J.-P. and Gheorghe, N. (1995) *Roma/Gypsies: A European Minority*, London: Minority Rights Group.

Lowe, R. and Shaw, W. (1993) *Travellers, Voices of the New Age Nomads*, London: Fourth Estate.

Lucassen, L., Willems, W. and Cottaar, A. (1998) *Gypsies and Other Itinerant Groups: A Socio-Historical Approach,* London: Macmillan.

MacLaughlin, J. (1995) *Travellers and Ireland*, Cork: Cork University Press.

McCann, M., Ó Síocháin, S. and Ruane, J. (eds) (1994) *Irish Travellers: Culture and Ethnicity*, Belfast: The Institute of Irish Studies, The Queen's University of Belfast and The Anthropological Association of Ireland.

Matras, Y. (2002) *Romani: A Linguistic Introduction*, Cambridge: Cambridge University Press.

Mayall, D. (1988) *Gypsy-Travellers in Nineteenth Century Society*, Cambridge:

Cambridge University Press.

Mayall, D. (2004) *Gypsy Identities 1500–2000: From Egipcyans and Moon-Men to the Ethnic Romany*, London: Routledge.

Morris, R. and Clements, L. (eds) (1999) *Gaining Ground: Law Reform for Gypsies and Travellers*, Hatfield: University of Hertfordshire Press.

Morris, R. and Clements, L. (2002) *At What Cost? The Economics of Gypsy and Traveller Encampments*, Bristol: Policy Press.

Okely, J. (1983) *The Traveller-Gypsies*, Cambridge: Cambridge University Press.

Power, C. (2004) *Room to Roam: England's Irish Travellers*, London: Action Group for Irish Youth.

Rehfisch, F. (ed.) (1975) *Gypsies, Tinkers and other Travellers*, London: Academic Press.

Sampson, J. (1926) *The Dialect of the Gypsies of Wales*, Oxford: Clarendon Press.

Saul, N. and Tebbutt, S. (eds) (2004) *The Role of the Romanies: Images and Counter-Images of Gypsies / Romanies in European Cultures*, Liverpool: Liverpool University Press.

Sibley, D. (1981) *Outsiders in Urban Society*, Oxford: Basil Blackwell.

Smith, L. (2004) *Romany Nevi-Wesh: An Informal History of the New Forest Gypsies*, Minstead: Nova Foresta Publishing.

Stewart, M. (1997) *The Time of the Gypsies*, Oxford: Westview Press.

Sutherland, A. (1975) *Gypsies: The Hidden Americans,* Prospect Heights, Ill.: Waveland Press.

Sway, M. (1988) *Familiar Strangers: Gypsy Life in America,* Urbana, Ill.: University of Illinois Press.

Tebbutt, S. (ed.) (1998) *Sinti and Roma: Gypsies in German-Speaking Society and Literature*, Oxford: Berghahn.

Tong, D. (ed.) (1998) *Gypsies: An Interdisciplinary Reader*, New York: Garland.

Vesey-Fitzgerald, B. (1973) *The Gypsies of Britain*, Newton Abbot: David and Charles. First published in 1944.

Weyrauch, W. (ed.) (2001) *Gypsy Law: Romani Legal Traditions and Culture*, Berkeley, Calif.: University of California Press.

Williams, P. (2003) *Gypsy World: The Silence of the Living and the Voices of the Dead*, Chicago, Ill.: University of Chicago Press.

Willems, W. (1997) *In Search of the True Gypsy: From Enlightenment to Final Solution,* London: Frank Cass.

Worthington, A. (ed.) (2005) *The Battle of the Beanfield*, Teignmouth: Enabler Publications.

Young, M. (1999) *Unwanted Journey: Why Central European Roma are Fleeing to the UK*, London: Refugee Council.

Yoors, J. (1987) *The Gypsies*, Prospect Heights, Ill.: Waveland Press. First published in 1967.

Index